LEGENDS

30th ANNIVERSARY EDITION

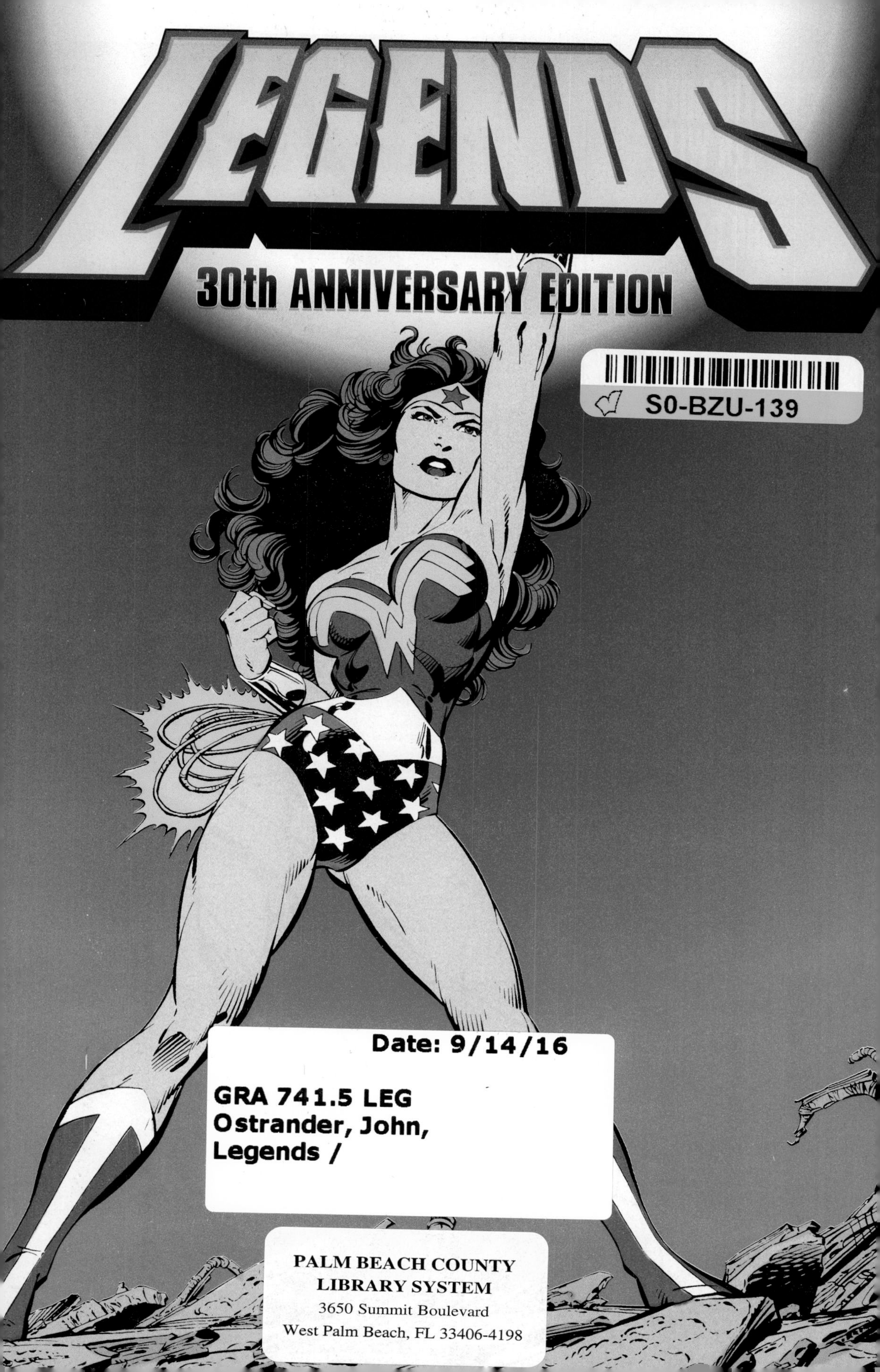

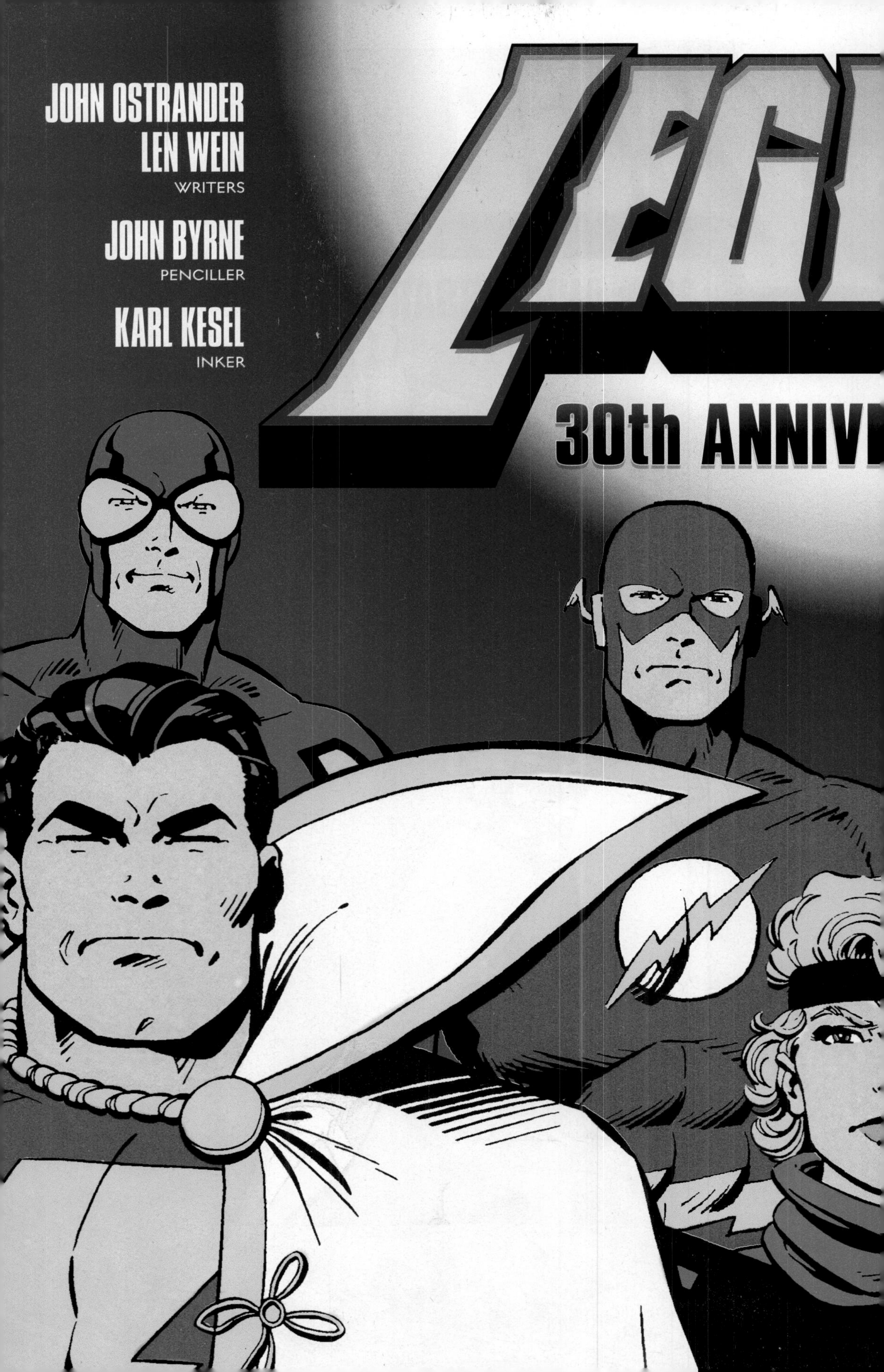

JOHN OSTRANDER
LEN WEIN
WRITERS
JOHN BYRNE
PENCILLER
KARL KESEL
INKER
30th ANNIV

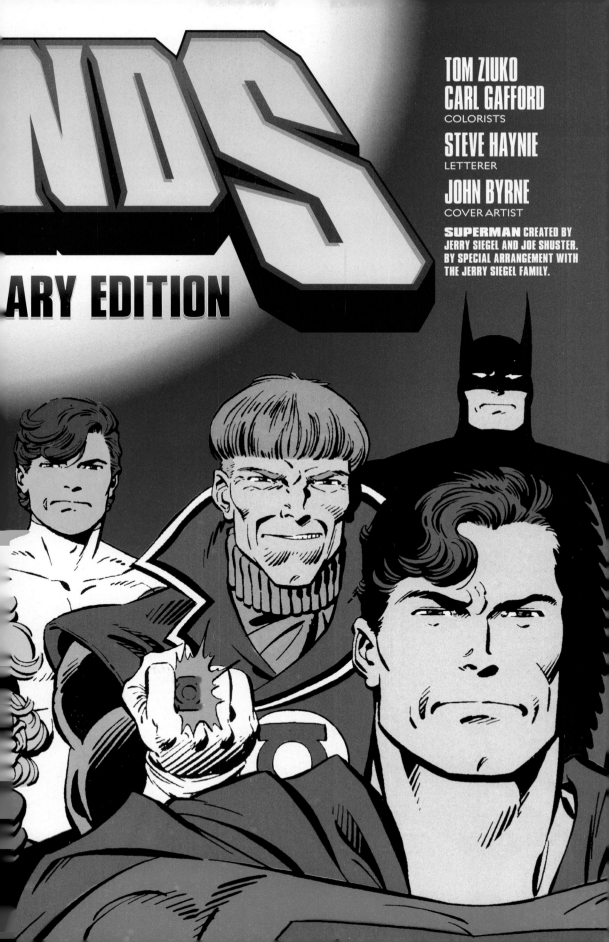

TOM ZIUKO
CARL GAFFORD
COLORISTS

STEVE HAYNIE
LETTERER

JOHN BYRNE
COVER ARTIST

SUPERMAN CREATED BY
JERRY SIEGEL AND JOE SHUSTER.
BY SPECIAL ARRANGEMENT WITH
THE JERRY SIEGEL FAMILY.

MIKE GOLD Editor – Original Series
JEB WOODARD Group Editor – Collected Editions
PAUL SANTOS Editor – Collected Edition
STEVE COOK Design Director – Books
CURTIS KING JR. Publication Design

BOB HARRAS Senior VP – Editor-in-Chief, DC Comics

DIANE NELSON President
DAN DIDIO and **JIM LEE** Co-Publishers
GEOFF JOHNS Chief Creative Officer
AMIT DESAI Senior VP – Marketing & Global Franchise Management
NAIRI GARDINER Senior VP – Finance
SAM ADES VP – Digital Marketing
BOBBIE CHASE VP – Talent Development
MARK CHIARELLO Senior VP – Art, Design & Collected Editions
JOHN CUNNINGHAM VP – Content Strategy
ANNE DEPIES VP – Strategy Planning & Reporting
DON FALLETTI VP – Manufacturing Operations
LAWRENCE GANEM VP – Editorial Administration & Talent Relations
ALISON GILL Senior VP – Manufacturing & Operations
HANK KANALZ Senior VP – Editorial Strategy & Administration
JAY KOGAN VP – Legal Affairs
DEREK MADDALENA Senior VP – Sales & Business Development
JACK MAHAN VP – Business Affairs
DAN MIRON VP – Sales Planning & Trade Development
NICK NAPOLITANO VP – Manufacturing Administration
CAROL ROEDER VP – Marketing
EDDIE SCANNELL VP – Mass Account & Digital Sales
COURTNEY SIMMONS Senior VP – Publicity & Communications
JIM (SKI) SOKOLOWSKI VP – Comic Book Specialty & Newsstand Sales
SANDY YI Senior VP – Global Franchise Management

LEGENDS 30TH ANNIVERSARY EDITION

Published by DC Comics. Compilation and all new material Copyright © 2016 DC Comics. All Rights Reserved.

Originally published in single magazine form in LEGENDS 1-6. Copyright © 1986, 1987 DC Comics. All Rights Reserved. All characters, their distinctive likenesses and related elements featured in this publication are trademarks of DC Comics. The stories, characters and incidents featured in this publication are entirely fictional. DC Comics does not read or accept unsolicited submissions of ideas, stories or artwork.

DC Comics,
2900 West Alameda Avenue,
Burbank, CA 91505
Printed by RR Donnelley, Owensville, MO, USA.
4/29/16. First printing. ISBN: 978-1-4012-6316-4

Library of Congress
Cataloging-in-Publication Data is available.

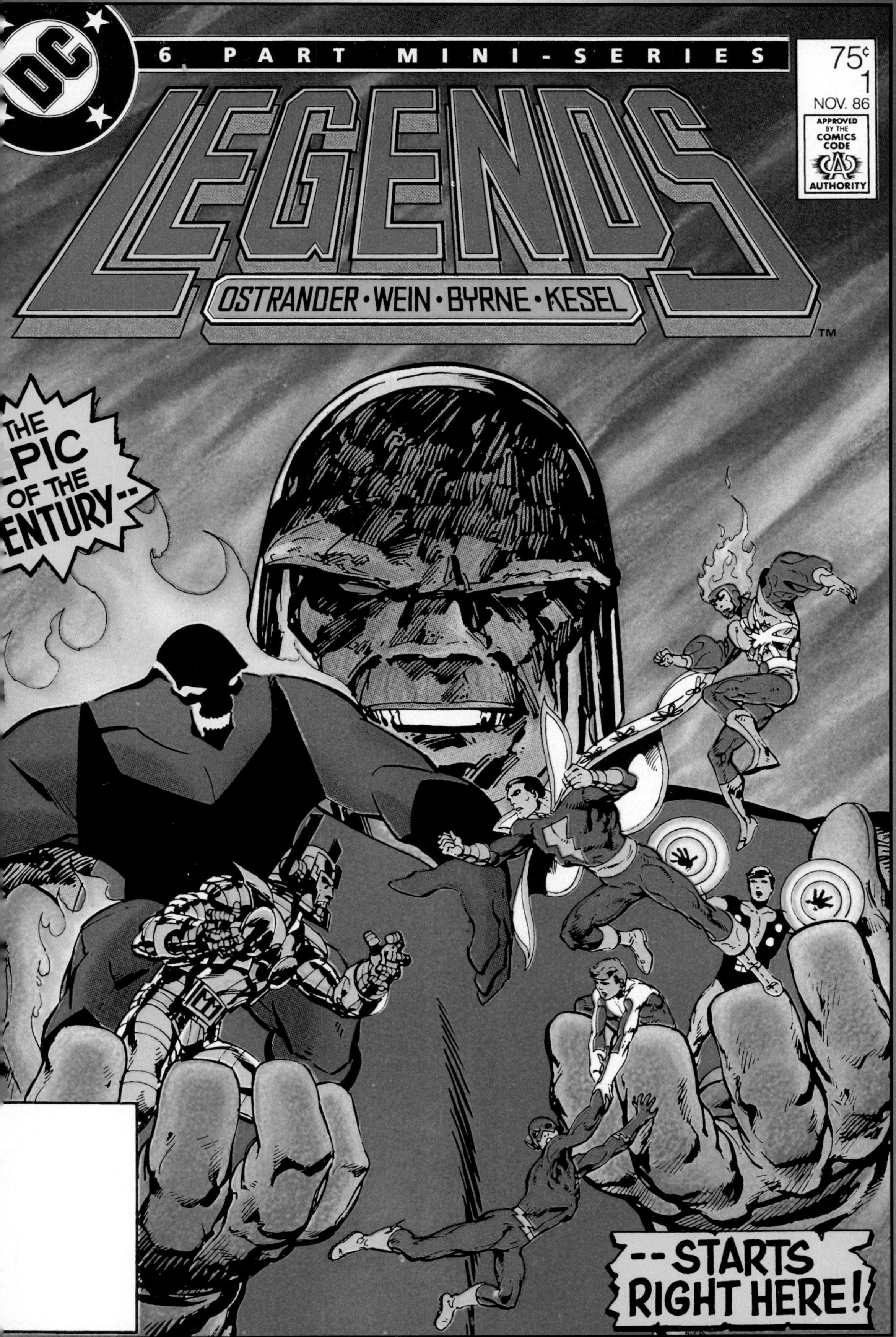
DC
6 PART MINI-SERIES
75¢
1
NOV. 86
APPROVED BY THE COMICS CODE AUTHORITY
LEGENDS
OSTRANDER • WEIN • BYRNE • KESEL
THE EPIC OF THE CENTURY--
--STARTS RIGHT HERE!

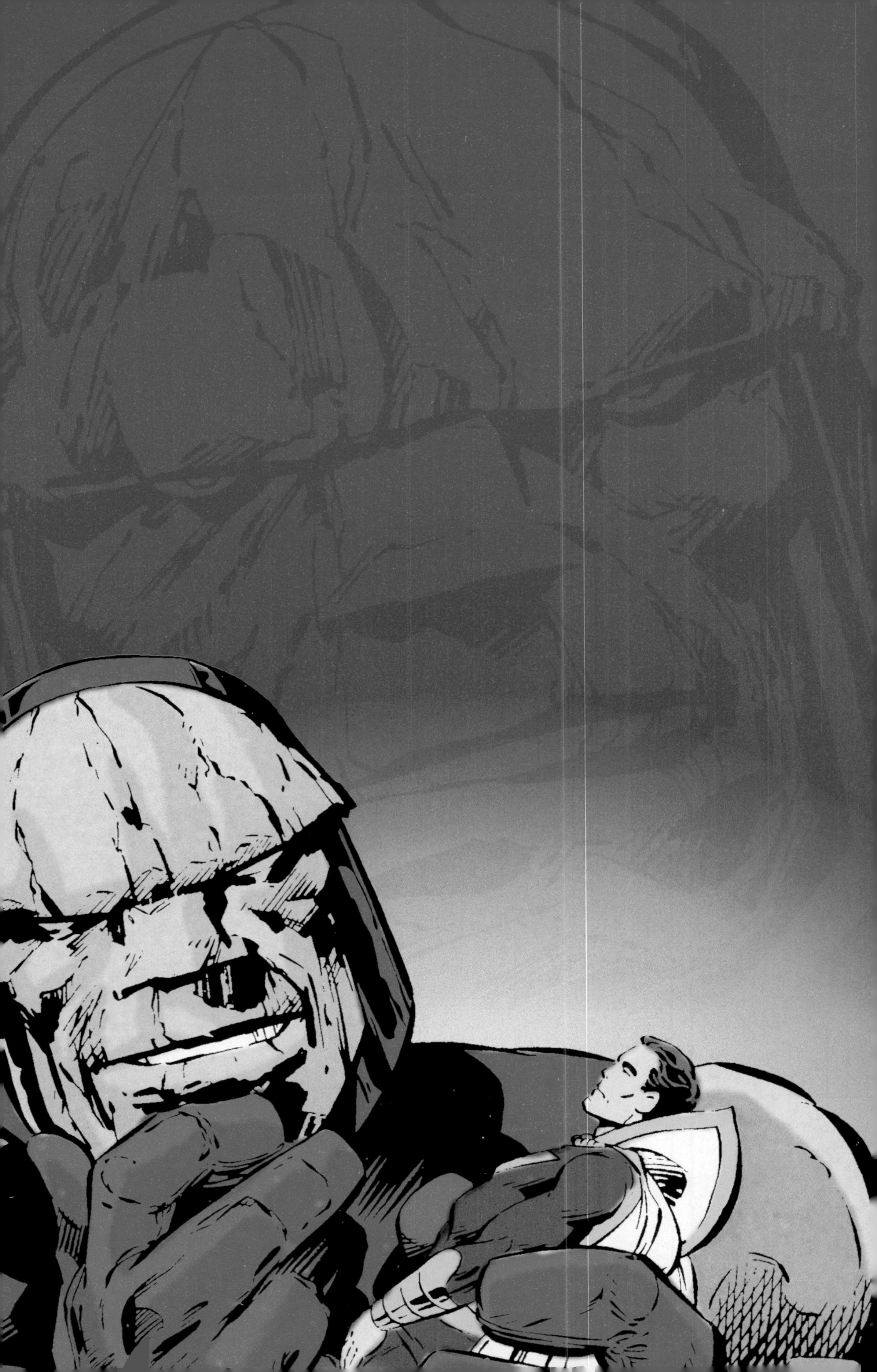

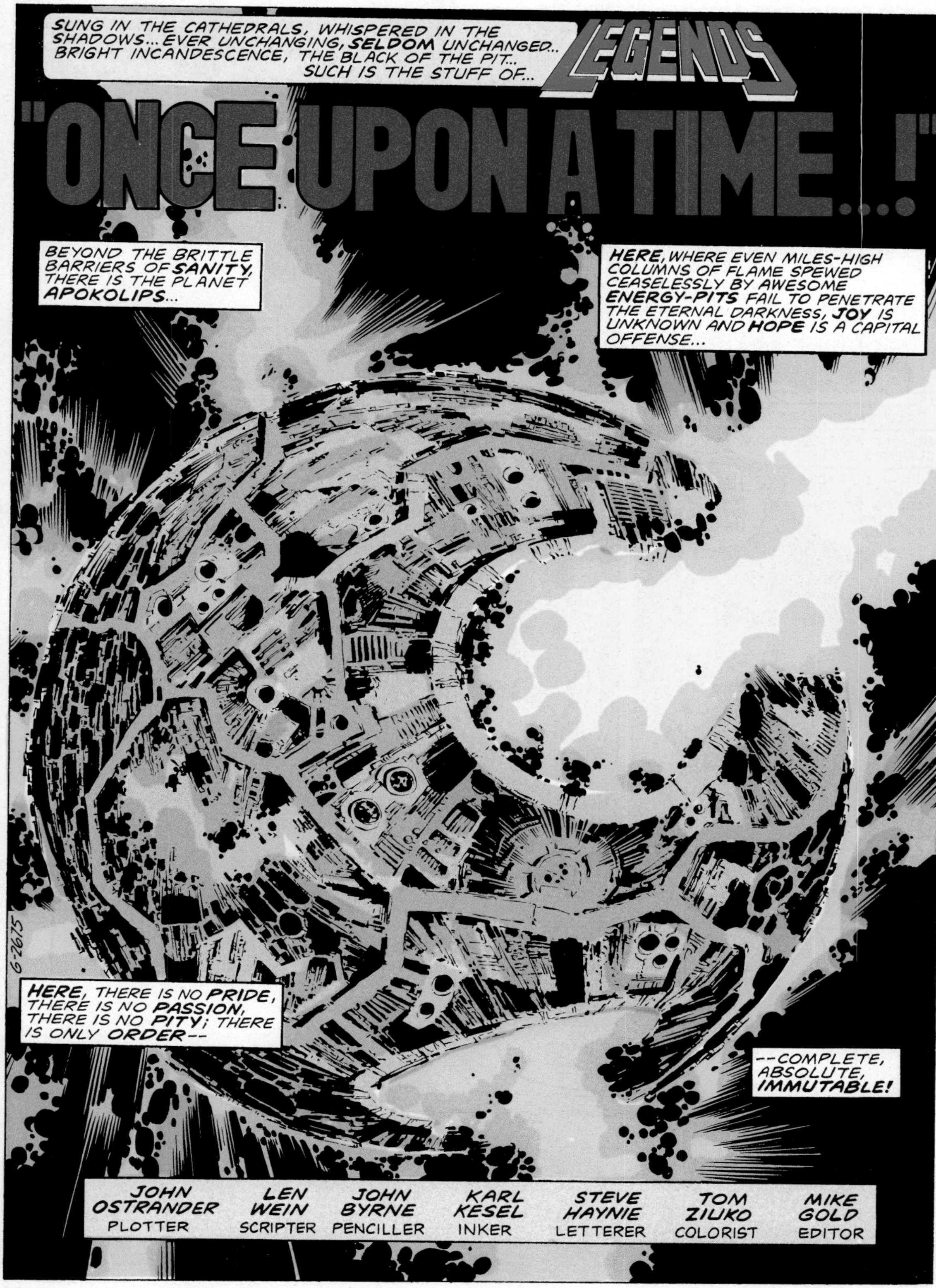
SUNG IN THE CATHEDRALS, WHISPERED IN THE SHADOWS... EVER UNCHANGING, SELDOM UNCHANGED... BRIGHT INCANDESCENCE, THE BLACK OF THE PIT... SUCH IS THE STUFF OF...
LEGENDS
"ONCE UPON A TIME...!"
BEYOND THE BRITTLE BARRIERS OF SANITY, THERE IS THE PLANET APOKOLIPS...
HERE, WHERE EVEN MILES-HIGH COLUMNS OF FLAME SPEWED CEASELESSLY BY AWESOME ENERGY-PITS FAIL TO PENETRATE THE ETERNAL DARKNESS, JOY IS UNKNOWN AND HOPE IS A CAPITAL OFFENSE...
HERE, THERE IS NO PRIDE, THERE IS NO PASSION, THERE IS NO PITY; THERE IS ONLY ORDER--
--COMPLETE, ABSOLUTE, IMMUTABLE!
JOHN OSTRANDER PLOTTER
LEN WEIN SCRIPTER
JOHN BYRNE PENCILLER
KARL KESEL INKER
STEVE HAYNIE LETTERER
TOM ZIUKO COLORIST
MIKE GOLD EDITOR
G-2675

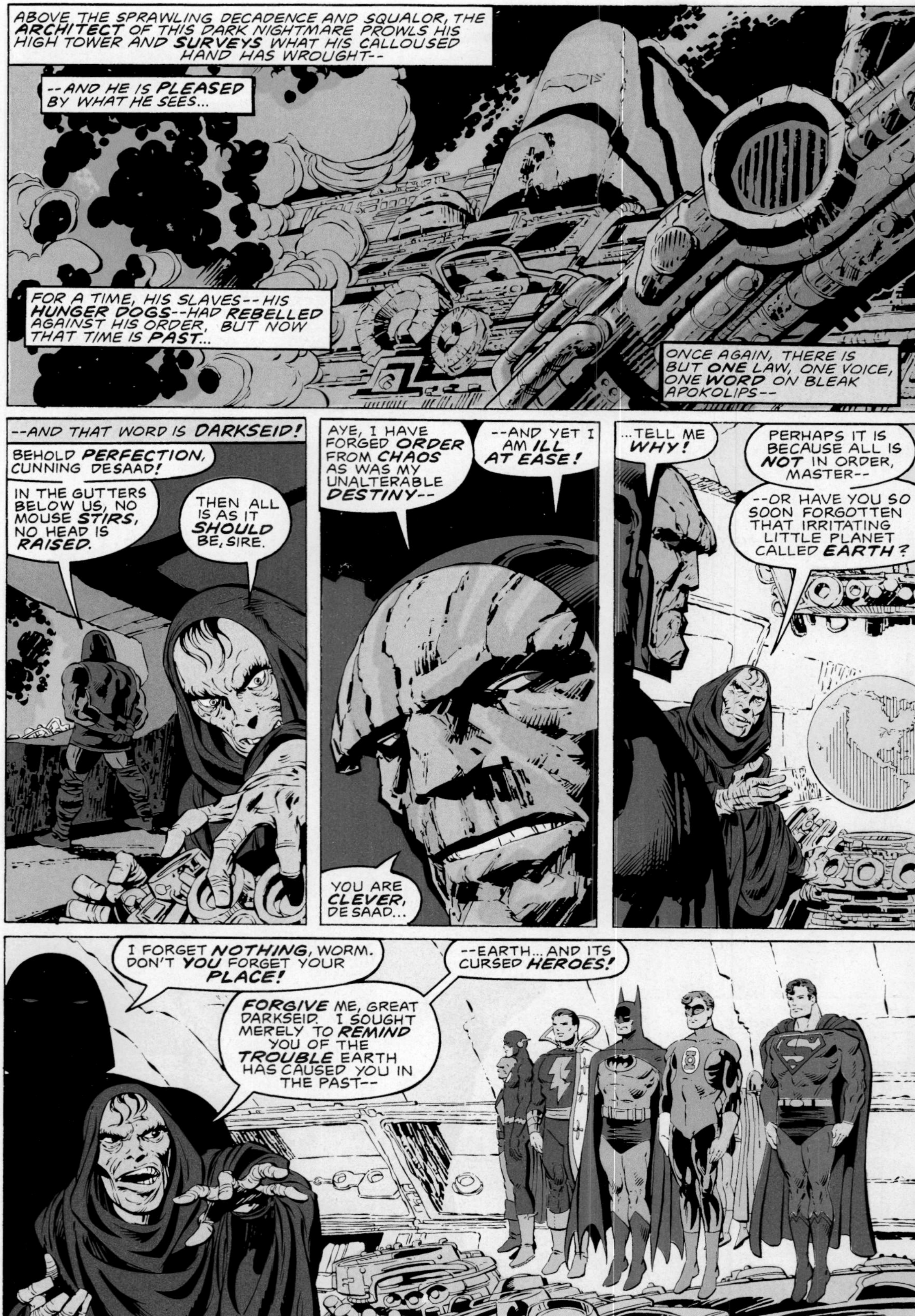
ABOVE THE SPRAWLING DECADENCE AND SQUALOR, THE ARCHITECT OF THIS DARK NIGHTMARE PROWLS HIS HIGH TOWER AND SURVEYS WHAT HIS CALLOUSED HAND HAS WROUGHT--
--AND HE IS PLEASED BY WHAT HE SEES...
FOR A TIME, HIS SLAVES--HIS HUNGER DOGS--HAD REBELLED AGAINST HIS ORDER, BUT NOW THAT TIME IS PAST...
ONCE AGAIN, THERE IS BUT ONE LAW, ONE VOICE, ONE WORD ON BLEAK APOKOLIPS--
--AND THAT WORD IS DARKSEID!
BEHOLD PERFECTION, CUNNING DESAAD!
IN THE GUTTERS BELOW US, NO MOUSE STIRS, NO HEAD IS RAISED.
THEN ALL IS AS IT SHOULD BE, SIRE.
AYE, I HAVE FORGED ORDER FROM CHAOS AS WAS MY UNALTERABLE DESTINY--
--AND YET I AM ILL AT EASE!
YOU ARE CLEVER, DESAAD...
...TELL ME WHY!
PERHAPS IT IS BECAUSE ALL IS NOT IN ORDER, MASTER--
--OR HAVE YOU SO SOON FORGOTTEN THAT IRRITATING LITTLE PLANET CALLED EARTH?
I FORGET NOTHING, WORM. DON'T YOU FORGET YOUR PLACE!
FORGIVE ME, GREAT DARKSEID. I SOUGHT MERELY TO REMIND YOU OF THE TROUBLE EARTH HAS CAUSED YOU IN THE PAST--
--EARTH... AND ITS CURSED HEROES!

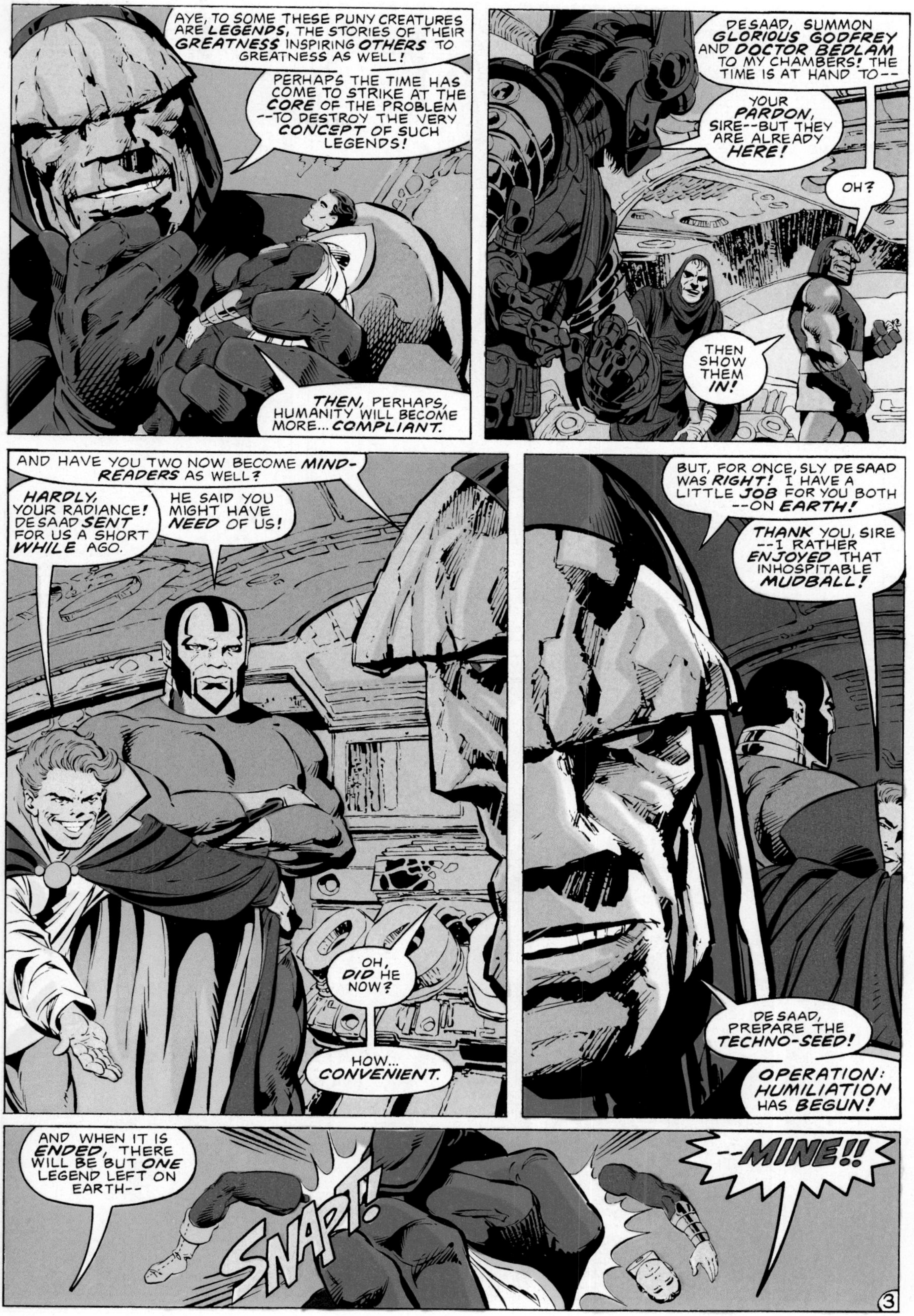
AYE, TO SOME THESE PUNY CREATURES ARE LEGENDS, THE STORIES OF THEIR GREATNESS INSPIRING OTHERS TO GREATNESS AS WELL!
PERHAPS THE TIME HAS COME TO STRIKE AT THE CORE OF THE PROBLEM --TO DESTROY THE VERY CONCEPT OF SUCH LEGENDS!
THEN, PERHAPS, HUMANITY WILL BECOME MORE... COMPLIANT.
DESAAD, SUMMON GLORIOUS GODFREY AND DOCTOR BEDLAM TO MY CHAMBERS! THE TIME IS AT HAND TO--
YOUR PARDON, SIRE--BUT THEY ARE ALREADY HERE!
OH?
THEN SHOW THEM IN!
AND HAVE YOU TWO NOW BECOME MIND-READERS AS WELL?
HARDLY, YOUR RADIANCE! DESAAD SENT FOR US A SHORT WHILE AGO.
HE SAID YOU MIGHT HAVE NEED OF US!
OH, DID HE NOW?
HOW... CONVENIENT.
BUT, FOR ONCE, SLY DESAAD WAS RIGHT! I HAVE A LITTLE JOB FOR YOU BOTH --ON EARTH!
THANK YOU, SIRE --I RATHER ENJOYED THAT INHOSPITABLE MUDBALL!
DESAAD, PREPARE THE TECHNO-SEED!
OPERATION: HUMILIATION HAS BEGUN!
AND WHEN IT IS ENDED, THERE WILL BE BUT ONE LEGEND LEFT ON EARTH--
SNAP!
--MINE!!
3

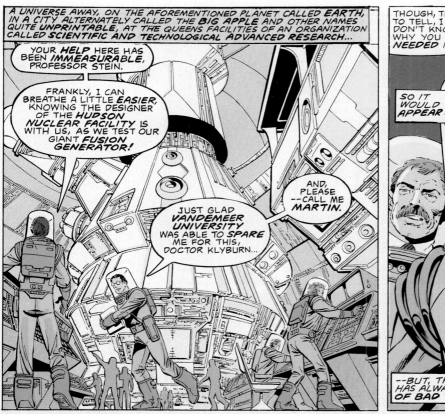

A UNIVERSE AWAY, ON THE AFOREMENTIONED PLANET CALLED *EARTH*, IN A CITY ALTERNATELY CALLED THE *BIG APPLE* AND OTHER NAMES QUITE *UNPRINTABLE*, AT THE QUEENS FACILITIES OF AN ORGANIZATION CALLED *SCIENTIFIC AND TECHNOLOGICAL ADVANCED RESEARCH...*

YOUR *HELP* HERE HAS BEEN *IMMEASURABLE*, PROFESSOR STEIN.

FRANKLY, I CAN BREATHE A LITTLE *EASIER*, KNOWING THE DESIGNER OF THE *HUDSON NUCLEAR FACILITY* IS WITH US, AS WE TEST OUR GIANT *FUSION GENERATOR!*

JUST GLAD *VANDEMEER UNIVERSITY* WAS ABLE TO *SPARE* ME FOR THIS, DOCTOR KLYBURN...

AND, PLEASE --CALL ME *MARTIN.*

THOUGH, TRUTH TO TELL, I REALLY *DON'T KNOW* WHY YOU *NEEDED* ME--

--SINCE THE LIMITED *FUSION PROCESS* YOU'VE BEGUN HERE SEEMS TO BE MOVING ALONG *FLAWLESSLY!*

SO IT *WOULD APPEAR* --

--BUT, THEN, MARTIN STEIN HAS ALWAYS BEEN A *MASTER OF BAD TIMING...*

...FOR *DARKSEID'S* TERRIBLE *TECHNO-SEED* CHOOSES PRECISELY THAT MOMENT TO MATERIALIZE IN THE VERY *HEART* OF THE NUCLEAR GENERATOR--

--AND THE *RESULT* IS SPONTANEOUS *CHAOS!*

THE GENERATOR'S GONE *BERSERK*--!

IT'S SUCKING IN ALL THE *POWER* IN THE ENTIRE *FACILITY*--

--AND-- MY GOD-- SOMETHING IS *GROWING* INSIDE IT--!!

SOMETHING--*INHUMAN!!*

BEHOLD THE FALLEN ANGEL KNOWN AS-- *BRIMSTONE!*

GAZE INTO MY *EYES*, YE MIGHTY --AND *DESPAIR!*

THIS IS *MADNESS!*

I'VE GOT TO SUMMON-- *FIRESTORM!*

4

CONTINUED ON 3RD PAGE FOLLOWING

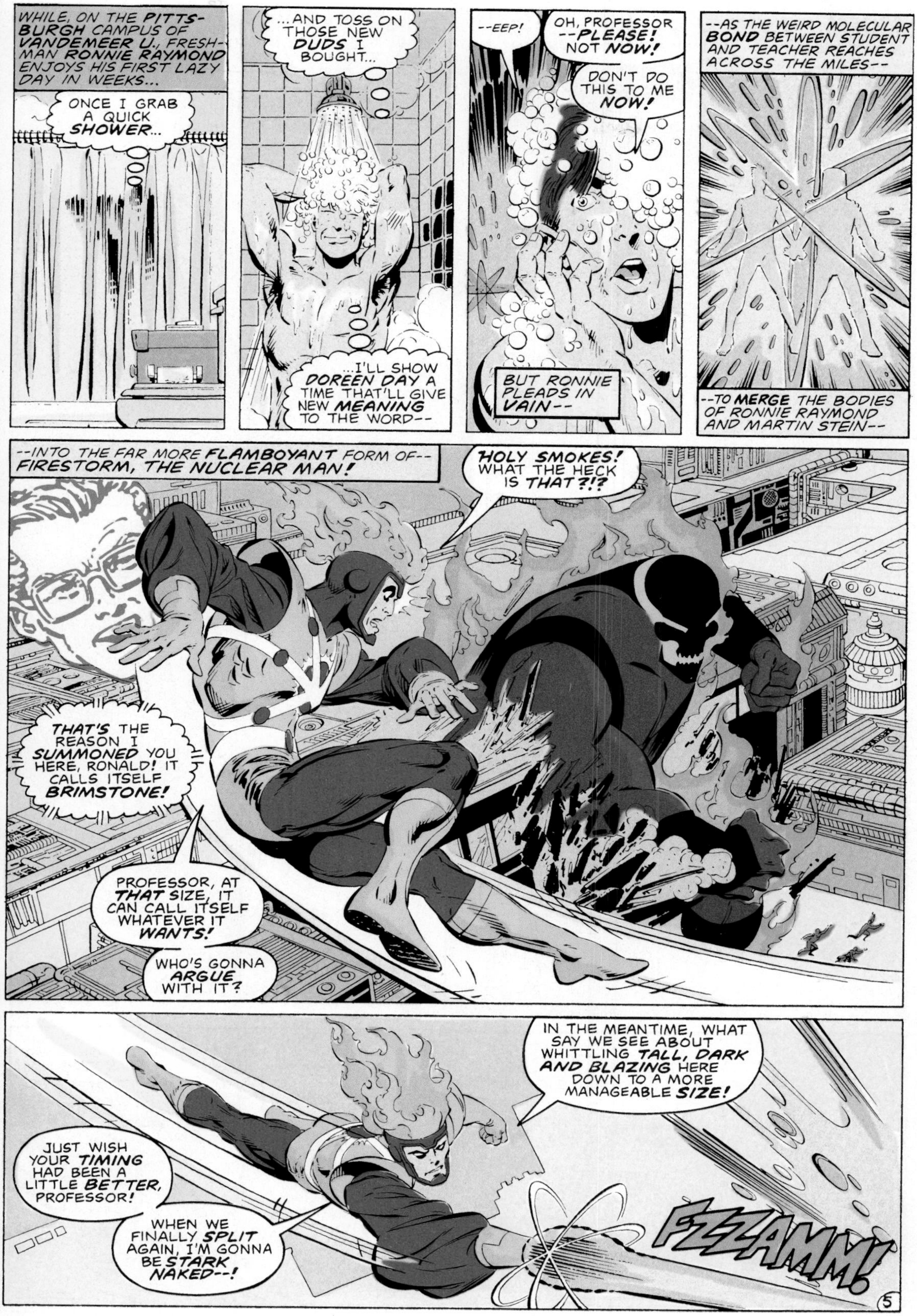

WHILE, ON THE PITTSBURGH CAMPUS OF VANDEMEER U., FRESHMAN RONNIE RAYMOND ENJOYS HIS FIRST LAZY DAY IN WEEKS...
ONCE I GRAB A QUICK SHOWER...
...AND TOSS ON THOSE NEW DUDS I BOUGHT...
...I'LL SHOW DOREEN DAY A TIME THAT'LL GIVE NEW MEANING TO THE WORD--
--EEP!
OH, PROFESSOR --PLEASE! NOT NOW!
DON'T DO THIS TO ME NOW!
BUT RONNIE PLEADS IN VAIN--
--AS THE WEIRD MOLECULAR BOND BETWEEN STUDENT AND TEACHER REACHES ACROSS THE MILES--
--TO MERGE THE BODIES OF RONNIE RAYMOND AND MARTIN STEIN--
--INTO THE FAR MORE FLAMBOYANT FORM OF-- FIRESTORM, THE NUCLEAR MAN!
HOLY SMOKES! WHAT THE HECK IS THAT?!?
THAT'S THE REASON I SUMMONED YOU HERE, RONALD! IT CALLS ITSELF BRIMSTONE!
PROFESSOR, AT THAT SIZE, IT CAN CALL ITSELF WHATEVER IT WANTS!
WHO'S GONNA ARGUE WITH IT?
IN THE MEANTIME, WHAT SAY WE SEE ABOUT WHITTLING TALL, DARK AND BLAZING HERE DOWN TO A MORE MANAGEABLE SIZE!
JUST WISH YOUR TIMING HAD BEEN A LITTLE BETTER, PROFESSOR!
WHEN WE FINALLY SPLIT AGAIN, I'M GONNA BE STARK NAKED--!
FZZAMM!
5

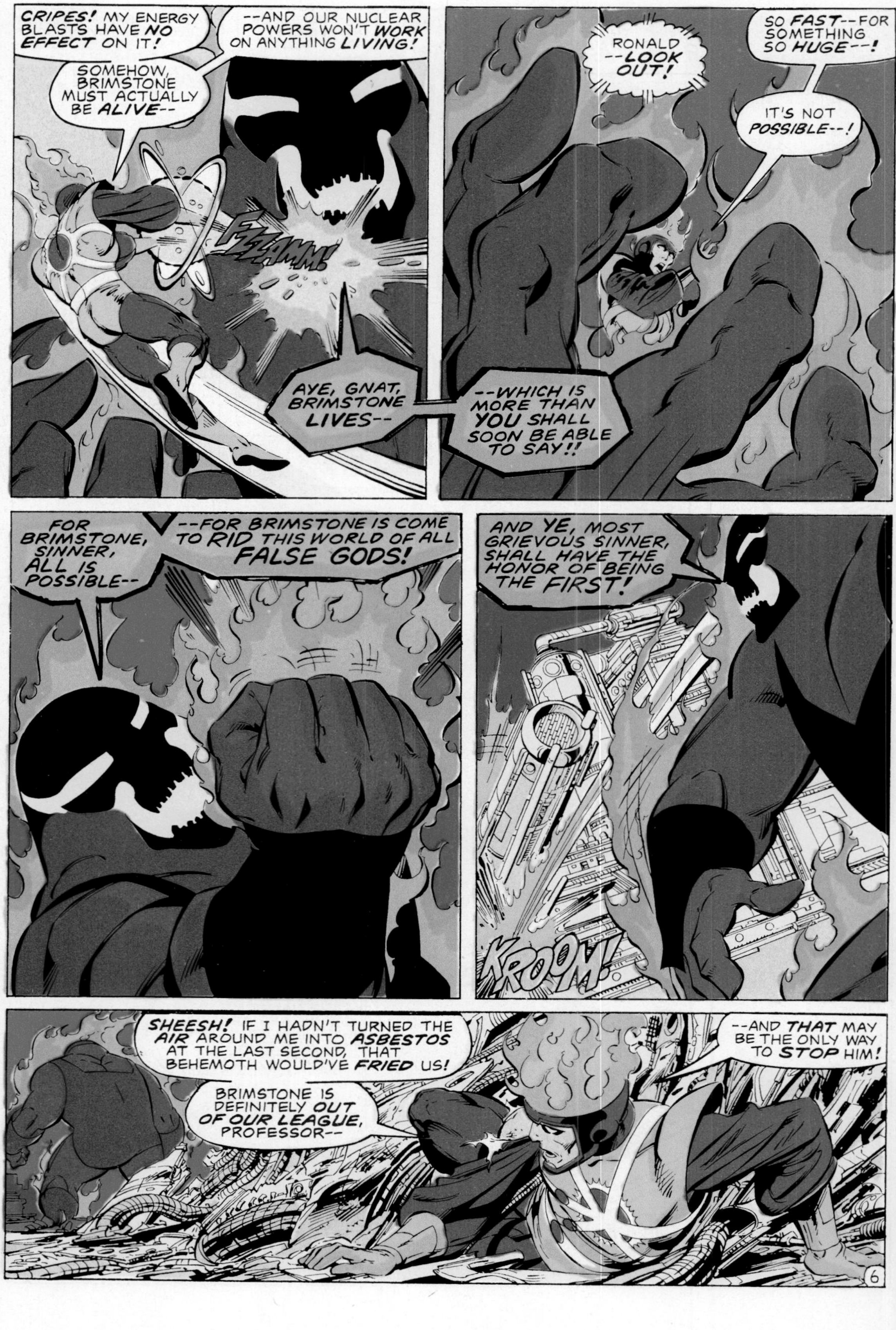
CRIPES! MY ENERGY BLASTS HAVE NO EFFECT ON IT!
--AND OUR NUCLEAR POWERS WON'T WORK ON ANYTHING LIVING!
SOMEHOW, BRIMSTONE MUST ACTUALLY BE ALIVE--
FZZLAMM!
AYE, GNAT, BRIMSTONE LIVES--
--WHICH IS MORE THAN YOU SHALL SOON BE ABLE TO SAY!!
RONALD --LOOK OUT!
SO FAST--FOR SOMETHING SO HUGE--!
IT'S NOT POSSIBLE--!
FOR BRIMSTONE, SINNER, ALL IS POSSIBLE--
--FOR BRIMSTONE IS COME TO RID THIS WORLD OF ALL FALSE GODS!
AND YE, MOST GRIEVOUS SINNER, SHALL HAVE THE HONOR OF BEING THE FIRST!
KROOM!
SHEESH! IF I HADN'T TURNED THE AIR AROUND ME INTO ASBESTOS AT THE LAST SECOND, THAT BEHEMOTH WOULD'VE FRIED US!
BRIMSTONE IS DEFINITELY OUT OF OUR LEAGUE, PROFESSOR--
--AND THAT MAY BE THE ONLY WAY TO STOP HIM!
6

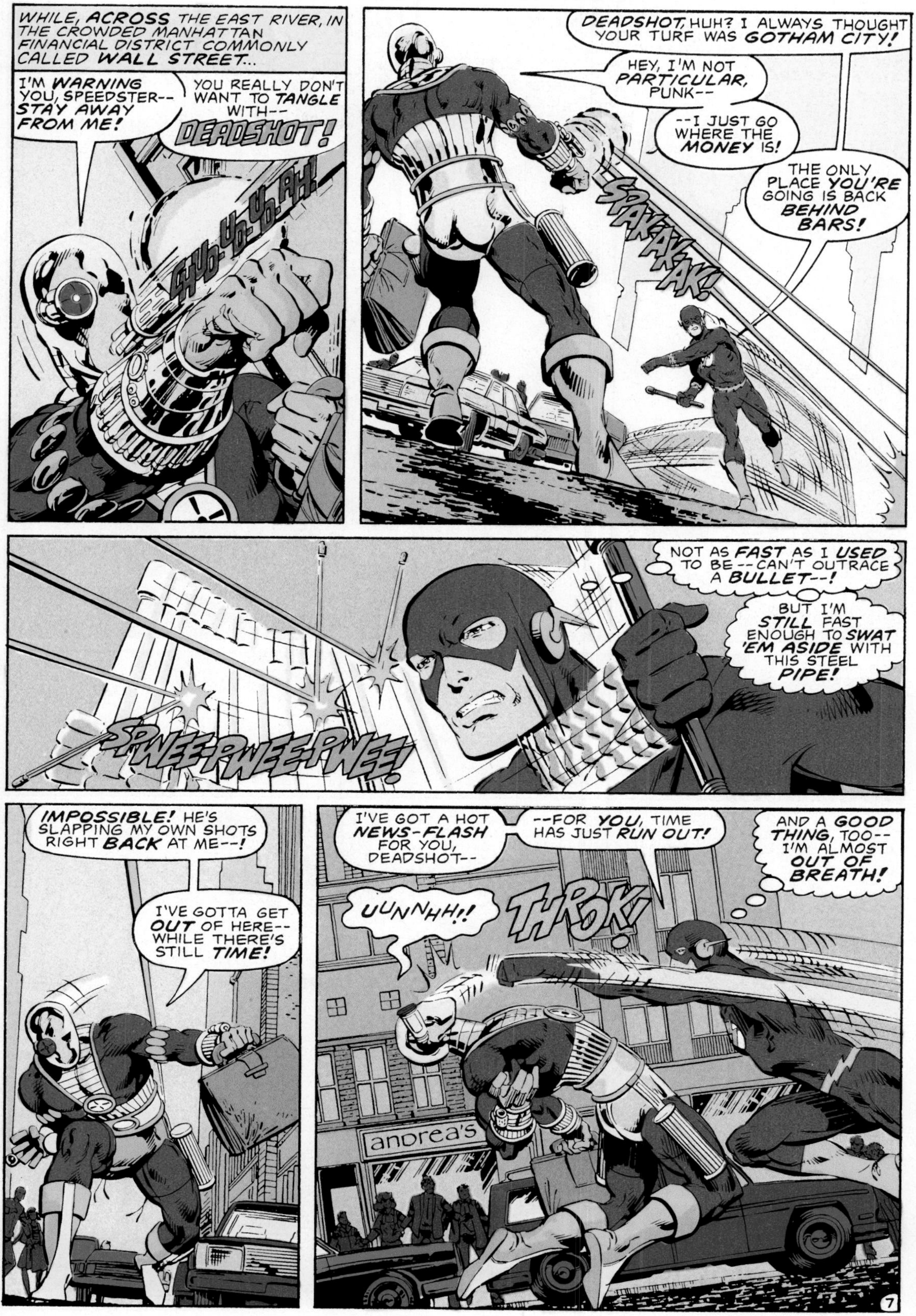
WHILE, ACROSS THE EAST RIVER, IN THE CROWDED MANHATTAN FINANCIAL DISTRICT COMMONLY CALLED WALL STREET...
I'M WARNING YOU, SPEEDSTER-- STAY AWAY FROM ME!
YOU REALLY DON'T WANT TO TANGLE WITH-- DEADSHOT!
CHUD-UD-UD-UD-AH!
DEADSHOT, HUH? I ALWAYS THOUGHT YOUR TURF WAS GOTHAM CITY!
HEY, I'M NOT PARTICULAR, PUNK--
--I JUST GO WHERE THE MONEY IS!
THE ONLY PLACE YOU'RE GOING IS BACK BEHIND BARS!
SPAKAKAK!
NOT AS FAST AS I USED TO BE--CAN'T OUTRACE A BULLET--!
BUT I'M STILL FAST ENOUGH TO SWAT 'EM ASIDE WITH THIS STEEL PIPE!
SPWEE-PWEE-PWEE!
IMPOSSIBLE! HE'S SLAPPING MY OWN SHOTS RIGHT BACK AT ME--!
I'VE GOTTA GET OUT OF HERE-- WHILE THERE'S STILL TIME!
I'VE GOT A HOT NEWS-FLASH FOR YOU, DEADSHOT--
--FOR YOU, TIME HAS JUST RUN OUT!
AND A GOOD THING, TOO-- I'M ALMOST OUT OF BREATH!
UUNNHH!!
THROK!
andrea's

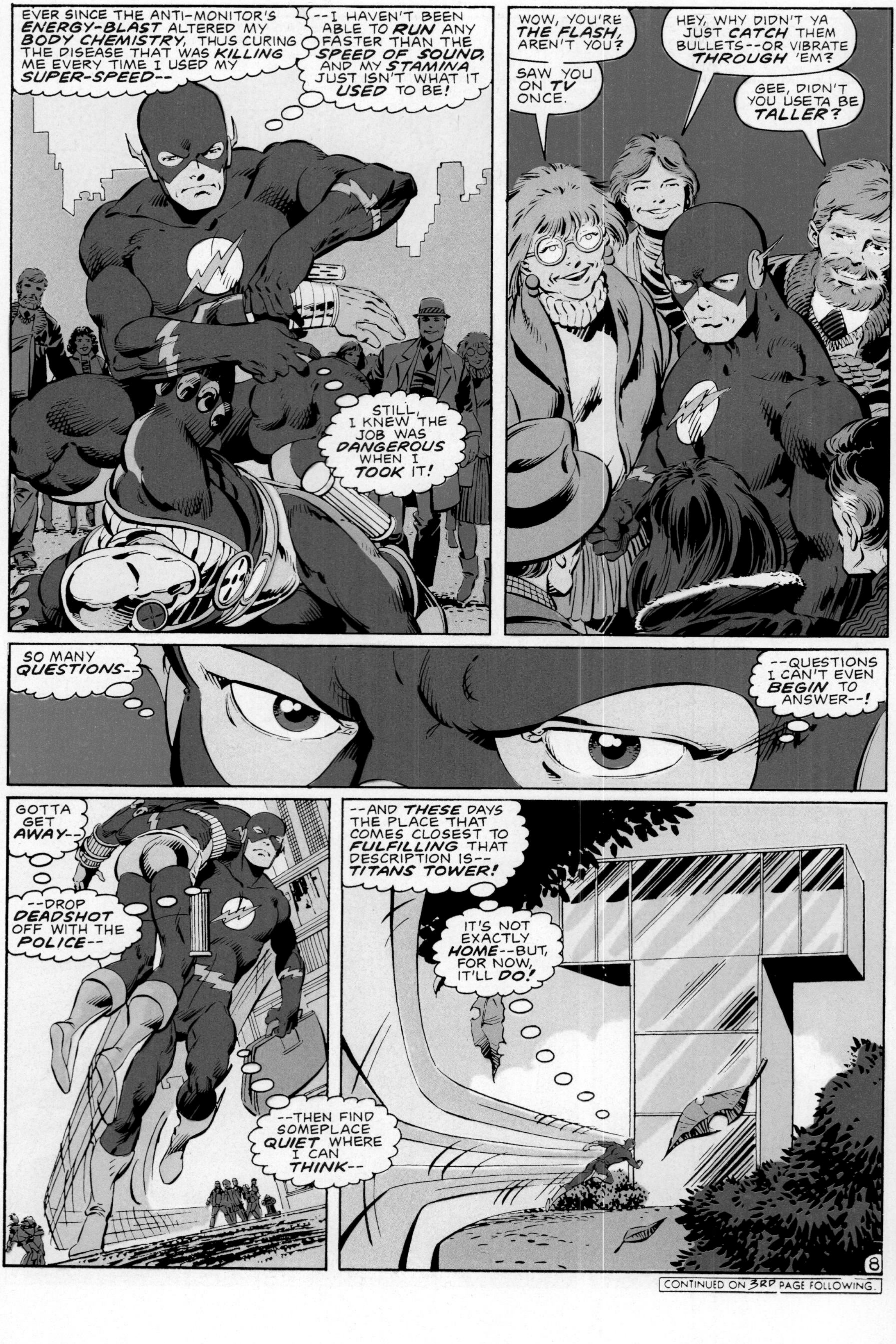
EVER SINCE THE ANTI-MONITOR'S ENERGY-BLAST ALTERED MY BODY CHEMISTRY, THUS CURING THE DISEASE THAT WAS KILLING ME EVERY TIME I USED MY SUPER-SPEED--
--I HAVEN'T BEEN ABLE TO RUN ANY FASTER THAN THE SPEED OF SOUND, AND MY STAMINA JUST ISN'T WHAT IT USED TO BE!
STILL, I KNEW THE JOB WAS DANGEROUS WHEN I TOOK IT!
WOW, YOU'RE THE FLASH, AREN'T YOU?
SAW YOU ON TV ONCE.
HEY, WHY DIDN'T YA JUST CATCH THEM BULLETS--OR VIBRATE THROUGH 'EM?
GEE, DIDN'T YOU USETA BE TALLER?
SO MANY QUESTIONS--
--QUESTIONS I CAN'T EVEN BEGIN TO ANSWER--!
GOTTA GET AWAY--
--DROP DEADSHOT OFF WITH THE POLICE--
--THEN FIND SOMEPLACE QUIET WHERE I CAN THINK--
--AND THESE DAYS THE PLACE THAT COMES CLOSEST TO FULFILLING THAT DESCRIPTION IS--TITANS TOWER!
IT'S NOT EXACTLY HOME--BUT, FOR NOW, IT'LL DO!

CONTINUED ON 3RD PAGE FOLLOWING.

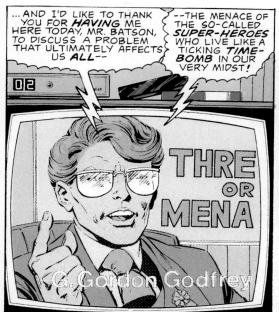

...AND I'D LIKE TO THANK YOU FOR *HAVING* ME HERE TODAY, MR. BATSON, TO DISCUSS A PROBLEM THAT ULTIMATELY AFFECTS US *ALL*--

--THE MENACE OF THE SO-CALLED *SUPER-HEROES* WHO LIVE LIKE A TICKING *TIME-BOMB* IN OUR VERY MIDST!

THRE OR MENA

G. Gordon Godfrey

MAN, THAT *G. GORDON GODFREY* GOON IS JUST WHAT THIS COUNTRY *NEEDS*--ANOTHER *CRAZY* WITH A *CAUSE!*

HEY, *BOZO*--YER *FATHER* WEARS YER MOTHER'S *ARMY BOOTS!*

ENJOYING YOURSELF, CHANGLING?

WELL, LET ME PUT IT *THIS* WAY, WALLY OL' PAL...

ALL THINGS CONSIDERED, I'D RATHER BE WATCHING A *McLEAN STEVENSON* RETROSPECTIVE!

SO HOW'RE *YOU* DOIN'?

YOU LOOK LIKE *GOD* JUST CAUGHT YOU STEALING HIS *HUBCAPS!*

OH, IT'S REALLY NOTHING IN *PARTICULAR,* GAR--

--JUST ANOTHER EXCITING EPISODE IN MY ONGOING *IDENTITY CRISIS!*

HEY, JUST GIVE ME A SECOND TO *CHANGE* INTO SOMEONE MORE *COMFORTABLE*--

--AND YOU CAN TELL *DOCTOR LOGAN* ALL *ABOUT* IT!

9

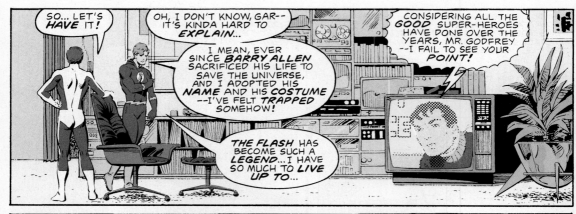

SO... LET'S *HAVE* IT!

OH, I DON'T KNOW, GAR-- IT'S KINDA HARD TO *EXPLAIN...*

I MEAN, EVER SINCE *BARRY ALLEN* SACRIFICED HIS LIFE TO SAVE THE UNIVERSE, AND I ADOPTED HIS *NAME* AND HIS *COSTUME* --I'VE FELT *TRAPPED* SOMEHOW!

THE FLASH HAS BECOME SUCH A *LEGEND...* I HAVE SO MUCH TO *LIVE* UP TO...

CONSIDERING ALL THE *GOOD* SUPER-HEROES HAVE DONE OVER THE YEARS, MR. GODFREY --I FAIL TO SEE YOUR *POINT!*

AND YOU'RE NOT SURE YOU CAN *CUT* IT, HUH?

IN TWENTY-FIVE WORDS OR LESS-- THAT'S ABOUT THE *SIZE* OF IT!

HEY--EASY *SOLUTION!* IF BEING *THE FLASH* IS YOUR PROBLEM, WHY NOT JUST BECOME SOMEBODY *ELSE?*

MY POINT IS SIMPLY *THIS,* MR. BATSON--THESE COSTUMED *MYSTERY-MEN* PROVIDE NEGATIVE *ROLE MODELS* FOR OUR CHILDREN...

GET YOURSELF A NEW *COSTUME...* A SPIFFY NEW NAME LIKE *BLUE BOLT* OR *SPEED DEMON* OR *CHARLIE HUSTLE* OR SOMETHING AND-- *POOF!*

NO MORE *LEGEND* TO WORRY ABOUT!

BUT THAT'S JUST THE *POINT,* GAR! IF I DO *THAT,* THE LEGEND *DIES*--

--AND I REFUSE TO *ALLOW* THAT TO *HAPPEN!*

...THEY EMPHASIZE *VIOLENCE* AS A *SOLUTION* TO THE WORLD'S PROBLEMS.

LISTEN, PAL--IF THAT *GEEK* ON THE BOOB-TUBE GETS HIS WAY, THERE WON'T BE *ANY* LEGENDS LEFT ALIVE!

YEAH, JUST WHO *IS* THIS G. GORDON GODFREY SUPPOSED TO--

--HUH??

AWW--DON'T TELL ME WE'VE BLOWN ANOTHER *FUSE!*

THEY ARE OUTMODED, MALADJUSTED *LONERS,* OUTLAWS WORKING *OUTSIDE* THE SYSTEM TO--

10

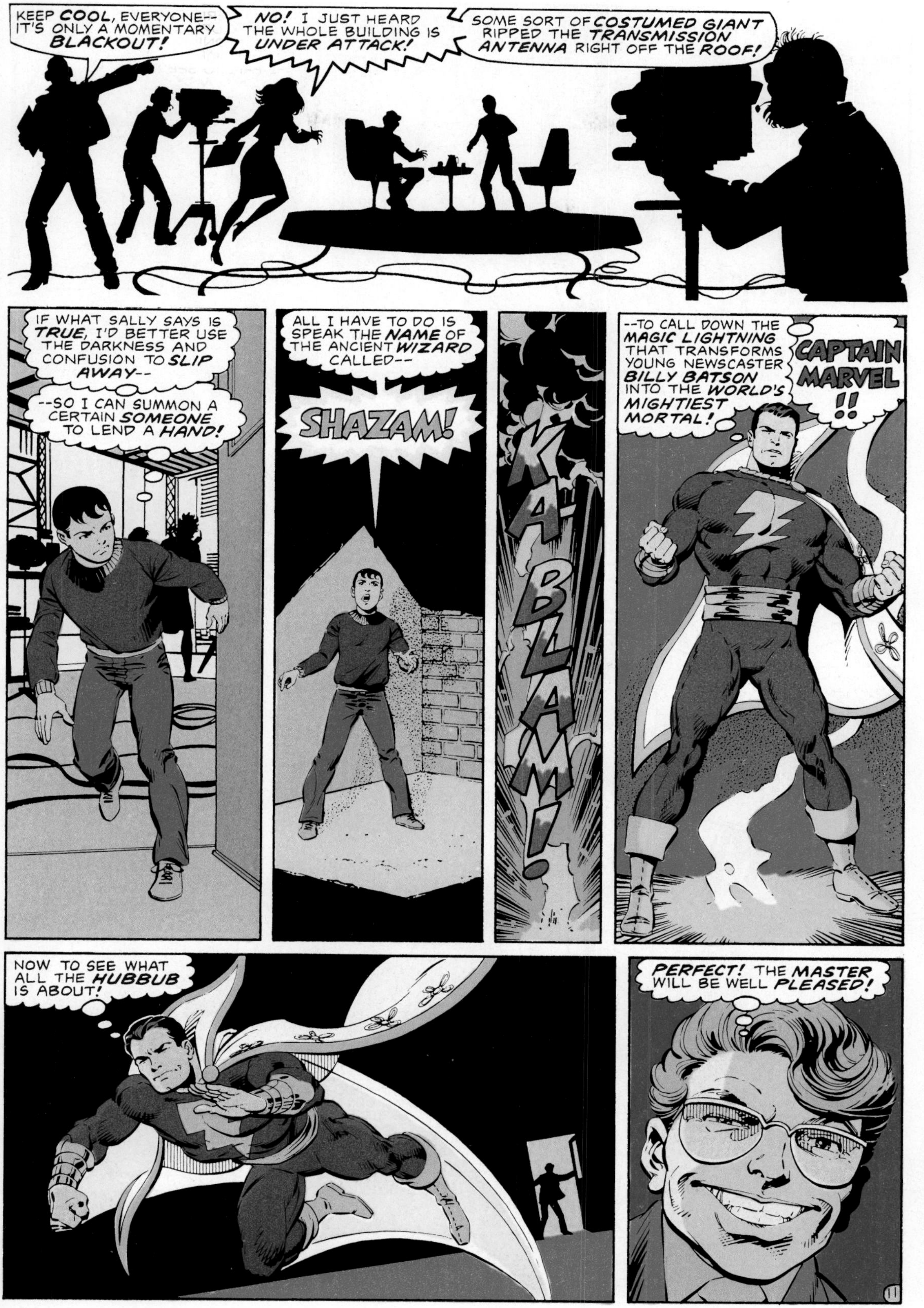
KEEP COOL, EVERYONE-- IT'S ONLY A MOMENTARY BLACKOUT!
NO! I JUST HEARD THE WHOLE BUILDING IS UNDER ATTACK!
SOME SORT OF COSTUMED GIANT RIPPED THE TRANSMISSION ANTENNA RIGHT OFF THE ROOF!
IF WHAT SALLY SAYS IS TRUE, I'D BETTER USE THE DARKNESS AND CONFUSION TO SLIP AWAY--
--SO I CAN SUMMON A CERTAIN SOMEONE TO LEND A HAND!
ALL I HAVE TO DO IS SPEAK THE NAME OF THE ANCIENT WIZARD CALLED--
SHAZAM!
KA-BLAM!
--TO CALL DOWN THE MAGIC LIGHTNING THAT TRANSFORMS YOUNG NEWSCASTER BILLY BATSON INTO THE WORLD'S MIGHTIEST MORTAL!
CAPTAIN MARVEL !!
NOW TO SEE WHAT ALL THE HUBBUB IS ABOUT!
PERFECT! THE MASTER WILL BE WELL PLEASED!

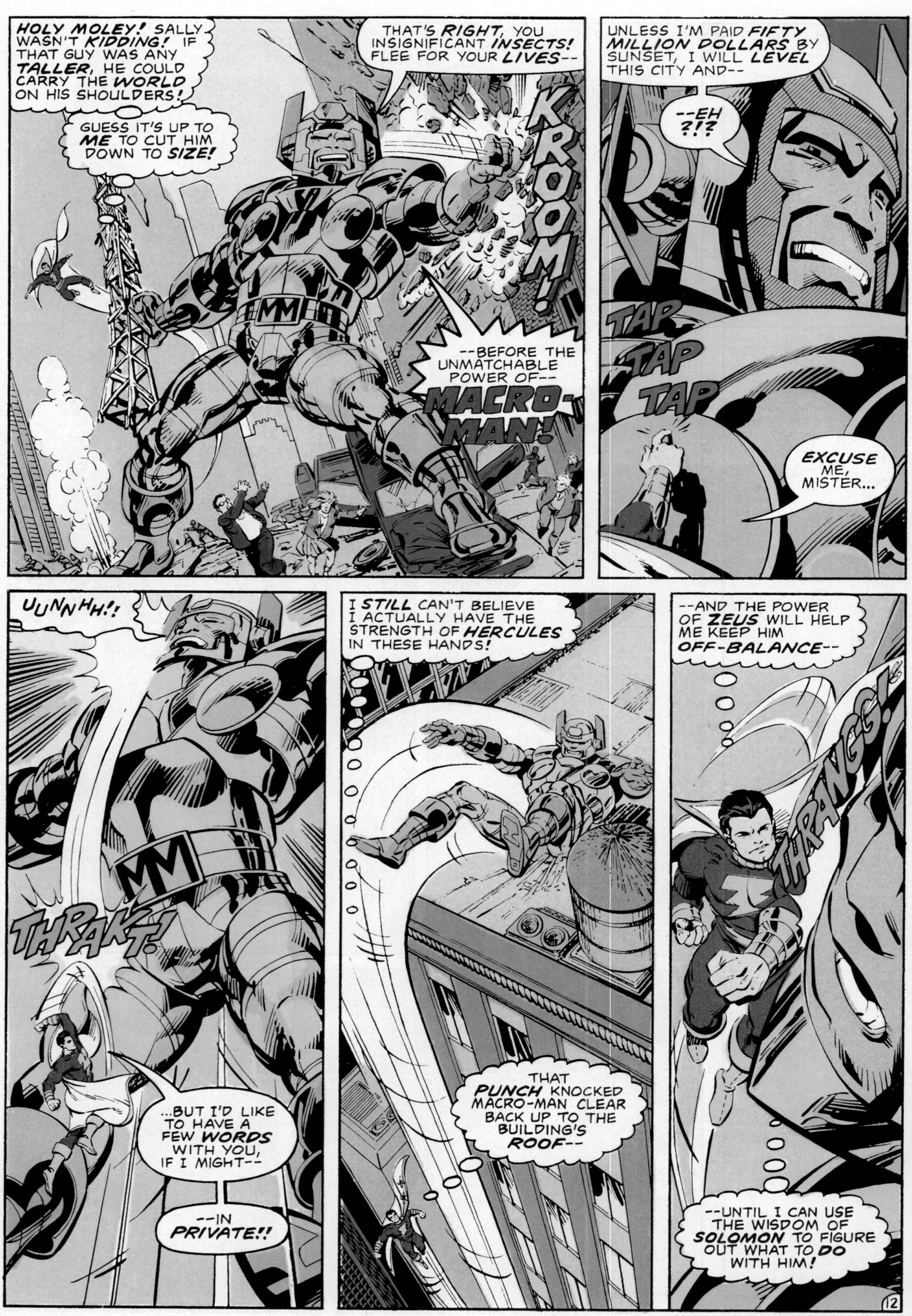

HOLY MOLEY! SALLY WASN'T KIDDING! IF THAT GUY WAS ANY TALLER, HE COULD CARRY THE WORLD ON HIS SHOULDERS!
GUESS IT'S UP TO ME TO CUT HIM DOWN TO SIZE!
THAT'S RIGHT, YOU INSIGNIFICANT INSECTS! FLEE FOR YOUR LIVES--
KROOM!
--BEFORE THE UNMATCHABLE POWER OF-- MACRO-MAN!
UNLESS I'M PAID FIFTY MILLION DOLLARS BY SUNSET, I WILL LEVEL THIS CITY AND--
--EH ?!?
TAP TAP TAP
EXCUSE ME, MISTER...
UUNNHH!!
THRAKT!
...BUT I'D LIKE TO HAVE A FEW WORDS WITH YOU, IF I MIGHT--
--IN PRIVATE!!
I STILL CAN'T BELIEVE I ACTUALLY HAVE THE STRENGTH OF HERCULES IN THESE HANDS!
THAT PUNCH KNOCKED MACRO-MAN CLEAR BACK UP TO THE BUILDING'S ROOF--
--AND THE POWER OF ZEUS WILL HELP ME KEEP HIM OFF-BALANCE--
THRANGG!
--UNTIL I CAN USE THE WISDOM OF SOLOMON TO FIGURE OUT WHAT TO DO WITH HIM!

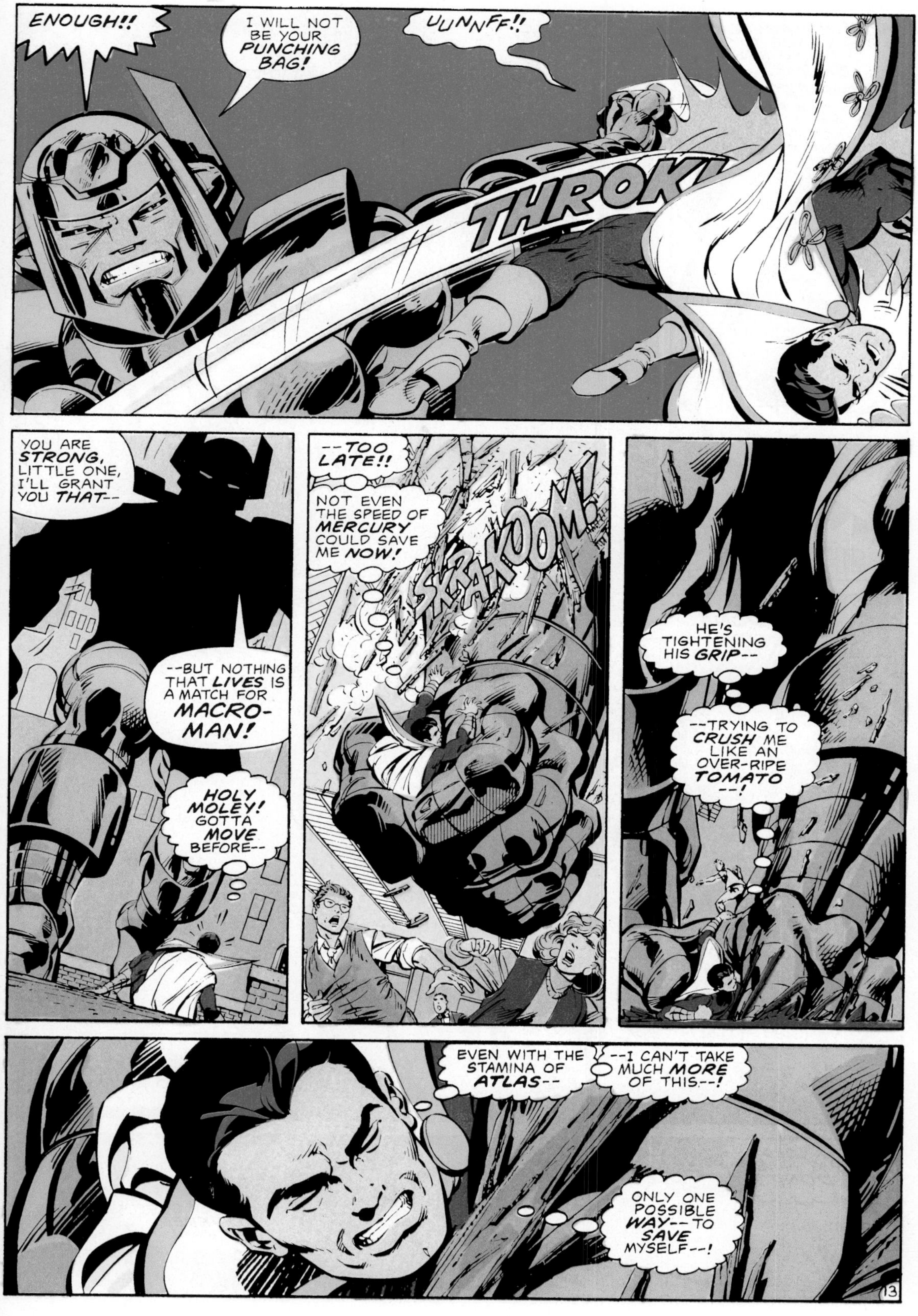
ENOUGH!!
I WILL NOT BE YOUR PUNCHING BAG!
UUNNFF!!
THROK!
YOU ARE STRONG, LITTLE ONE, I'LL GRANT YOU THAT--
--BUT NOTHING THAT LIVES IS A MATCH FOR MACRO-MAN!
HOLY MOLEY! GOTTA MOVE BEFORE--
--TOO LATE!!
NOT EVEN THE SPEED OF MERCURY COULD SAVE ME NOW!
SKRAKOOM!
HE'S TIGHTENING HIS GRIP--
--TRYING TO CRUSH ME LIKE AN OVER-RIPE TOMATO --!
EVEN WITH THE STAMINA OF ATLAS--
--I CAN'T TAKE MUCH MORE OF THIS--!
ONLY ONE POSSIBLE WAY--TO SAVE MYSELF--!

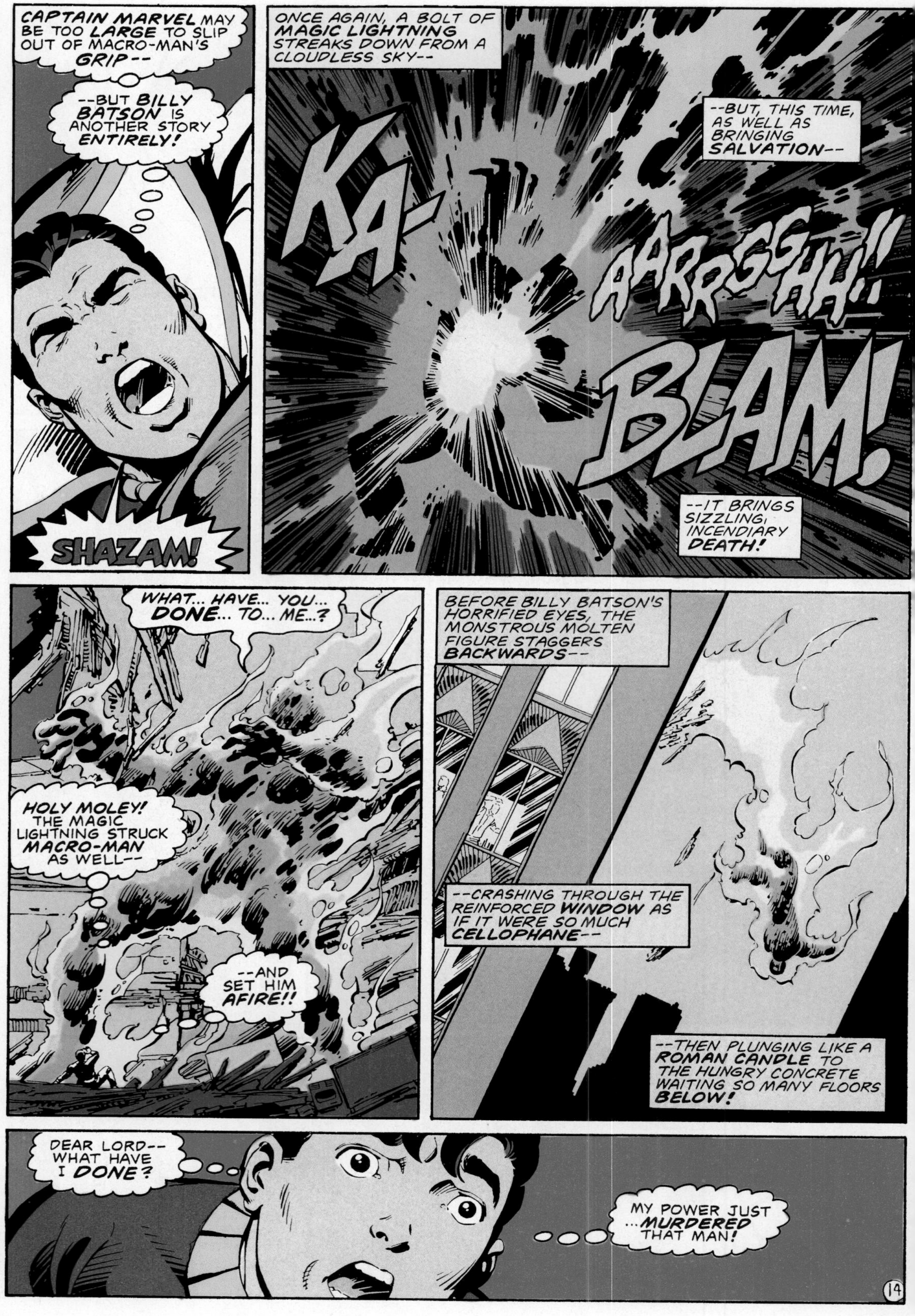

CAPTAIN MARVEL MAY BE TOO LARGE TO SLIP OUT OF MACRO-MAN'S GRIP--
--BUT BILLY BATSON IS ANOTHER STORY ENTIRELY!
SHAZAM!
ONCE AGAIN, A BOLT OF MAGIC LIGHTNING STREAKS DOWN FROM A CLOUDLESS SKY--
--BUT, THIS TIME, AS WELL AS BRINGING SALVATION--
KA-
AARRGGHH!!
BLAM!
--IT BRINGS SIZZLING, INCENDIARY DEATH!
WHAT... HAVE... YOU... DONE... TO... ME..?
HOLY MOLEY! THE MAGIC LIGHTNING STRUCK MACRO-MAN AS WELL--
--AND SET HIM AFIRE!!
BEFORE BILLY BATSON'S HORRIFIED EYES, THE MONSTROUS MOLTEN FIGURE STAGGERS BACKWARDS--
--CRASHING THROUGH THE REINFORCED WINDOW AS IF IT WERE SO MUCH CELLOPHANE--
--THEN PLUNGING LIKE A ROMAN CANDLE TO THE HUNGRY CONCRETE WAITING SO MANY FLOORS BELOW!
DEAR LORD-- WHAT HAVE I DONE?
MY POWER JUST ...MURDERED THAT MAN!

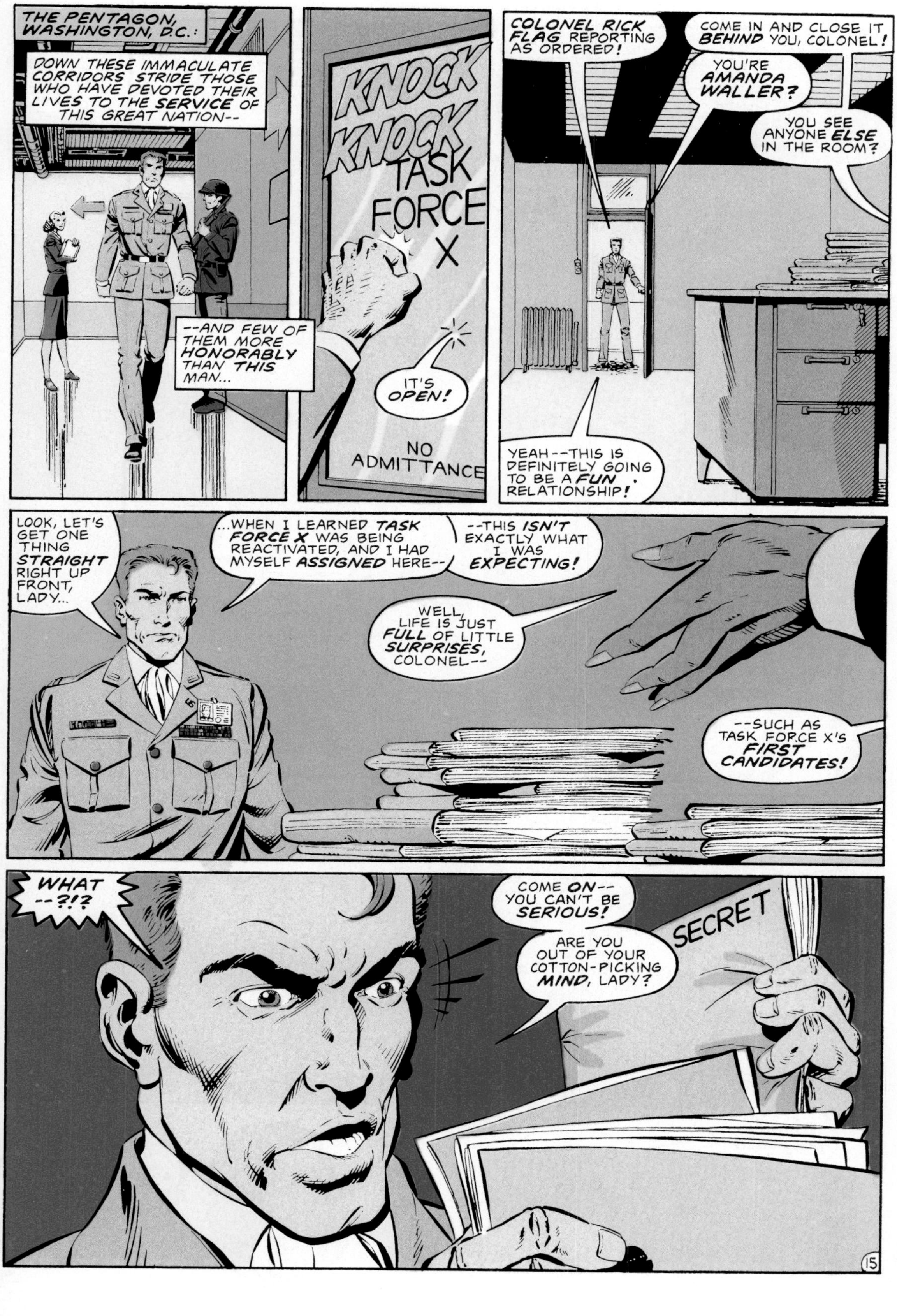
THE PENTAGON, WASHINGTON, D.C.:
DOWN THESE IMMACULATE CORRIDORS STRIDE THOSE WHO HAVE DEVOTED THEIR LIVES TO THE SERVICE OF THIS GREAT NATION--
--AND FEW OF THEM MORE HONORABLY THAN THIS MAN...
KNOCK KNOCK
TASK FORCE X
IT'S OPEN!
NO ADMITTANCE
COLONEL RICK FLAG REPORTING AS ORDERED!
COME IN AND CLOSE IT BEHIND YOU, COLONEL!
YOU'RE AMANDA WALLER?
YOU SEE ANYONE ELSE IN THE ROOM?
YEAH--THIS IS DEFINITELY GOING TO BE A FUN RELATIONSHIP!
LOOK, LET'S GET ONE THING STRAIGHT RIGHT UP FRONT, LADY...
...WHEN I LEARNED TASK FORCE X WAS BEING REACTIVATED, AND I HAD MYSELF ASSIGNED HERE--
--THIS ISN'T EXACTLY WHAT I WAS EXPECTING!
WELL, LIFE IS JUST FULL OF LITTLE SURPRISES, COLONEL--
--SUCH AS TASK FORCE X'S FIRST CANDIDATES!
WHAT--?!?
COME ON--YOU CAN'T BE SERIOUS!
ARE YOU OUT OF YOUR COTTON-PICKING MIND, LADY?
SECRET

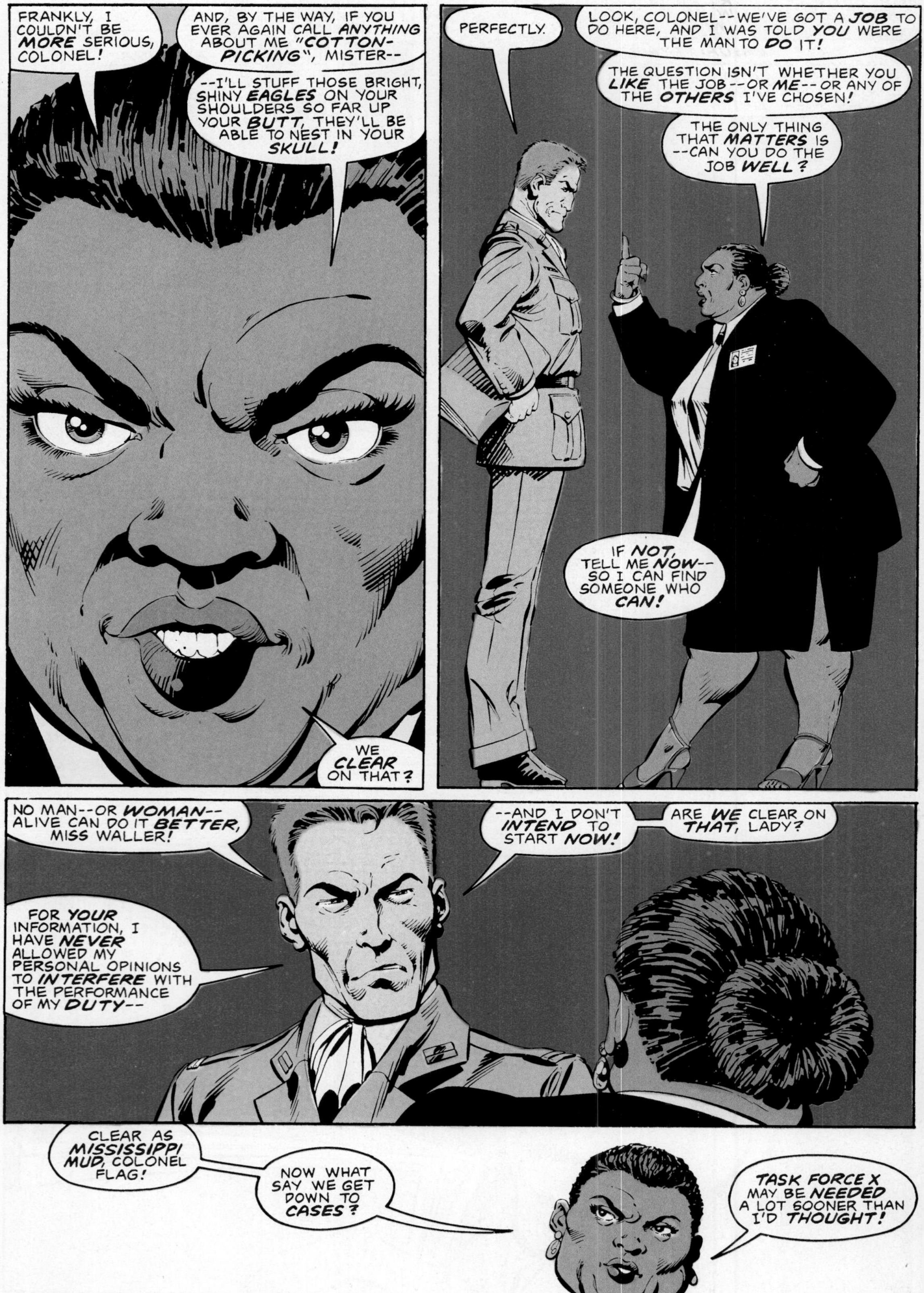
FRANKLY, I COULDN'T BE MORE SERIOUS, COLONEL!
AND, BY THE WAY, IF YOU EVER AGAIN CALL ANYTHING ABOUT ME "COTTON-PICKING", MISTER--
--I'LL STUFF THOSE BRIGHT, SHINY EAGLES ON YOUR SHOULDERS SO FAR UP YOUR BUTT, THEY'LL BE ABLE TO NEST IN YOUR SKULL!
WE CLEAR ON THAT?
PERFECTLY.
LOOK, COLONEL--WE'VE GOT A JOB TO DO HERE, AND I WAS TOLD YOU WERE THE MAN TO DO IT!
THE QUESTION ISN'T WHETHER YOU LIKE THE JOB--OR ME--OR ANY OF THE OTHERS I'VE CHOSEN!
THE ONLY THING THAT MATTERS IS --CAN YOU DO THE JOB WELL?
IF NOT, TELL ME NOW-- SO I CAN FIND SOMEONE WHO CAN!
NO MAN--OR WOMAN-- ALIVE CAN DO IT BETTER, MISS WALLER!
FOR YOUR INFORMATION, I HAVE NEVER ALLOWED MY PERSONAL OPINIONS TO INTERFERE WITH THE PERFORMANCE OF MY DUTY--
--AND I DON'T INTEND TO START NOW!
ARE WE CLEAR ON THAT, LADY?
CLEAR AS MISSISSIPPI MUD, COLONEL FLAG!
NOW WHAT SAY WE GET DOWN TO CASES?
TASK FORCE X MAY BE NEEDED A LOT SOONER THAN I'D THOUGHT!

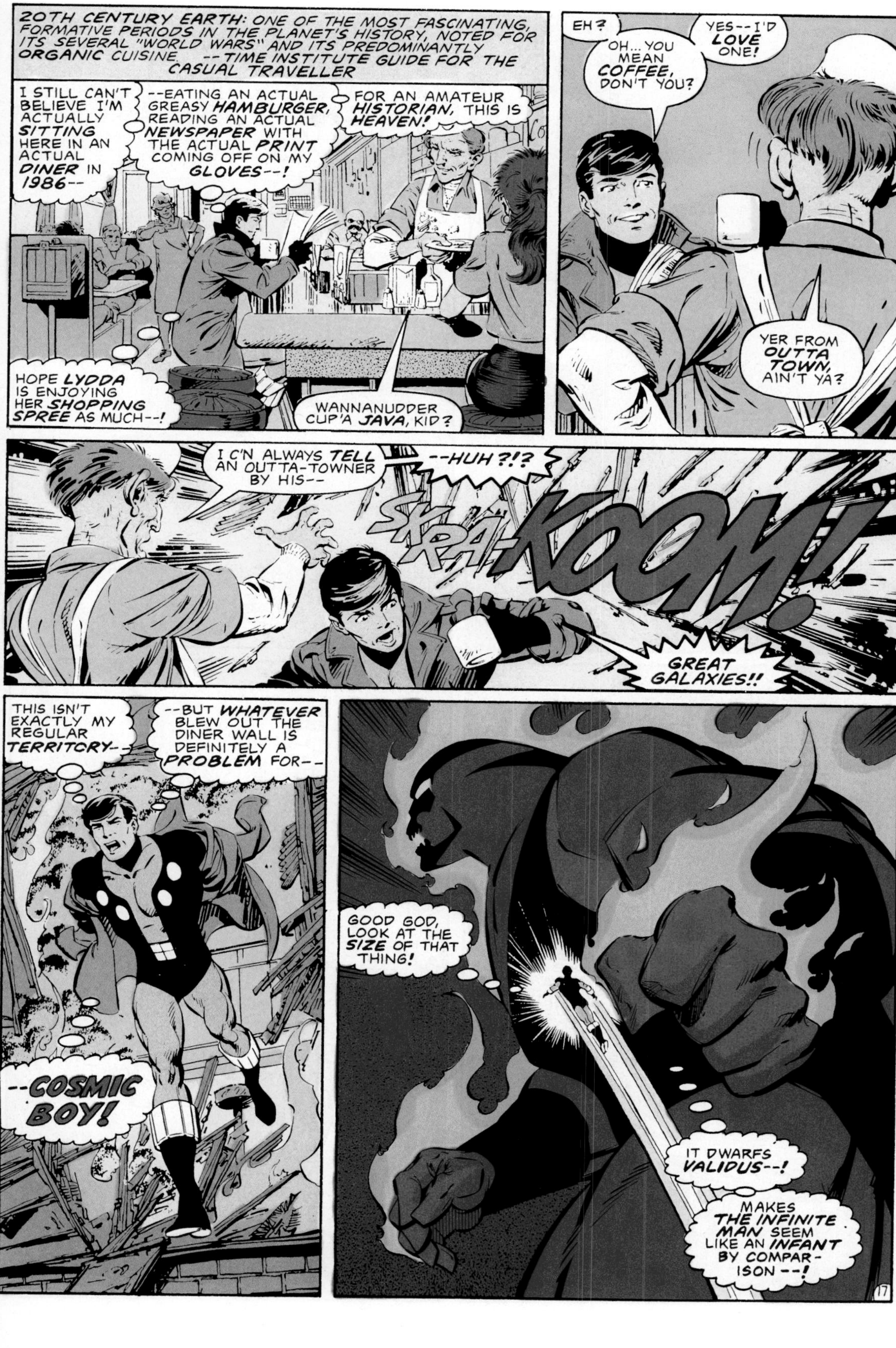

20TH CENTURY EARTH: ONE OF THE MOST FASCINATING, FORMATIVE PERIODS IN THE PLANET'S HISTORY, NOTED FOR ITS SEVERAL "WORLD WARS" AND ITS PREDOMINANTLY ORGANIC CUISINE. --TIME INSTITUTE GUIDE FOR THE CASUAL TRAVELLER
I STILL CAN'T BELIEVE I'M ACTUALLY SITTING HERE IN AN ACTUAL DINER IN 1986--
--EATING AN ACTUAL GREASY HAMBURGER, READING AN ACTUAL NEWSPAPER WITH THE ACTUAL PRINT COMING OFF ON MY GLOVES--!
FOR AN AMATEUR HISTORIAN, THIS IS HEAVEN!
HOPE LYDDA IS ENJOYING HER SHOPPING SPREE AS MUCH--!
WANNANUDDER CUP'A JAVA, KID?
EH?
OH... YOU MEAN COFFEE, DON'T YOU?
YES--I'D LOVE ONE!
YER FROM OUTTA TOWN, AIN'T YA?
I C'N ALWAYS TELL AN OUTTA-TOWNER BY HIS--
--HUH?!?
SKRA-KOOM!
GREAT GALAXIES!!
THIS ISN'T EXACTLY MY REGULAR TERRITORY--
--BUT WHATEVER BLEW OUT THE DINER WALL IS DEFINITELY A PROBLEM FOR--
--COSMIC BOY!
GOOD GOD, LOOK AT THE SIZE OF THAT THING!
IT DWARFS VALIDUS--!
MAKES THE INFINITE MAN SEEM LIKE AN INFANT BY COMPAR-ISON--!

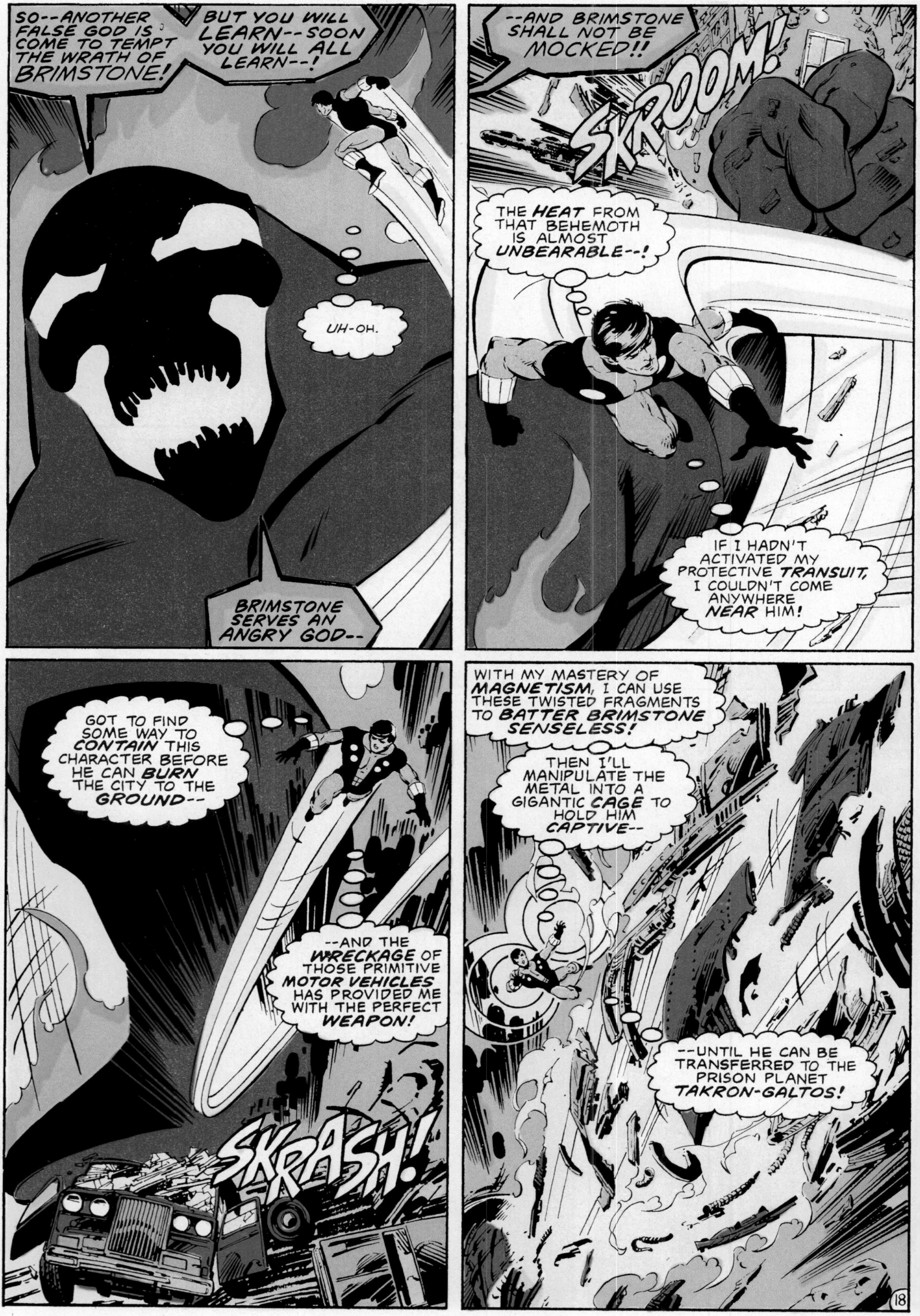
SO--ANOTHER FALSE GOD IS COME TO TEMPT THE WRATH OF BRIMSTONE!
BUT YOU WILL LEARN--SOON YOU WILL ALL LEARN--!
UH-OH.
BRIMSTONE SERVES AN ANGRY GOD--
--AND BRIMSTONE SHALL NOT BE MOCKED!!
SKROOM!
THE HEAT FROM THAT BEHEMOTH IS ALMOST UNBEARABLE--!
IF I HADN'T ACTIVATED MY PROTECTIVE TRANSUIT, I COULDN'T COME ANYWHERE NEAR HIM!
GOT TO FIND SOME WAY TO CONTAIN THIS CHARACTER BEFORE HE CAN BURN THE CITY TO THE GROUND--
--AND THE WRECKAGE OF THOSE PRIMITIVE MOTOR VEHICLES HAS PROVIDED ME WITH THE PERFECT WEAPON!
SKRASH!
WITH MY MASTERY OF MAGNETISM, I CAN USE THESE TWISTED FRAGMENTS TO BATTER BRIMSTONE SENSELESS!
THEN I'LL MANIPULATE THE METAL INTO A GIGANTIC CAGE TO HOLD HIM CAPTIVE--
--UNTIL HE CAN BE TRANSFERRED TO THE PRISON PLANET TAKRON-GALTOS!

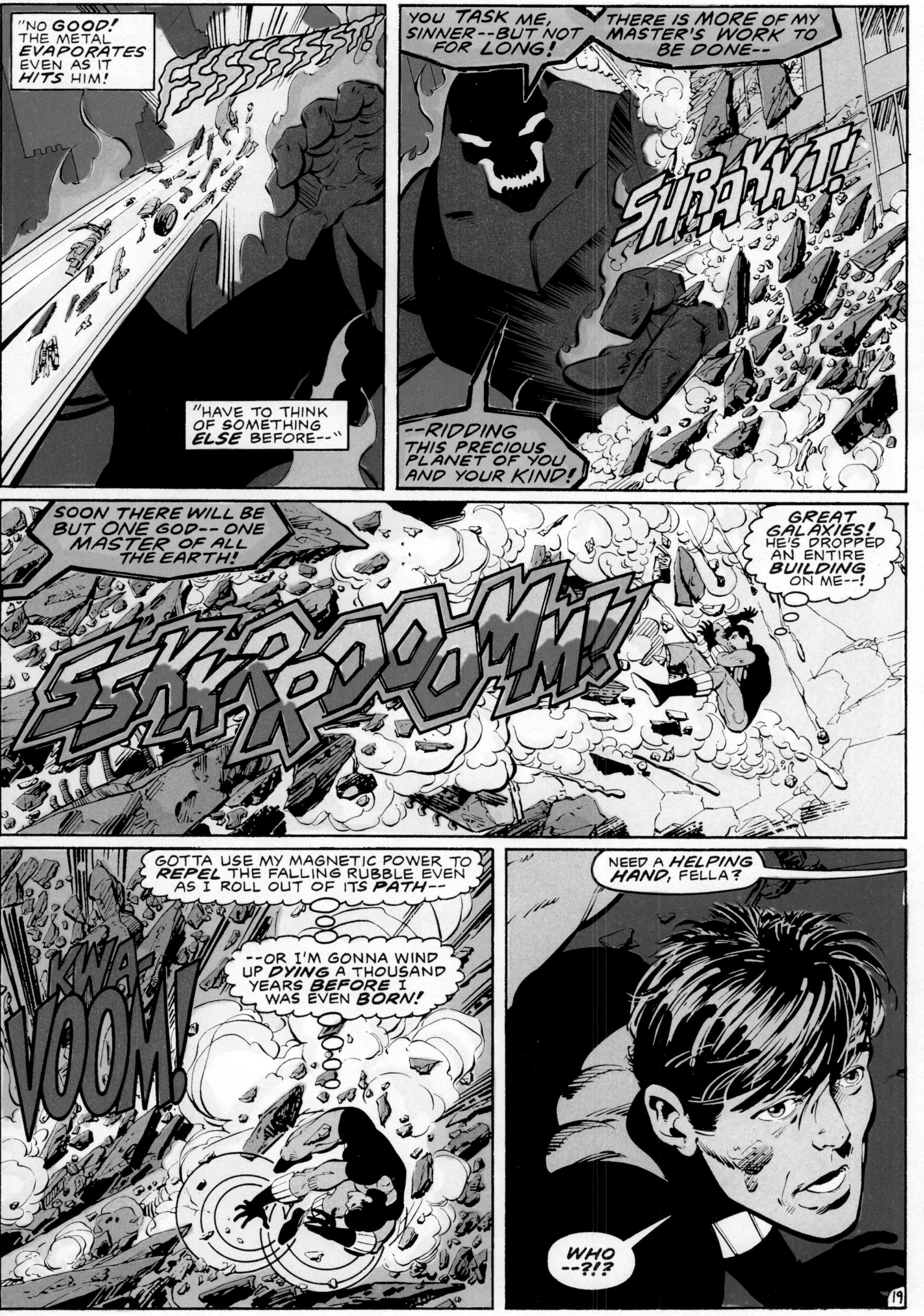
"NO GOOD! THE METAL EVAPORATES EVEN AS IT HITS HIM!
FSSSSSSSST!
"HAVE TO THINK OF SOMETHING ELSE BEFORE--"
YOU TASK ME, SINNER--BUT NOT FOR LONG!
THERE IS MORE OF MY MASTER'S WORK TO BE DONE--
SHRAKKT!
--RIDDING THIS PRECIOUS PLANET OF YOU AND YOUR KIND!
SOON THERE WILL BE BUT ONE GOD-- ONE MASTER OF ALL THE EARTH!
GREAT GALAXIES! HE'S DROPPED AN ENTIRE BUILDING ON ME--!
SSKRROOOMM!
GOTTA USE MY MAGNETIC POWER TO REPEL THE FALLING RUBBLE EVEN AS I ROLL OUT OF ITS PATH--
--OR I'M GONNA WIND UP DYING A THOUSAND YEARS BEFORE I WAS EVEN BORN!
KWA-VOOM!
NEED A HELPING HAND, FELLA?
WHO --?!?

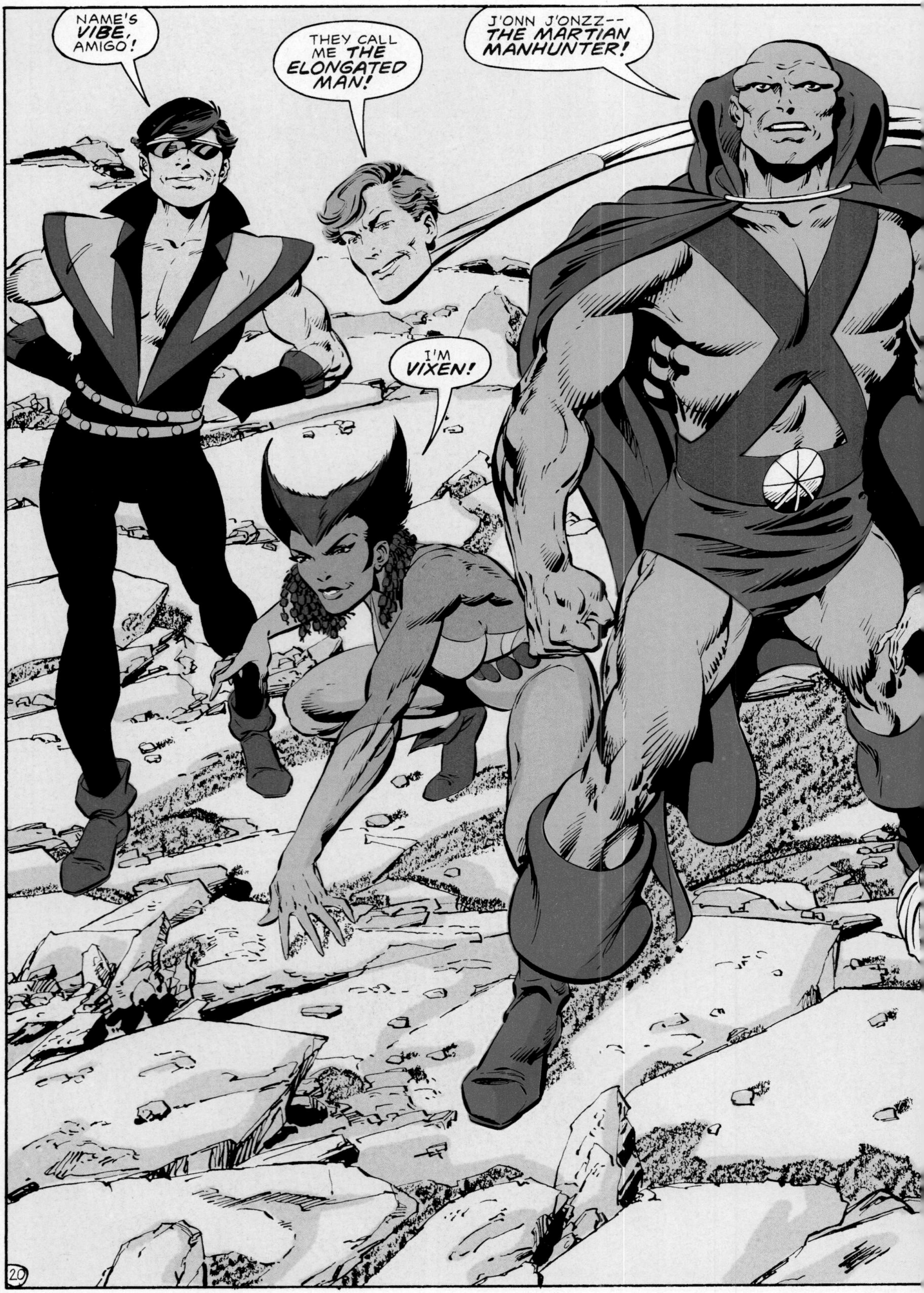
NAME'S VIBE, AMIGO!
THEY CALL ME THE ELONGATED MAN!
J'ONN J'ONZZ-- THE MARTIAN MANHUNTER!
I'M VIXEN!
20

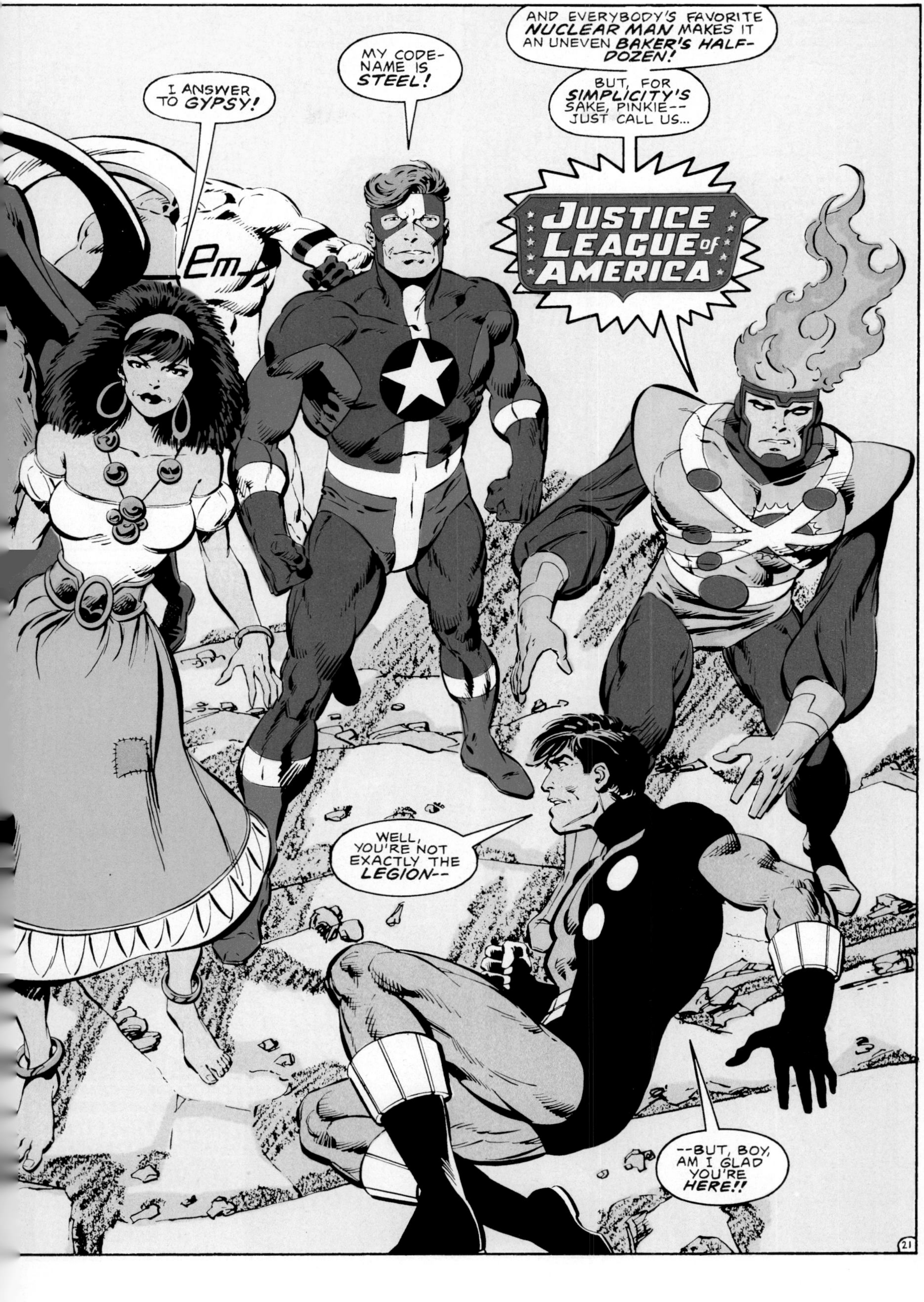
I ANSWER TO GYPSY!
MY CODE-NAME IS STEEL!
AND EVERYBODY'S FAVORITE NUCLEAR MAN MAKES IT AN UNEVEN BAKER'S HALF-DOZEN!
BUT, FOR SIMPLICITY'S SAKE, PINKIE-- JUST CALL US...
JUSTICE LEAGUE of AMERICA
WELL, YOU'RE NOT EXACTLY THE LEGION--
--BUT, BOY, AM I GLAD YOU'RE HERE!!
21

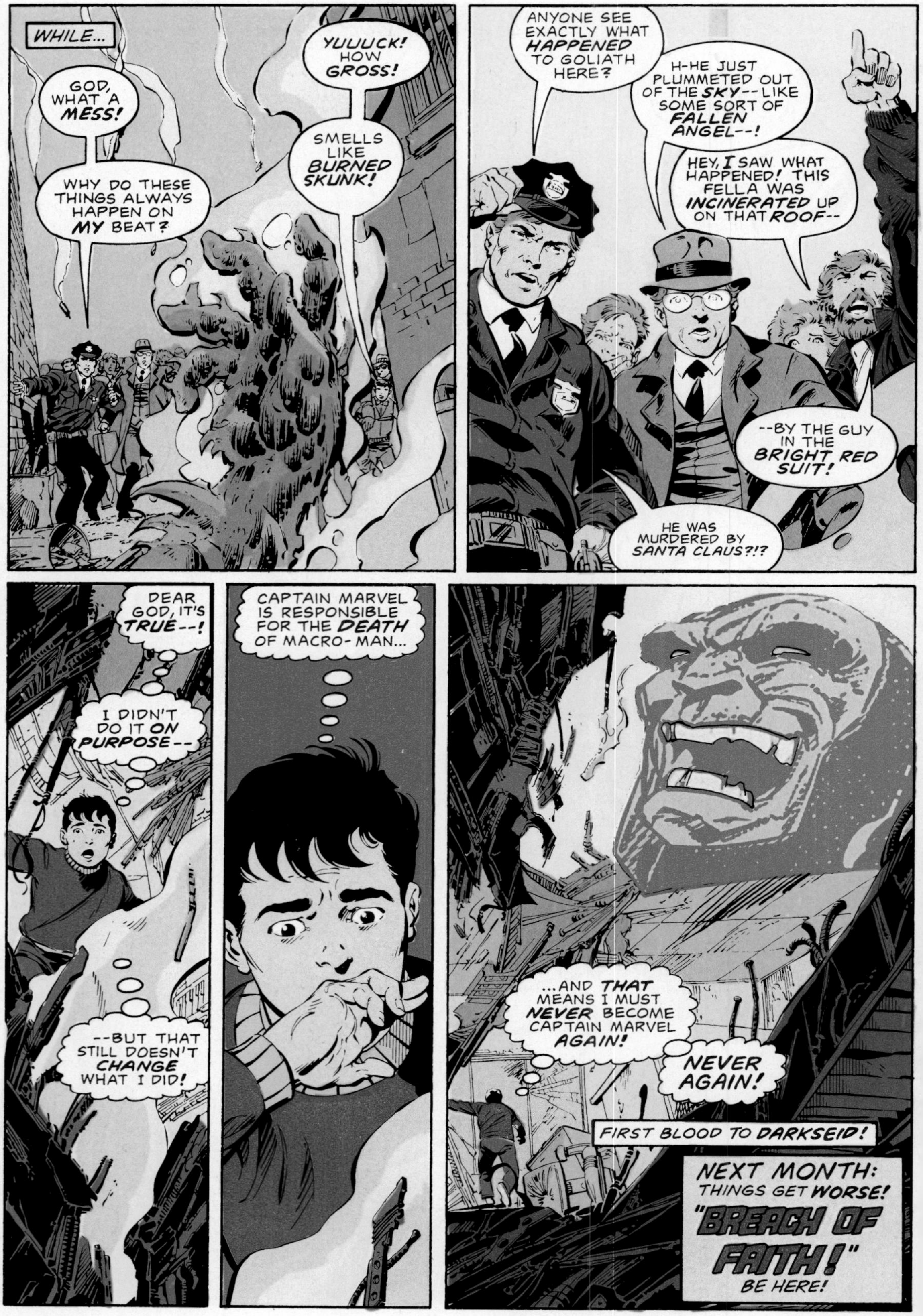
WHILE...
GOD, WHAT A MESS!
WHY DO THESE THINGS ALWAYS HAPPEN ON MY BEAT?
YUUUCK! HOW GROSS!
SMELLS LIKE BURNED SKUNK!
ANYONE SEE EXACTLY WHAT HAPPENED TO GOLIATH HERE?
H-HE JUST PLUMMETED OUT OF THE SKY--LIKE SOME SORT OF FALLEN ANGEL--!
HEY, I SAW WHAT HAPPENED! THIS FELLA WAS INCINERATED UP ON THAT ROOF--
--BY THE GUY IN THE BRIGHT RED SUIT!
HE WAS MURDERED BY SANTA CLAUS?!?
DEAR GOD, IT'S TRUE--!
I DIDN'T DO IT ON PURPOSE--
--BUT THAT STILL DOESN'T CHANGE WHAT I DID!
CAPTAIN MARVEL IS RESPONSIBLE FOR THE DEATH OF MACRO-MAN...
...AND THAT MEANS I MUST NEVER BECOME CAPTAIN MARVEL AGAIN!
NEVER AGAIN!
FIRST BLOOD TO DARKSEID!
NEXT MONTH: THINGS GET WORSE!
"BREACH OF FAITH!" BE HERE!

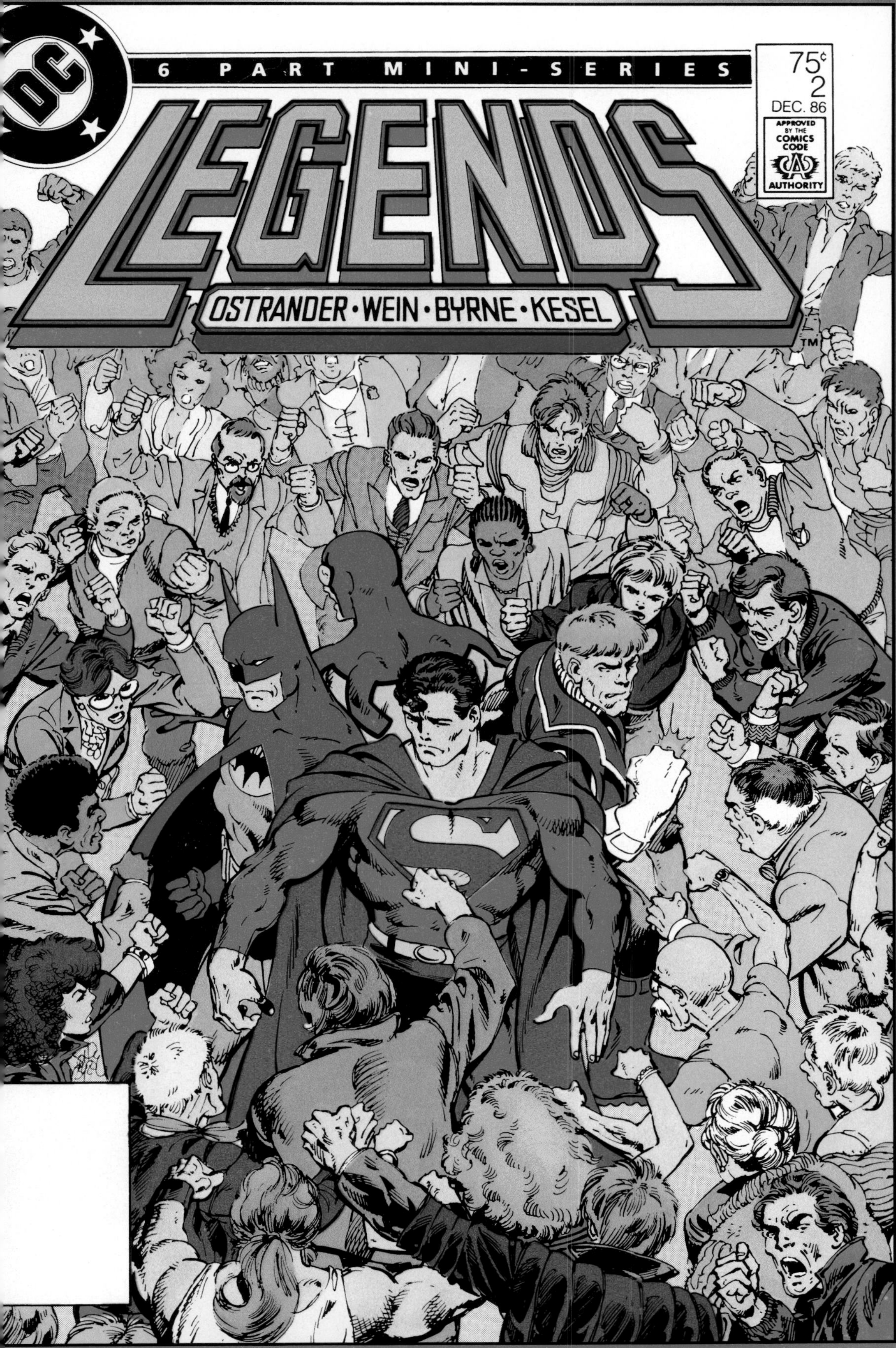
6 PART MINI-SERIES
75¢
2
DEC. 86
APPROVED BY THE COMICS CODE AUTHORITY
DC
LEGENDS
OSTRANDER • WEIN • BYRNE • KESEL
TM

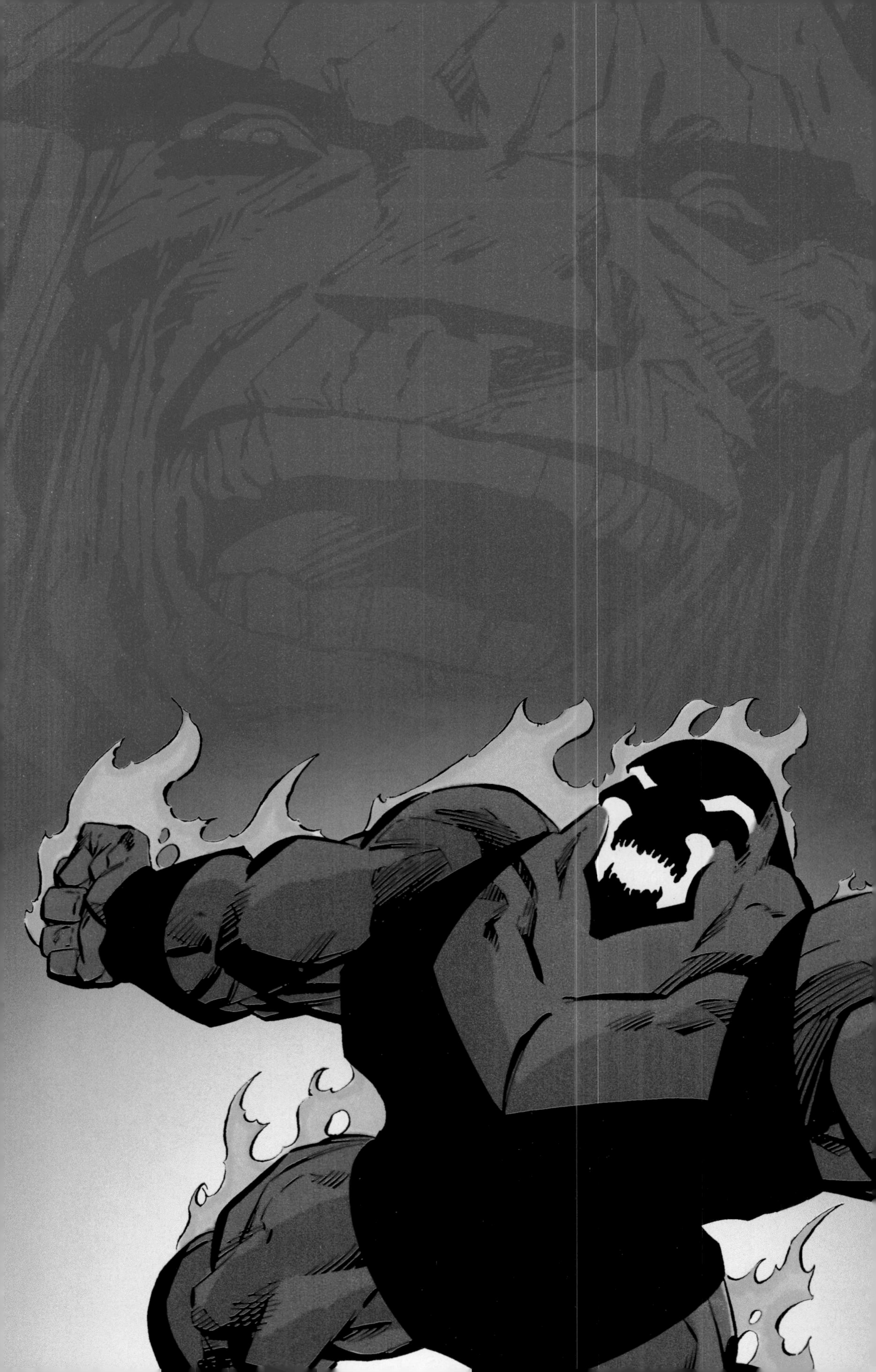

SUNG IN THE CATHEDRALS, WHISPERED IN THE SHADOWS... EVER UNCHANGING, *SELDOM* UNCHANGED... BRIGHT INCANDESCENCE, THE BLACK OF THE PIT... *SUCH* IS THE STUFF OF...

LEGENDS

"BREACH OF FAITH!"

WHAT IS THE *SOUND* OF THE *END OF THE WORLD*?

TO THE STILL-SMOLDERING HUSK THAT WAS ONCE KNOWN AS *MACRO-MAN*, IT WAS THE ANGRY CLASH OF *THUNDER* ACCOMPANYING A JAGGED BOLT OF *MAGIC LIGHTNING*--

--LIGHTNING THAT ALL BUT *INCINERATED* HIS MONSTROUS FORM, EVEN AS IT *HURLED* HIM FROM A BATTLE-TORN *ROOFTOP*--

--TO *IMPACT* WITH A *THUNDER OF HIS OWN* AGAINST THE FILTHY *PAVEMENT*, WAITING FAR BELOW!

FOR MACRO-MAN, AT LEAST, THE WORLD ENDED WITH A *BANG*, NOT A *WHIMPER!*

POLICE LINE DO NOT CROSS

JOHN OSTRANDER	LEN WEIN	JOHN BYRNE	KARL KESEL	STEVE HAYNIE	TOM ZIUKO	MIKE GOLD
PLOTTER	SCRIPTER	PENCILLER	INKER	LETTERER	COLORIST	EDITOR

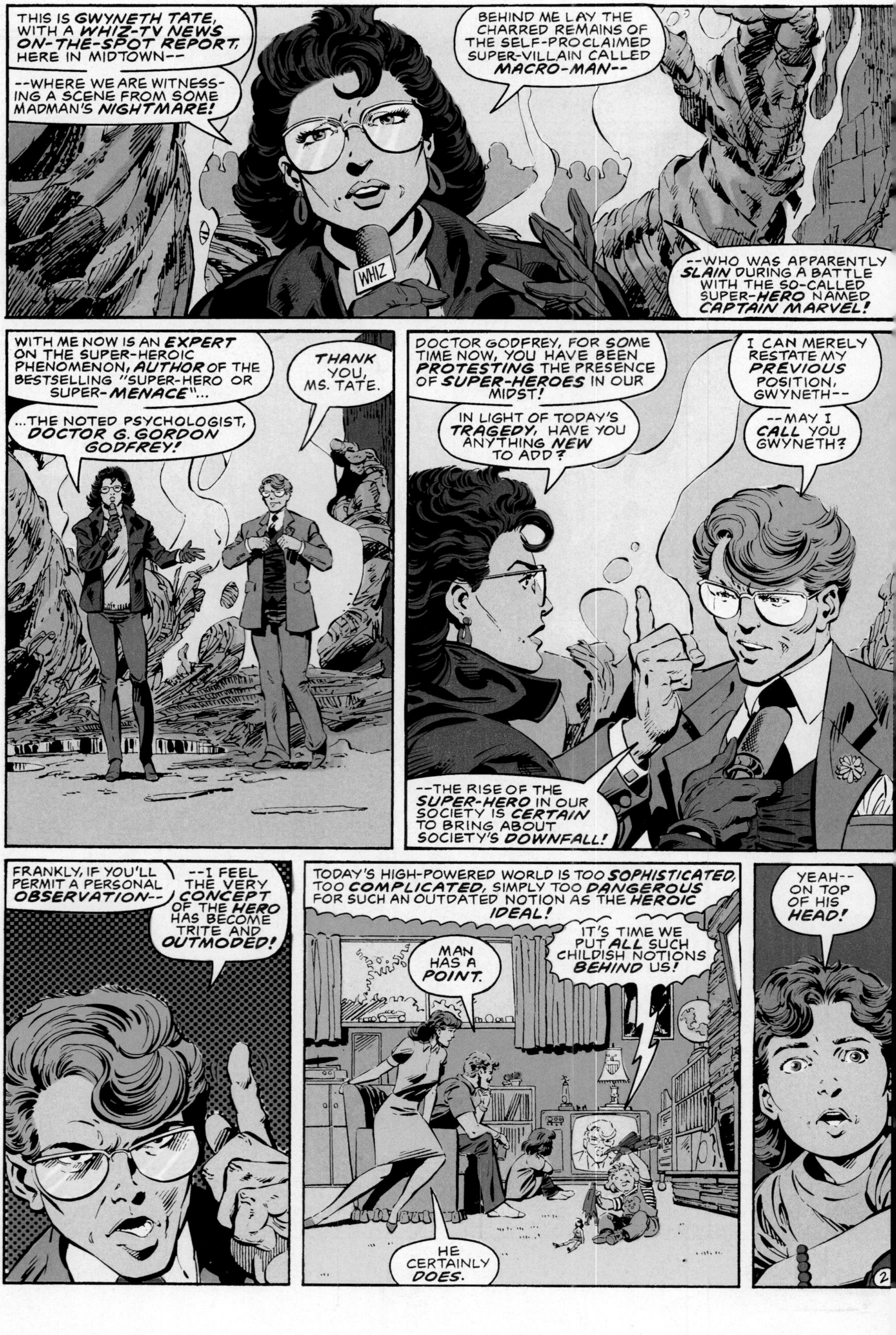

THIS IS GWYNETH TATE, WITH A WHIZ-TV NEWS ON-THE-SPOT REPORT, HERE IN MIDTOWN--
--WHERE WE ARE WITNESSING A SCENE FROM SOME MADMAN'S NIGHTMARE!
BEHIND ME LAY THE CHARRED REMAINS OF THE SELF-PROCLAIMED SUPER-VILLAIN CALLED MACRO-MAN--
WHIZ
--WHO WAS APPARENTLY SLAIN DURING A BATTLE WITH THE SO-CALLED SUPER-HERO NAMED CAPTAIN MARVEL!
WITH ME NOW IS AN EXPERT ON THE SUPER-HEROIC PHENOMENON, AUTHOR OF THE BESTSELLING "SUPER-HERO OR SUPER-MENACE"...
...THE NOTED PSYCHOLOGIST, DOCTOR G. GORDON GODFREY!
THANK YOU, MS. TATE.
DOCTOR GODFREY, FOR SOME TIME NOW, YOU HAVE BEEN PROTESTING THE PRESENCE OF SUPER-HEROES IN OUR MIDST!
IN LIGHT OF TODAY'S TRAGEDY, HAVE YOU ANYTHING NEW TO ADD?
I CAN MERELY RESTATE MY PREVIOUS POSITION, GWYNETH--
--MAY I CALL YOU GWYNETH?
--THE RISE OF THE SUPER-HERO IN OUR SOCIETY IS CERTAIN TO BRING ABOUT SOCIETY'S DOWNFALL!
FRANKLY, IF YOU'LL PERMIT A PERSONAL OBSERVATION--
--I FEEL THE VERY CONCEPT OF THE HERO HAS BECOME TRITE AND OUTMODED!
TODAY'S HIGH-POWERED WORLD IS TOO SOPHISTICATED, TOO COMPLICATED, SIMPLY TOO DANGEROUS FOR SUCH AN OUTDATED NOTION AS THE HEROIC IDEAL!
IT'S TIME WE PUT ALL SUCH CHILDISH NOTIONS BEHIND US!
MAN HAS A POINT.
HE CERTAINLY DOES.
YEAH-- ON TOP OF HIS HEAD!
2

WHAT HAS THE HEROIC IDEAL EVER BRED BESIDES *WAR* AND *MISERY*? I'M TELLING YOU WE DON'T *NEED* HEROES!

AND UNLESS THE *GOVERNMENT* PUTS AN *END* TO THE ACTIVITIES OF THESE COSTUMED VIGILANTES *SOON*--

--WE, THE PEOPLE, *WILL!!*

GUY MAKES *SENSE.*

WELL, I DON'T *KNOW*..

HEY, 'BOUT *TIME* SOMEONE STOOD UP FOR US *ORDINARY JOES!*

T CROSS

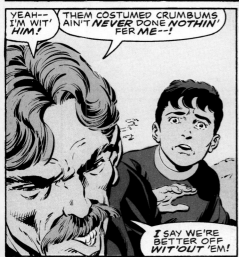

YEAH-- I'M WIT' *HIM!*

THEM COSTUMED CRUMBUMS AIN'T *NEVER* DONE *NOTHIN'* FER *ME*--!

I SAY WE'RE BETTER OFF *WIT'OUT* 'EM!

GO, GODFREY!!

DOWN WITH SUPER-HEROES!!

NO.

NO.

NO!

NO!!

I--I CAN'T *BELIEVE* IT--!

IT TOOK SO *LITTLE* TO TURN THOSE PEOPLE INTO A BLOODTHIRSTY *MOB*--!

AND *YET*-- MAYBE THEY'RE *RIGHT!*

AFTER ALL, *I* WAS A *SUPER-HERO*, BRIEFLY--

--*BEFORE* I BECAME--

--A *MURDERER!!*

AND ONCE AGAIN, THE MEMORIES RETURN, UNBIDDEN--

--MEMORIES OF THE *TELEVISION TALK SHOW* HOSTED ONLY A SHORT WHILE AGO BY YOUTHFUL NEWS COMMENTATOR, *BILLY BATSON*--

--HIS *GUEST*, THE SELFSAME *G. GORDON GODFREY* WHO NOW STIRS THE CROWD TO *FRENZY*...

THE *DEBATE* HAD BEEN GOING ABOUT AS *WELL* AS COULD BE *EXPECTED*--

WHIZ COLORACE

③

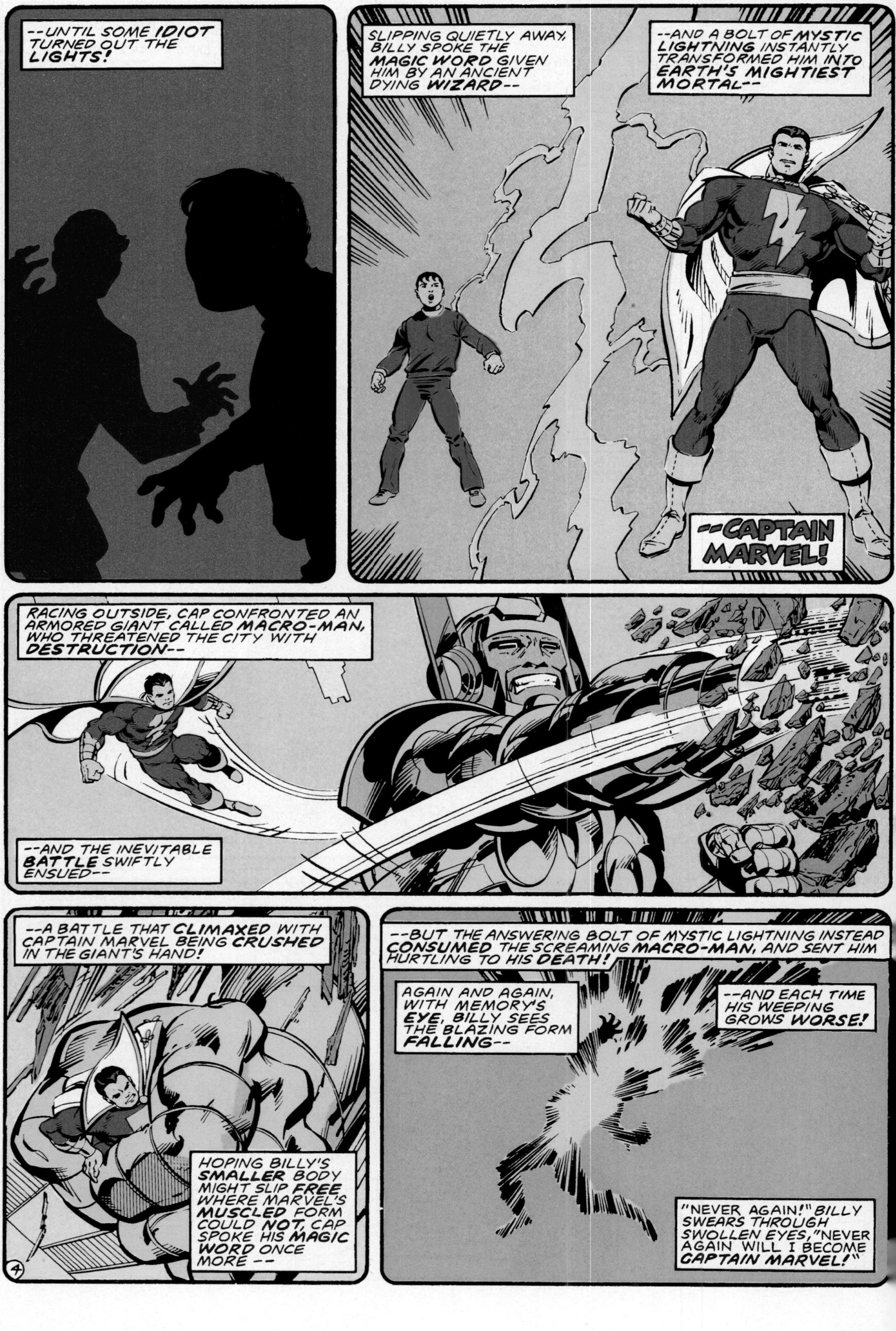
--UNTIL SOME IDIOT TURNED OUT THE LIGHTS!
SLIPPING QUIETLY AWAY, BILLY SPOKE THE MAGIC WORD GIVEN HIM BY AN ANCIENT DYING WIZARD--
--AND A BOLT OF MYSTIC LIGHTNING INSTANTLY TRANSFORMED HIM INTO EARTH'S MIGHTIEST MORTAL--
--CAPTAIN MARVEL!
RACING OUTSIDE, CAP CONFRONTED AN ARMORED GIANT CALLED MACRO-MAN, WHO THREATENED THE CITY WITH DESTRUCTION--
--AND THE INEVITABLE BATTLE SWIFTLY ENSUED--
--A BATTLE THAT CLIMAXED WITH CAPTAIN MARVEL BEING CRUSHED IN THE GIANT'S HAND!
HOPING BILLY'S SMALLER BODY MIGHT SLIP FREE WHERE MARVEL'S MUSCLED FORM COULD NOT, CAP SPOKE HIS MAGIC WORD ONCE MORE --
--BUT THE ANSWERING BOLT OF MYSTIC LIGHTNING INSTEAD CONSUMED THE SCREAMING MACRO-MAN, AND SENT HIM HURTLING TO HIS DEATH!
AGAIN AND AGAIN, WITH MEMORY'S EYE, BILLY SEES THE BLAZING FORM FALLING--
--AND EACH TIME HIS WEEPING GROWS WORSE!
"NEVER AGAIN!" BILLY SWEARS THROUGH SWOLLEN EYES, "NEVER AGAIN WILL I BECOME CAPTAIN MARVEL!"
4

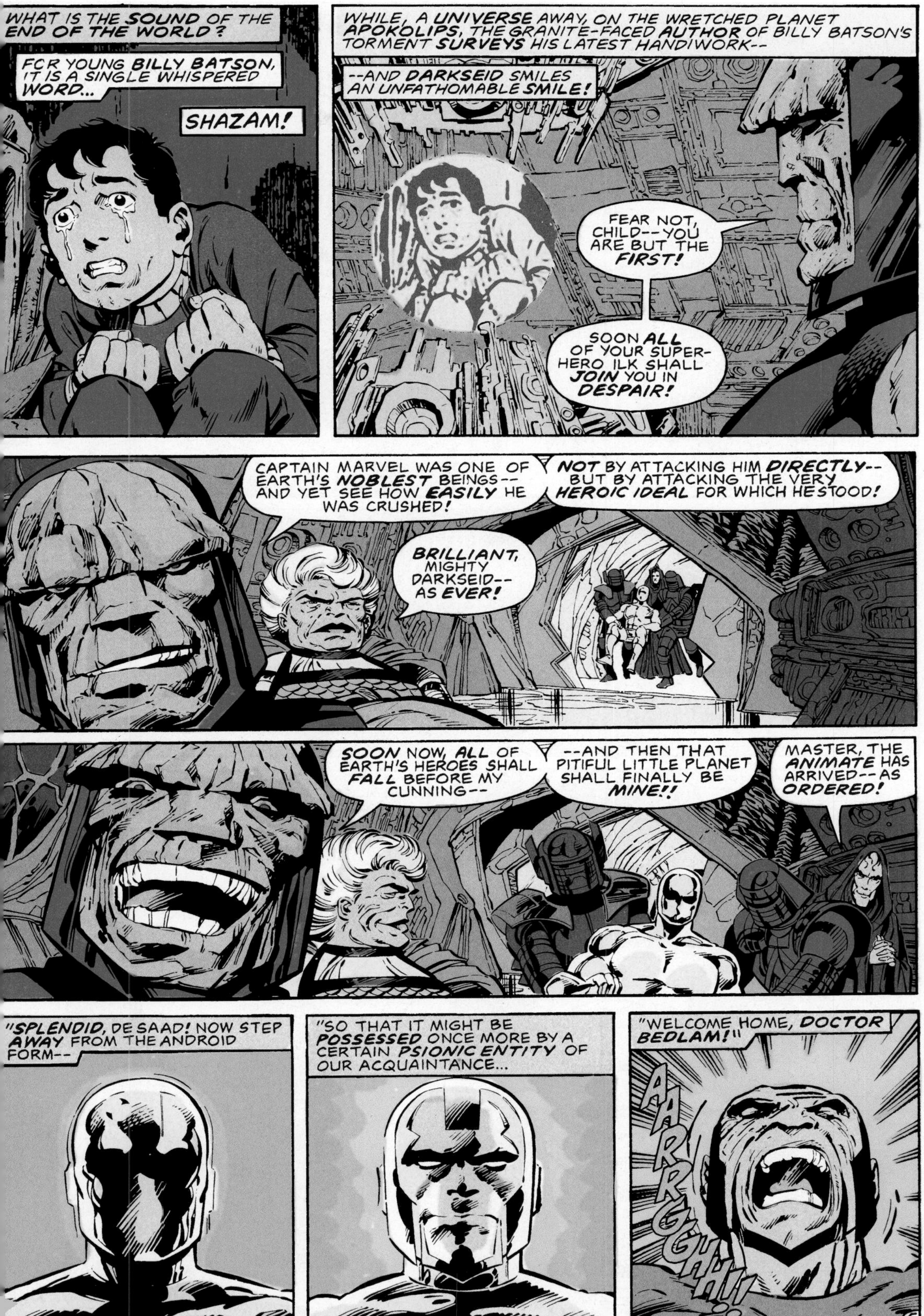
WHAT IS THE SOUND OF THE END OF THE WORLD?
FOR YOUNG BILLY BATSON, IT IS A SINGLE WHISPERED WORD...
SHAZAM!
WHILE, A UNIVERSE AWAY, ON THE WRETCHED PLANET APOKOLIPS, THE GRANITE-FACED AUTHOR OF BILLY BATSON'S TORMENT SURVEYS HIS LATEST HANDIWORK--
--AND DARKSEID SMILES AN UNFATHOMABLE SMILE!
FEAR NOT, CHILD--YOU ARE BUT THE FIRST!
SOON ALL OF YOUR SUPER-HERO ILK SHALL JOIN YOU IN DESPAIR!
CAPTAIN MARVEL WAS ONE OF EARTH'S NOBLEST BEINGS--AND YET SEE HOW EASILY HE WAS CRUSHED!
NOT BY ATTACKING HIM DIRECTLY--BUT BY ATTACKING THE VERY HEROIC IDEAL FOR WHICH HE STOOD!
BRILLIANT, MIGHTY DARKSEID--AS EVER!
SOON NOW, ALL OF EARTH'S HEROES SHALL FALL BEFORE MY CUNNING--
--AND THEN THAT PITIFUL LITTLE PLANET SHALL FINALLY BE MINE!!
MASTER, THE ANIMATE HAS ARRIVED--AS ORDERED!
"SPLENDID, DE SAAD! NOW STEP AWAY FROM THE ANDROID FORM--
"SO THAT IT MIGHT BE POSSESSED ONCE MORE BY A CERTAIN PSIONIC ENTITY OF OUR ACQUAINTANCE...
"WELCOME HOME, DOCTOR BEDLAM!"
AARRGGHH!!
5

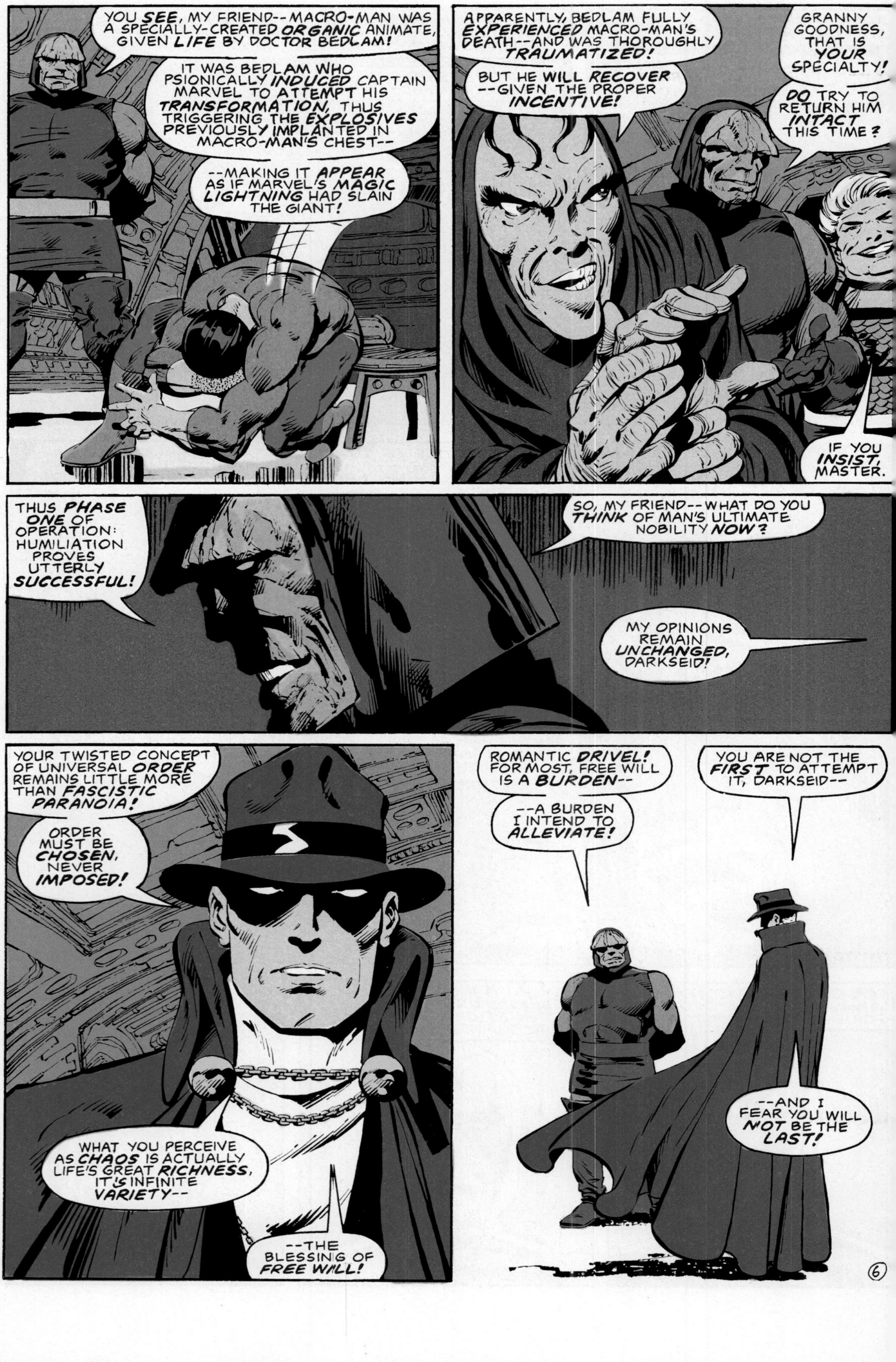
YOU SEE, MY FRIEND--MACRO-MAN WAS A SPECIALLY-CREATED ORGANIC ANIMATE, GIVEN LIFE BY DOCTOR BEDLAM!
IT WAS BEDLAM WHO PSIONICALLY INDUCED CAPTAIN MARVEL TO ATTEMPT HIS TRANSFORMATION, THUS TRIGGERING THE EXPLOSIVES PREVIOUSLY IMPLANTED IN MACRO-MAN'S CHEST--
--MAKING IT APPEAR AS IF MARVEL'S MAGIC LIGHTNING HAD SLAIN THE GIANT!
APPARENTLY, BEDLAM FULLY EXPERIENCED MACRO-MAN'S DEATH--AND WAS THOROUGHLY TRAUMATIZED!
BUT HE WILL RECOVER --GIVEN THE PROPER INCENTIVE!
GRANNY GOODNESS, THAT IS YOUR SPECIALTY!
DO TRY TO RETURN HIM INTACT THIS TIME?
IF YOU INSIST, MASTER.
THUS PHASE ONE OF OPERATION: HUMILIATION PROVES UTTERLY SUCCESSFUL!
SO, MY FRIEND--WHAT DO YOU THINK OF MAN'S ULTIMATE NOBILITY NOW?
MY OPINIONS REMAIN UNCHANGED, DARKSEID!
YOUR TWISTED CONCEPT OF UNIVERSAL ORDER REMAINS LITTLE MORE THAN FASCISTIC PARANOIA!
ORDER MUST BE CHOSEN, NEVER IMPOSED!
WHAT YOU PERCEIVE AS CHAOS IS ACTUALLY LIFE'S GREAT RICHNESS, IT'S INFINITE VARIETY--
--THE BLESSING OF FREE WILL!
ROMANTIC DRIVEL! FOR MOST, FREE WILL IS A BURDEN--
--A BURDEN I INTEND TO ALLEVIATE!
YOU ARE NOT THE FIRST TO ATTEMPT IT, DARKSEID--
--AND I FEAR YOU WILL NOT BE THE LAST!
6

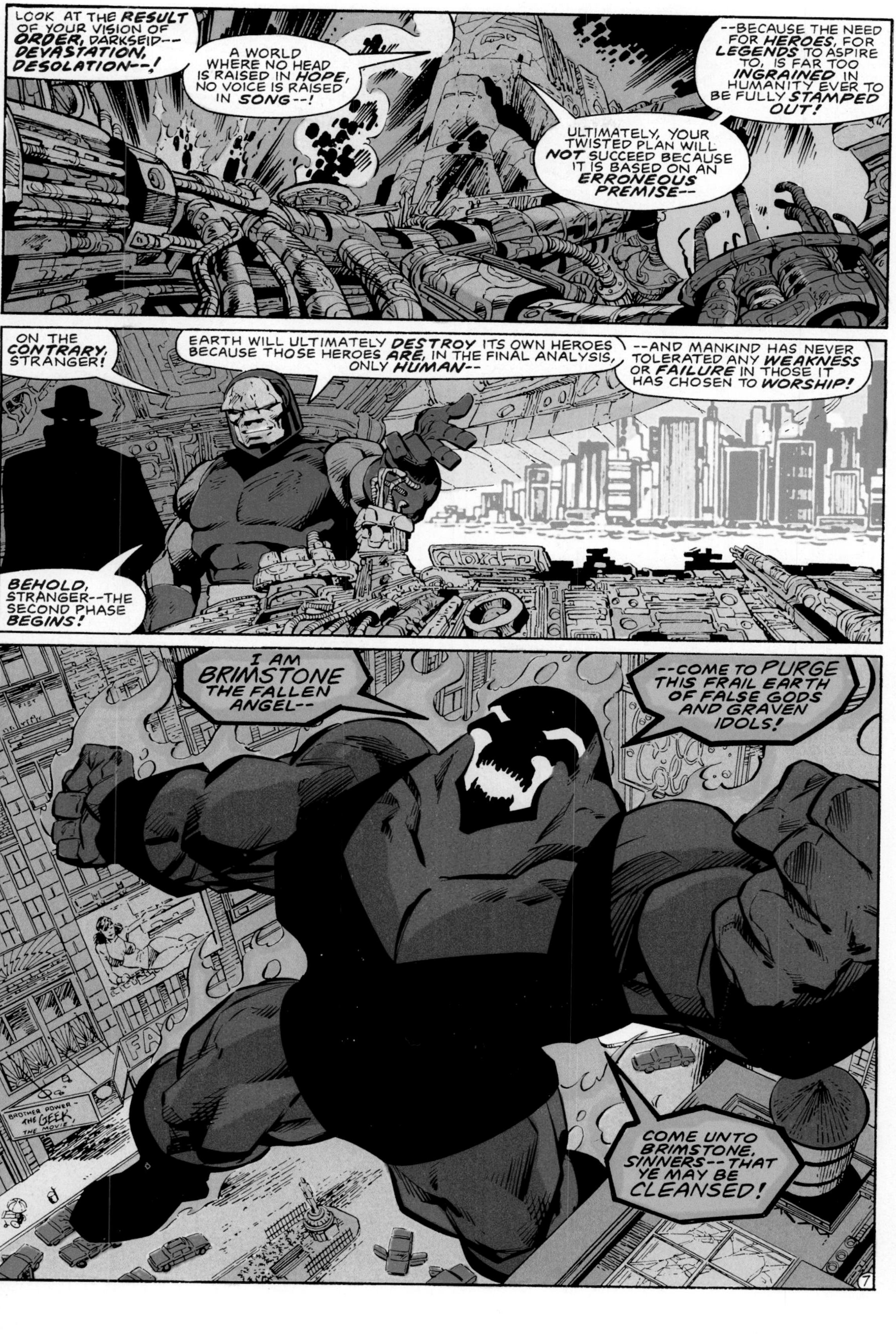
LOOK AT THE RESULT OF YOUR VISION OF ORDER, DARKSEID-- DEVASTATION, DESOLATION--!
A WORLD WHERE NO HEAD IS RAISED IN HOPE, NO VOICE IS RAISED IN SONG--!
ULTIMATELY, YOUR TWISTED PLAN WILL NOT SUCCEED BECAUSE IT IS BASED ON AN ERRONEOUS PREMISE--
--BECAUSE THE NEED FOR HEROES, FOR LEGENDS TO ASPIRE TO, IS FAR TOO INGRAINED IN HUMANITY EVER TO BE FULLY STAMPED OUT!
ON THE CONTRARY, STRANGER!
EARTH WILL ULTIMATELY DESTROY ITS OWN HEROES BECAUSE THOSE HEROES ARE, IN THE FINAL ANALYSIS, ONLY HUMAN--
--AND MANKIND HAS NEVER TOLERATED ANY WEAKNESS OR FAILURE IN THOSE IT HAS CHOSEN TO WORSHIP!
BEHOLD, STRANGER--THE SECOND PHASE BEGINS!
I AM BRIMSTONE THE FALLEN ANGEL--
--COME TO PURGE THIS FRAIL EARTH OF FALSE GODS AND GRAVEN IDOLS!
BROTHER POWER - THE GEEK, THE MOVIE
COME UNTO BRIMSTONE, SINNERS--THAT YE MAY BE CLEANSED!

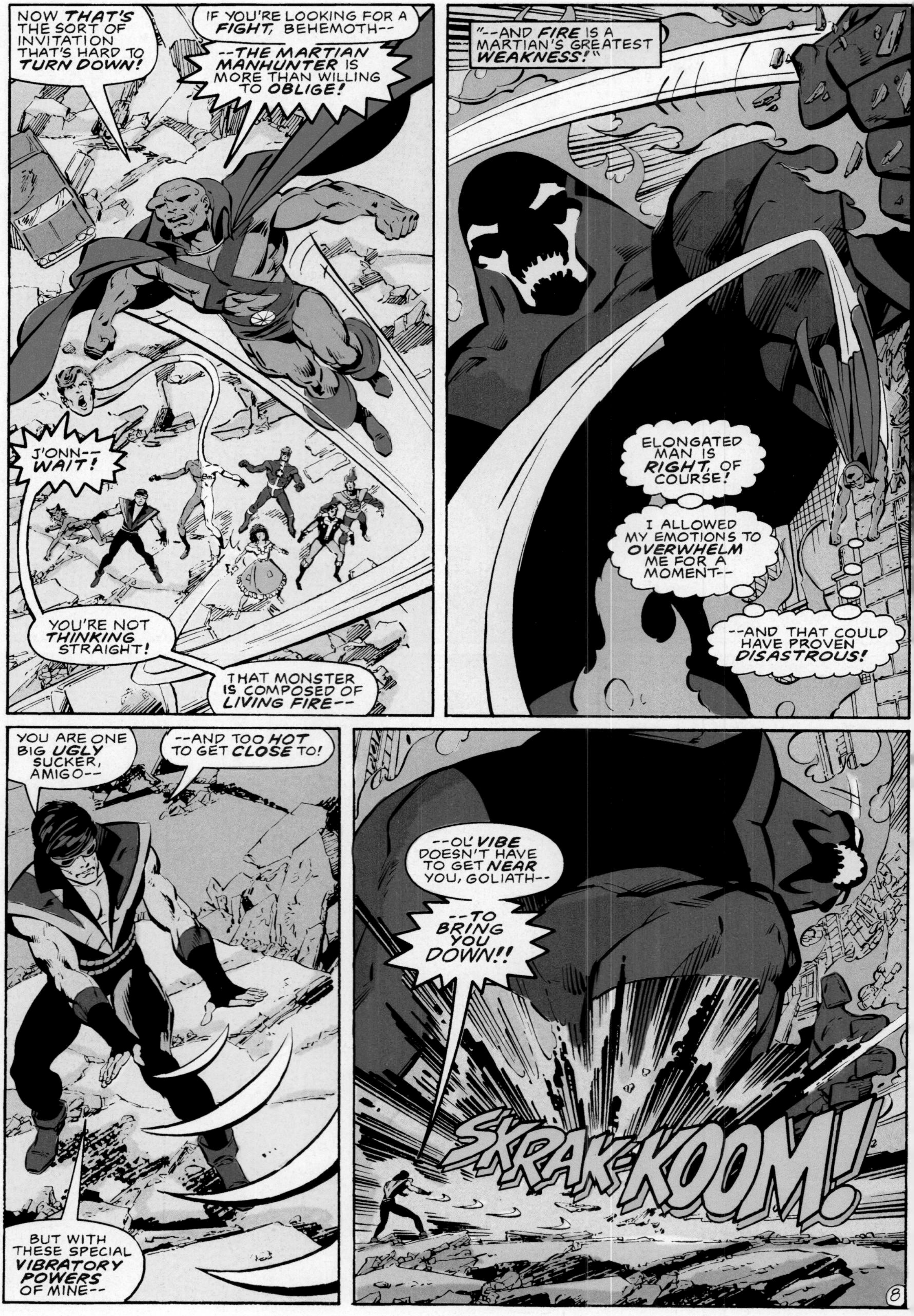
NOW THAT'S THE SORT OF INVITATION THAT'S HARD TO TURN DOWN!
IF YOU'RE LOOKING FOR A FIGHT, BEHEMOTH--
--THE MARTIAN MANHUNTER IS MORE THAN WILLING TO OBLIGE!
J'ONN--WAIT!
YOU'RE NOT THINKING STRAIGHT!
THAT MONSTER IS COMPOSED OF LIVING FIRE--
"--AND FIRE IS A MARTIAN'S GREATEST WEAKNESS!"
ELONGATED MAN IS RIGHT, OF COURSE!
I ALLOWED MY EMOTIONS TO OVERWHELM ME FOR A MOMENT--
--AND THAT COULD HAVE PROVEN DISASTROUS!
YOU ARE ONE BIG UGLY SUCKER, AMIGO--
--AND TOO HOT TO GET CLOSE TO!
BUT WITH THESE SPECIAL VIBRATORY POWERS OF MINE--
--OL' VIBE DOESN'T HAVE TO GET NEAR YOU, GOLIATH--
--TO BRING YOU DOWN!!
SKRAK-KOOM!

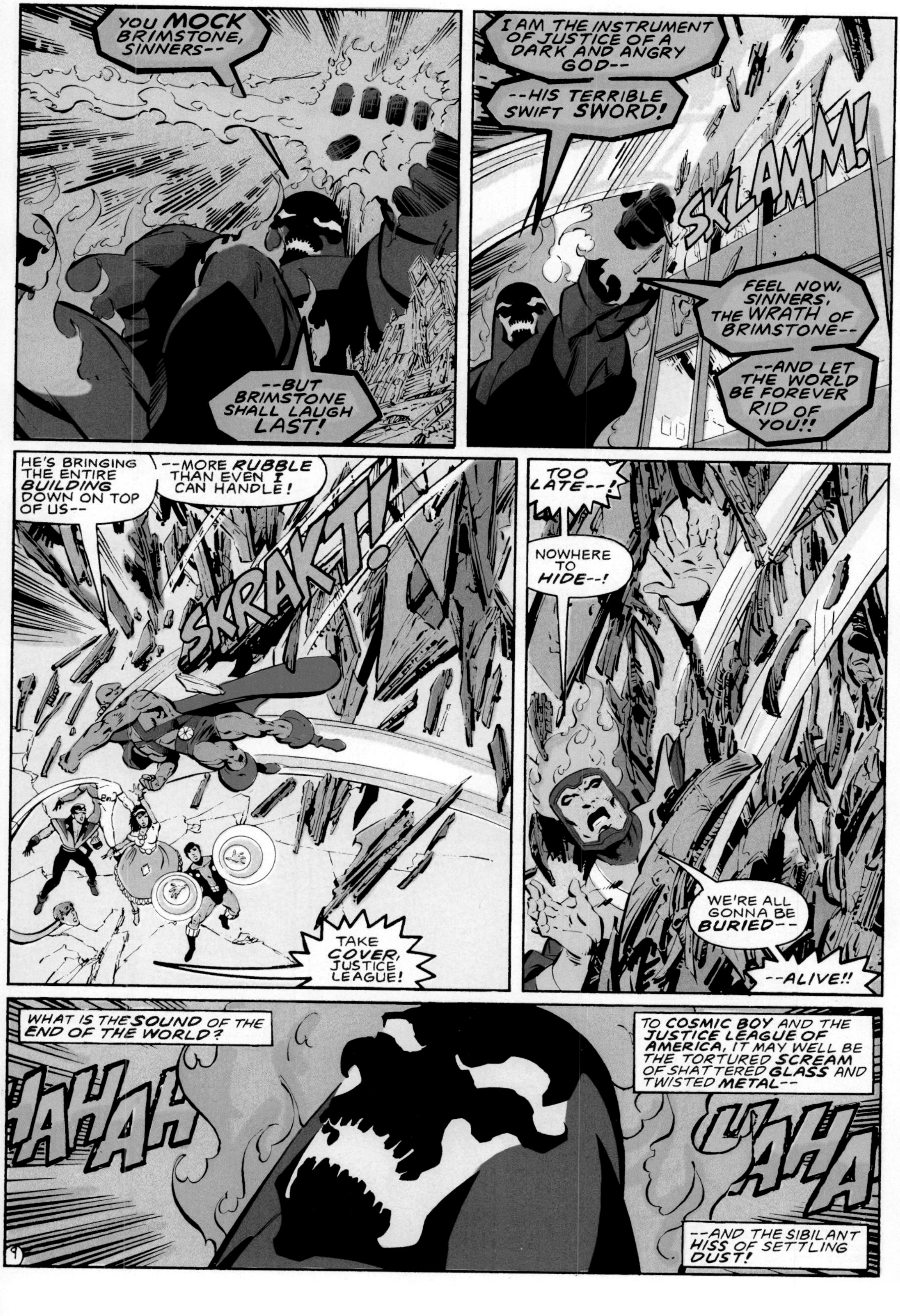

YOU MOCK BRIMSTONE, SINNERS--
--BUT BRIMSTONE SHALL LAUGH LAST!
I AM THE INSTRUMENT OF JUSTICE OF A DARK AND ANGRY GOD--
--HIS TERRIBLE SWIFT SWORD!
SKLAMM!
FEEL NOW, SINNERS, THE WRATH OF BRIMSTONE--
--AND LET THE WORLD BE FOREVER RID OF YOU!!
HE'S BRINGING THE ENTIRE BUILDING DOWN ON TOP OF US--
--MORE RUBBLE THAN EVEN I CAN HANDLE!
SKRAKT!
TAKE COVER, JUSTICE LEAGUE!
TOO LATE--!
NOWHERE TO HIDE--!
WE'RE ALL GONNA BE BURIED--
--ALIVE!!
WHAT IS THE SOUND OF THE END OF THE WORLD?
HAHAH
TO COSMIC BOY AND THE JUSTICE LEAGUE OF AMERICA, IT MAY WELL BE THE TORTURED SCREAM OF SHATTERED GLASS AND TWISTED METAL--
HAHA
--AND THE SIBILANT HISS OF SETTLING DUST!
9

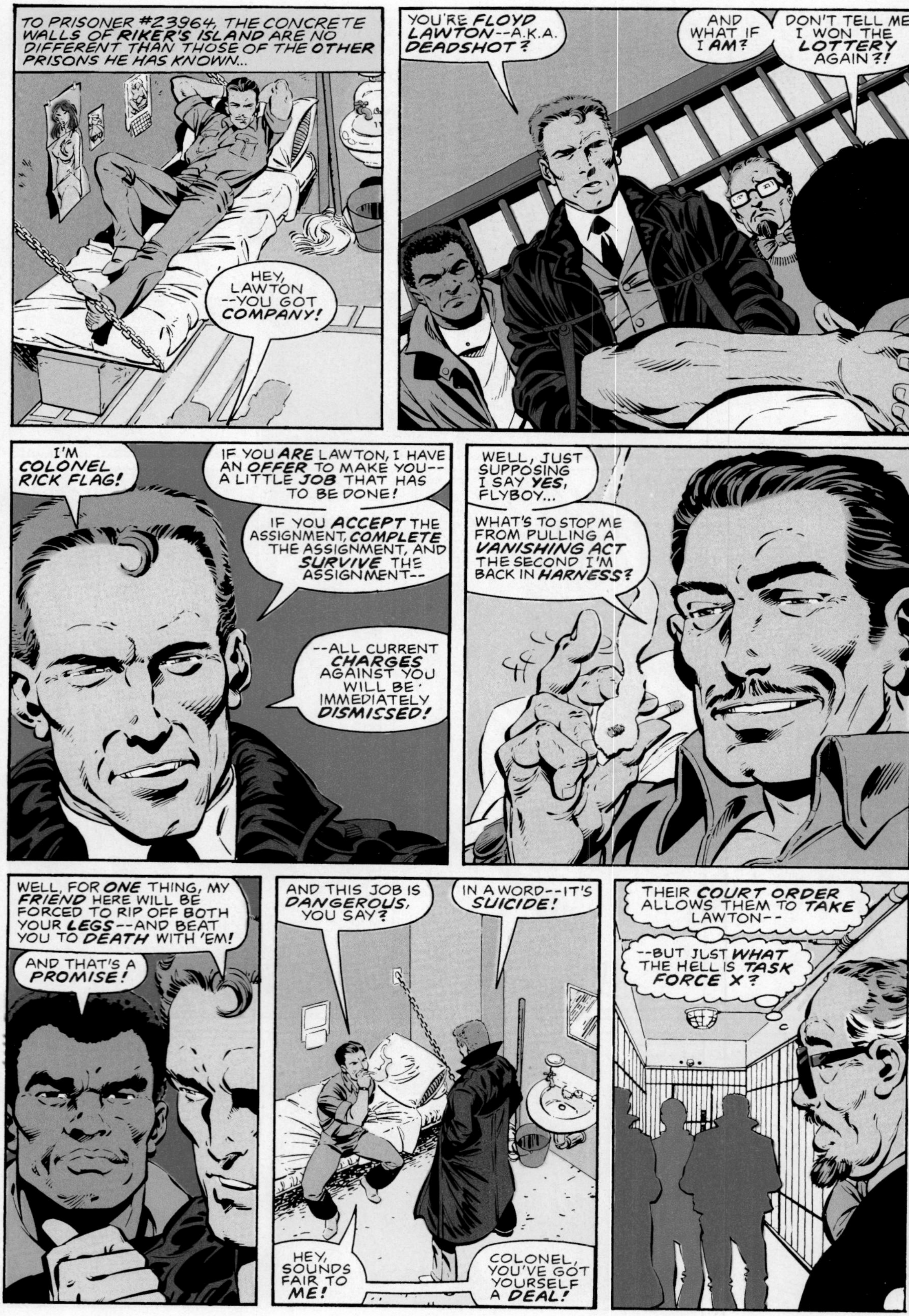
TO PRISONER #23964, THE CONCRETE WALLS OF RIKER'S ISLAND ARE NO DIFFERENT THAN THOSE OF THE OTHER PRISONS HE HAS KNOWN...
HEY, LAWTON --YOU GOT COMPANY!
YOU'RE FLOYD LAWTON--A.K.A. DEADSHOT?
AND WHAT IF I AM?
DON'T TELL ME I WON THE LOTTERY AGAIN?!
I'M COLONEL RICK FLAG!
IF YOU ARE LAWTON, I HAVE AN OFFER TO MAKE YOU-- A LITTLE JOB THAT HAS TO BE DONE!
IF YOU ACCEPT THE ASSIGNMENT, COMPLETE THE ASSIGNMENT, AND SURVIVE THE ASSIGNMENT--
--ALL CURRENT CHARGES AGAINST YOU WILL BE IMMEDIATELY DISMISSED!
WELL, JUST SUPPOSING I SAY YES, FLYBOY...
WHAT'S TO STOP ME FROM PULLING A VANISHING ACT THE SECOND I'M BACK IN HARNESS?
WELL, FOR ONE THING, MY FRIEND HERE WILL BE FORCED TO RIP OFF BOTH YOUR LEGS--AND BEAT YOU TO DEATH WITH 'EM!
AND THAT'S A PROMISE!
AND THIS JOB IS DANGEROUS, YOU SAY?
IN A WORD--IT'S SUICIDE!
HEY, SOUNDS FAIR TO ME!
COLONEL, YOU'VE GOT YOURSELF A DEAL!
THEIR COURT ORDER ALLOWS THEM TO TAKE LAWTON--
--BUT JUST WHAT THE HELL IS TASK FORCE X?

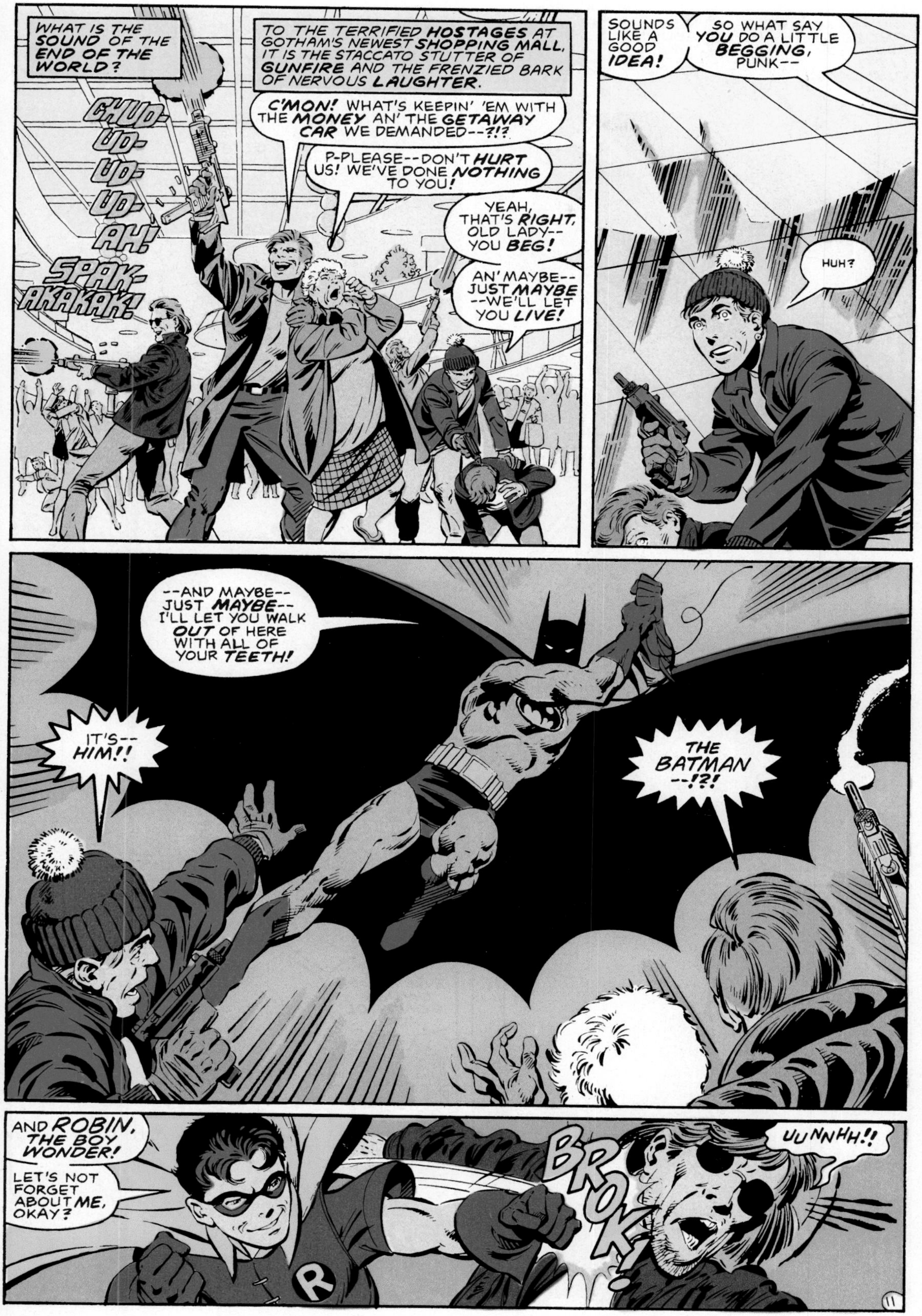
WHAT IS THE SOUND OF THE END OF THE WORLD?
TO THE TERRIFIED HOSTAGES AT GOTHAM'S NEWEST SHOPPING MALL, IT IS THE STACCATO STUTTER OF GUNFIRE AND THE FRENZIED BARK OF NERVOUS LAUGHTER.
CHUD-UD-UD-UD-AH!
SPAK-AKAKAK!
C'MON! WHAT'S KEEPIN' 'EM WITH THE MONEY AN' THE GETAWAY CAR WE DEMANDED--?!?
P-PLEASE--DON'T HURT US! WE'VE DONE NOTHING TO YOU!
YEAH, THAT'S RIGHT, OLD LADY--YOU BEG!
AN' MAYBE--JUST MAYBE--WE'LL LET YOU LIVE!
SOUNDS LIKE A GOOD IDEA!
SO WHAT SAY YOU DO A LITTLE BEGGING, PUNK--
HUH?
--AND MAYBE--JUST MAYBE--I'LL LET YOU WALK OUT OF HERE WITH ALL OF YOUR TEETH!
IT'S--HIM!!
THE BATMAN--!?!
AND ROBIN, THE BOY WONDER!
LET'S NOT FORGET ABOUT ME, OKAY?
BROK!
UUNNHH!!
11

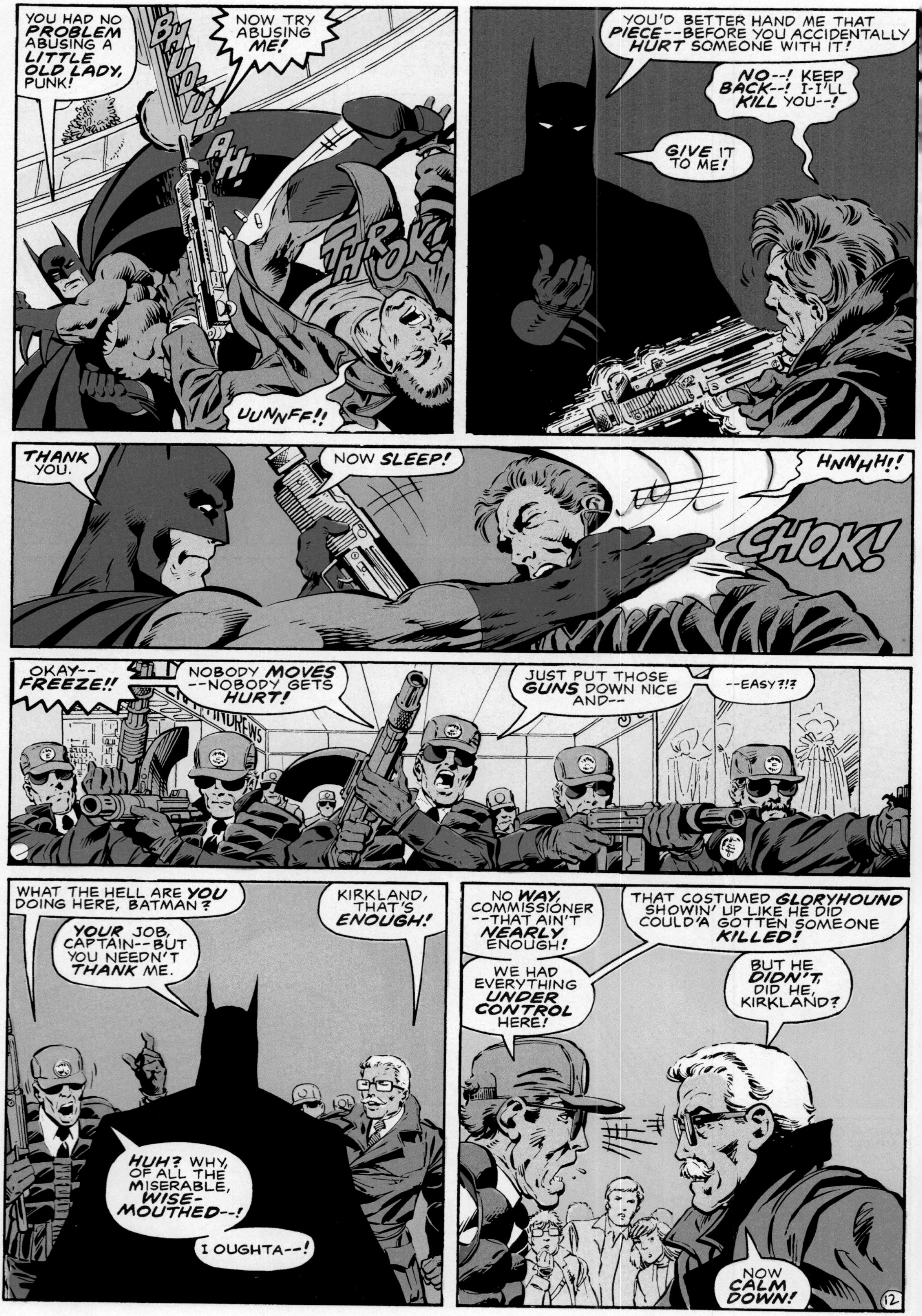

YOU HAD NO PROBLEM ABUSING A LITTLE OLD LADY, PUNK!
BUDUDUDAH!
NOW TRY ABUSING ME!
THROK!
UUNNFF!!
YOU'D BETTER HAND ME THAT PIECE--BEFORE YOU ACCIDENTALLY HURT SOMEONE WITH IT!
NO--! KEEP BACK--! I-I'LL KILL YOU--!
GIVE IT TO ME!
THANK YOU.
NOW SLEEP!
HNNHH!!
CHOK!
OKAY-- FREEZE!!
NOBODY MOVES --NOBODY GETS HURT!
JUST PUT THOSE GUNS DOWN NICE AND--
--EASY?!?
WHAT THE HELL ARE YOU DOING HERE, BATMAN?
YOUR JOB, CAPTAIN--BUT YOU NEEDN'T THANK ME.
KIRKLAND, THAT'S ENOUGH!
HUH? WHY, OF ALL THE MISERABLE, WISE-MOUTHED--!
I OUGHTA--!
NO WAY, COMMISSIONER --THAT AIN'T NEARLY ENOUGH!
THAT COSTUMED GLORYHOUND SHOWIN' UP LIKE HE DID COULD'A GOTTEN SOMEONE KILLED!
WE HAD EVERYTHING UNDER CONTROL HERE!
BUT HE DIDN'T, DID HE, KIRKLAND?
NOW CALM DOWN!
12

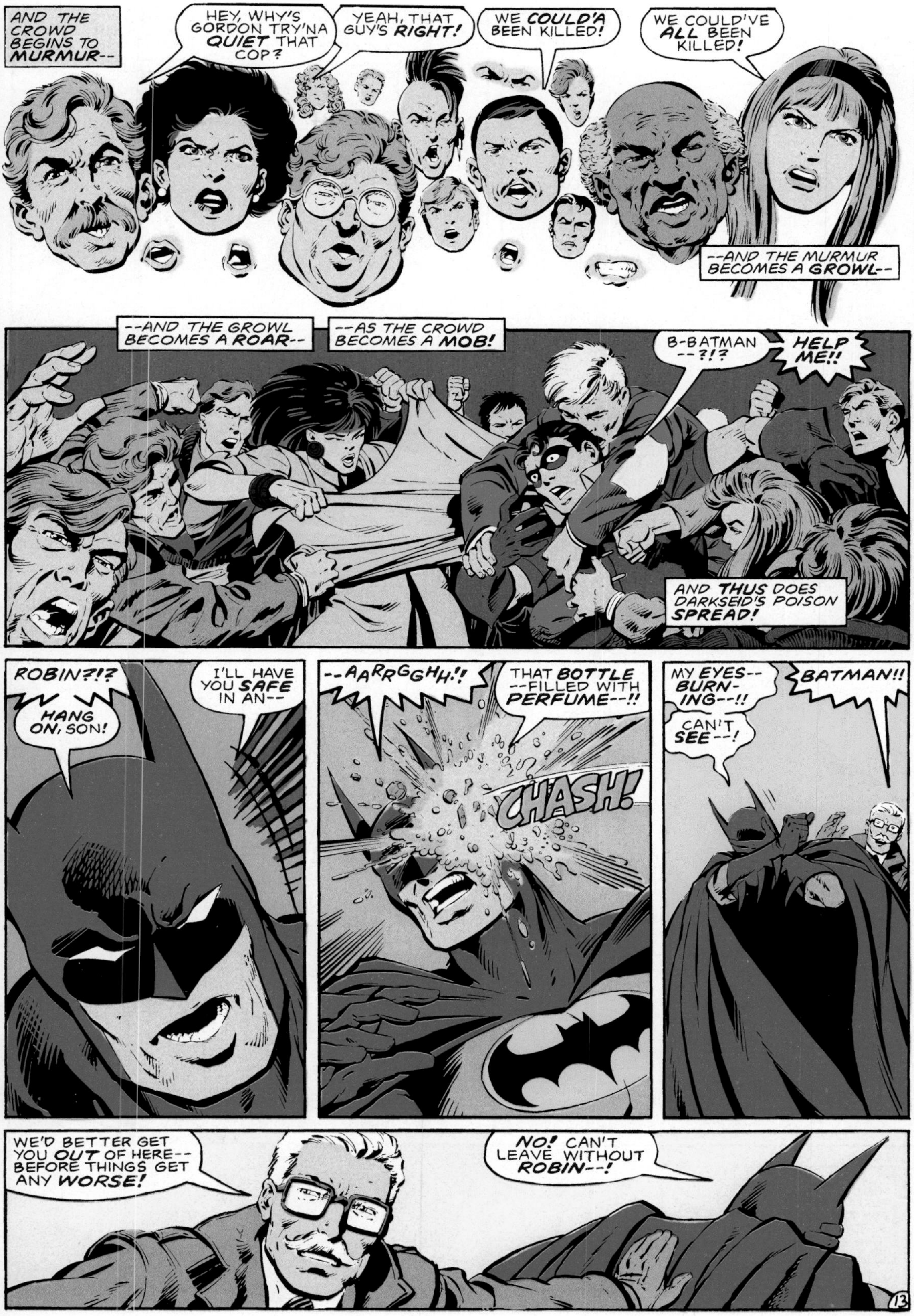
AND THE CROWD BEGINS TO MURMUR--
HEY, WHY'S GORDON TRY'NA QUIET THAT COP?
YEAH, THAT GUY'S RIGHT!
WE COULD'A BEEN KILLED!
WE COULD'VE ALL BEEN KILLED!
--AND THE MURMUR BECOMES A GROWL--
--AND THE GROWL BECOMES A ROAR--
--AS THE CROWD BECOMES A MOB!
B-BATMAN --?!?
HELP ME!!
AND THUS DOES DARKSEID'S POISON SPREAD!
ROBIN?!?
HANG ON, SON!
I'LL HAVE YOU SAFE IN AN--
--AARRGGHH!!
THAT BOTTLE --FILLED WITH PERFUME--!!
CHASH!
MY EYES-- BURN-ING--!!
CAN'T SEE--!
BATMAN!!
WE'D BETTER GET YOU OUT OF HERE-- BEFORE THINGS GET ANY WORSE!
NO! CAN'T LEAVE WITHOUT ROBIN--!
13

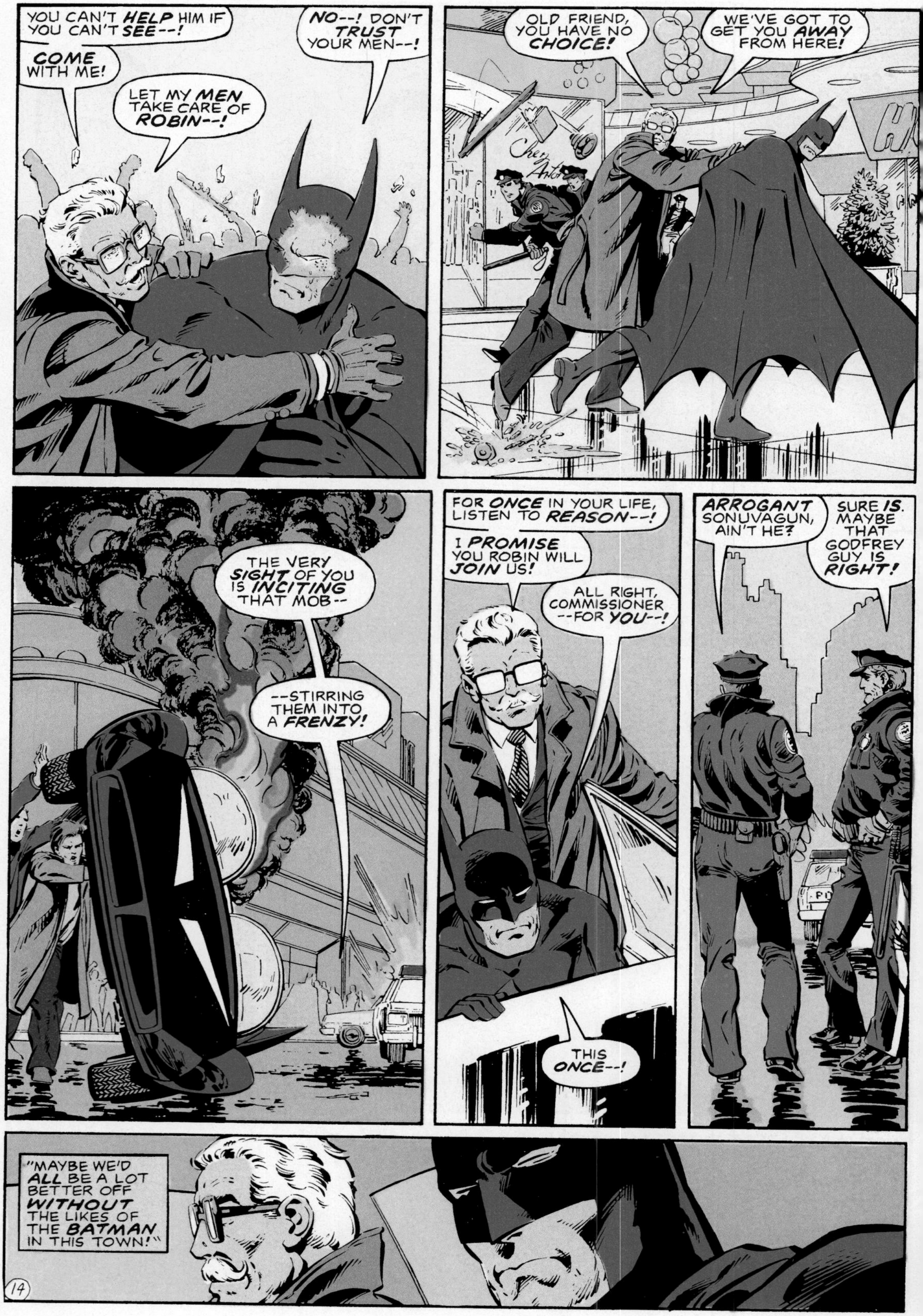
YOU CAN'T HELP HIM IF YOU CAN'T SEE--!
COME WITH ME!
LET MY MEN TAKE CARE OF ROBIN--!
NO--! DON'T TRUST YOUR MEN--!
OLD FRIEND, YOU HAVE NO CHOICE!
WE'VE GOT TO GET YOU AWAY FROM HERE!
THE VERY SIGHT OF YOU IS INCITING THAT MOB--
--STIRRING THEM INTO A FRENZY!
FOR ONCE IN YOUR LIFE, LISTEN TO REASON--!
I PROMISE YOU ROBIN WILL JOIN US!
ALL RIGHT, COMMISSIONER --FOR YOU--!
THIS ONCE--!
ARROGANT SONUVAGUN, AIN'T HE?
SURE IS. MAYBE THAT GODFREY GUY IS RIGHT!
"MAYBE WE'D ALL BE A LOT BETTER OFF WITHOUT THE LIKES OF THE BATMAN IN THIS TOWN!"
14

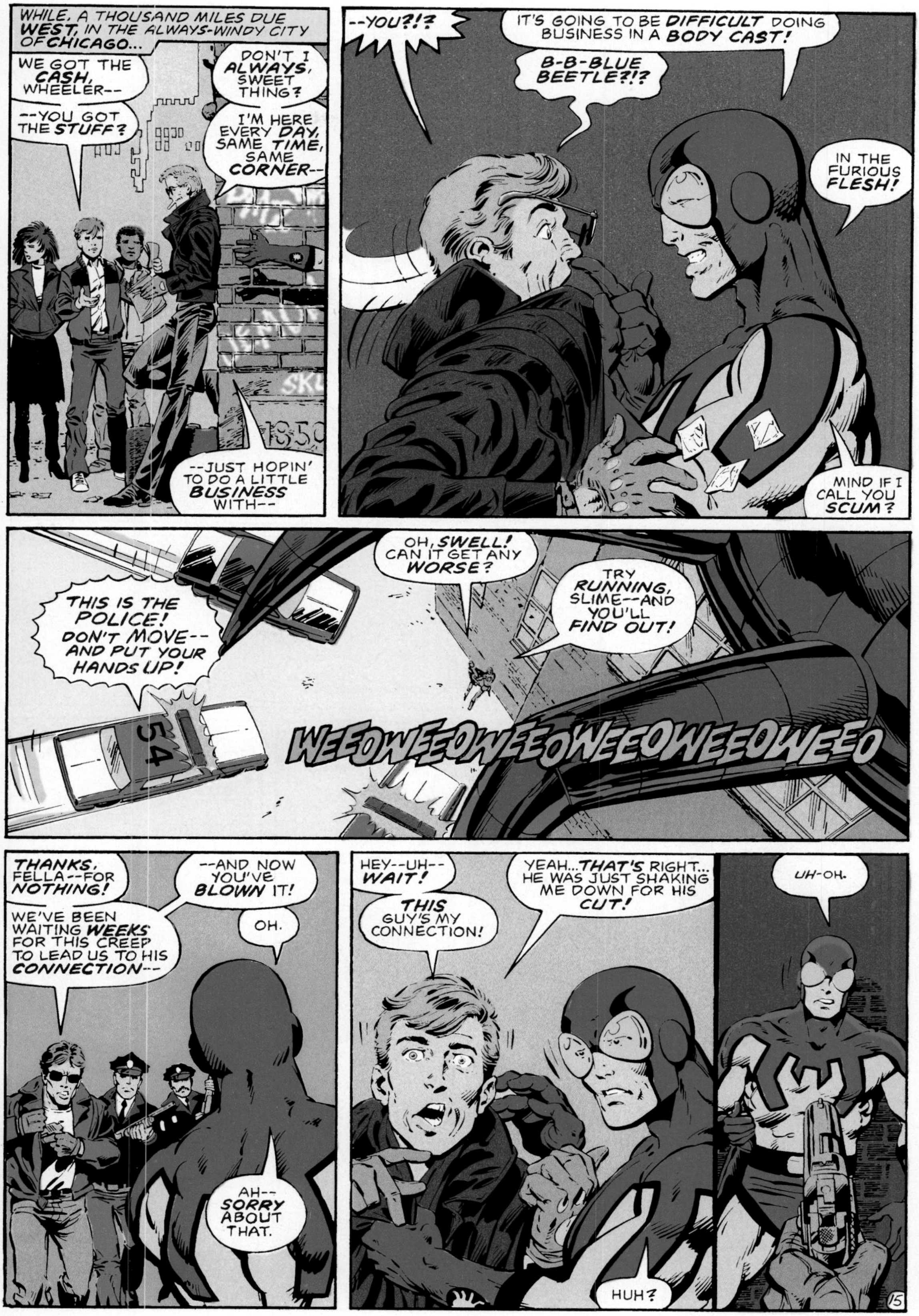
WHILE, A THOUSAND MILES DUE WEST, IN THE ALWAYS-WINDY CITY OF CHICAGO...
WE GOT THE CASH, WHEELER--
--YOU GOT THE STUFF?
DON'T I ALWAYS, SWEET THING?
I'M HERE EVERY DAY, SAME TIME, SAME CORNER--
--JUST HOPIN' TO DO A LITTLE BUSINESS WITH--
--YOU?!?
IT'S GOING TO BE DIFFICULT DOING BUSINESS IN A BODY CAST!
B-B-BLUE BEETLE?!?
IN THE FURIOUS FLESH!
MIND IF I CALL YOU SCUM?
THIS IS THE POLICE! DON'T MOVE-- AND PUT YOUR HANDS UP!
OH, SWELL! CAN IT GET ANY WORSE?
TRY RUNNING, SLIME--AND YOU'LL FIND OUT!
54
WEEOWEEOWEEOWEEOWEEOWEEO
THANKS, FELLA--FOR NOTHING!
WE'VE BEEN WAITING WEEKS FOR THIS CREEP TO LEAD US TO HIS CONNECTION--
--AND NOW YOU'VE BLOWN IT!
OH.
AH-- SORRY ABOUT THAT.
HEY--UH-- WAIT!
THIS GUY'S MY CONNECTION!
YEAH...THAT'S RIGHT... HE WAS JUST SHAKING ME DOWN FOR HIS CUT!
HUH?
UH-OH.
15

DON'T *MOVE*, BUG-EYES! YOU'RE *UNDER* AR--

--HEY!!

GEE, I'D REALLY *LOVE* TO STICK AROUND AND *EXPLAIN*, FELLAS--

--BUT SOMETHING TELLS ME YOU'RE IN NO MOOD TO *LISTEN!*

I MEAN, I KNOW YOU'RE *ANGRY* THAT I *BOTCHED* YOUR OPERATION HERE--

--BUT DON'T YOU THINK TRYING TO *ANNIHILATE* ME IS JUST A LITTLE BIT *EXTREME*?

SPWEEE!

SPAK!

SPADOING!

USED THE *ELECTRONIC FINGERTIP CONTROLS* IN MY GLOVES TO SUMMON MY *SKY-WIRE*--

--SO I CAN *REEL* MYSELF UP INTO MY BULLETPROOF *BUG*--

--AND GET THE *HECK*--

OWWW!

TWINNNG!

--OF HERE!

THEY *SHOT* AT ME! THEY ACTUALLY TRIED TO *KILL* ME--

--AND I WAS ONLY TRYING TO *HELP!*

SPRING!

SPING!

KAPHWEEE! KA-PWEEE!

METAL-MESH FABRIC OF MY COSTUME *PROTECTED* ME FROM THE BULLET'S *IMPACT*--

--BUT THIS *ARM* IS STILL GONNA BE *SORE* FOR A FEW DAYS!

MAYBE I'D BETTER DO SOME FAST *RETHINK-ING*--

--BEFORE THE *BLUE BEETLE* BECOMES THE *DEATH* OF ME!

16

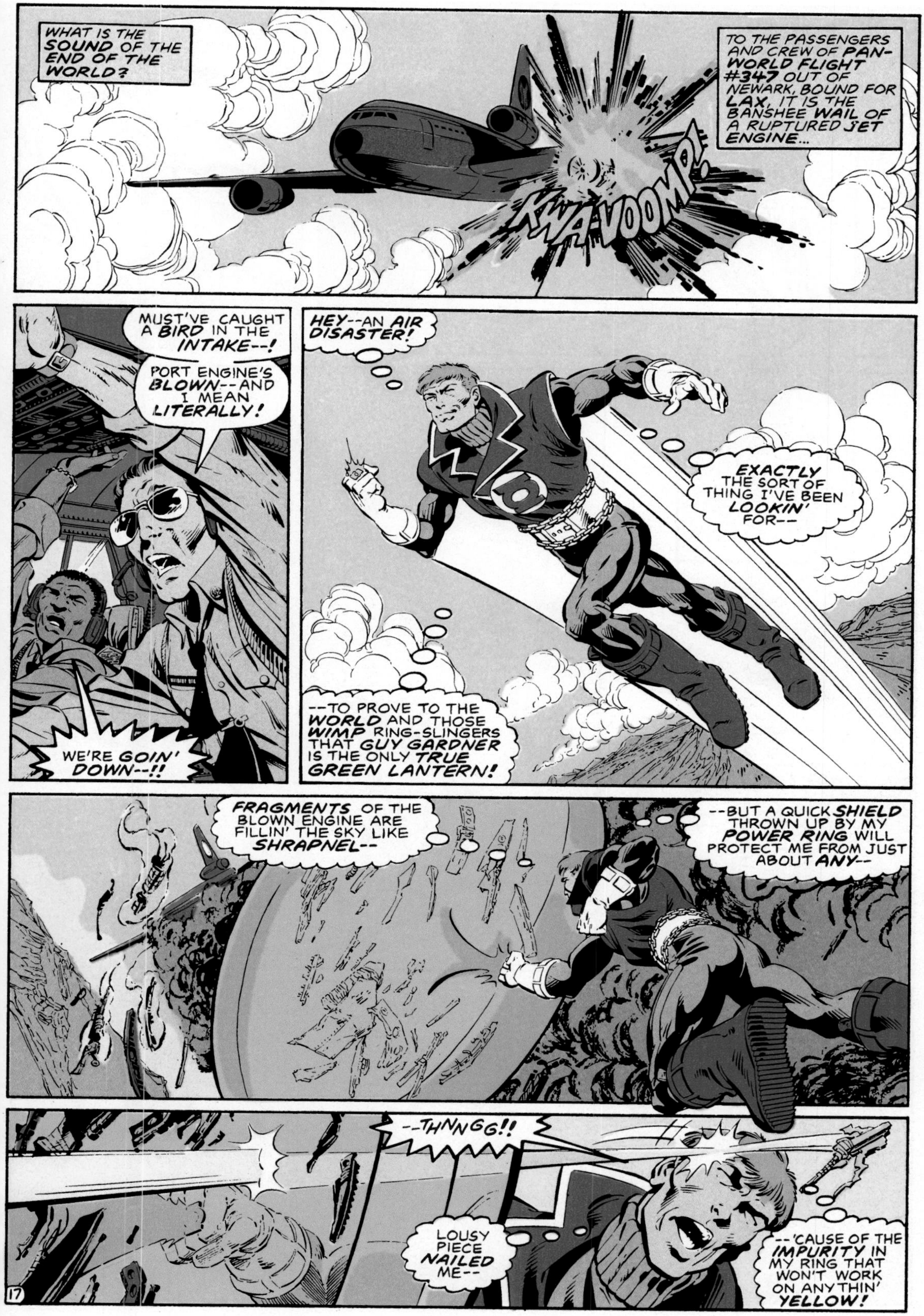
WHAT IS THE SOUND OF THE END OF THE WORLD?
TO THE PASSENGERS AND CREW OF PAN-WORLD FLIGHT #347 OUT OF NEWARK, BOUND FOR LAX, IT IS THE BANSHEE WAIL OF A RUPTURED JET ENGINE...
KWA-VOOMP!
MUST'VE CAUGHT A BIRD IN THE INTAKE--!
PORT ENGINE'S BLOWN--AND I MEAN LITERALLY!
WE'RE GOIN' DOWN--!!
HEY--AN AIR DISASTER!
EXACTLY THE SORT OF THING I'VE BEEN LOOKIN' FOR--
--TO PROVE TO THE WORLD AND THOSE WIMP RING-SLINGERS THAT GUY GARDNER IS THE ONLY TRUE GREEN LANTERN!
FRAGMENTS OF THE BLOWN ENGINE ARE FILLIN' THE SKY LIKE SHRAPNEL--
--BUT A QUICK SHIELD THROWN UP BY MY POWER RING WILL PROTECT ME FROM JUST ABOUT ANY--
--THNNGG!!
LOUSY PIECE NAILED ME--
--'CAUSE OF THE IMPURITY IN MY RING THAT WON'T WORK ON ANYTHIN' YELLOW!
17

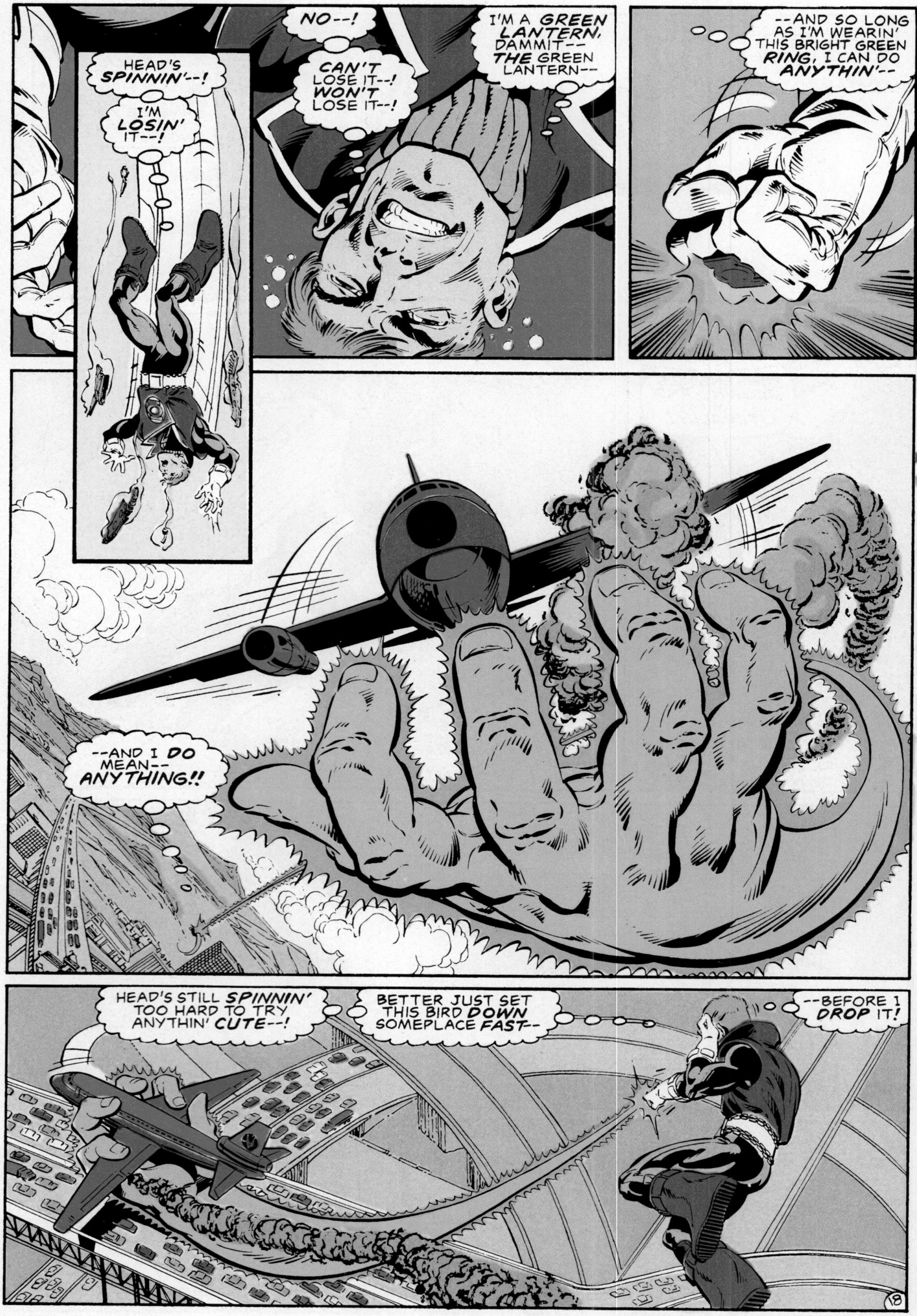
HEAD'S SPINNIN'--!
I'M LOSIN' IT--!
NO--!
CAN'T LOSE IT--! WON'T LOSE IT--!
I'M A GREEN LANTERN, DAMMIT-- THE GREEN LANTERN--
--AND SO LONG AS I'M WEARIN' THIS BRIGHT GREEN RING, I CAN DO ANYTHIN'--
--AND I DO MEAN-- ANYTHING!!
HEAD'S STILL SPINNIN' TOO HARD TO TRY ANYTHIN' CUTE--!
BETTER JUST SET THIS BIRD DOWN SOMEPLACE FAST--
--BEFORE I DROP IT!

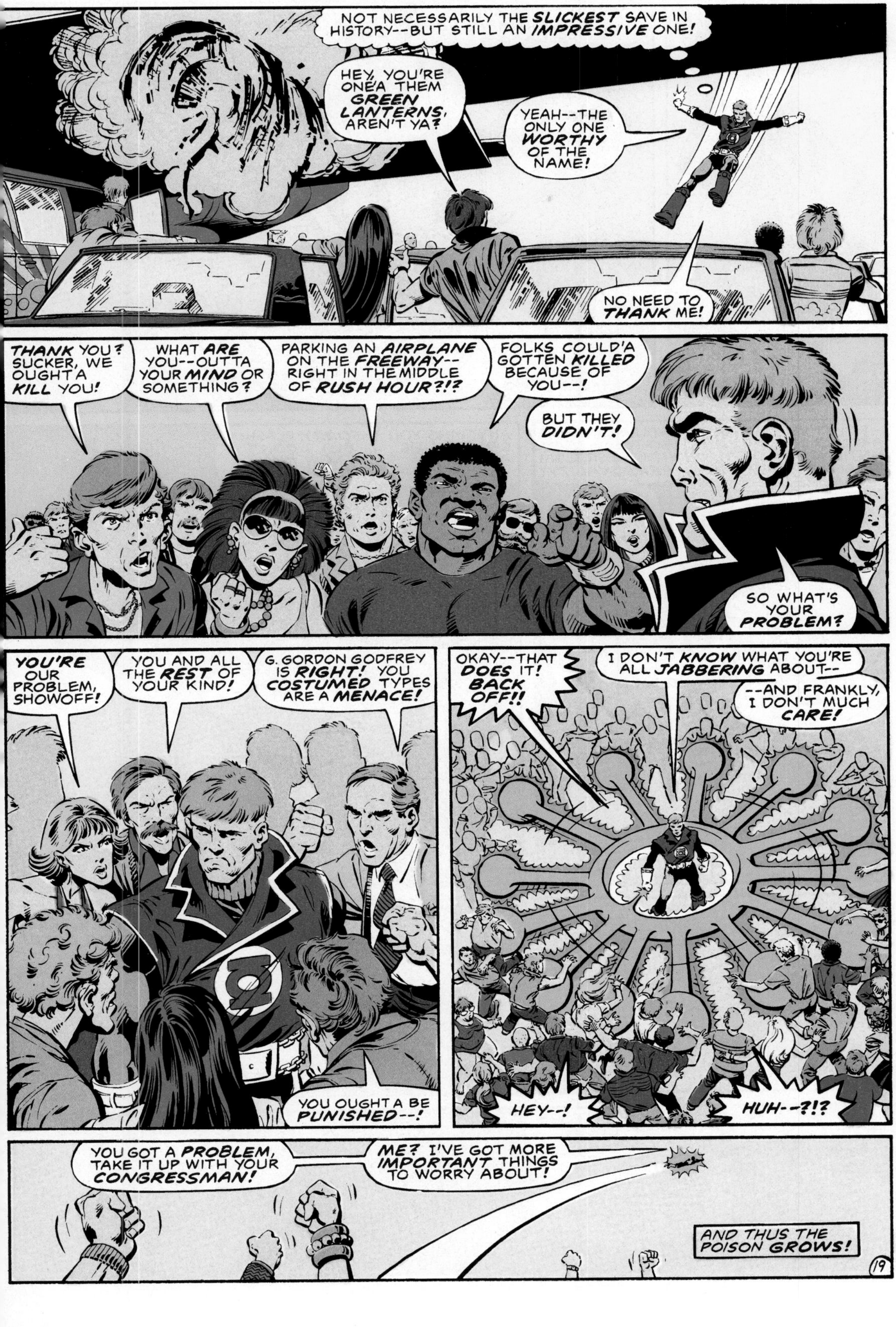
NOT NECESSARILY THE SLICKEST SAVE IN HISTORY--BUT STILL AN IMPRESSIVE ONE!
HEY, YOU'RE ONE'A THEM GREEN LANTERNS, AREN'T YA?
YEAH--THE ONLY ONE WORTHY OF THE NAME!
NO NEED TO THANK ME!
THANK YOU? SUCKER, WE OUGHT A KILL YOU!
WHAT ARE YOU--OUTTA YOUR MIND OR SOMETHING?
PARKING AN AIRPLANE ON THE FREEWAY-- RIGHT IN THE MIDDLE OF RUSH HOUR?!?
FOLKS COULD'A GOTTEN KILLED BECAUSE OF YOU--!
BUT THEY DIDN'T!
SO WHAT'S YOUR PROBLEM?
YOU'RE OUR PROBLEM, SHOWOFF!
YOU AND ALL THE REST OF YOUR KIND!
G. GORDON GODFREY IS RIGHT! YOU COSTUMED TYPES ARE A MENACE!
YOU OUGHT A BE PUNISHED--!
OKAY--THAT DOES IT! BACK OFF!!
I DON'T KNOW WHAT YOU'RE ALL JABBERING ABOUT--
--AND FRANKLY, I DON'T MUCH CARE!
HEY--!
HUH--?!?
YOU GOT A PROBLEM, TAKE IT UP WITH YOUR CONGRESSMAN!
ME? I'VE GOT MORE IMPORTANT THINGS TO WORRY ABOUT!
AND THUS THE POISON GROWS!

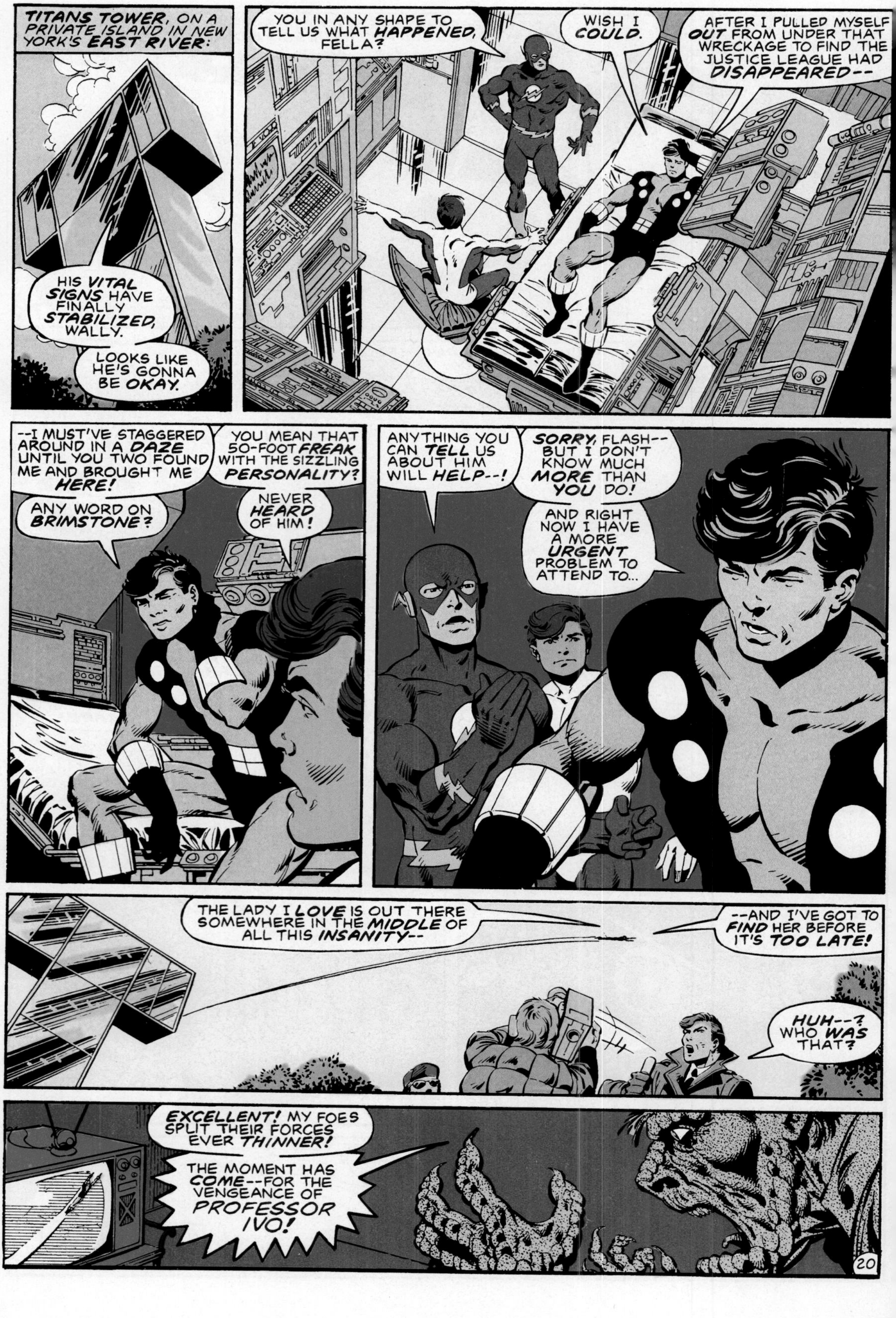

TITANS TOWER, ON A PRIVATE ISLAND IN NEW YORK'S EAST RIVER:
HIS VITAL SIGNS HAVE FINALLY STABILIZED, WALLY.
LOOKS LIKE HE'S GONNA BE OKAY.
YOU IN ANY SHAPE TO TELL US WHAT HAPPENED, FELLA?
WISH I COULD.
AFTER I PULLED MYSELF OUT FROM UNDER THAT WRECKAGE TO FIND THE JUSTICE LEAGUE HAD DISAPPEARED--
--I MUST'VE STAGGERED AROUND IN A DAZE UNTIL YOU TWO FOUND ME AND BROUGHT ME HERE!
YOU MEAN THAT 50-FOOT FREAK WITH THE SIZZLING PERSONALITY?
ANY WORD ON BRIMSTONE?
NEVER HEARD OF HIM!
ANYTHING YOU CAN TELL US ABOUT HIM WILL HELP--!
SORRY, FLASH--BUT I DON'T KNOW MUCH MORE THAN YOU DO!
AND RIGHT NOW I HAVE A MORE URGENT PROBLEM TO ATTEND TO...
THE LADY I LOVE IS OUT THERE SOMEWHERE IN THE MIDDLE OF ALL THIS INSANITY--
--AND I'VE GOT TO FIND HER BEFORE IT'S TOO LATE!
HUH--? WHO WAS THAT?
EXCELLENT! MY FOES SPLIT THEIR FORCES EVER THINNER!
THE MOMENT HAS COME--FOR THE VENGEANCE OF PROFESSOR IVO!

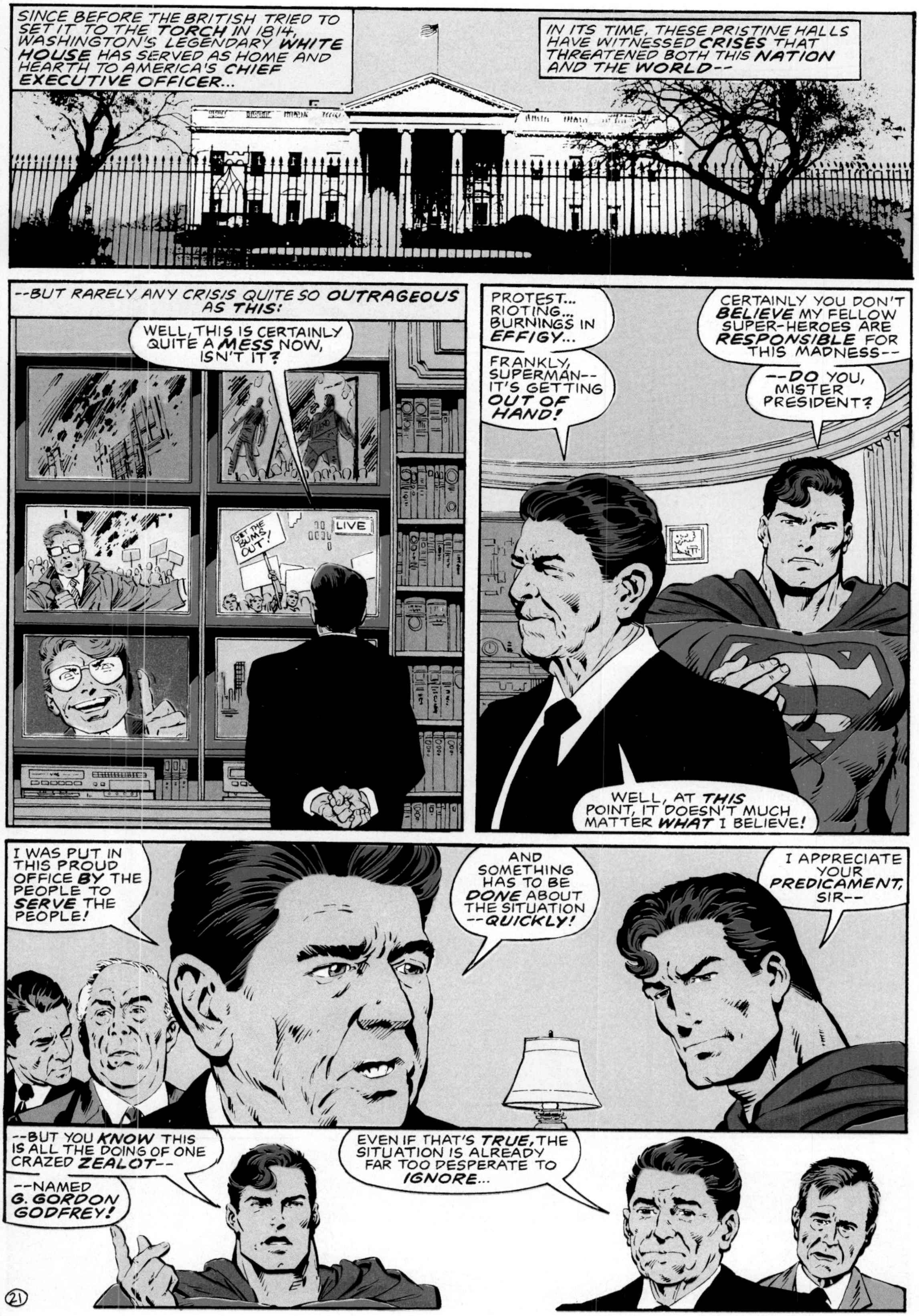

SINCE BEFORE THE BRITISH TRIED TO SET IT TO THE TORCH IN 1814, WASHINGTON'S LEGENDARY WHITE HOUSE HAS SERVED AS HOME AND HEARTH TO AMERICA'S CHIEF EXECUTIVE OFFICER...
IN ITS TIME, THESE PRISTINE HALLS HAVE WITNESSED CRISES THAT THREATENED BOTH THIS NATION AND THE WORLD--
--BUT RARELY ANY CRISIS QUITE SO OUTRAGEOUS AS THIS:
WELL, THIS IS CERTAINLY QUITE A MESS NOW, ISN'T IT?
GET THE BUMS OUT!
LIVE
PROTEST... RIOTING... BURNINGS IN EFFIGY...
FRANKLY, SUPERMAN-- IT'S GETTING OUT OF HAND!
CERTAINLY YOU DON'T BELIEVE MY FELLOW SUPER-HEROES ARE RESPONSIBLE FOR THIS MADNESS--
--DO YOU, MISTER PRESIDENT?
WELL, AT THIS POINT, IT DOESN'T MUCH MATTER WHAT I BELIEVE!
I WAS PUT IN THIS PROUD OFFICE BY THE PEOPLE TO SERVE THE PEOPLE!
AND SOMETHING HAS TO BE DONE ABOUT THE SITUATION --QUICKLY!
I APPRECIATE YOUR PREDICAMENT, SIR--
--BUT YOU KNOW THIS IS ALL THE DOING OF ONE CRAZED ZEALOT--
--NAMED G. GORDON GODFREY!
EVEN IF THAT'S TRUE, THE SITUATION IS ALREADY FAR TOO DESPERATE TO IGNORE...

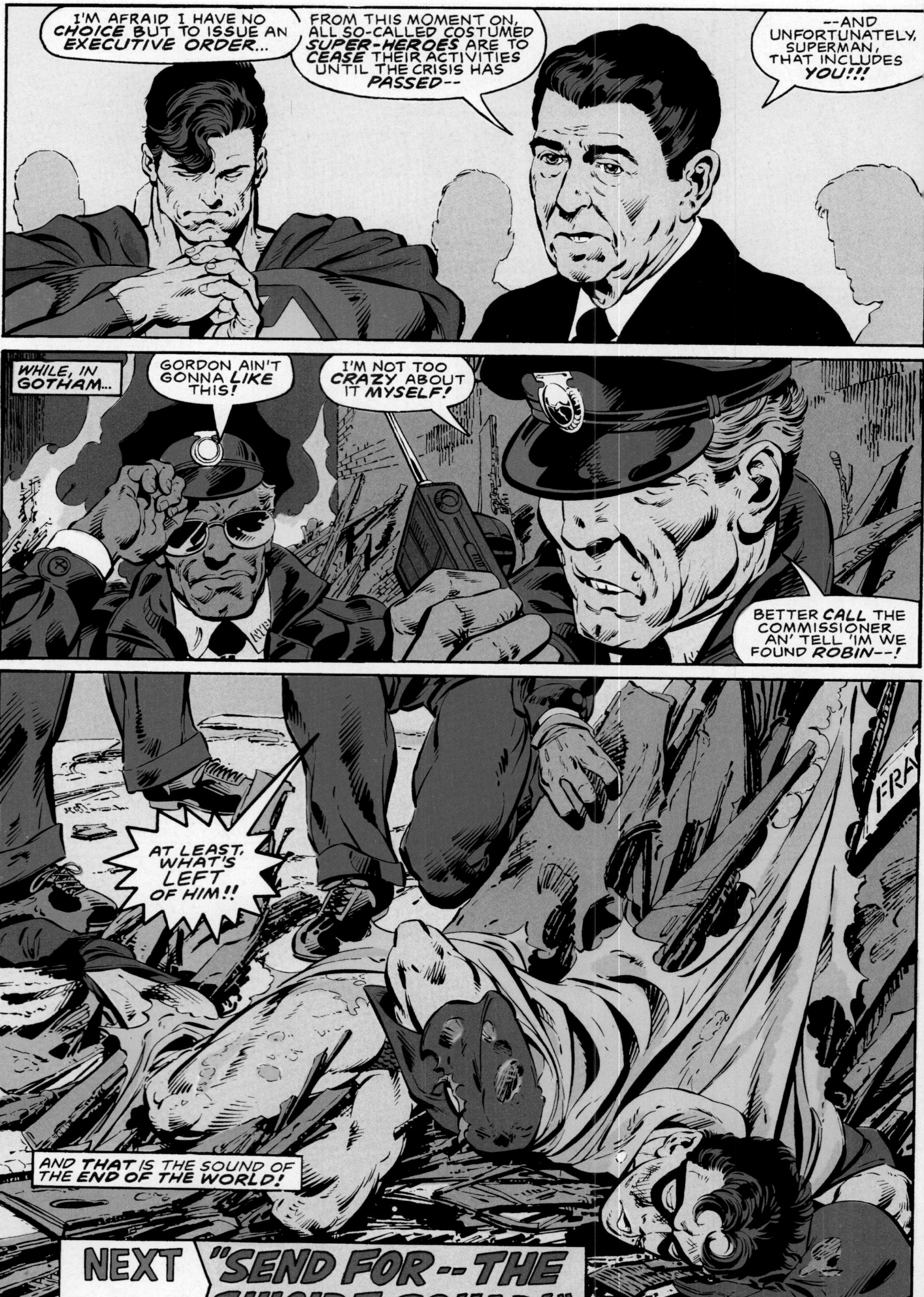
I'M AFRAID I HAVE NO CHOICE BUT TO ISSUE AN EXECUTIVE ORDER...
FROM THIS MOMENT ON, ALL SO-CALLED COSTUMED SUPER-HEROES ARE TO CEASE THEIR ACTIVITIES UNTIL THE CRISIS HAS PASSED--
--AND UNFORTUNATELY, SUPERMAN, THAT INCLUDES YOU!!!
WHILE, IN GOTHAM...
GORDON AIN'T GONNA LIKE THIS!
I'M NOT TOO CRAZY ABOUT IT MYSELF!
BETTER CALL THE COMMISSIONER AN' TELL 'IM WE FOUND ROBIN--!
AT LEAST, WHAT'S LEFT OF HIM!!
AND THAT IS THE SOUND OF THE END OF THE WORLD!
NEXT "SEND FOR--THE SUICIDE SQUAD!"

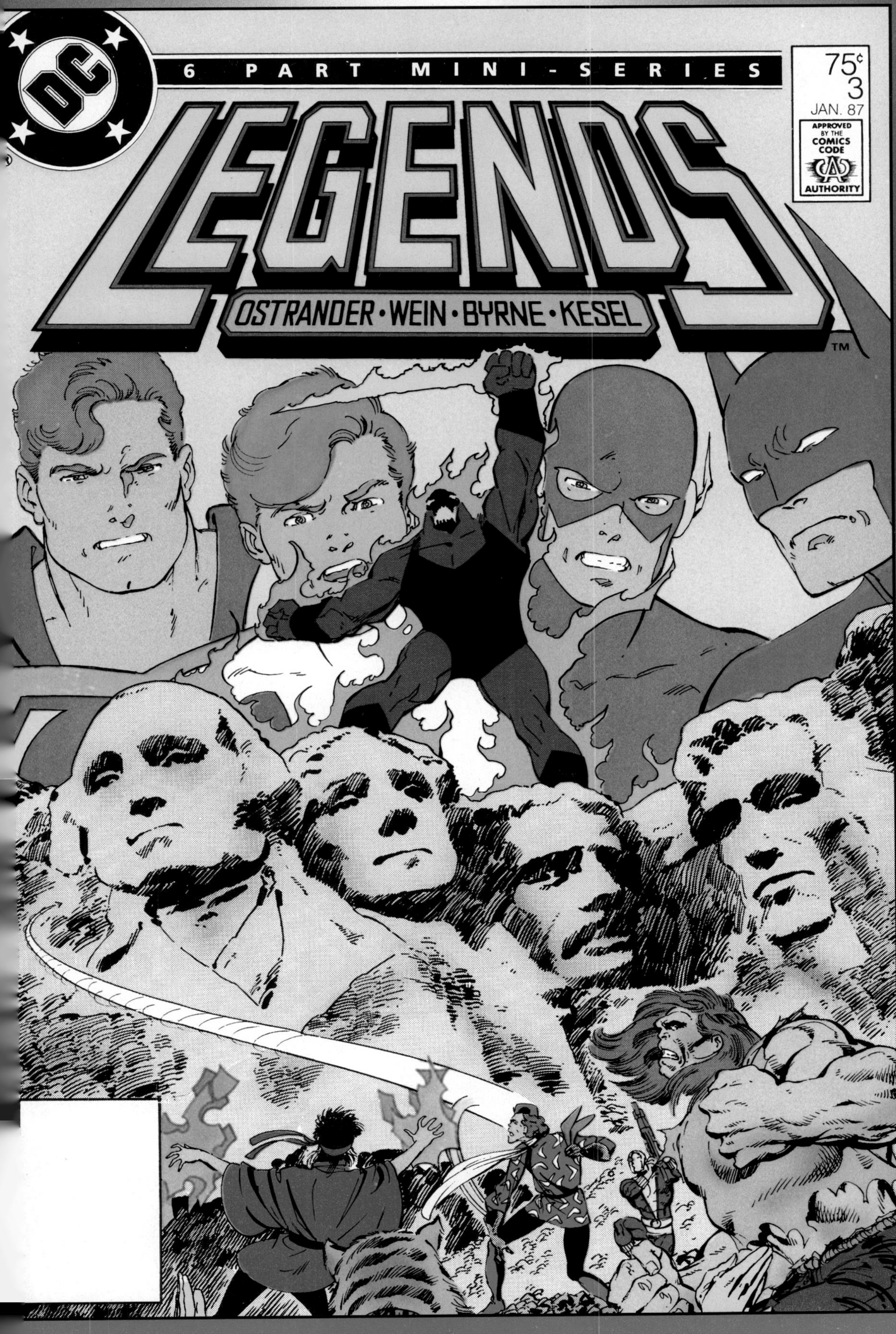
6 PART MINI-SERIES
75¢
3
JAN. 87
APPROVED BY THE COMICS CODE AUTHORITY
LEGENDS
OSTRANDER • WEIN • BYRNE • KESEL
TM

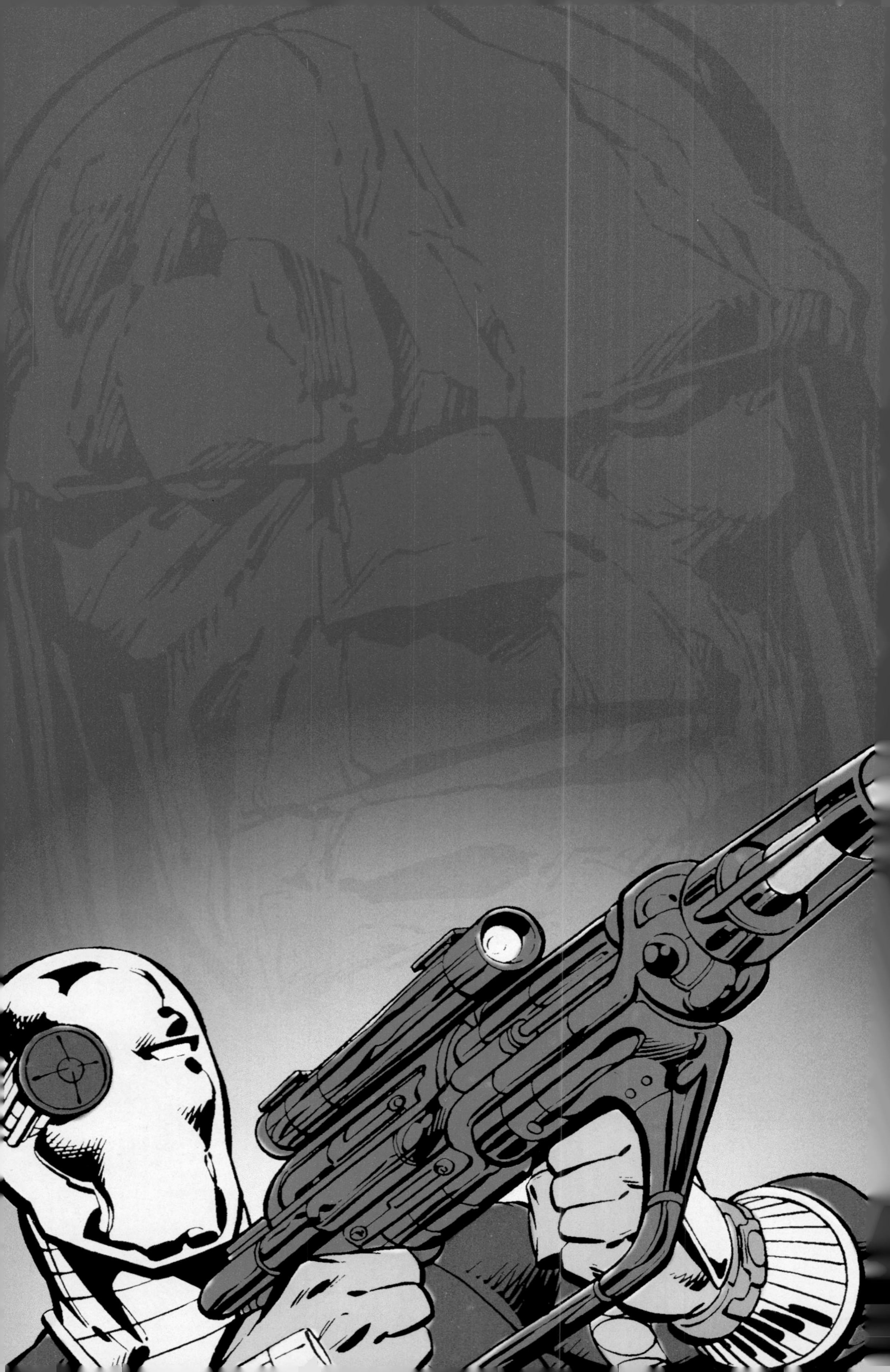

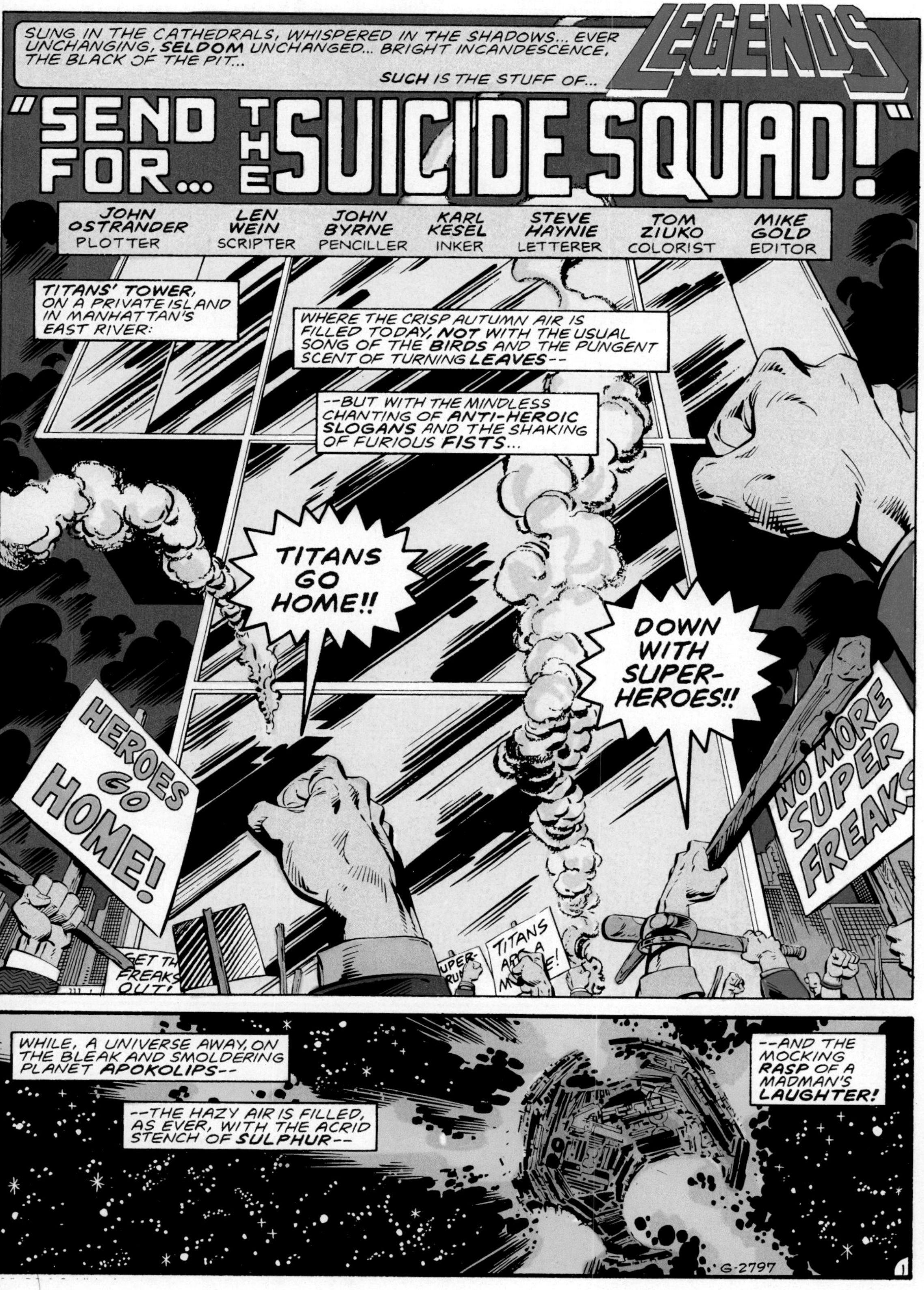
SUNG IN THE CATHEDRALS, WHISPERED IN THE SHADOWS... EVER UNCHANGING, SELDOM UNCHANGED... BRIGHT INCANDESCENCE, THE BLACK OF THE PIT...
SUCH IS THE STUFF OF...
LEGENDS
"SEND FOR... THE SUICIDE SQUAD!"
JOHN OSTRANDER PLOTTER
LEN WEIN SCRIPTER
JOHN BYRNE PENCILLER
KARL KESEL INKER
STEVE HAYNIE LETTERER
TOM ZIUKO COLORIST
MIKE GOLD EDITOR
TITANS' TOWER, ON A PRIVATE ISLAND IN MANHATTAN'S EAST RIVER:
WHERE THE CRISP AUTUMN AIR IS FILLED TODAY, NOT WITH THE USUAL SONG OF THE BIRDS AND THE PUNGENT SCENT OF TURNING LEAVES--
--BUT WITH THE MINDLESS CHANTING OF ANTI-HEROIC SLOGANS AND THE SHAKING OF FURIOUS FISTS...
TITANS GO HOME!!
DOWN WITH SUPER-HEROES!!
HEROES GO HOME!
NO MORE SUPER FREAKS
WHILE, A UNIVERSE AWAY, ON THE BLEAK AND SMOLDERING PLANET APOKOLIPS--
--THE HAZY AIR IS FILLED, AS EVER, WITH THE ACRID STENCH OF SULPHUR--
--AND THE MOCKING RASP OF A MADMAN'S LAUGHTER!
G-2797
1

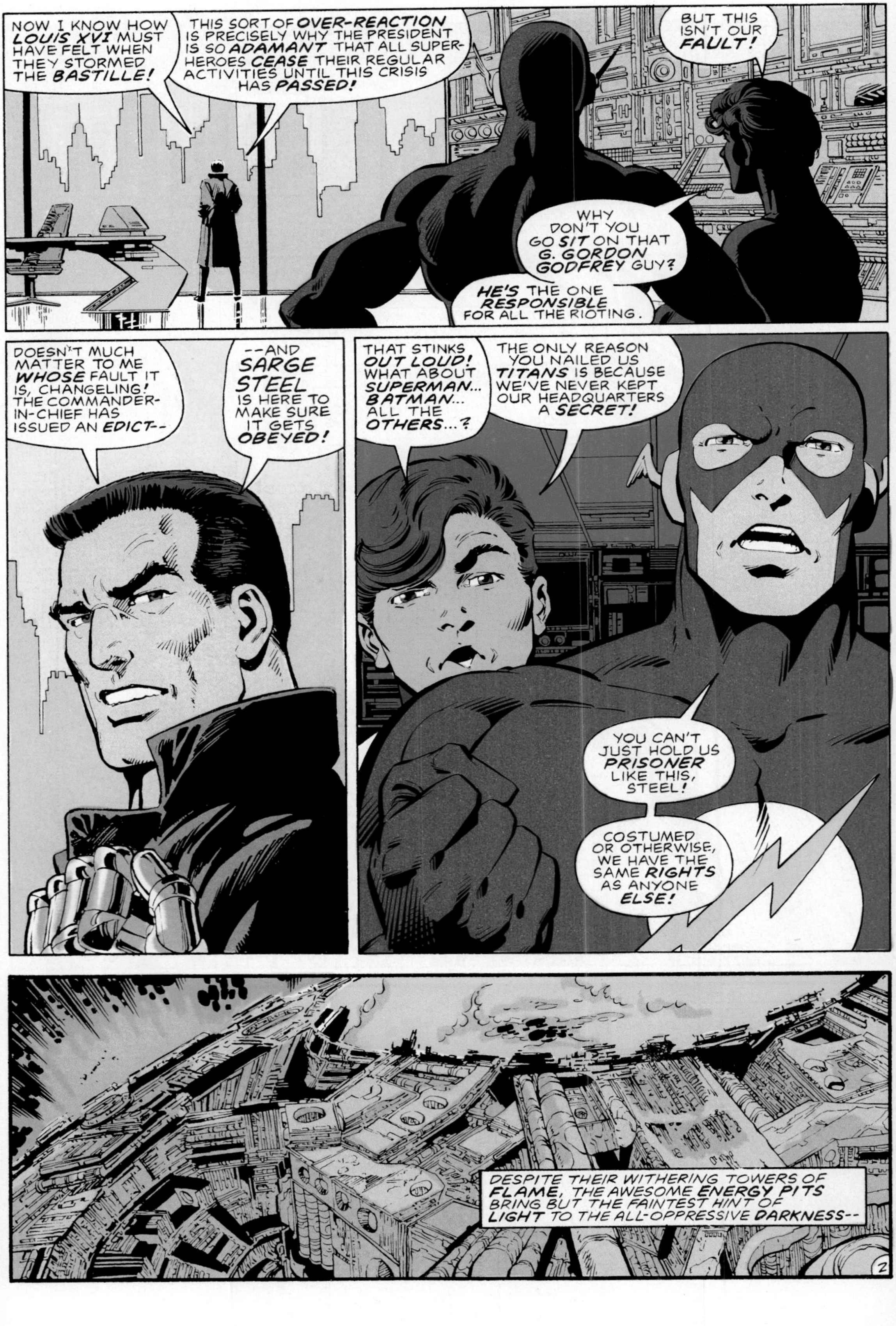
NOW I KNOW HOW LOUIS XVI MUST HAVE FELT WHEN THEY STORMED THE BASTILLE!
THIS SORT OF OVER-REACTION IS PRECISELY WHY THE PRESIDENT IS SO ADAMANT THAT ALL SUPER-HEROES CEASE THEIR REGULAR ACTIVITIES UNTIL THIS CRISIS HAS PASSED!
BUT THIS ISN'T OUR FAULT!
WHY DON'T YOU GO SIT ON THAT G. GORDON GODFREY GUY?
HE'S THE ONE RESPONSIBLE FOR ALL THE RIOTING.
DOESN'T MUCH MATTER TO ME WHOSE FAULT IT IS, CHANGELING! THE COMMANDER-IN-CHIEF HAS ISSUED AN EDICT--
--AND SARGE STEEL IS HERE TO MAKE SURE IT GETS OBEYED!
THAT STINKS OUT LOUD! WHAT ABOUT SUPERMAN... BATMAN... ALL THE OTHERS...?
THE ONLY REASON YOU NAILED US TITANS IS BECAUSE WE'VE NEVER KEPT OUR HEADQUARTERS A SECRET!
YOU CAN'T JUST HOLD US PRISONER LIKE THIS, STEEL!
COSTUMED OR OTHERWISE, WE HAVE THE SAME RIGHTS AS ANYONE ELSE!
DESPITE THEIR WITHERING TOWERS OF FLAME, THE AWESOME ENERGY PITS BRING BUT THE FAINTEST HINT OF LIGHT TO THE ALL-OPPRESSIVE DARKNESS--
2

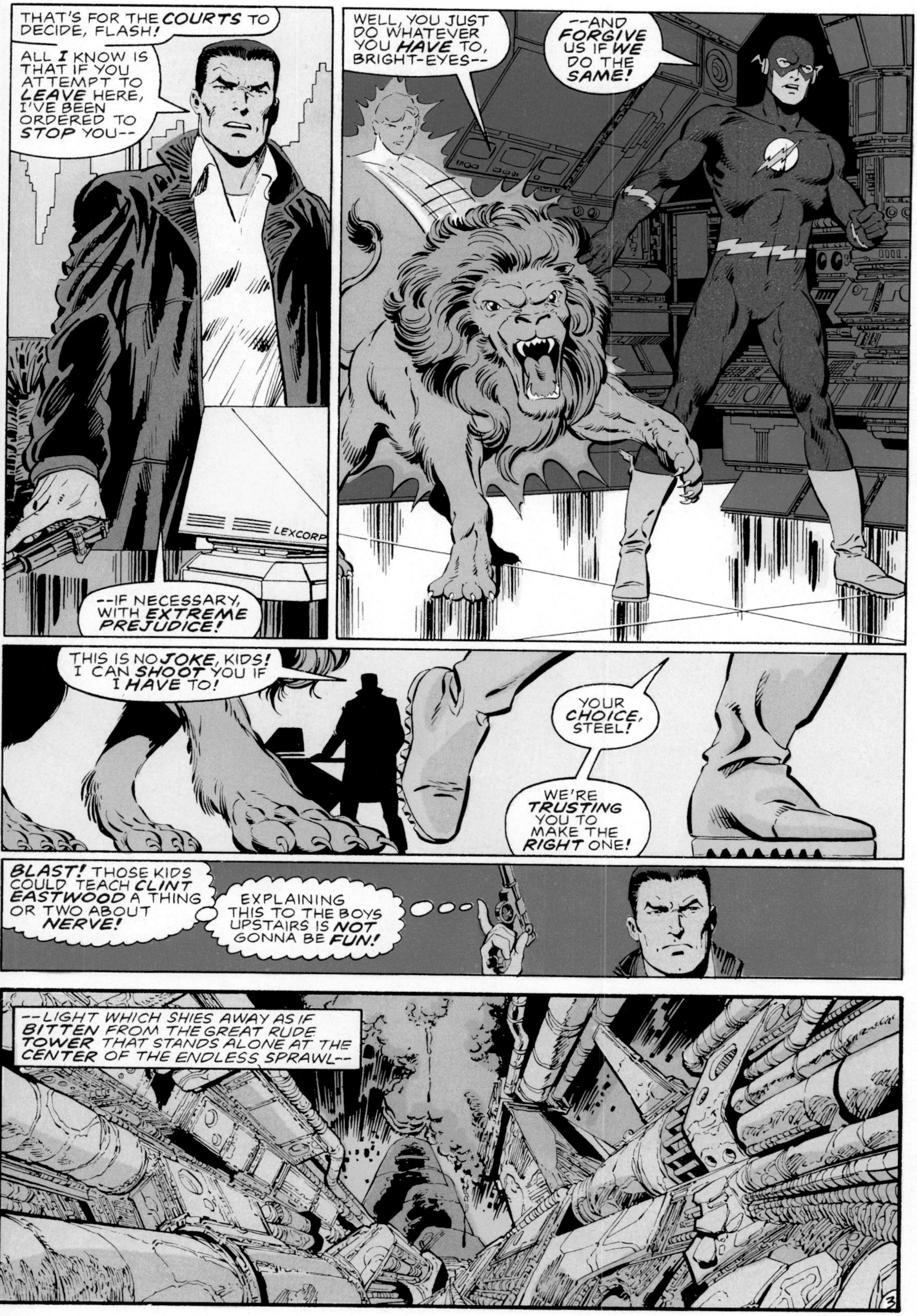
THAT'S FOR THE COURTS TO DECIDE, FLASH!
ALL I KNOW IS THAT IF YOU ATTEMPT TO LEAVE HERE, I'VE BEEN ORDERED TO STOP YOU--
LEXCORP
--IF NECESSARY, WITH EXTREME PREJUDICE!
WELL, YOU JUST DO WHATEVER YOU HAVE TO, BRIGHT-EYES--
--AND FORGIVE US IF WE DO THE SAME!
THIS IS NO JOKE, KIDS! I CAN SHOOT YOU IF I HAVE TO!
YOUR CHOICE, STEEL!
WE'RE TRUSTING YOU TO MAKE THE RIGHT ONE!
BLAST! THOSE KIDS COULD TEACH CLINT EASTWOOD A THING OR TWO ABOUT NERVE!
EXPLAINING THIS TO THE BOYS UPSTAIRS IS NOT GONNA BE FUN!
--LIGHT WHICH SHIES AWAY AS IF BITTEN FROM THE GREAT RUDE TOWER THAT STANDS ALONE AT THE CENTER OF THE ENDLESS SPRAWL--
3

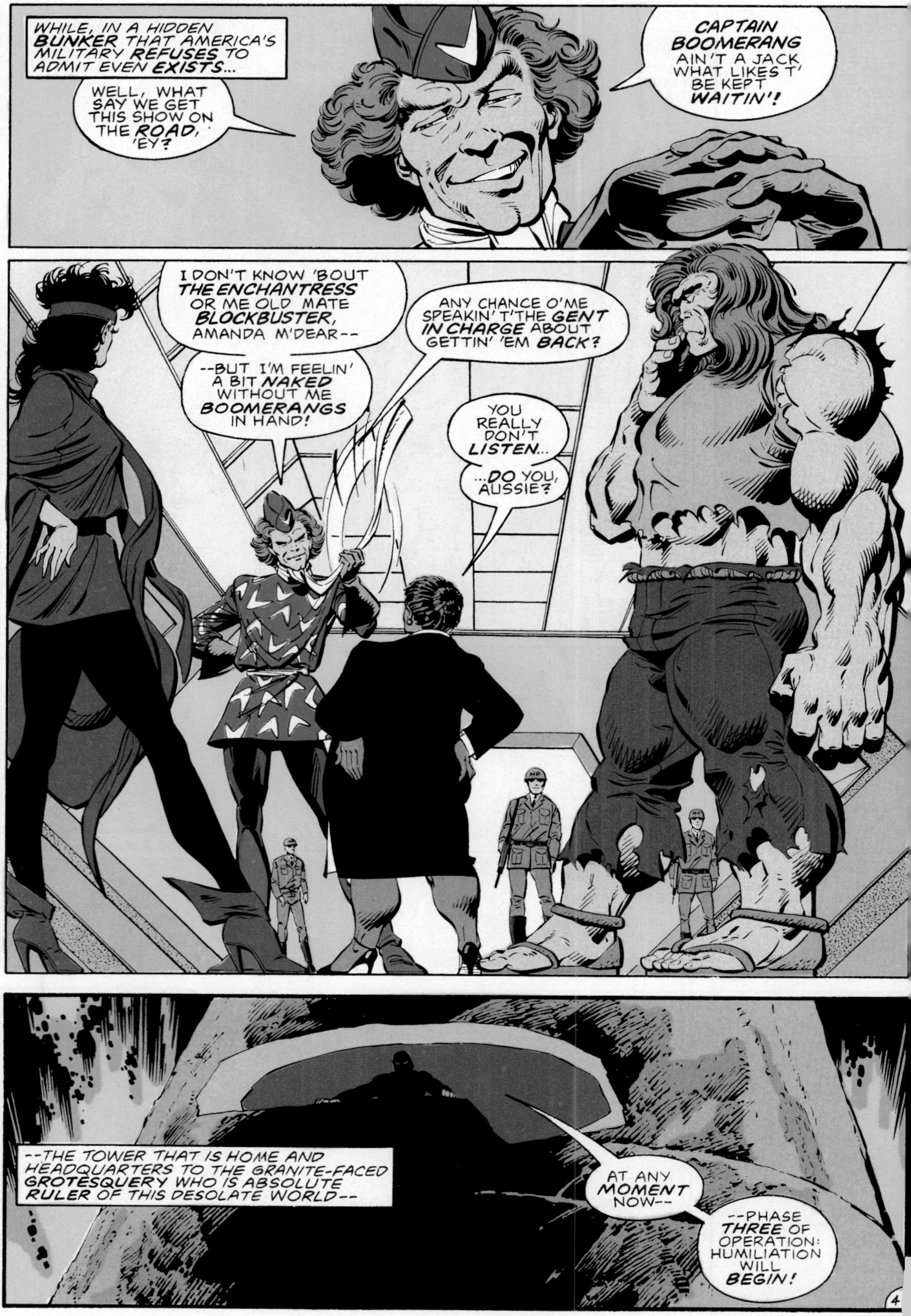

WHILE, IN A HIDDEN BUNKER THAT AMERICA'S MILITARY REFUSES TO ADMIT EVEN EXISTS...
WELL, WHAT SAY WE GET THIS SHOW ON THE ROAD, 'EY?
CAPTAIN BOOMERANG AIN'T A JACK WHAT LIKES T' BE KEPT WAITIN'!
I DON'T KNOW 'BOUT THE ENCHANTRESS OR ME OLD MATE BLOCKBUSTER, AMANDA M'DEAR--
--BUT I'M FEELIN' A BIT NAKED WITHOUT ME BOOMERANGS IN HAND!
ANY CHANCE O'ME SPEAKIN' T'THE GENT IN CHARGE ABOUT GETTIN' 'EM BACK?
YOU REALLY DON'T LISTEN...
...DO YOU, AUSSIE?
--THE TOWER THAT IS HOME AND HEADQUARTERS TO THE GRANITE-FACED GROTESQUERY WHO IS ABSOLUTE RULER OF THIS DESOLATE WORLD--
AT ANY MOMENT NOW--
--PHASE THREE OF OPERATION: HUMILIATION WILL BEGIN!

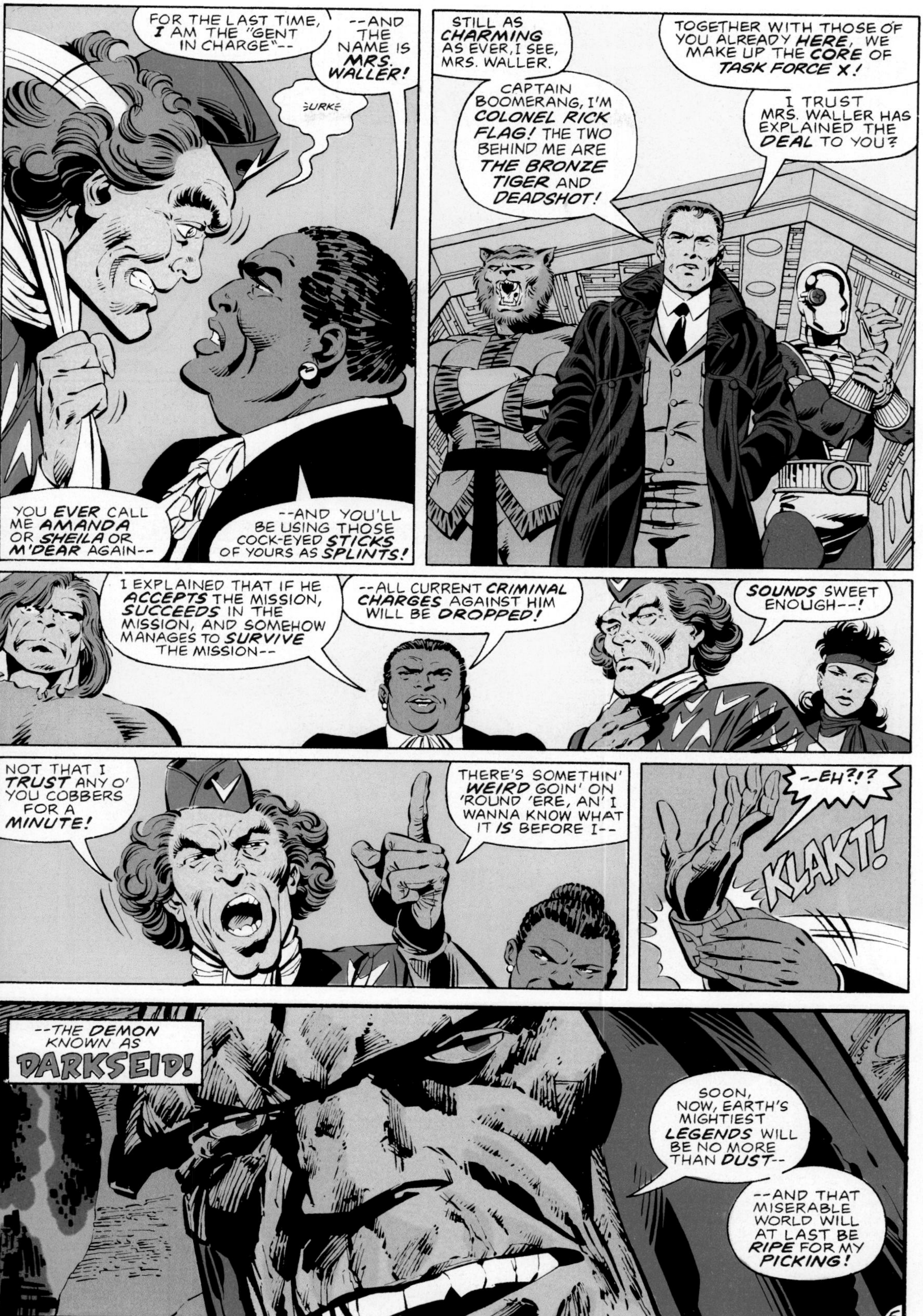
FOR THE LAST TIME, I AM THE "GENT IN CHARGE"--
--AND THE NAME IS MRS. WALLER!
URK
YOU EVER CALL ME AMANDA OR SHEILA OR M'DEAR AGAIN--
--AND YOU'LL BE USING THOSE COCK-EYED STICKS OF YOURS AS SPLINTS!
STILL AS CHARMING AS EVER, I SEE, MRS. WALLER.
CAPTAIN BOOMERANG, I'M COLONEL RICK FLAG! THE TWO BEHIND ME ARE THE BRONZE TIGER AND DEADSHOT!
TOGETHER WITH THOSE OF YOU ALREADY HERE, WE MAKE UP THE CORE OF TASK FORCE X!
I TRUST MRS. WALLER HAS EXPLAINED THE DEAL TO YOU?
I EXPLAINED THAT IF HE ACCEPTS THE MISSION, SUCCEEDS IN THE MISSION, AND SOMEHOW MANAGES TO SURVIVE THE MISSION--
--ALL CURRENT CRIMINAL CHARGES AGAINST HIM WILL BE DROPPED!
SOUNDS SWEET ENOUGH--!
NOT THAT I TRUST ANY O' YOU COBBERS FOR A MINUTE!
THERE'S SOMETHIN' WEIRD GOIN' ON 'ROUND 'ERE, AN' I WANNA KNOW WHAT IT IS BEFORE I--
--EH?!?
KLAKT!
--THE DEMON KNOWN AS DARKSEID!
SOON, NOW, EARTH'S MIGHTIEST LEGENDS WILL BE NO MORE THAN DUST--
--AND THAT MISERABLE WORLD WILL AT LAST BE RIPE FOR MY PICKING!
5

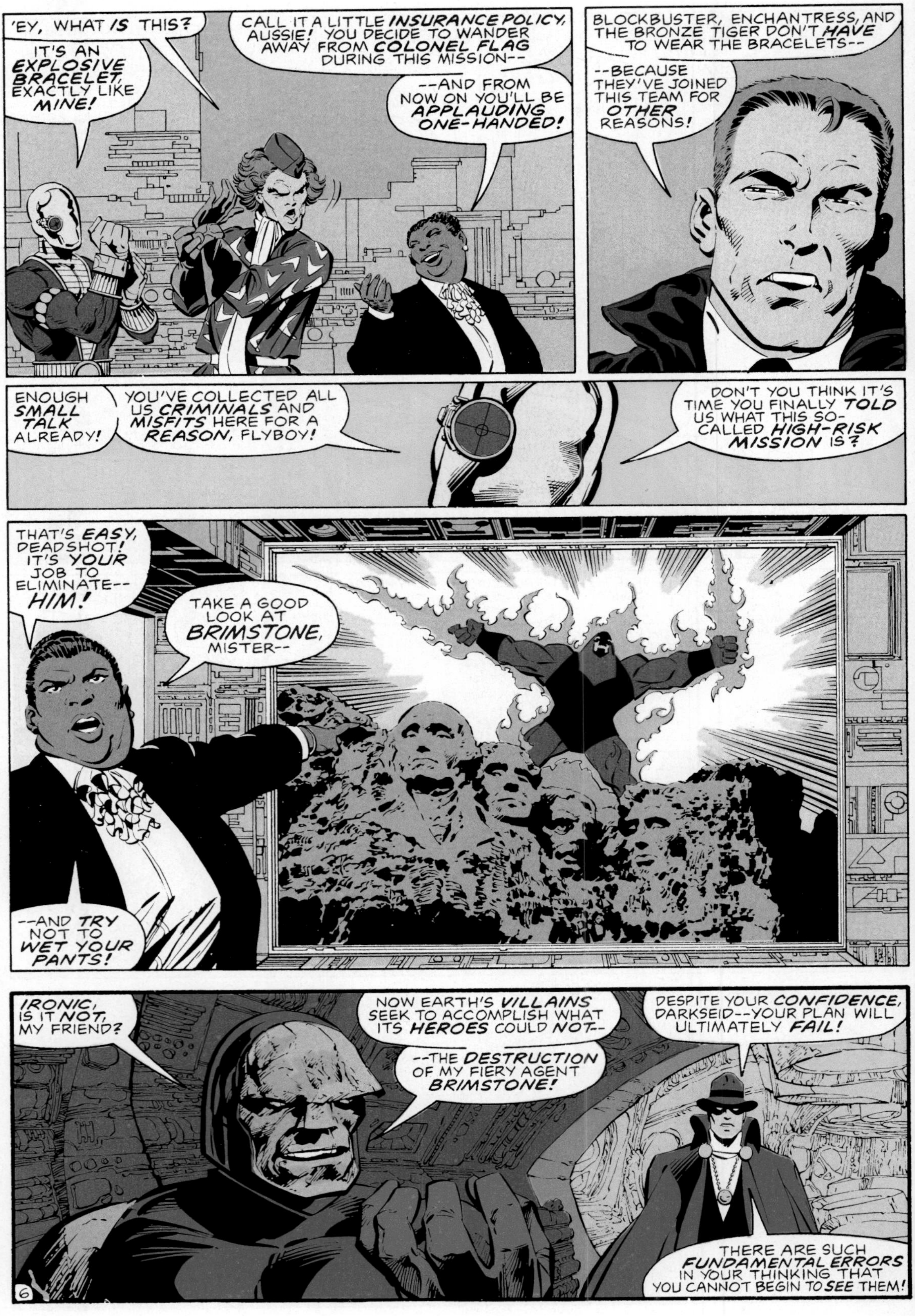
'EY, WHAT IS THIS?
IT'S AN EXPLOSIVE BRACELET, EXACTLY LIKE MINE!
CALL IT A LITTLE INSURANCE POLICY, AUSSIE! YOU DECIDE TO WANDER AWAY FROM COLONEL FLAG DURING THIS MISSION--
--AND FROM NOW ON YOU'LL BE APPLAUDING ONE-HANDED!
BLOCKBUSTER, ENCHANTRESS, AND THE BRONZE TIGER DON'T HAVE TO WEAR THE BRACELETS--
--BECAUSE THEY'VE JOINED THIS TEAM FOR OTHER REASONS!
ENOUGH SMALL TALK ALREADY!
YOU'VE COLLECTED ALL US CRIMINALS AND MISFITS HERE FOR A REASON, FLYBOY!
DON'T YOU THINK IT'S TIME YOU FINALLY TOLD US WHAT THIS SO-CALLED HIGH-RISK MISSION IS?
THAT'S EASY, DEADSHOT! IT'S YOUR JOB TO ELIMINATE-- HIM!
TAKE A GOOD LOOK AT BRIMSTONE, MISTER--
--AND TRY NOT TO WET YOUR PANTS!
IRONIC, IS IT NOT, MY FRIEND?
NOW EARTH'S VILLAINS SEEK TO ACCOMPLISH WHAT ITS HEROES COULD NOT--
--THE DESTRUCTION OF MY FIERY AGENT BRIMSTONE!
DESPITE YOUR CONFIDENCE, DARKSEID--YOUR PLAN WILL ULTIMATELY FAIL!
THERE ARE SUCH FUNDAMENTAL ERRORS IN YOUR THINKING THAT YOU CANNOT BEGIN TO SEE THEM!
6

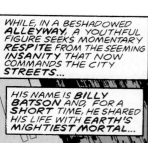

WHILE, IN A BESHADOWED **ALLEYWAY,** A YOUTHFUL FIGURE SEEKS MOMENTARY **RESPITE** FROM THE SEEMING **INSANITY** THAT NOW COMMANDS THE CITY **STREETS...**

HIS NAME IS **BILLY BATSON** AND, FOR A **SHORT** TIME, HE SHARED HIS LIFE WITH **EARTH'S MIGHTIEST MORTAL...**

YES, FOR A **SHORT** TIME...

IT'S SO **CRAZY** OUT THERE... ALL THE **FIGHTING**... ALL THE **RIOTING...**

I COULD SAY THE ANCIENT WIZARD'S **MAGIC WORD...** BECOME **CAPTAIN MARVEL** AGAIN... MAYBE PUT A **STOP** TO THIS **MADNESS...**

...BUT I **CAN'T**...I **CAN'T!**

THE **LAST** TIME I BECAME CAPTAIN MARVEL, THE MAGIC LIGHTNING **KILLED** SOMEONE...

...AND I CAN'T EVER RISK THAT HAPPENING **AGAIN**...

...**NEVER AGAIN!!**

HI! YOU **OKAY?**

MY NAME IS **LISA!** I GOT **SEPARATED** FROM MY MOM AND DAD BY THE **CROWD** --AND I'M A LITTLE **SCARED!**

WHAT'S **YOUR** NAME?

IT'S **BILLY,** LISA--

--AND **I'M** SCARED, **TOO!**

MY THINKING IS **FLAWLESS,** STRANGER-- MY PLANNING **IMPECCABLE!**

BUT YOU CAN SEE FOR **YOURSELF,** IF YOU WISH--!

DESAAD, ACTIVATE THE **RETRO-SCREEN!**

AS YOU **DESIRE,** MASTER--SO SHALL IT BE **DONE!**

7

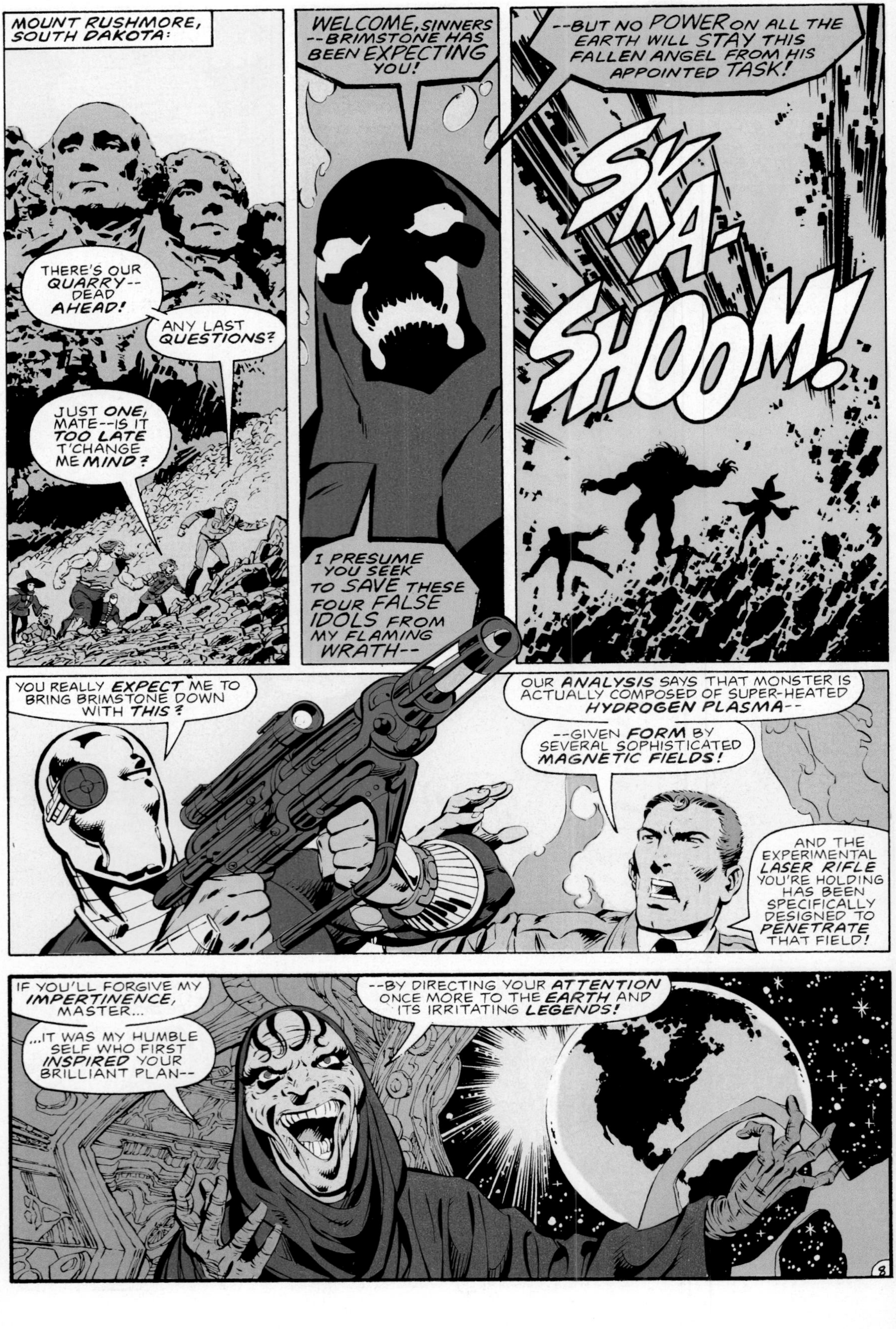
MOUNT RUSHMORE, SOUTH DAKOTA:
THERE'S OUR QUARRY-- DEAD AHEAD!
ANY LAST QUESTIONS?
JUST ONE, MATE--IS IT TOO LATE T'CHANGE ME MIND?
WELCOME, SINNERS --BRIMSTONE HAS BEEN EXPECTING YOU!
I PRESUME YOU SEEK TO SAVE THESE FOUR FALSE IDOLS FROM MY FLAMING WRATH--
--BUT NO POWER ON ALL THE EARTH WILL STAY THIS FALLEN ANGEL FROM HIS APPOINTED TASK!
SKA-SHOOM!
YOU REALLY EXPECT ME TO BRING BRIMSTONE DOWN WITH THIS?
OUR ANALYSIS SAYS THAT MONSTER IS ACTUALLY COMPOSED OF SUPER-HEATED HYDROGEN PLASMA--
--GIVEN FORM BY SEVERAL SOPHISTICATED MAGNETIC FIELDS!
AND THE EXPERIMENTAL LASER RIFLE YOU'RE HOLDING HAS BEEN SPECIFICALLY DESIGNED TO PENETRATE THAT FIELD!
IF YOU'LL FORGIVE MY IMPERTINENCE, MASTER...
...IT WAS MY HUMBLE SELF WHO FIRST INSPIRED YOUR BRILLIANT PLAN--
--BY DIRECTING YOUR ATTENTION ONCE MORE TO THE EARTH AND ITS IRRITATING LEGENDS!
8

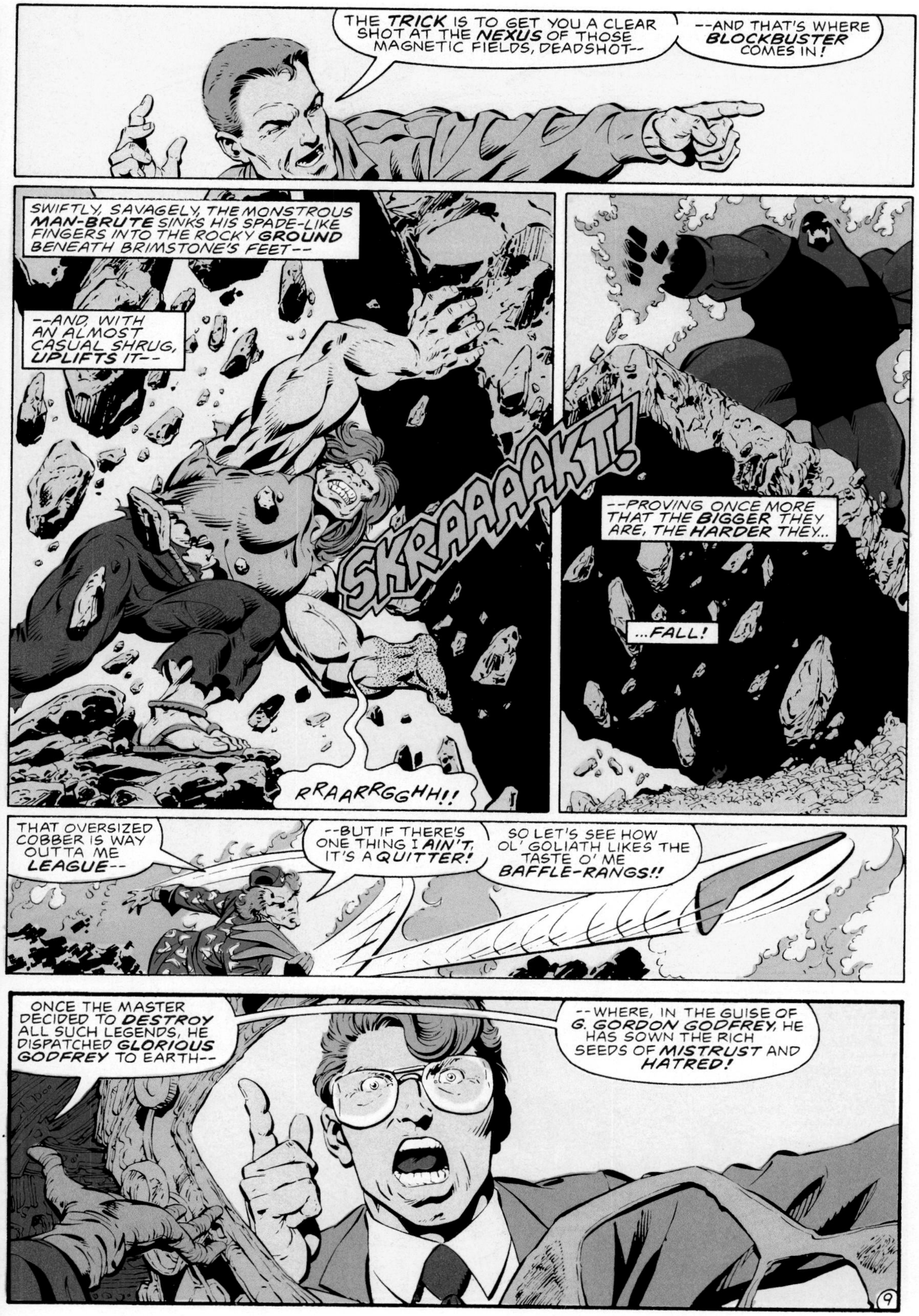
THE TRICK IS TO GET YOU A CLEAR SHOT AT THE NEXUS OF THOSE MAGNETIC FIELDS, DEADSHOT--
--AND THAT'S WHERE BLOCKBUSTER COMES IN!
SWIFTLY, SAVAGELY, THE MONSTROUS MAN-BRUTE SINKS HIS SPADE-LIKE FINGERS INTO THE ROCKY GROUND BENEATH BRIMSTONE'S FEET--
--AND, WITH AN ALMOST CASUAL SHRUG, UPLIFTS IT--
SKRAAAAKT!
RRAARRGGHH!!
--PROVING ONCE MORE THAT THE BIGGER THEY ARE, THE HARDER THEY...
...FALL!
THAT OVERSIZED COBBER IS WAY OUTTA ME LEAGUE--
--BUT IF THERE'S ONE THING I AIN'T, IT'S A QUITTER!
SO LET'S SEE HOW OL' GOLIATH LIKES THE TASTE O' ME BAFFLE-RANGS!!
ONCE THE MASTER DECIDED TO DESTROY ALL SUCH LEGENDS, HE DISPATCHED GLORIOUS GODFREY TO EARTH--
--WHERE, IN THE GUISE OF G. GORDON GODFREY, HE HAS SOWN THE RICH SEEDS OF MISTRUST AND HATRED!
9

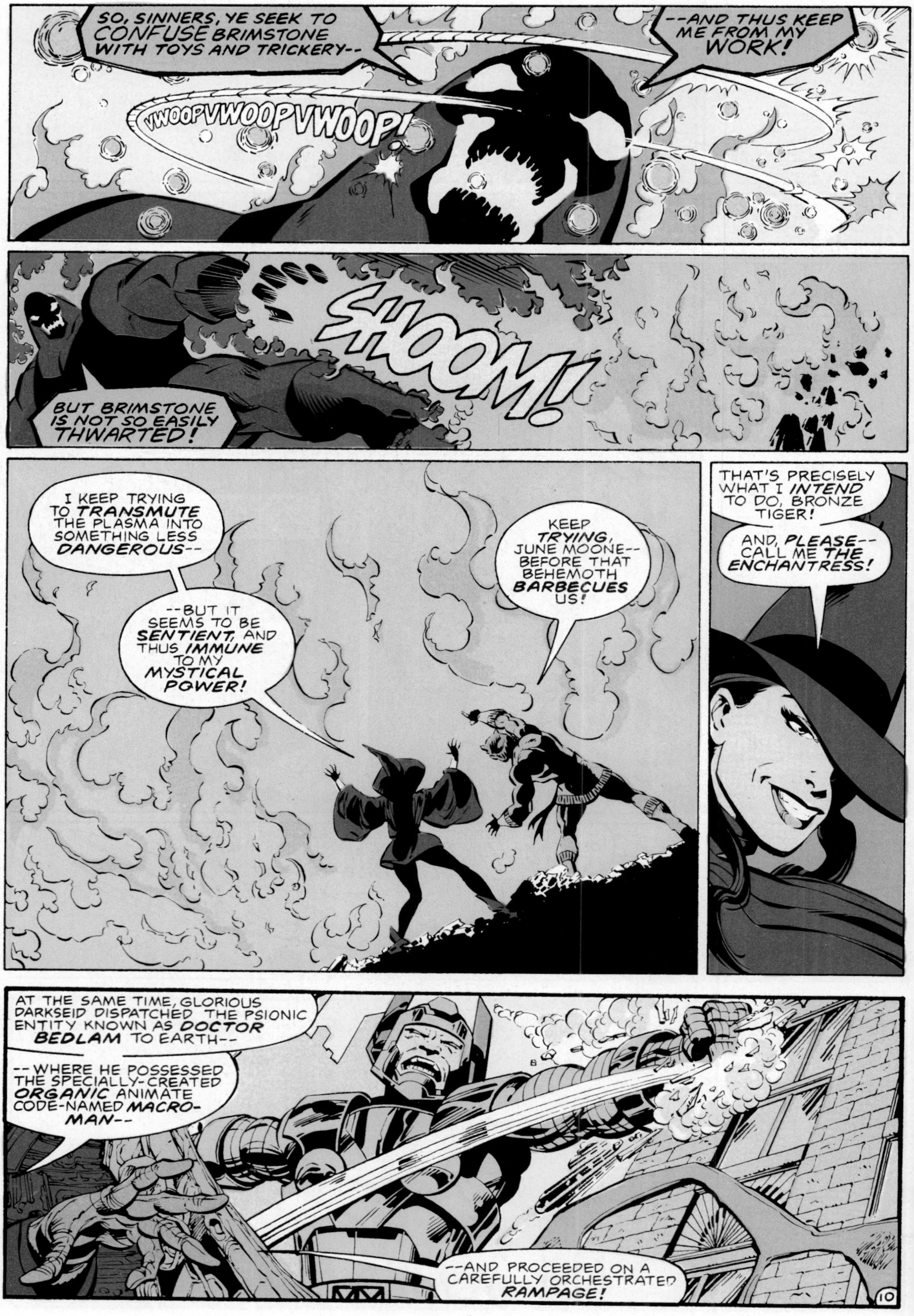

SO, SINNERS, YE SEEK TO CONFUSE BRIMSTONE WITH TOYS AND TRICKERY--
--AND THUS KEEP ME FROM MY WORK!
VWOOPVWOOPVWOOP!
SHOOM!
BUT BRIMSTONE IS NOT SO EASILY THWARTED!
I KEEP TRYING TO TRANSMUTE THE PLASMA INTO SOMETHING LESS DANGEROUS--
--BUT IT SEEMS TO BE SENTIENT, AND THUS IMMUNE TO MY MYSTICAL POWER!
KEEP TRYING, JUNE MOONE-- BEFORE THAT BEHEMOTH BARBECUES US!
THAT'S PRECISELY WHAT I INTEND TO DO, BRONZE TIGER!
AND, PLEASE-- CALL ME THE ENCHANTRESS!
AT THE SAME TIME, GLORIOUS DARKSEID DISPATCHED THE PSIONIC ENTITY KNOWN AS DOCTOR BEDLAM TO EARTH--
--WHERE HE POSSESSED THE SPECIALLY-CREATED ORGANIC ANIMATE CODE-NAMED MACRO-MAN--
--AND PROCEEDED ON A CAREFULLY ORCHESTRATED RAMPAGE!

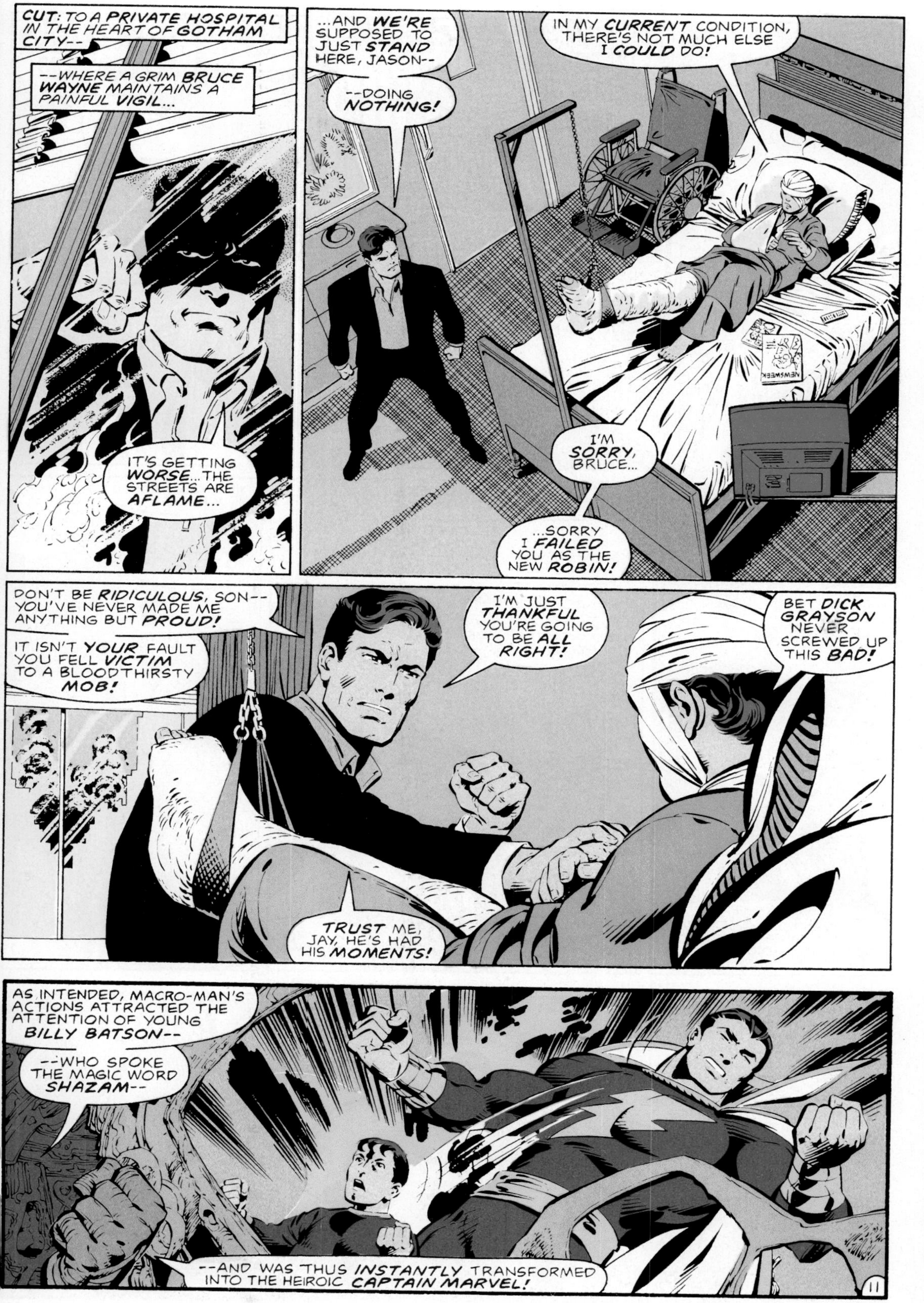
CUT: TO A PRIVATE HOSPITAL IN THE HEART OF GOTHAM CITY--
--WHERE A GRIM BRUCE WAYNE MAINTAINS A PAINFUL VIGIL...
IT'S GETTING WORSE... THE STREETS ARE AFLAME...
...AND WE'RE SUPPOSED TO JUST STAND HERE, JASON--
--DOING NOTHING!
IN MY CURRENT CONDITION, THERE'S NOT MUCH ELSE I COULD DO!
I'M SORRY, BRUCE...
...SORRY I FAILED YOU AS THE NEW ROBIN!
DON'T BE RIDICULOUS, SON-- YOU'VE NEVER MADE ME ANYTHING BUT PROUD!
IT ISN'T YOUR FAULT YOU FELL VICTIM TO A BLOODTHIRSTY MOB!
I'M JUST THANKFUL YOU'RE GOING TO BE ALL RIGHT!
BET DICK GRAYSON NEVER SCREWED UP THIS BAD!
TRUST ME, JAY, HE'S HAD HIS MOMENTS!
AS INTENDED, MACRO-MAN'S ACTIONS ATTRACTED THE ATTENTION OF YOUNG BILLY BATSON--
--WHO SPOKE THE MAGIC WORD SHAZAM--
--AND WAS THUS INSTANTLY TRANSFORMED INTO THE HEIROIC CAPTAIN MARVEL!
NEWSWEEK

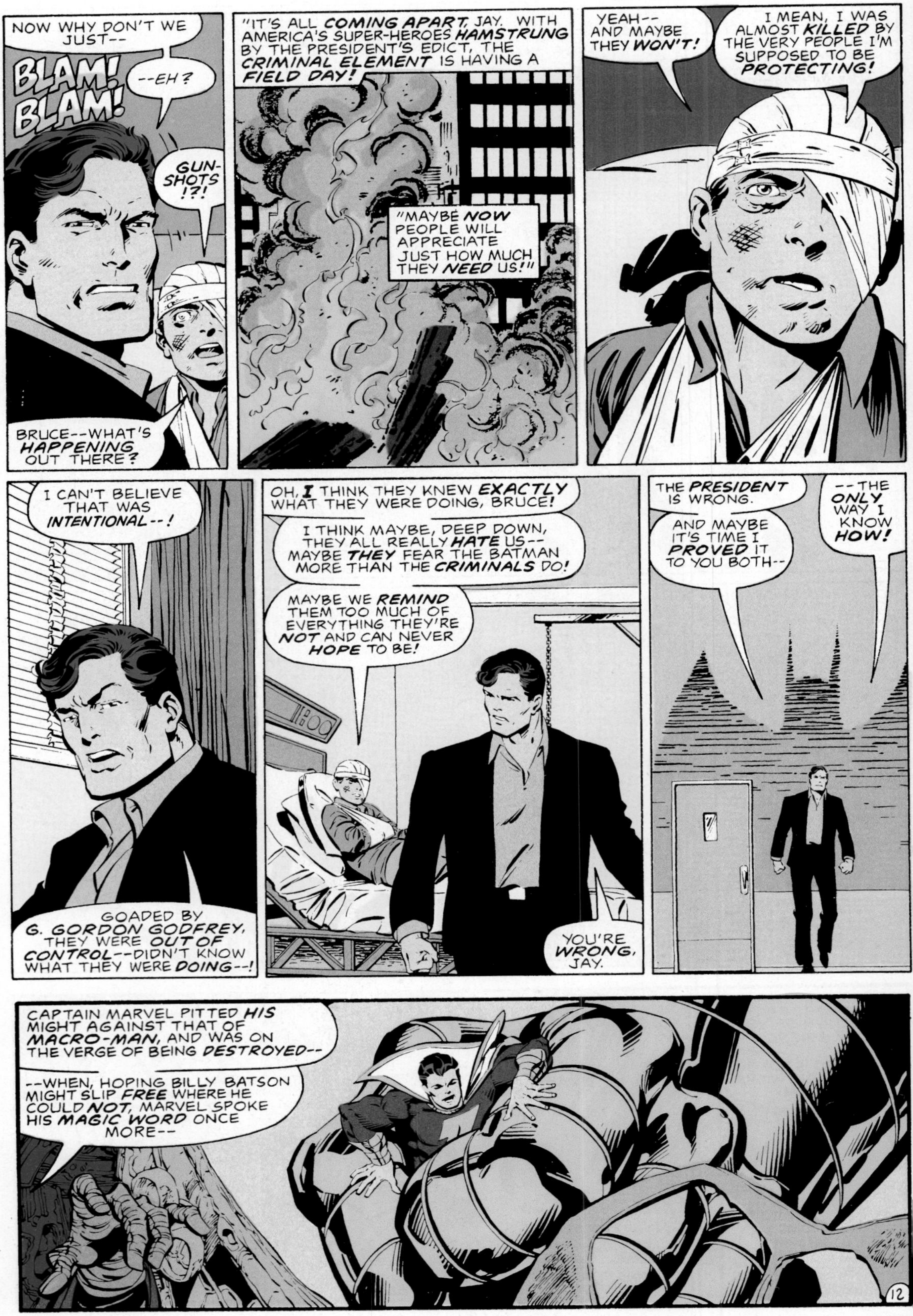

NOW WHY DON'T WE JUST--
BLAM! BLAM!
--EH?
GUN-SHOTS!?!
BRUCE--WHAT'S HAPPENING OUT THERE?
"IT'S ALL COMING APART, JAY. WITH AMERICA'S SUPER-HEROES HAMSTRUNG BY THE PRESIDENT'S EDICT, THE CRIMINAL ELEMENT IS HAVING A FIELD DAY!
"MAYBE NOW PEOPLE WILL APPRECIATE JUST HOW MUCH THEY NEED US!"
YEAH-- AND MAYBE THEY WON'T!
I MEAN, I WAS ALMOST KILLED BY THE VERY PEOPLE I'M SUPPOSED TO BE PROTECTING!
I CAN'T BELIEVE THAT WAS INTENTIONAL--!
GOADED BY G. GORDON GODFREY, THEY WERE OUT OF CONTROL--DIDN'T KNOW WHAT THEY WERE DOING--!
OH, I THINK THEY KNEW EXACTLY WHAT THEY WERE DOING, BRUCE!
I THINK MAYBE, DEEP DOWN, THEY ALL REALLY HATE US-- MAYBE THEY FEAR THE BATMAN MORE THAN THE CRIMINALS DO!
MAYBE WE REMIND THEM TOO MUCH OF EVERYTHING THEY'RE NOT AND CAN NEVER HOPE TO BE!
YOU'RE WRONG, JAY.
THE PRESIDENT IS WRONG.
AND MAYBE IT'S TIME I PROVED IT TO YOU BOTH--
--THE ONLY WAY I KNOW HOW!
CAPTAIN MARVEL PITTED HIS MIGHT AGAINST THAT OF MACRO-MAN, AND WAS ON THE VERGE OF BEING DESTROYED--
--WHEN, HOPING BILLY BATSON MIGHT SLIP FREE WHERE HE COULD NOT, MARVEL SPOKE HIS MAGIC WORD ONCE MORE--
12

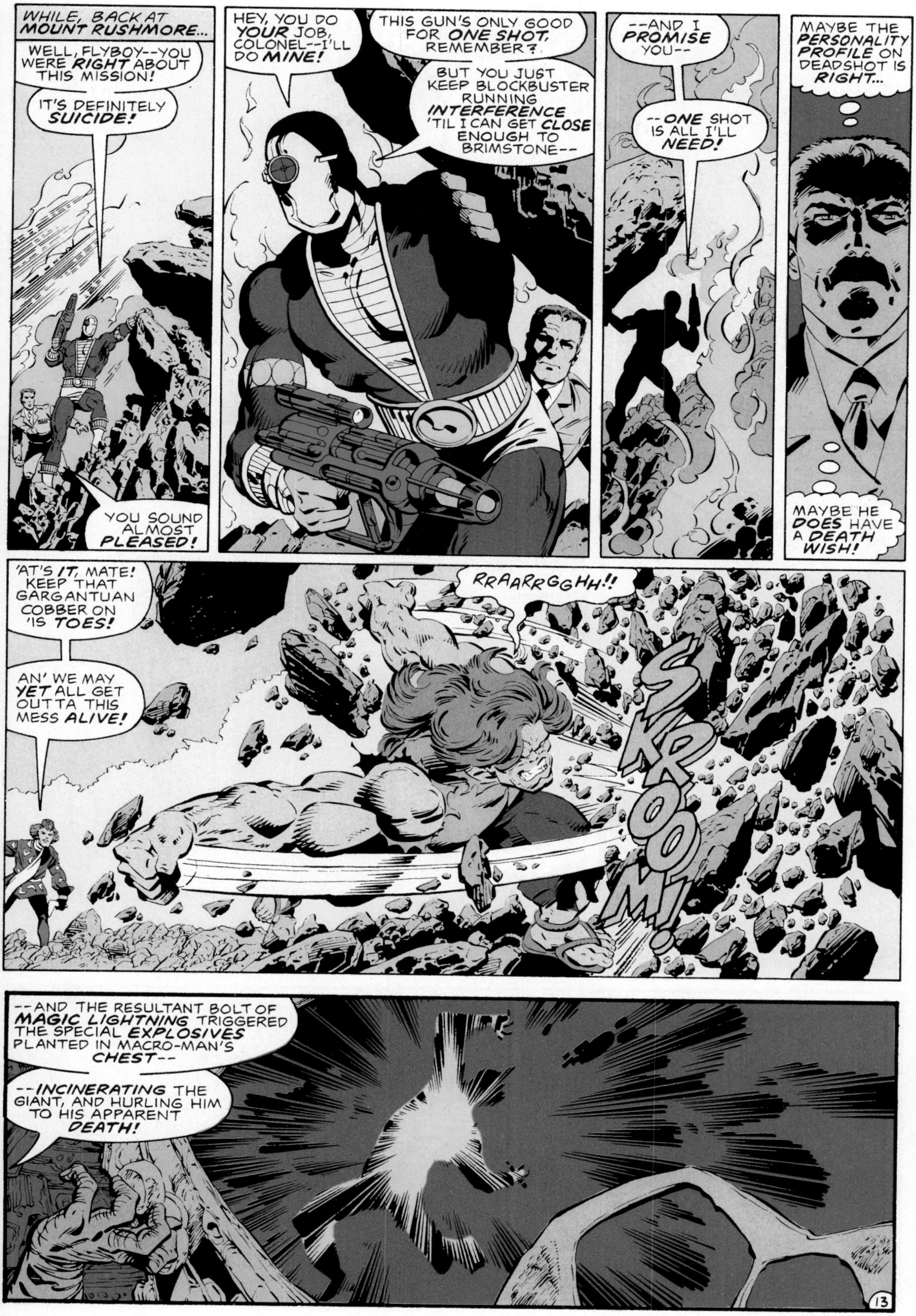
WHILE, BACK AT MOUNT RUSHMORE...
WELL, FLYBOY--YOU WERE RIGHT ABOUT THIS MISSION!
IT'S DEFINITELY SUICIDE!
YOU SOUND ALMOST PLEASED!
HEY, YOU DO YOUR JOB, COLONEL--I'LL DO MINE!
THIS GUN'S ONLY GOOD FOR ONE SHOT, REMEMBER?
BUT YOU JUST KEEP BLOCKBUSTER RUNNING INTERFERENCE 'TIL I CAN GET CLOSE ENOUGH TO BRIMSTONE--
--AND I PROMISE YOU--
--ONE SHOT IS ALL I'LL NEED!
MAYBE THE PERSONALITY PROFILE ON DEADSHOT IS RIGHT...
MAYBE HE DOES HAVE A DEATH WISH!
'AT'S IT, MATE! KEEP THAT GARGANTUAN COBBER ON 'IS TOES!
AN' WE MAY YET ALL GET OUTTA THIS MESS ALIVE!
RRAARRGGHH!!
SKROOOM!
--AND THE RESULTANT BOLT OF MAGIC LIGHTNING TRIGGERED THE SPECIAL EXPLOSIVES PLANTED IN MACRO-MAN'S CHEST--
--INCINERATING THE GIANT, AND HURLING HIM TO HIS APPARENT DEATH!
13

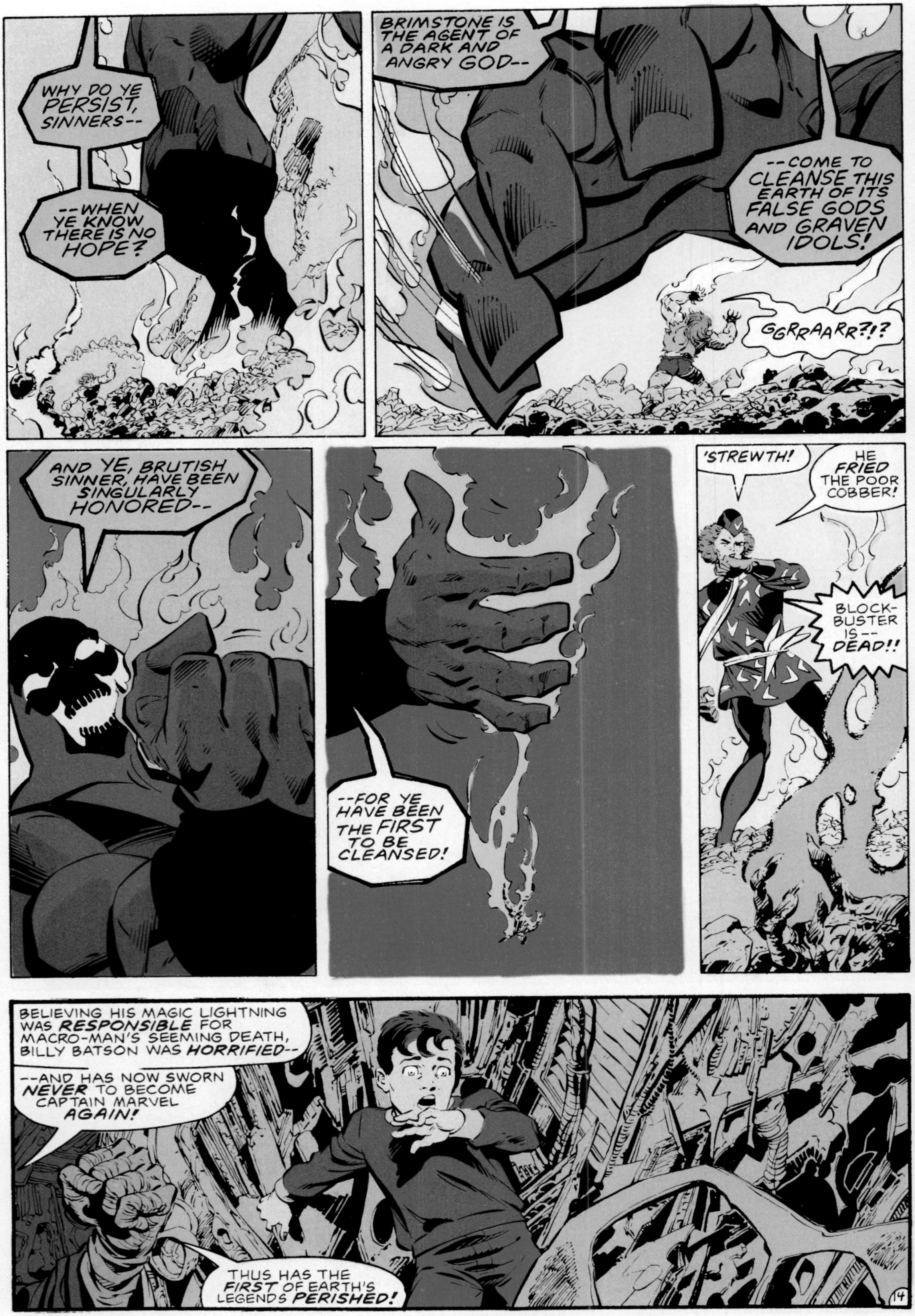
WHY DO YE PERSIST, SINNERS--
--WHEN YE KNOW THERE IS NO HOPE?
BRIMSTONE IS THE AGENT OF A DARK AND ANGRY GOD--
--COME TO CLEANSE THIS EARTH OF ITS FALSE GODS AND GRAVEN IDOLS!
GGRRAARR?!?
AND YE, BRUTISH SINNER, HAVE BEEN SINGULARLY HONORED--
--FOR YE HAVE BEEN THE FIRST TO BE CLEANSED!
'STREWTH!
HE FRIED THE POOR COBBER!
BLOCK-BUSTER IS-- DEAD!!
BELIEVING HIS MAGIC LIGHTNING WAS RESPONSIBLE FOR MACRO-MAN'S SEEMING DEATH, BILLY BATSON WAS HORRIFIED--
--AND HAS NOW SWORN NEVER TO BECOME CAPTAIN MARVEL AGAIN!
THUS HAS THE FIRST OF EARTH'S LEGENDS PERISHED!
14

"THERE! I'VE GOT BRIMSTONE'S *MAGNETIC NEXUS* LINED UP IN MY *SIGHTS*--

"BUT THERE'S SOME SORT OF *GIZMO* RIGHT ON THE *BULL'S EYE!*"

THEN WHAT ARE YOU *WAITING* FOR, DEADSHOT? THAT MONSTER IS ALMOST ON *TOP* OF US!

SHOOT ALREADY-- *SHOOT!!*

WHATEVER YOU *SAY*...

...SPOILSPORT!

SPWEEEEE

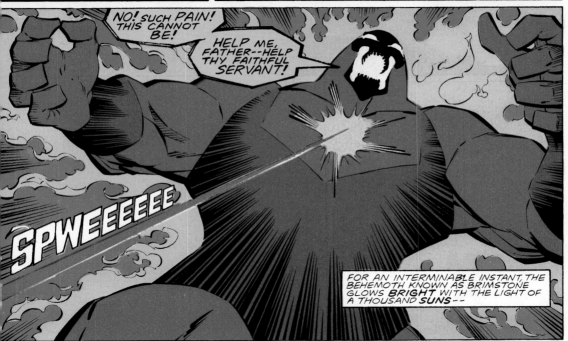

NO! SUCH PAIN! THIS CANNOT *BE!*

HELP ME, FATHER--HELP THY *FAITHFUL SERVANT!*

SPWEEEEEE

FOR AN *INTERMINABLE* INSTANT, THE BEHEMOTH KNOWN AS BRIMSTONE GLOWS *BRIGHT* WITH THE LIGHT OF A *THOUSAND SUNS*--

MEANWHILE, THE MASTER ALSO UNLEASHED *BRIMSTONE* UPON THE EARTH--

--A SUPER-HEATED *CONSTRUCT* OF SENTIENT PLASMA WHO BELIEVED ITSELF THE *FALLEN ANGEL* OF AN ANGRY *GOD!*

15

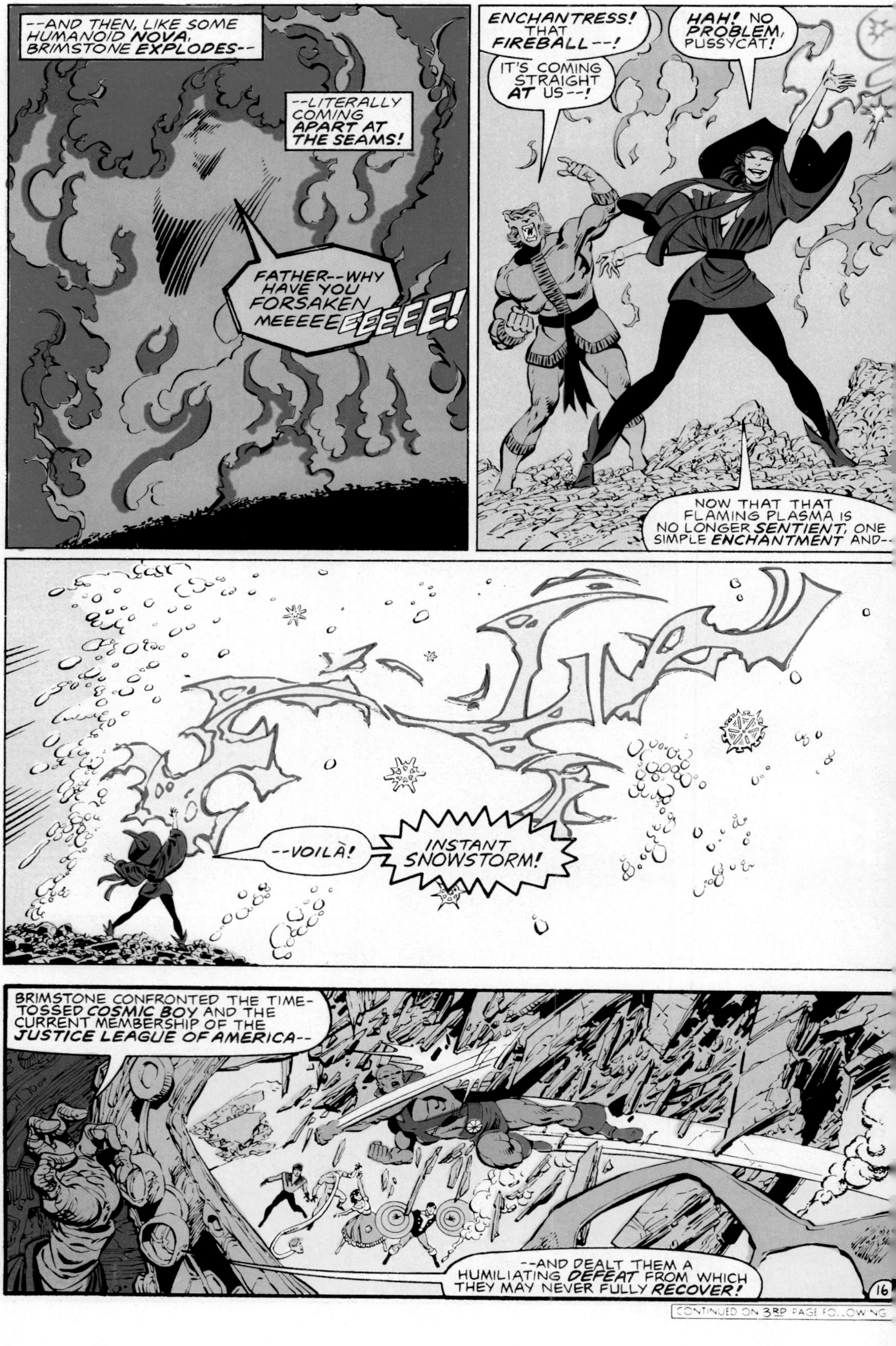
--AND THEN, LIKE SOME HUMANOID NOVA, BRIMSTONE EXPLODES--
--LITERALLY COMING APART AT THE SEAMS!
FATHER--WHY HAVE YOU FORSAKEN MEEEEEEEEEEE!
ENCHANTRESS! THAT FIREBALL--!
IT'S COMING STRAIGHT AT US--!
HAH! NO PROBLEM, PUSSYCAT!
NOW THAT THAT FLAMING PLASMA IS NO LONGER SENTIENT, ONE SIMPLE ENCHANTMENT AND--
--VOILÀ!
INSTANT SNOWSTORM!
BRIMSTONE CONFRONTED THE TIME-TOSSED COSMIC BOY AND THE CURRENT MEMBERSHIP OF THE JUSTICE LEAGUE OF AMERICA--
--AND DEALT THEM A HUMILIATING DEFEAT FROM WHICH THEY MAY NEVER FULLY RECOVER!
16
CONTINUED ON 3RD PAGE FOLLOWING

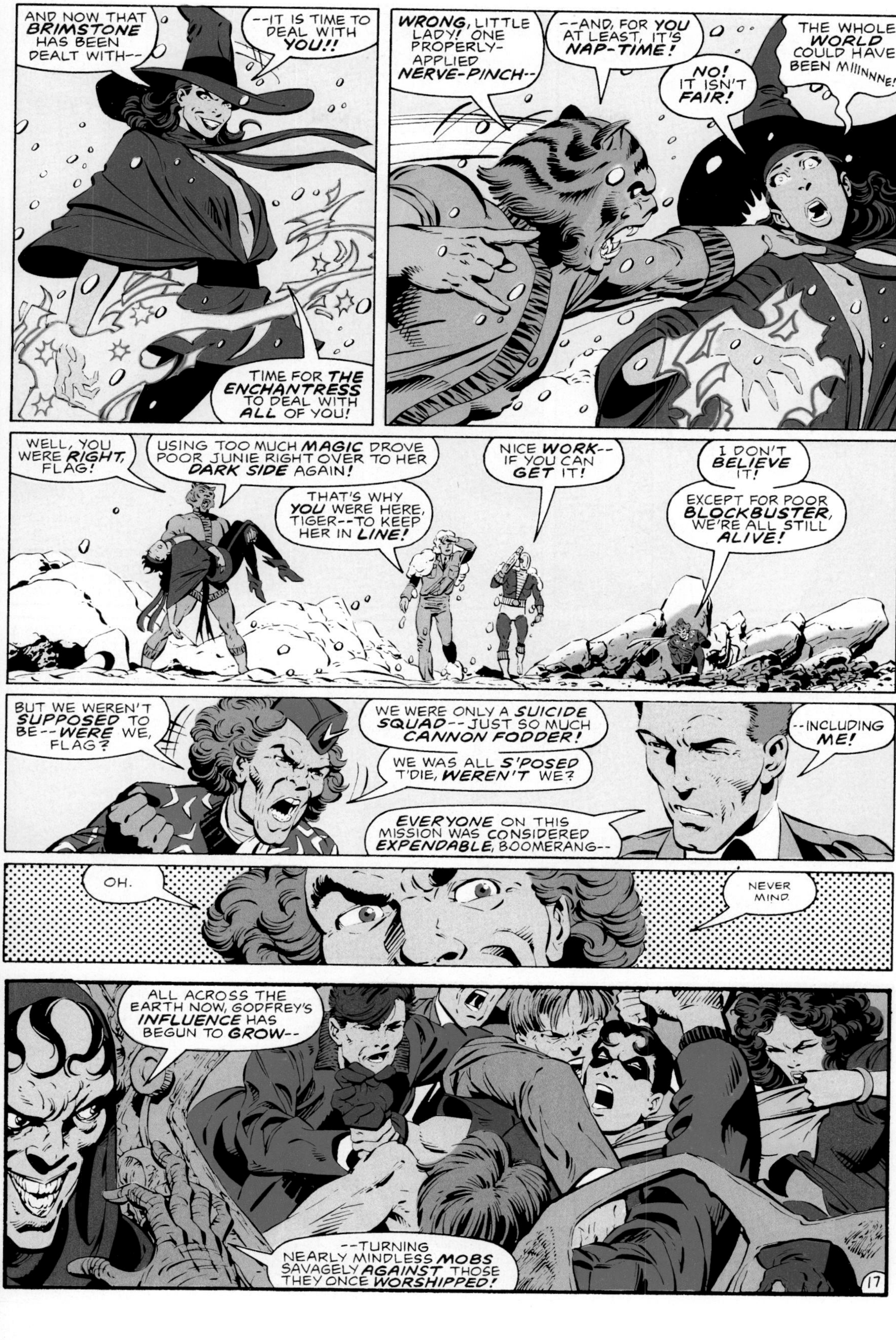
AND NOW THAT BRIMSTONE HAS BEEN DEALT WITH--
--IT IS TIME TO DEAL WITH YOU!!
TIME FOR THE ENCHANTRESS TO DEAL WITH ALL OF YOU!
WRONG, LITTLE LADY! ONE PROPERLY-APPLIED NERVE-PINCH--
--AND, FOR YOU AT LEAST, IT'S NAP-TIME!
NO! IT ISN'T FAIR!
THE WHOLE WORLD COULD HAVE BEEN MIIINNNE!
WELL, YOU WERE RIGHT, FLAG!
USING TOO MUCH MAGIC DROVE POOR JUNIE RIGHT OVER TO HER DARK SIDE AGAIN!
THAT'S WHY YOU WERE HERE, TIGER--TO KEEP HER IN LINE!
NICE WORK-- IF YOU CAN GET IT!
I DON'T BELIEVE IT!
EXCEPT FOR POOR BLOCKBUSTER, WE'RE ALL STILL ALIVE!
BUT WE WEREN'T SUPPOSED TO BE--WERE WE, FLAG?
WE WERE ONLY A SUICIDE SQUAD--JUST SO MUCH CANNON FODDER!
WE WAS ALL S'POSED T'DIE, WEREN'T WE?
--INCLUDING ME!
EVERYONE ON THIS MISSION WAS CONSIDERED EXPENDABLE, BOOMERANG--
OH.
NEVER MIND.
ALL ACROSS THE EARTH NOW, GODFREY'S INFLUENCE HAS BEGUN TO GROW--
--TURNING NEARLY MINDLESS MOBS SAVAGELY AGAINST THOSE THEY ONCE WORSHIPPED!
17

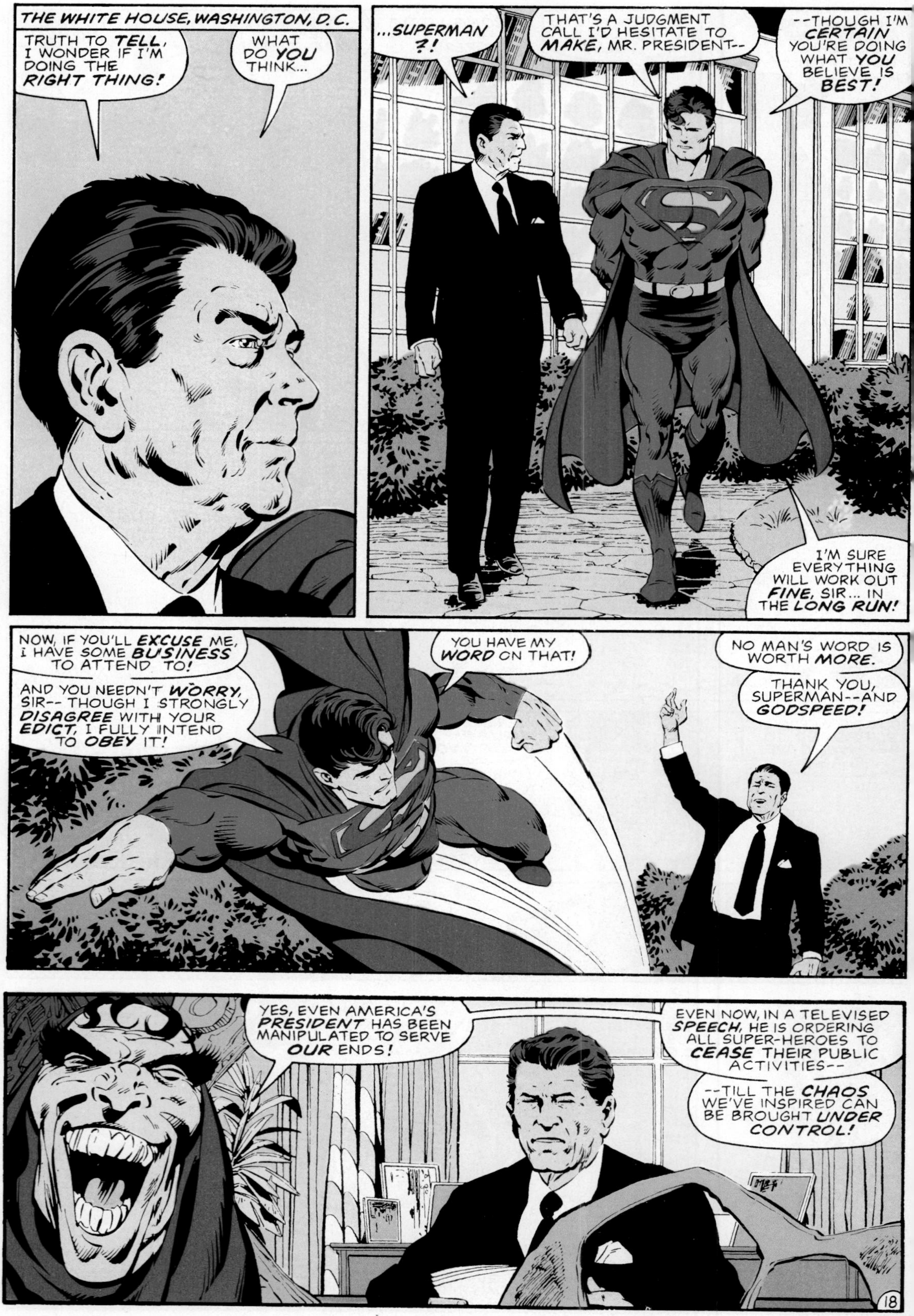
THE WHITE HOUSE, WASHINGTON, D.C.
TRUTH TO TELL, I WONDER IF I'M DOING THE RIGHT THING!
WHAT DO YOU THINK...
...SUPERMAN ?!
THAT'S A JUDGMENT CALL I'D HESITATE TO MAKE, MR. PRESIDENT--
--THOUGH I'M CERTAIN YOU'RE DOING WHAT YOU BELIEVE IS BEST!
I'M SURE EVERYTHING WILL WORK OUT FINE, SIR... IN THE LONG RUN!
NOW, IF YOU'LL EXCUSE ME, I HAVE SOME BUSINESS TO ATTEND TO!
AND YOU NEEDN'T WORRY, SIR-- THOUGH I STRONGLY DISAGREE WITH YOUR EDICT, I FULLY INTEND TO OBEY IT!
YOU HAVE MY WORD ON THAT!
NO MAN'S WORD IS WORTH MORE.
THANK YOU, SUPERMAN--AND GODSPEED!
YES, EVEN AMERICA'S PRESIDENT HAS BEEN MANIPULATED TO SERVE OUR ENDS!
EVEN NOW, IN A TELEVISED SPEECH, HE IS ORDERING ALL SUPER-HEROES TO CEASE THEIR PUBLIC ACTIVITIES--
--TILL THE CHAOS WE'VE INSPIRED CAN BE BROUGHT UNDER CONTROL!
18

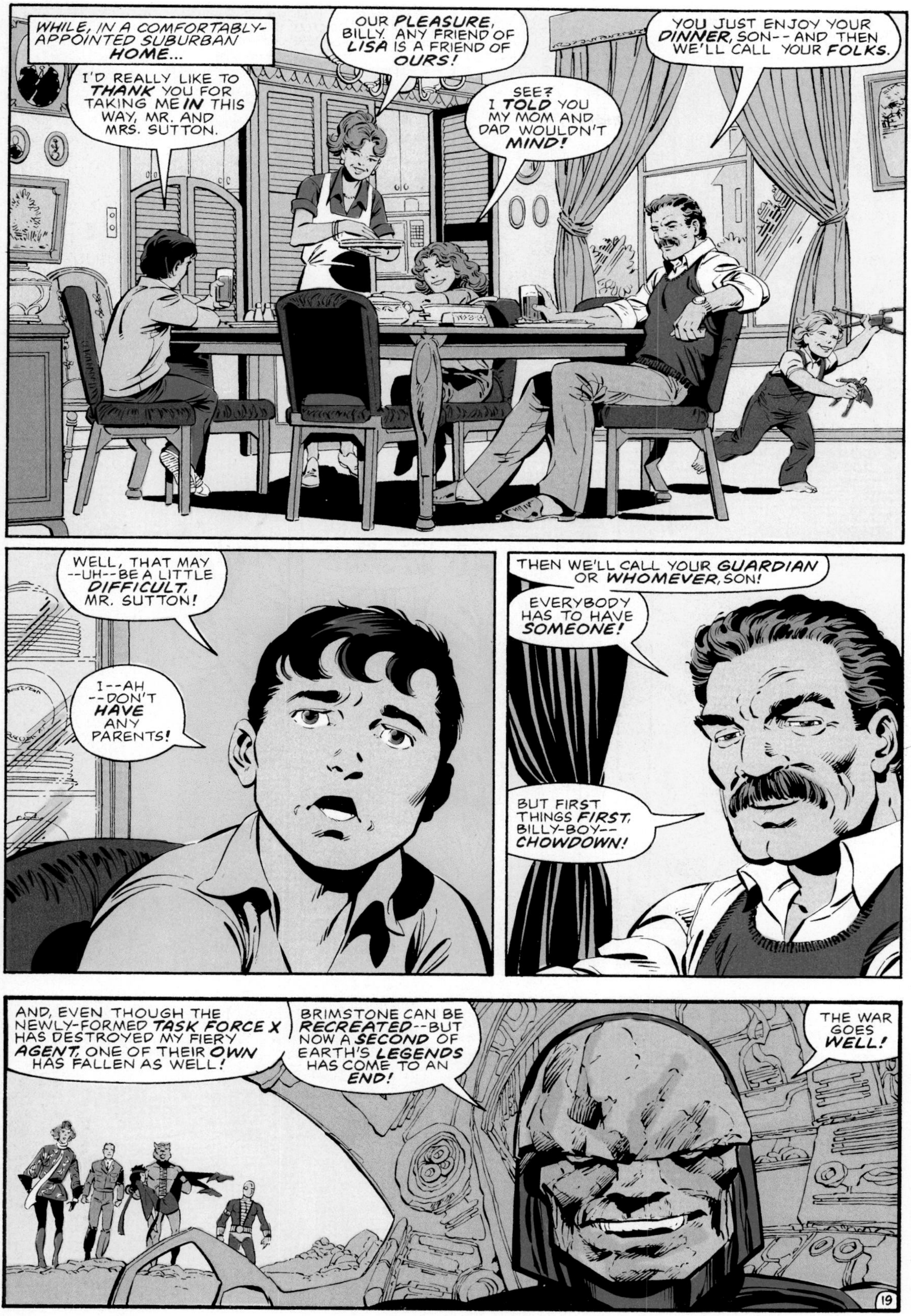
WHILE, IN A COMFORTABLY-APPOINTED SUBURBAN HOME...
I'D REALLY LIKE TO THANK YOU FOR TAKING ME IN THIS WAY, MR. AND MRS. SUTTON.
OUR PLEASURE, BILLY. ANY FRIEND OF LISA IS A FRIEND OF OURS!
SEE? I TOLD YOU MY MOM AND DAD WOULDN'T MIND!
YOU JUST ENJOY YOUR DINNER, SON--AND THEN WE'LL CALL YOUR FOLKS.
WELL, THAT MAY --UH--BE A LITTLE DIFFICULT, MR. SUTTON!
I--AH --DON'T HAVE ANY PARENTS!
THEN WE'LL CALL YOUR GUARDIAN OR WHOMEVER, SON!
EVERYBODY HAS TO HAVE SOMEONE!
BUT FIRST THINGS FIRST, BILLY-BOY-- CHOWDOWN!
AND, EVEN THOUGH THE NEWLY-FORMED TASK FORCE X HAS DESTROYED MY FIERY AGENT, ONE OF THEIR OWN HAS FALLEN AS WELL!
BRIMSTONE CAN BE RECREATED--BUT NOW A SECOND OF EARTH'S LEGENDS HAS COME TO AN END!
THE WAR GOES WELL!

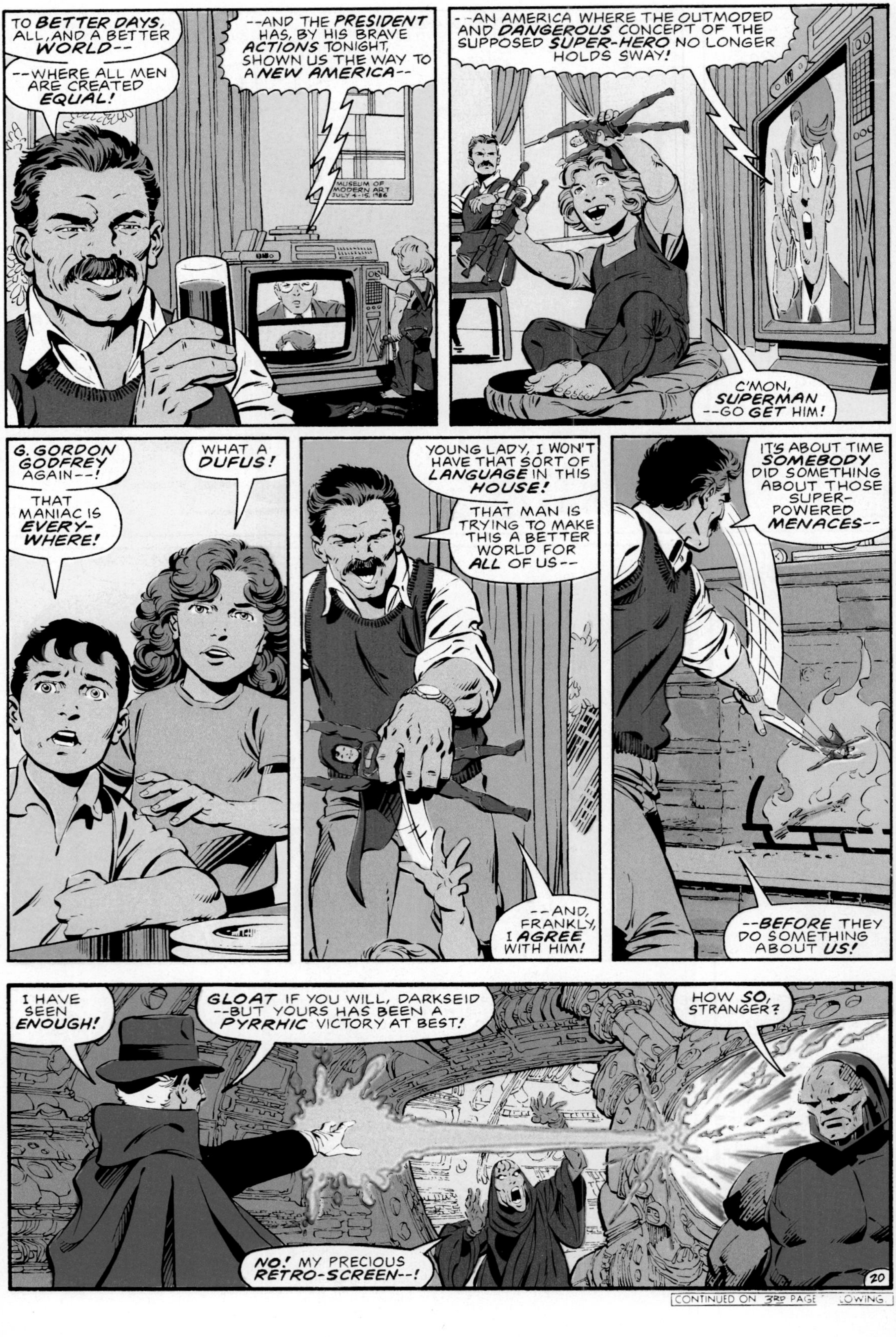
TO BETTER DAYS, ALL, AND A BETTER WORLD--
--WHERE ALL MEN ARE CREATED EQUAL!
--AND THE PRESIDENT HAS, BY HIS BRAVE ACTIONS TONIGHT, SHOWN US THE WAY TO A NEW AMERICA--
MUSEUM OF MODERN ART JULY 4-15, 1986
--AN AMERICA WHERE THE OUTMODED AND DANGEROUS CONCEPT OF THE SUPPOSED SUPER-HERO NO LONGER HOLDS SWAY!
C'MON, SUPERMAN --GO GET HIM!
G. GORDON GODFREY AGAIN--!
THAT MANIAC IS EVERY-WHERE!
WHAT A DUFUS!
YOUNG LADY, I WON'T HAVE THAT SORT OF LANGUAGE IN THIS HOUSE!
THAT MAN IS TRYING TO MAKE THIS A BETTER WORLD FOR ALL OF US--
--AND, FRANKLY, I AGREE WITH HIM!
IT'S ABOUT TIME SOMEBODY DID SOMETHING ABOUT THOSE SUPER-POWERED MENACES--
--BEFORE THEY DO SOMETHING ABOUT US!
I HAVE SEEN ENOUGH!
GLOAT IF YOU WILL, DARKSEID --BUT YOURS HAS BEEN A PYRRHIC VICTORY AT BEST!
HOW SO, STRANGER?
NO! MY PRECIOUS RETRO-SCREEN--!
20

CONTINUED ON 3RD PAGE FOLLOWING

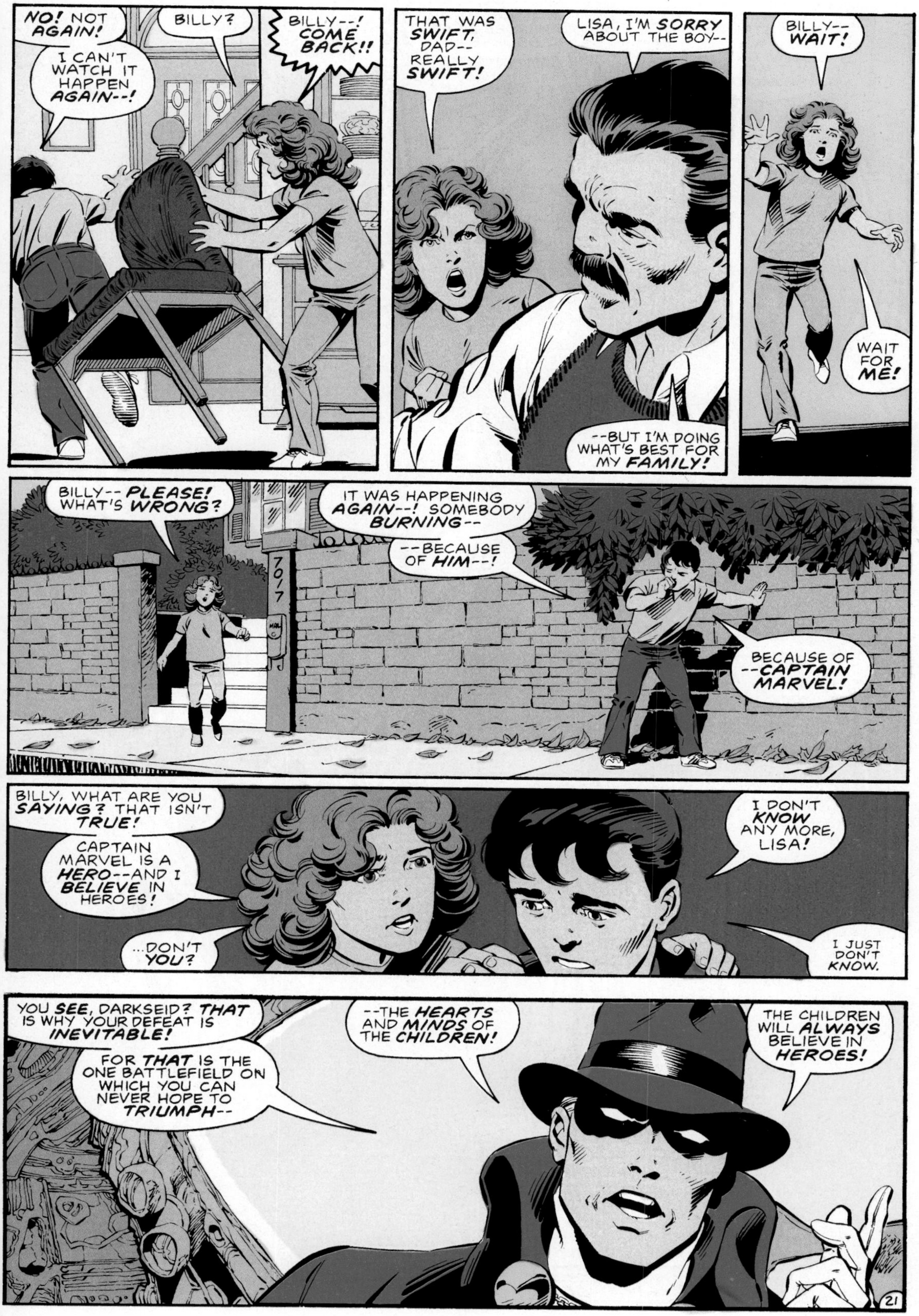
NO! NOT AGAIN!
I CAN'T WATCH IT HAPPEN AGAIN--!
BILLY?
BILLY--! COME BACK!!
THAT WAS SWIFT, DAD-- REALLY SWIFT!
LISA, I'M SORRY ABOUT THE BOY--
--BUT I'M DOING WHAT'S BEST FOR MY FAMILY!
BILLY-- WAIT!
WAIT FOR ME!
BILLY-- PLEASE! WHAT'S WRONG?
IT WAS HAPPENING AGAIN--! SOMEBODY BURNING--
--BECAUSE OF HIM--!
BECAUSE OF --CAPTAIN MARVEL!
7017
BILLY, WHAT ARE YOU SAYING? THAT ISN'T TRUE!
CAPTAIN MARVEL IS A HERO--AND I BELIEVE IN HEROES!
...DON'T YOU?
I DON'T KNOW ANY MORE, LISA!
I JUST DON'T KNOW.
YOU SEE, DARKSEID? THAT IS WHY YOUR DEFEAT IS INEVITABLE!
FOR THAT IS THE ONE BATTLEFIELD ON WHICH YOU CAN NEVER HOPE TO TRIUMPH--
--THE HEARTS AND MINDS OF THE CHILDREN!
THE CHILDREN WILL ALWAYS BELIEVE IN HEROES!

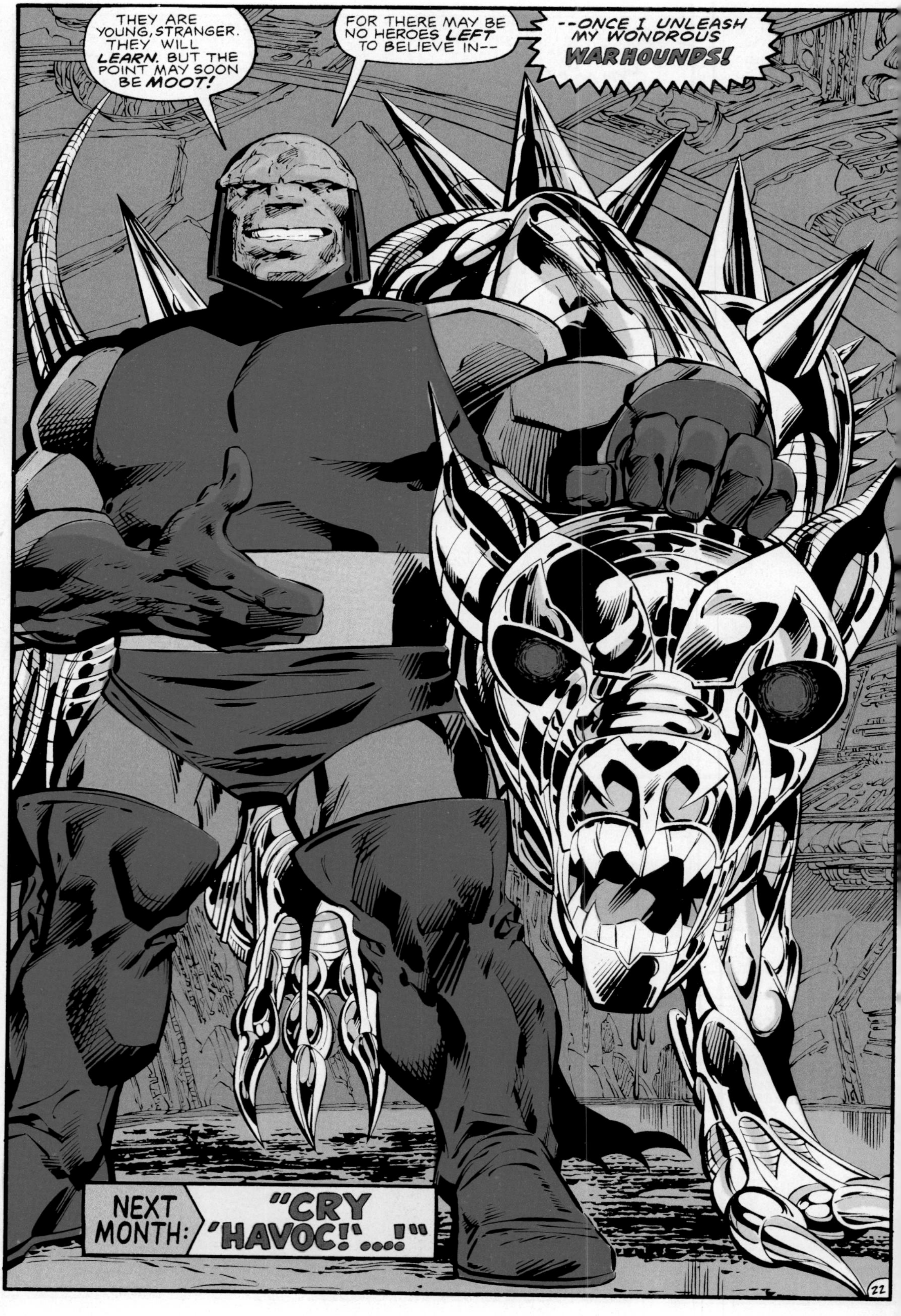
THEY ARE YOUNG, STRANGER. THEY WILL LEARN. BUT THE POINT MAY SOON BE MOOT!
FOR THERE MAY BE NO HEROES LEFT TO BELIEVE IN--
--ONCE I UNLEASH MY WONDROUS WARHOUNDS!
NEXT MONTH:
"CRY 'HAVOC!'...!"
22

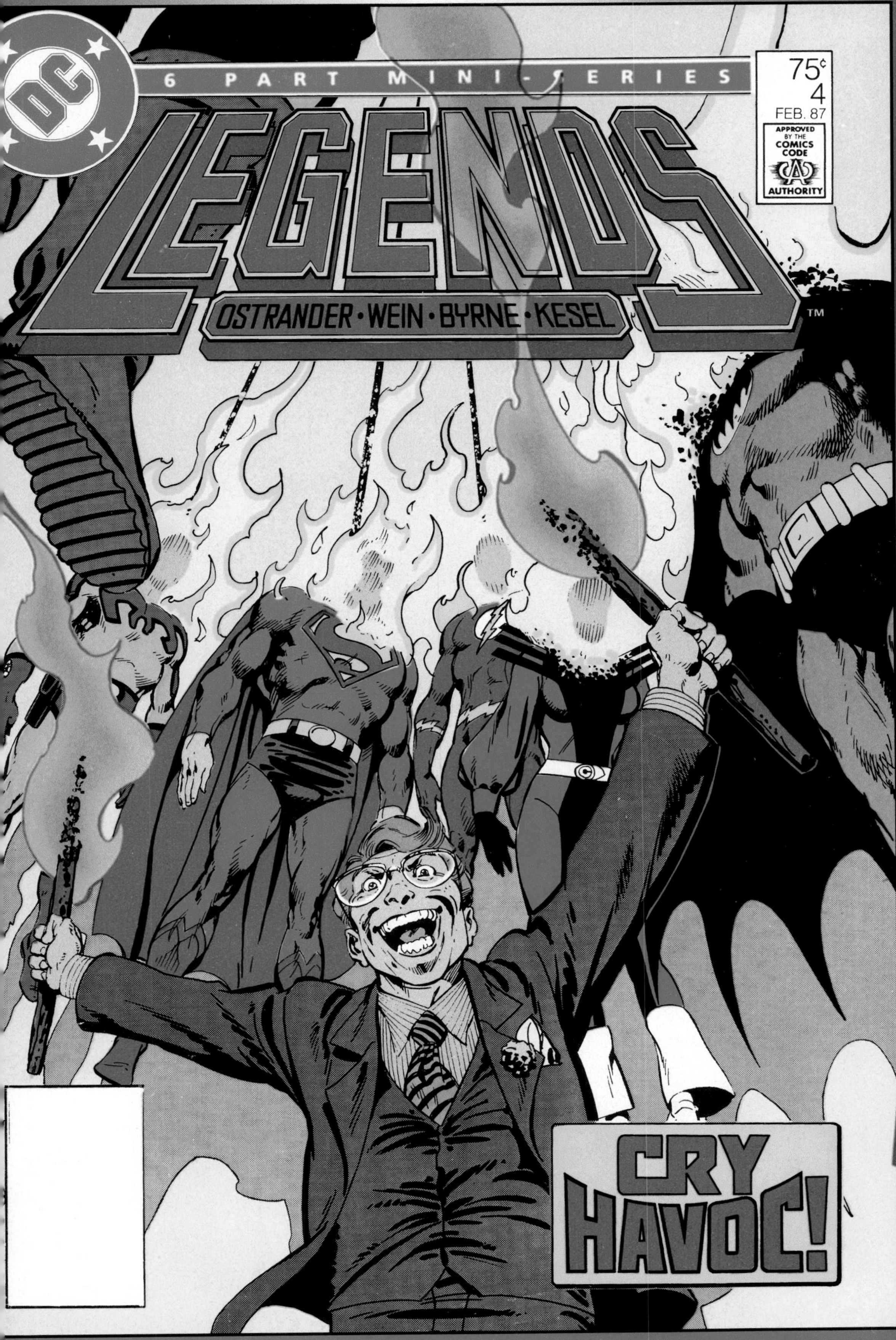
DC
6 PART MINI-SERIES
75¢
4
FEB. 87
APPROVED BY THE COMICS CODE AUTHORITY
LEGENDS
TM
OSTRANDER • WEIN • BYRNE • KESEL
CRY HAVOC!

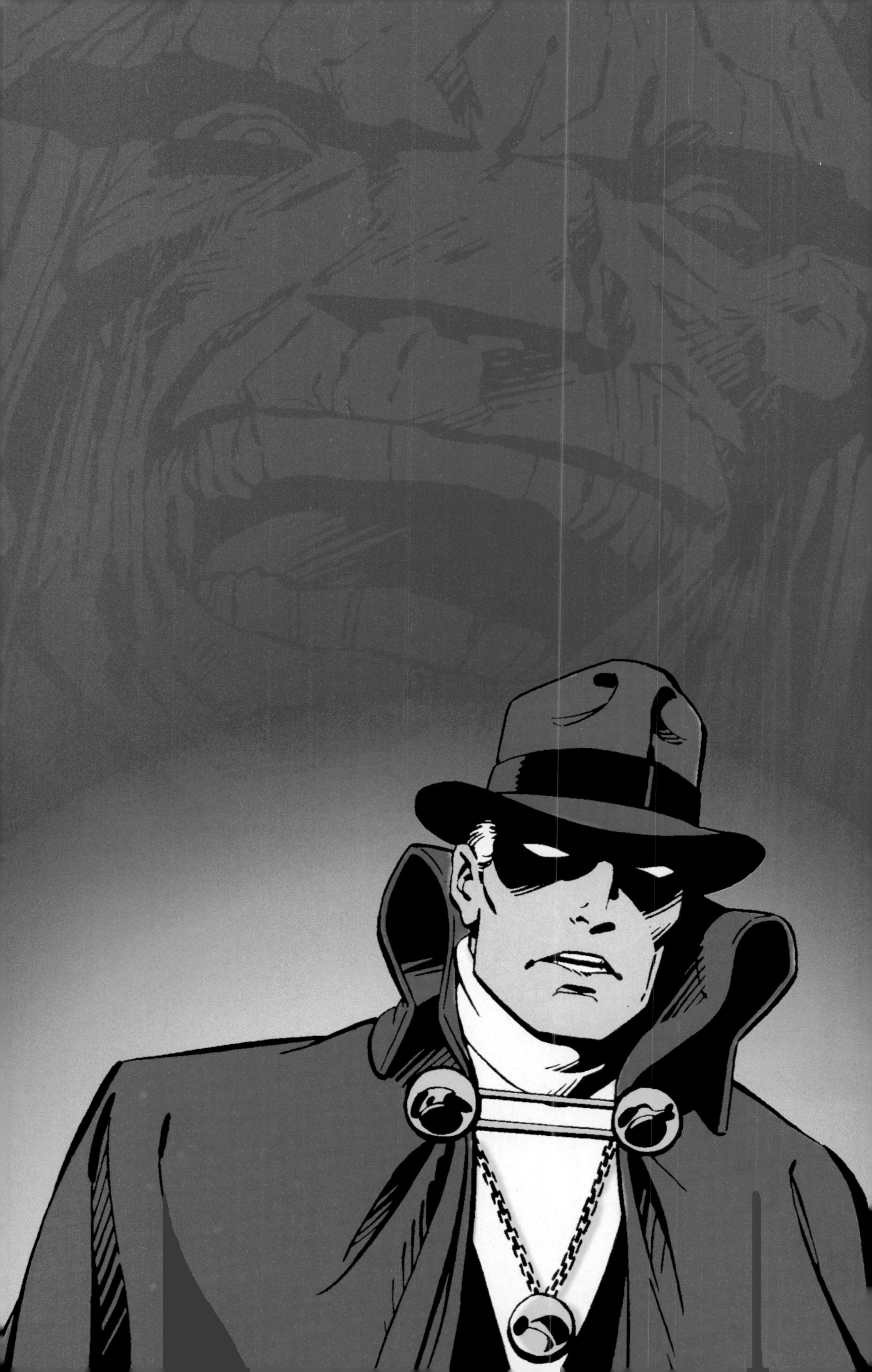

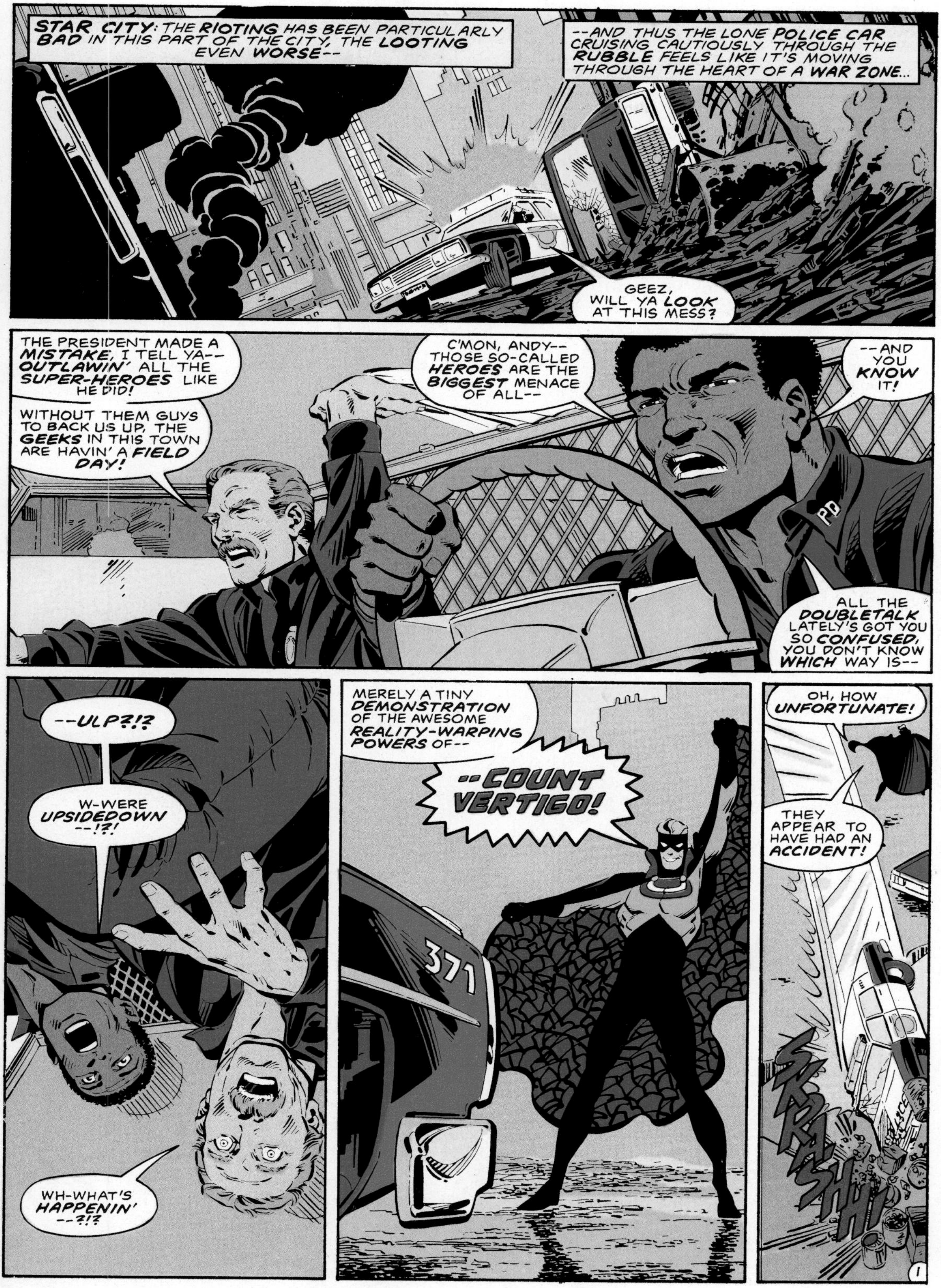
STAR CITY: THE RIOTING HAS BEEN PARTICULARLY BAD IN THIS PART OF THE CITY, THE LOOTING EVEN WORSE--
--AND THUS THE LONE POLICE CAR CRUISING CAUTIOUSLY THROUGH THE RUBBLE FEELS LIKE IT'S MOVING THROUGH THE HEART OF A WAR ZONE...
GEEZ, WILL YA LOOK AT THIS MESS?
THE PRESIDENT MADE A MISTAKE, I TELL YA-- OUTLAWIN' ALL THE SUPER-HEROES LIKE HE DID!
WITHOUT THEM GUYS TO BACK US UP, THE GEEKS IN THIS TOWN ARE HAVIN' A FIELD DAY!
C'MON, ANDY-- THOSE SO-CALLED HEROES ARE THE BIGGEST MENACE OF ALL--
--AND YOU KNOW IT!
ALL THE DOUBLETALK LATELY'S GOT YOU SO CONFUSED, YOU DON'T KNOW WHICH WAY IS--
--ULP?!?
W-WERE UPSIDEDOWN --!?!
WH-WHAT'S HAPPENIN' --?!?
MERELY A TINY DEMONSTRATION OF THE AWESOME REALITY-WARPING POWERS OF--
--COUNT VERTIGO!
371
OH, HOW UNFORTUNATE!
THEY APPEAR TO HAVE HAD AN ACCIDENT!
SKRASHH!

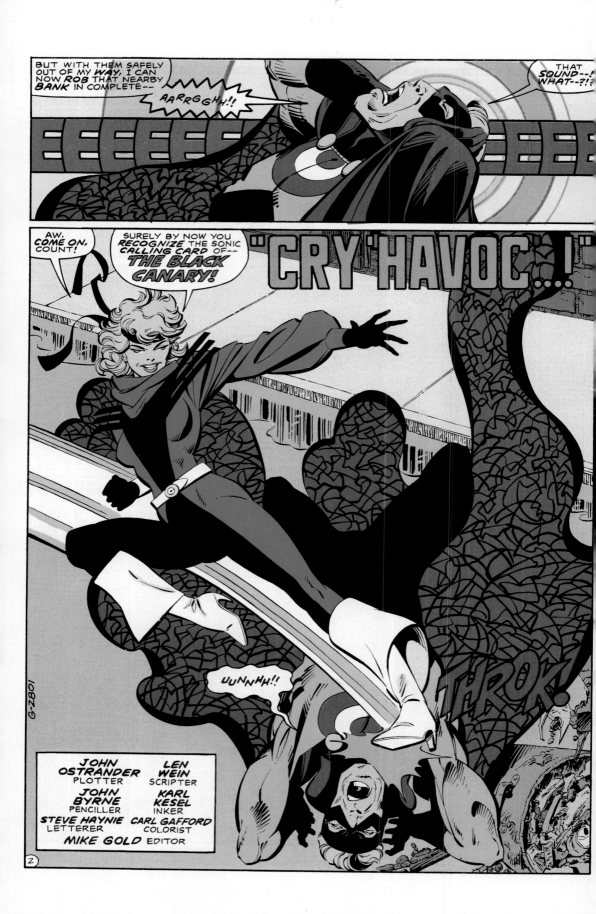

BUT WITH THEM SAFELY OUT OF MY *WAY,* I CAN NOW *ROB* THAT NEARBY *BANK* IN COMPLETE--

AARRGGHH!!

THAT *SOUND--!* WHAT--?!?

EEEEEE EEEEE

AW, COME ON, COUNT!

SURELY BY NOW YOU *RECOGNIZE* THE SONIC CALLING CARD OF-- *THE BLACK CANARY!*

"CRY HAVOC...!"

UUNNHH!!

THROK!

JOHN **OSTRANDER** PLOTTER

LEN **WEIN** SCRIPTER

JOHN **BYRNE** PENCILLER

KARL **KESEL** INKER

STEVE **HAYNIE** LETTERER

CARL **GAFFORD** COLORIST

MIKE **GOLD** EDITOR

G-ZBOI

2

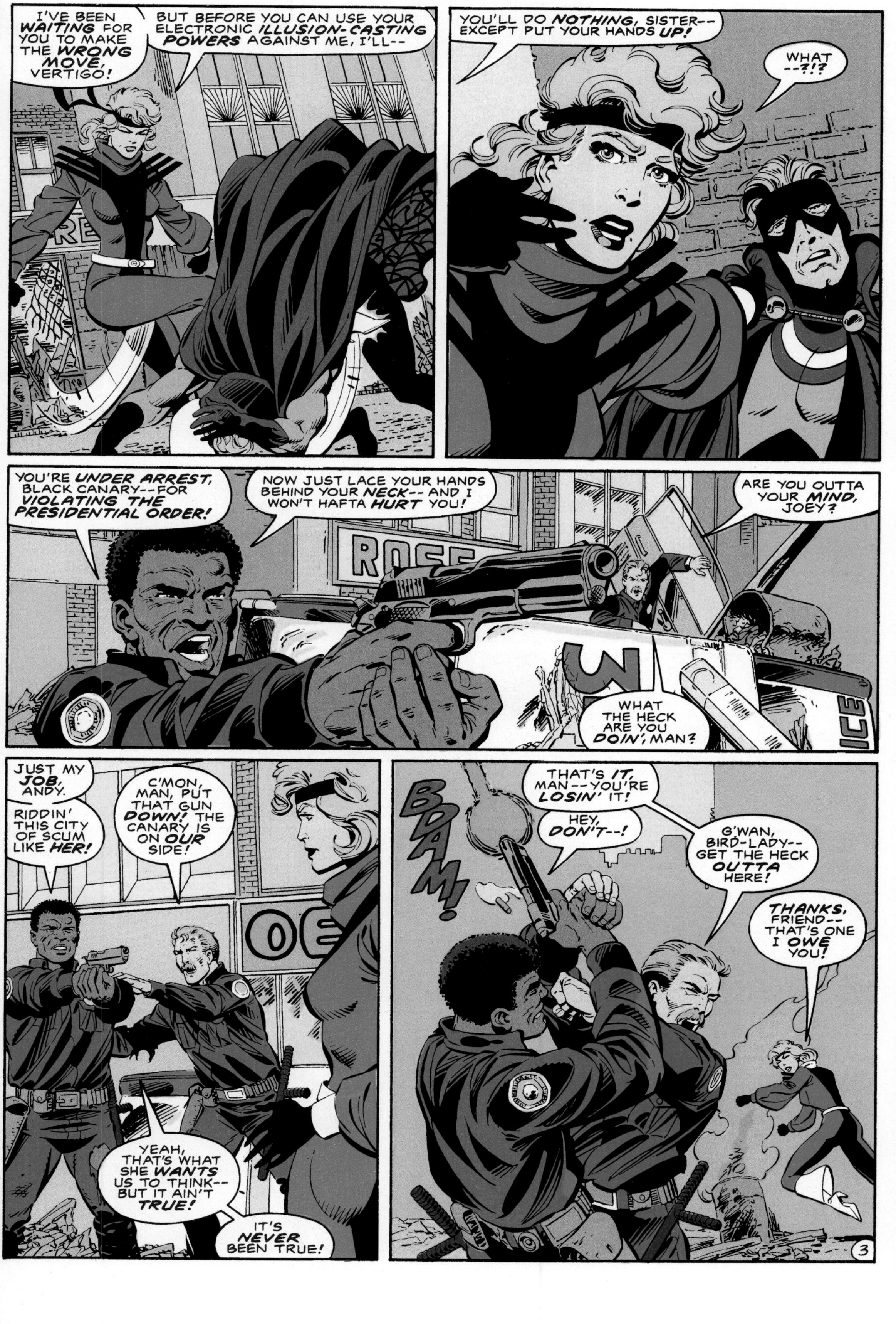
I'VE BEEN WAITING FOR YOU TO MAKE THE WRONG MOVE, VERTIGO!
BUT BEFORE YOU CAN USE YOUR ELECTRONIC ILLUSION-CASTING POWERS AGAINST ME, I'LL--
YOU'LL DO NOTHING, SISTER-- EXCEPT PUT YOUR HANDS UP!
WHAT --?!?
YOU'RE UNDER ARREST, BLACK CANARY--FOR VIOLATING THE PRESIDENTIAL ORDER!
NOW JUST LACE YOUR HANDS BEHIND YOUR NECK-- AND I WON'T HAFTA HURT YOU!
ARE YOU OUTTA YOUR MIND, JOEY?
WHAT THE HECK ARE YOU DOIN', MAN?
JUST MY JOB, ANDY.
RIDDIN' THIS CITY OF SCUM LIKE HER!
C'MON, MAN, PUT THAT GUN DOWN! THE CANARY IS ON OUR SIDE!
YEAH, THAT'S WHAT SHE WANTS US TO THINK-- BUT IT AIN'T TRUE!
IT'S NEVER BEEN TRUE!
BDAM!
THAT'S IT, MAN--YOU'RE LOSIN' IT!
HEY, DON'T--!
G'WAN, BIRD-LADY-- GET THE HECK OUTTA HERE!
THANKS, FRIEND-- THAT'S ONE I OWE YOU!

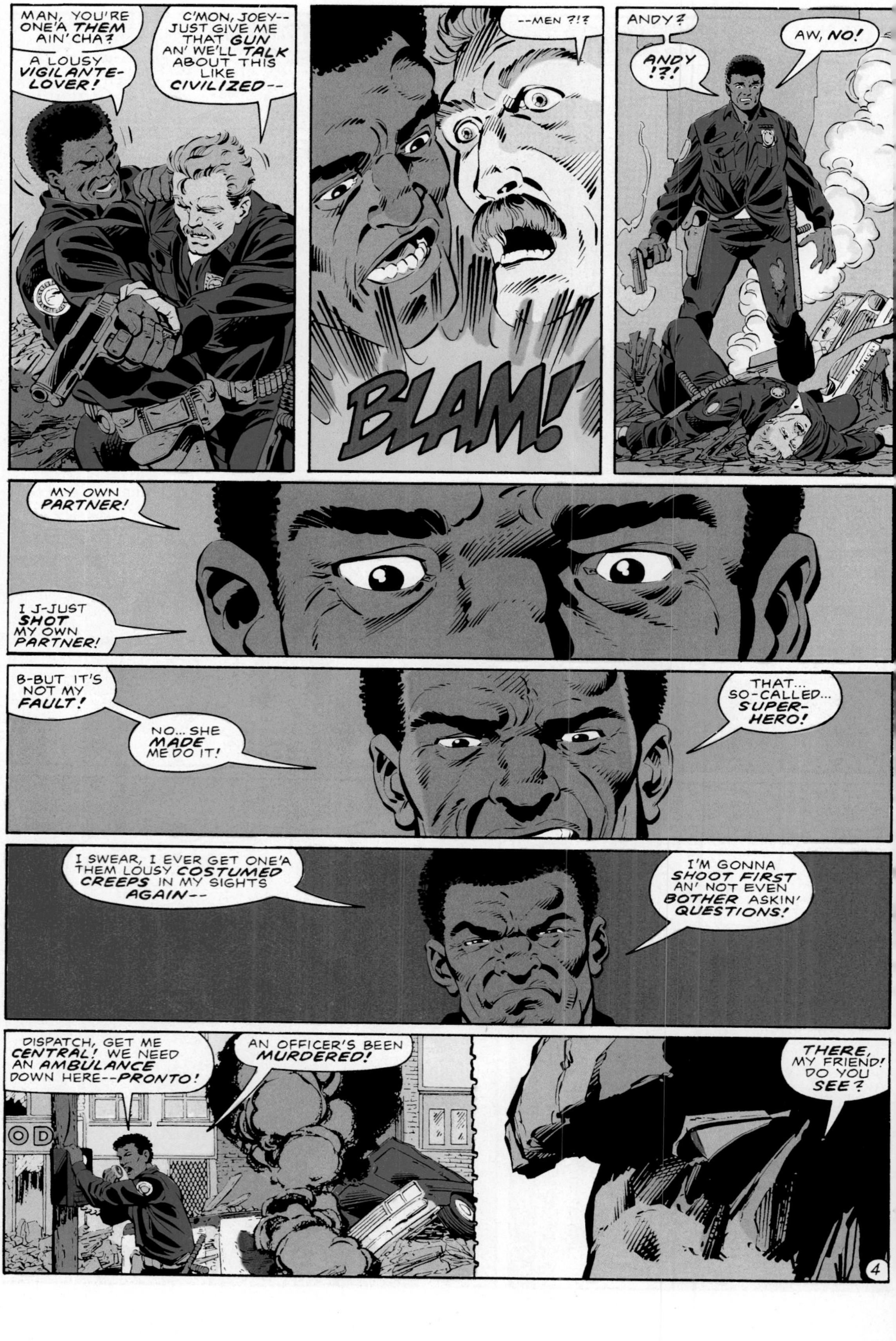
MAN, YOU'RE ONE'A THEM AIN'CHA?
A LOUSY VIGILANTE-LOVER!
C'MON, JOEY-- JUST GIVE ME THAT GUN AN' WE'LL TALK ABOUT THIS LIKE CIVILIZED--
--MEN ?!?
BLAM!
ANDY?
ANDY !?!
AW, NO!
MY OWN PARTNER!
I J-JUST SHOT MY OWN PARTNER!
B-BUT IT'S NOT MY FAULT!
NO... SHE MADE ME DO IT!
THAT... SO-CALLED... SUPER-HERO!
I SWEAR, I EVER GET ONE'A THEM LOUSY COSTUMED CREEPS IN MY SIGHTS AGAIN--
I'M GONNA SHOOT FIRST AN' NOT EVEN BOTHER ASKIN' QUESTIONS!
DISPATCH, GET ME CENTRAL! WE NEED AN AMBULANCE DOWN HERE--PRONTO!
AN OFFICER'S BEEN MURDERED!
THERE, MY FRIEND! DO YOU SEE?

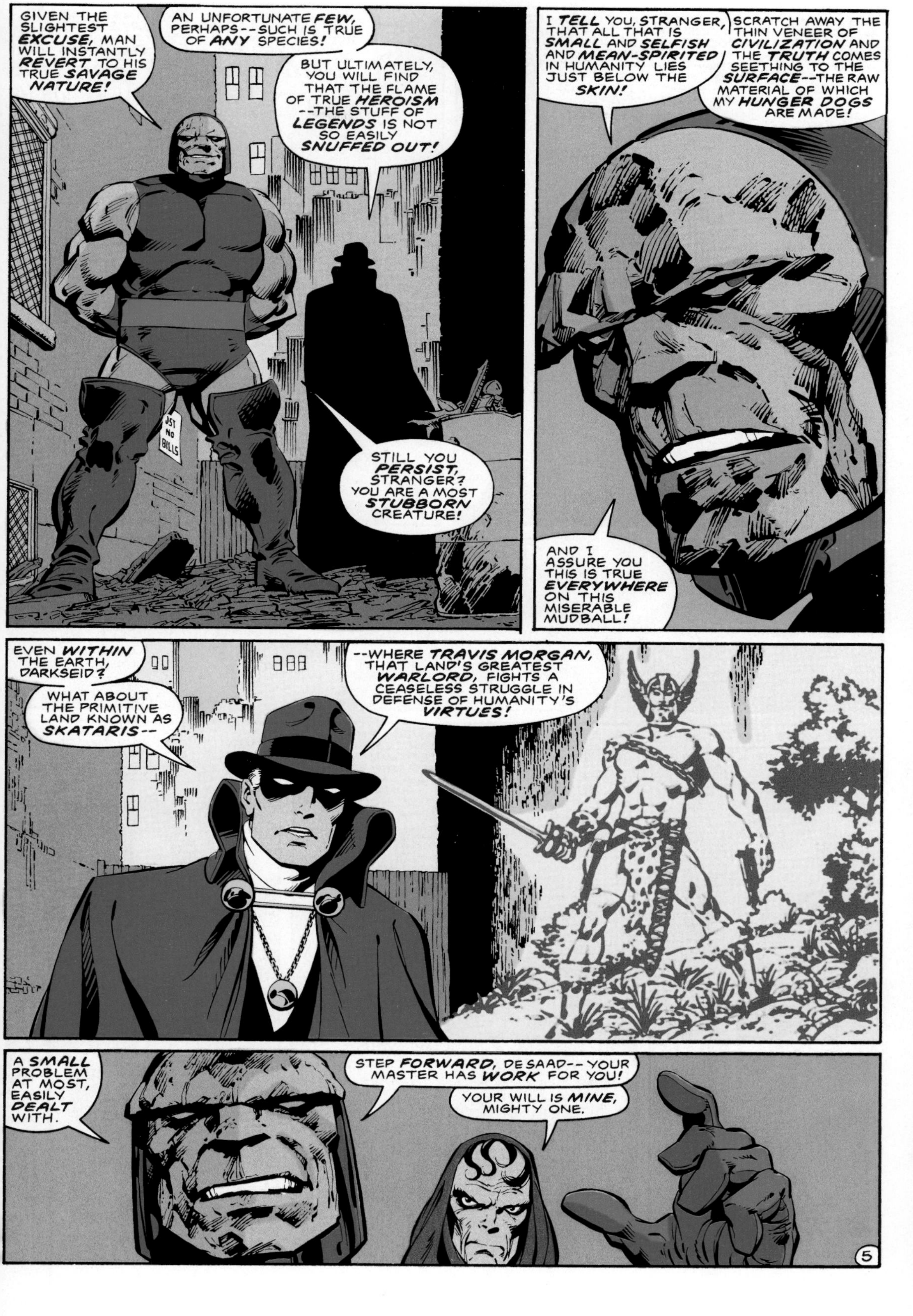
GIVEN THE SLIGHTEST EXCUSE, MAN WILL INSTANTLY REVERT TO HIS TRUE SAVAGE NATURE!
AN UNFORTUNATE FEW, PERHAPS--SUCH IS TRUE OF ANY SPECIES!
BUT ULTIMATELY, YOU WILL FIND THAT THE FLAME OF TRUE HEROISM --THE STUFF OF LEGENDS IS NOT SO EASILY SNUFFED OUT!
JST NO BILLS
STILL YOU PERSIST, STRANGER? YOU ARE A MOST STUBBORN CREATURE!
I TELL YOU, STRANGER, THAT ALL THAT IS SMALL AND SELFISH AND MEAN-SPIRITED IN HUMANITY LIES JUST BELOW THE SKIN!
SCRATCH AWAY THE THIN VENEER OF CIVILIZATION AND THE TRUTH COMES SEETHING TO THE SURFACE--THE RAW MATERIAL OF WHICH MY HUNGER DOGS ARE MADE!
AND I ASSURE YOU THIS IS TRUE EVERYWHERE ON THIS MISERABLE MUDBALL!
EVEN WITHIN THE EARTH, DARKSEID?
WHAT ABOUT THE PRIMITIVE LAND KNOWN AS SKATARIS--
--WHERE TRAVIS MORGAN, THAT LAND'S GREATEST WARLORD, FIGHTS A CEASELESS STRUGGLE IN DEFENSE OF HUMANITY'S VIRTUES!
A SMALL PROBLEM AT MOST, EASILY DEALT WITH.
STEP FORWARD, DE SAAD--YOUR MASTER HAS WORK FOR YOU!
YOUR WILL IS MINE, MIGHTY ONE.

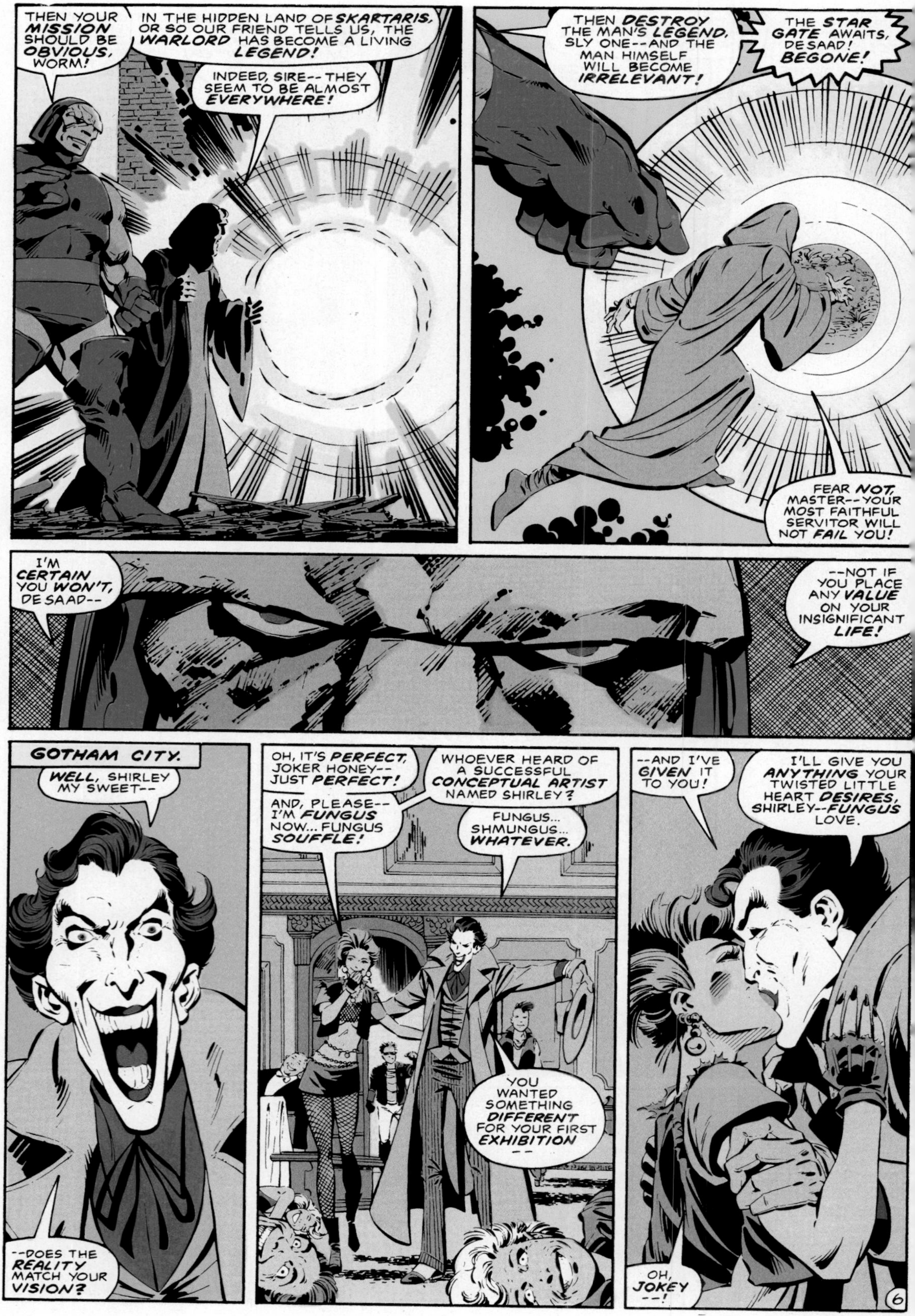
THEN YOUR MISSION SHOULD BE OBVIOUS, WORM!
IN THE HIDDEN LAND OF SKARTARIS, OR SO OUR FRIEND TELLS US, THE WARLORD HAS BECOME A LIVING LEGEND!
INDEED, SIRE-- THEY SEEM TO BE ALMOST EVERYWHERE!
THEN DESTROY THE MAN'S LEGEND, SLY ONE--AND THE MAN HIMSELF WILL BECOME IRRELEVANT!
THE STAR GATE AWAITS, DESAAD! BEGONE!
FEAR NOT, MASTER--YOUR MOST FAITHFUL SERVITOR WILL NOT FAIL YOU!
I'M CERTAIN YOU WON'T, DESAAD--
--NOT IF YOU PLACE ANY VALUE ON YOUR INSIGNIFICANT LIFE!
GOTHAM CITY.
WELL, SHIRLEY MY SWEET--
--DOES THE REALITY MATCH YOUR VISION?
OH, IT'S PERFECT, JOKER HONEY--JUST PERFECT!
WHOEVER HEARD OF A SUCCESSFUL CONCEPTUAL ARTIST NAMED SHIRLEY?
AND, PLEASE-- I'M FUNGUS NOW... FUNGUS SOUFFLE!
FUNGUS... SHMUNGUS... WHATEVER.
YOU WANTED SOMETHING DIFFERENT FOR YOUR FIRST EXHIBITION --
--AND I'VE GIVEN IT TO YOU!
I'LL GIVE YOU ANYTHING YOUR TWISTED LITTLE HEART DESIRES, SHIRLEY--FUNGUS LOVE.
OH, JOKEY--!
6

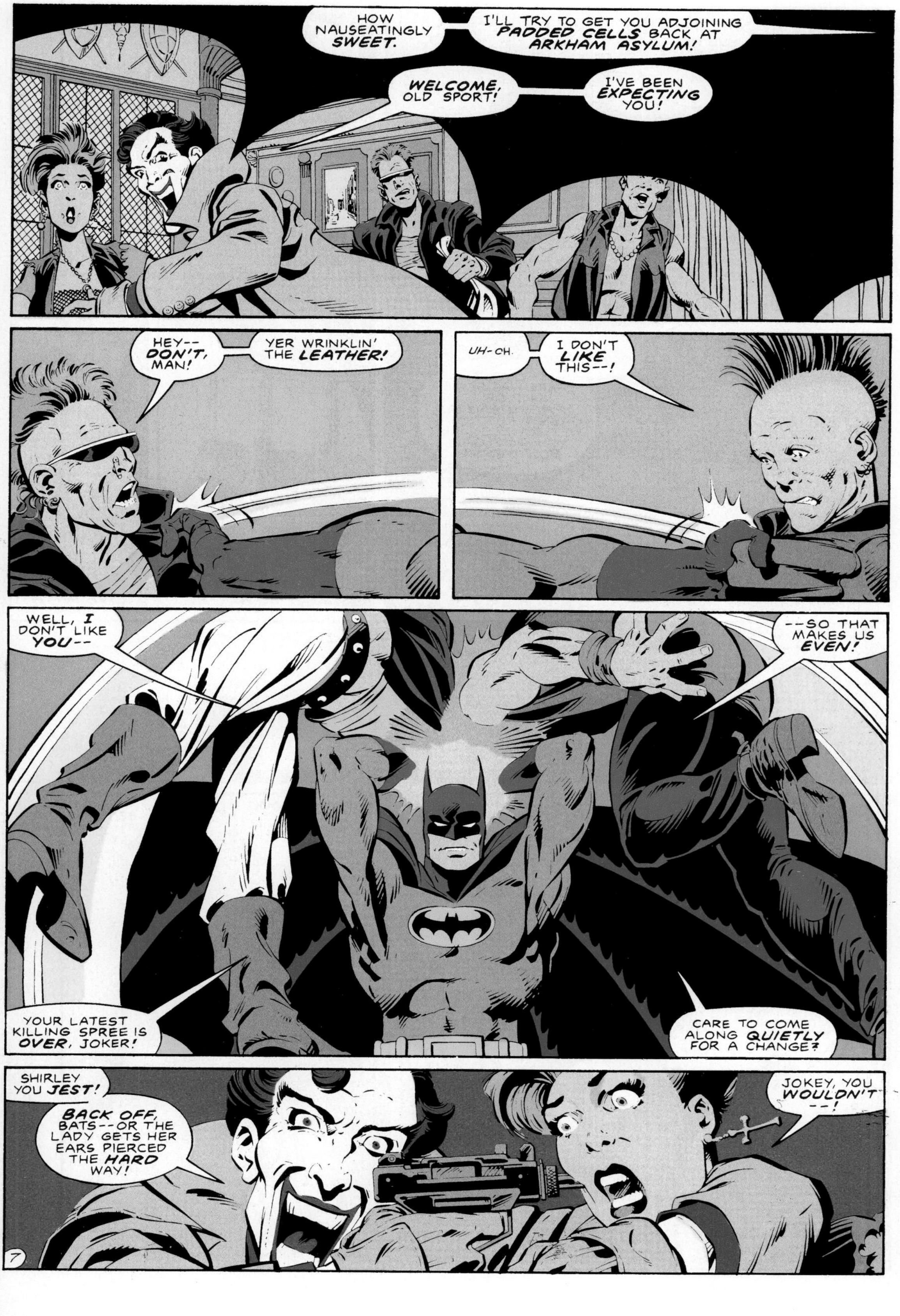
HOW NAUSEATINGLY SWEET.
I'LL TRY TO GET YOU ADJOINING PADDED CELLS BACK AT ARKHAM ASYLUM!
WELCOME, OLD SPORT!
I'VE BEEN EXPECTING YOU!
HEY-- DON'T, MAN!
YER WRINKLIN' THE LEATHER!
UH-OH.
I DON'T LIKE THIS--!
WELL, I DON'T LIKE YOU--
--SO THAT MAKES US EVEN!
YOUR LATEST KILLING SPREE IS OVER, JOKER!
CARE TO COME ALONG QUIETLY FOR A CHANGE?
SHIRLEY YOU JEST!
BACK OFF, BATS--OR THE LADY GETS HER EARS PIERCED THE HARD WAY!
JOKEY, YOU WOULDN'T --!

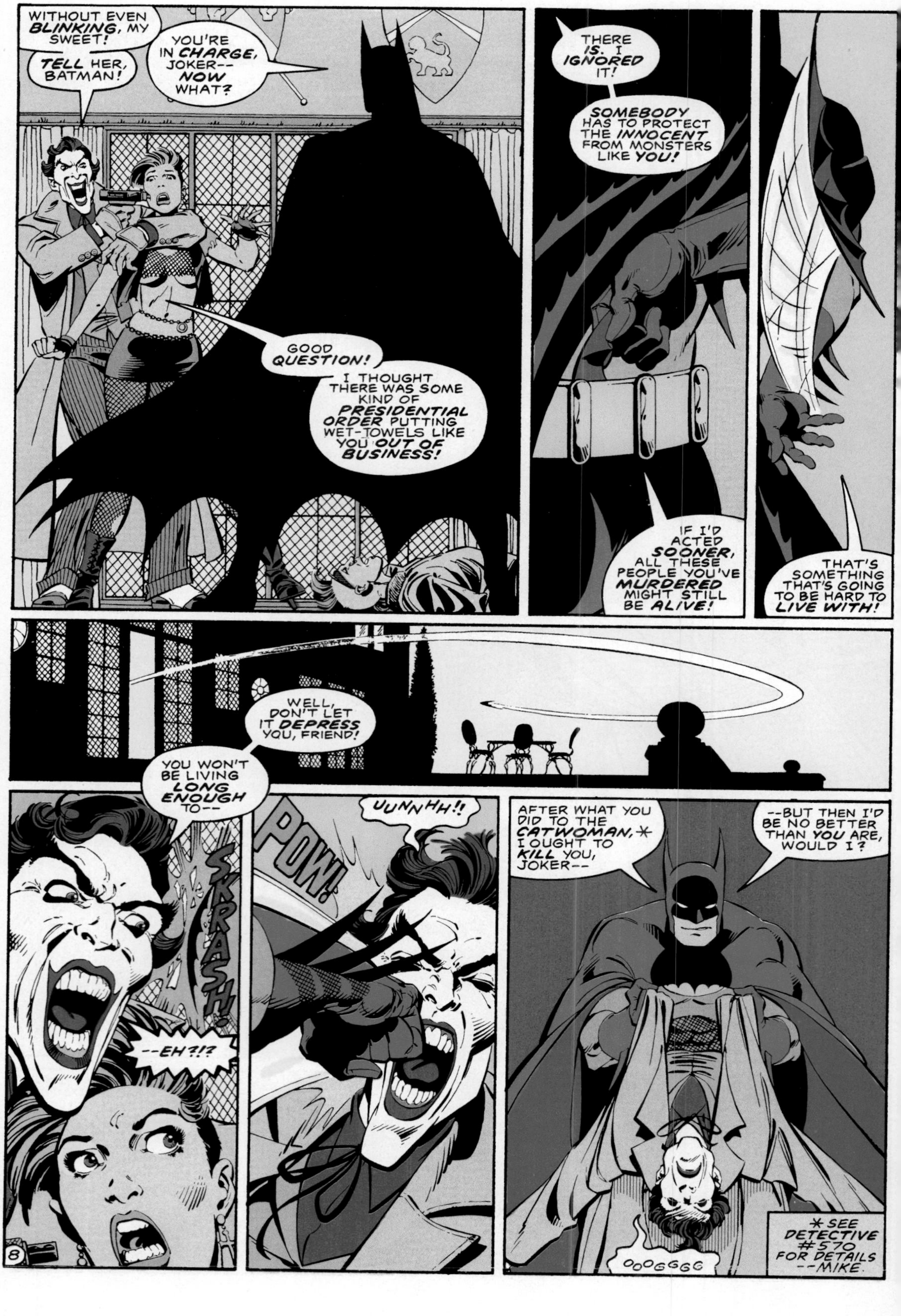
WITHOUT EVEN BLINKING, MY SWEET!
TELL HER, BATMAN!
YOU'RE IN CHARGE, JOKER-- NOW WHAT?
GOOD QUESTION!
I THOUGHT THERE WAS SOME KIND OF PRESIDENTIAL ORDER PUTTING WET-TOWELS LIKE YOU OUT OF BUSINESS!
THERE IS. I IGNORED IT!
SOMEBODY HAS TO PROTECT THE INNOCENT FROM MONSTERS LIKE YOU!
IF I'D ACTED SOONER, ALL THESE PEOPLE YOU'VE MURDERED MIGHT STILL BE ALIVE!
THAT'S SOMETHING THAT'S GOING TO BE HARD TO LIVE WITH!
WELL, DON'T LET IT DEPRESS YOU, FRIEND!
YOU WON'T BE LIVING LONG ENOUGH TO--
SKRASH!
--EH?!?
POW!
UUNNHH!!
AFTER WHAT YOU DID TO THE CATWOMAN,* I OUGHT TO KILL YOU, JOKER--
--BUT THEN I'D BE NO BETTER THAN YOU ARE, WOULD I?
OOOGGGG
*SEE DETECTIVE #570 FOR DETAILS --MIKE.
8

LOS ANGELES: WHERE PHYSICAL FITNESS, EVEN IN THE EXTREME, IS AS MUCH A PART OF DAILY LIFE AS RUSH-HOUR TRAFFIC...

OKAY, FELLAS-- HIT IT WITH ALL YOU'VE GOT!

WHICH, IN OUR CASE, IS PLENTY!

YOU GOT IT, EMMA SUE, HONEY!

NLER INC.

ALLLL-RIIIIIIGHT!

WHONG.

AIN'T NO ARMORED DOOR MADE THAT CAN STAND UP TO THE POWER OF-- MS. MAGNIFICENT AND HER PRETTY BOYS!

NOW TO DEMONSTRATE THE SAME KIND OF STYLE THAT MADE ME THREE-TIME WORLD WOMEN'S BODY-BUILDING CHAMPION--

CANFIELD'S SECURITY

WRUNCH!

--AND WE CAN START COLLECTING--

RRRAAWWW

WWWRRR

--MAMA?!?

9

IT'S A **MONSTER** --A **BIG** MONSTER --!

B-BUT THERE WAS 'S'POSED TO BE **GOLD** IN THERE-- AN' **JEWELS** AN'--!

SECURITY

HELP ME!!

SOMEBODY-- **ANYBODY**-- PLEASE **HELP** ME!!

TRY SAYIN' **PRETTY PLEASE** WITH LOTS OF **SUGAR** ON IT, SUGAR!

IT WON'T **HELP**--

--BUT IT COULDN'T **HURT!**

Y-YOU CREATED THAT MONSTER--WITH THAT LITTLE **RING**?!?

WHO-- **WHAT**-- ARE YOU --?!?

NAME'S **GUY GARDNER**, SUGAR--

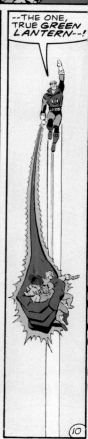

--THE ONE, TRUE **GREEN LANTERN**--!

10

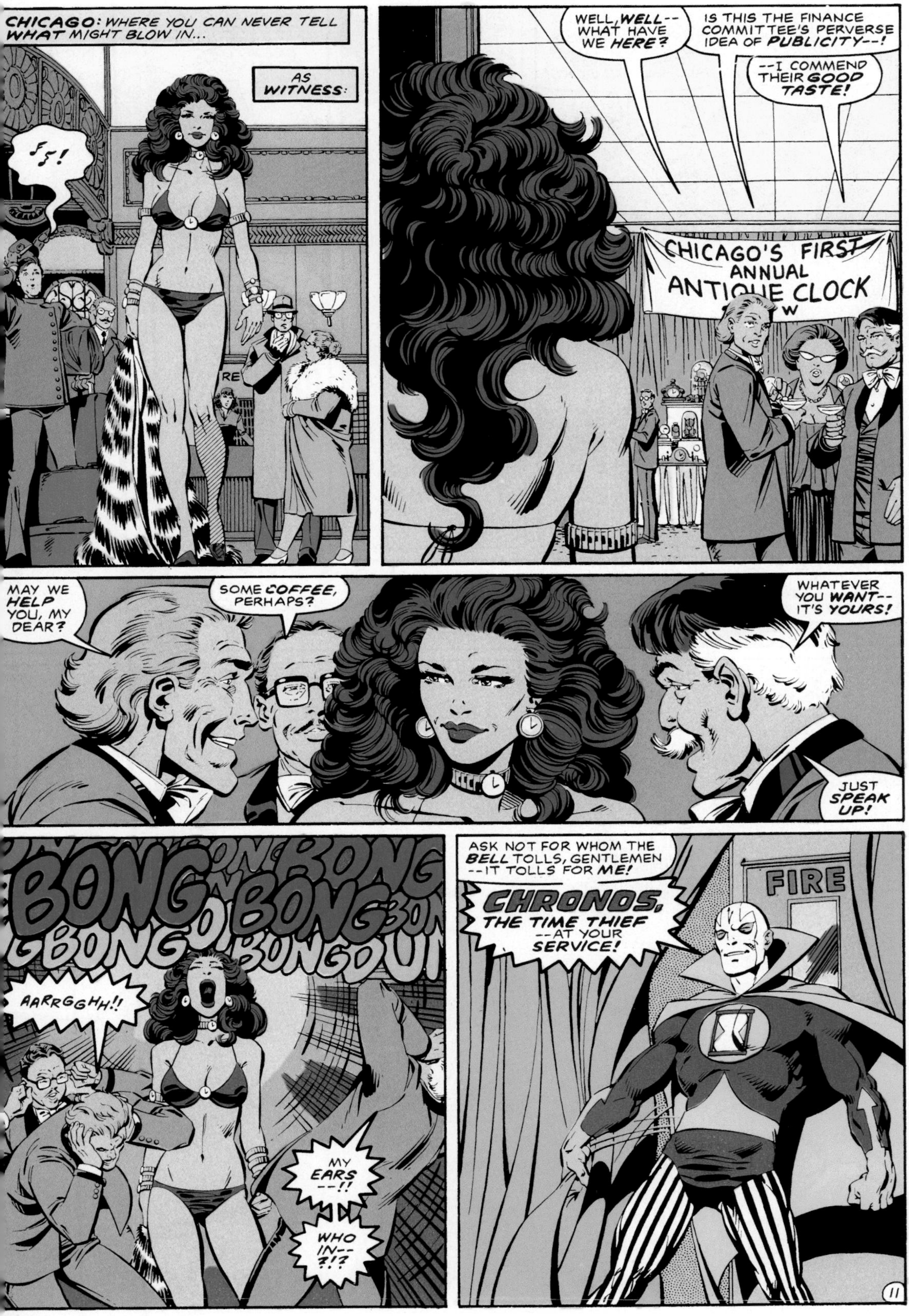
CHICAGO: WHERE YOU CAN NEVER TELL WHAT MIGHT BLOW IN...
AS WITNESS:
WELL, WELL--WHAT HAVE WE HERE?
IS THIS THE FINANCE COMMITTEE'S PERVERSE IDEA OF PUBLICITY--!
--I COMMEND THEIR GOOD TASTE!
CHICAGO'S FIRST ANNUAL ANTIQUE CLOCK
MAY WE HELP YOU, MY DEAR?
SOME COFFEE, PERHAPS?
WHATEVER YOU WANT--IT'S YOURS!
JUST SPEAK UP!
BONG BONG BONG BONG BONG
AARRGGHH!!
MY EARS--!!
WHO IN--?!?
ASK NOT FOR WHOM THE BELL TOLLS, GENTLEMEN--IT TOLLS FOR ME!
CHRONOS, THE TIME THIEF--AT YOUR SERVICE!
FIRE

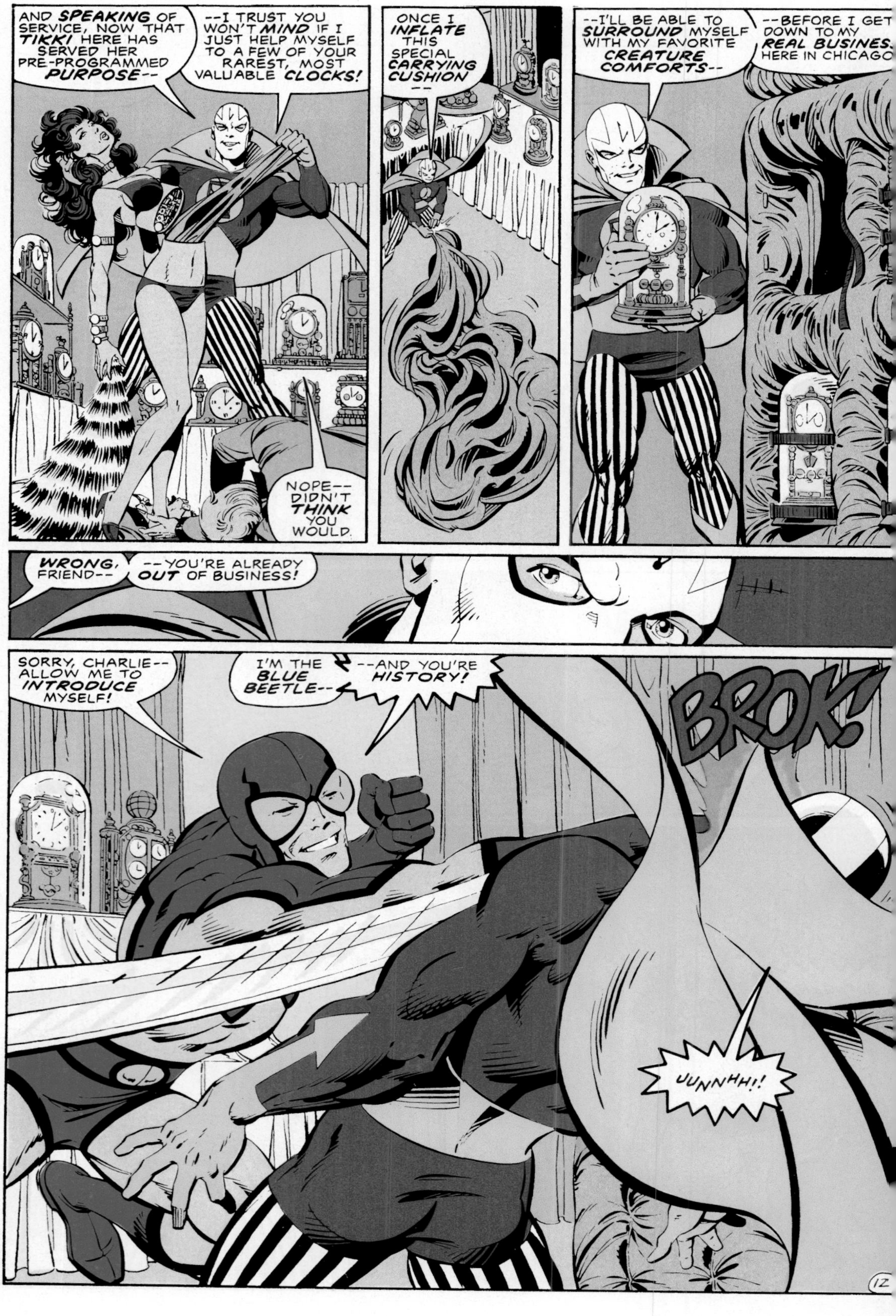
AND SPEAKING OF SERVICE, NOW THAT TIKKI HERE HAS SERVED HER PRE-PROGRAMMED PURPOSE--
--I TRUST YOU WON'T MIND IF I JUST HELP MYSELF TO A FEW OF YOUR RAREST, MOST VALUABLE CLOCKS!
NOPE-- DIDN'T THINK YOU WOULD.
ONCE I INFLATE THIS SPECIAL CARRYING CUSHION --
--I'LL BE ABLE TO SURROUND MYSELF WITH MY FAVORITE CREATURE COMFORTS--
--BEFORE I GET DOWN TO MY REAL BUSINES HERE IN CHICAGO
WRONG, FRIEND--
--YOU'RE ALREADY OUT OF BUSINESS!
SORRY, CHARLIE-- ALLOW ME TO INTRODUCE MYSELF!
I'M THE BLUE BEETLE--
--AND YOU'RE HISTORY!
BROK!
UUNNHH!

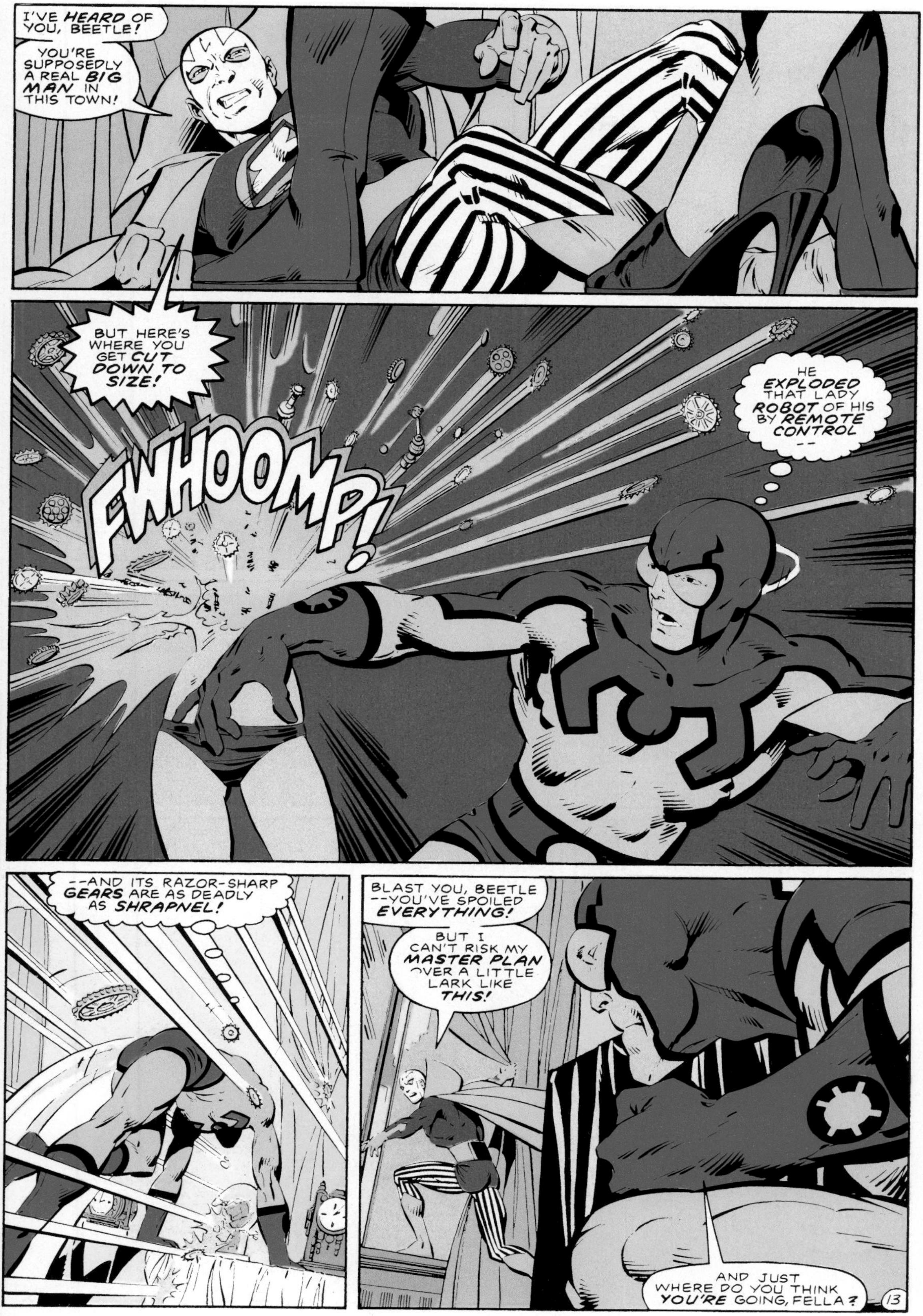
I'VE HEARD OF YOU, BEETLE!
YOU'RE SUPPOSEDLY A REAL BIG MAN IN THIS TOWN!
BUT HERE'S WHERE YOU GET CUT DOWN TO SIZE!
FWHOOMP!
HE EXPLODED THAT LADY ROBOT OF HIS BY REMOTE CONTROL --
--AND ITS RAZOR-SHARP GEARS ARE AS DEADLY AS SHRAPNEL!
BLAST YOU, BEETLE --YOU'VE SPOILED EVERYTHING!
BUT I CAN'T RISK MY MASTER PLAN OVER A LITTLE LARK LIKE THIS!
AND JUST WHERE DO YOU THINK YOU'RE GOING, FELLA?

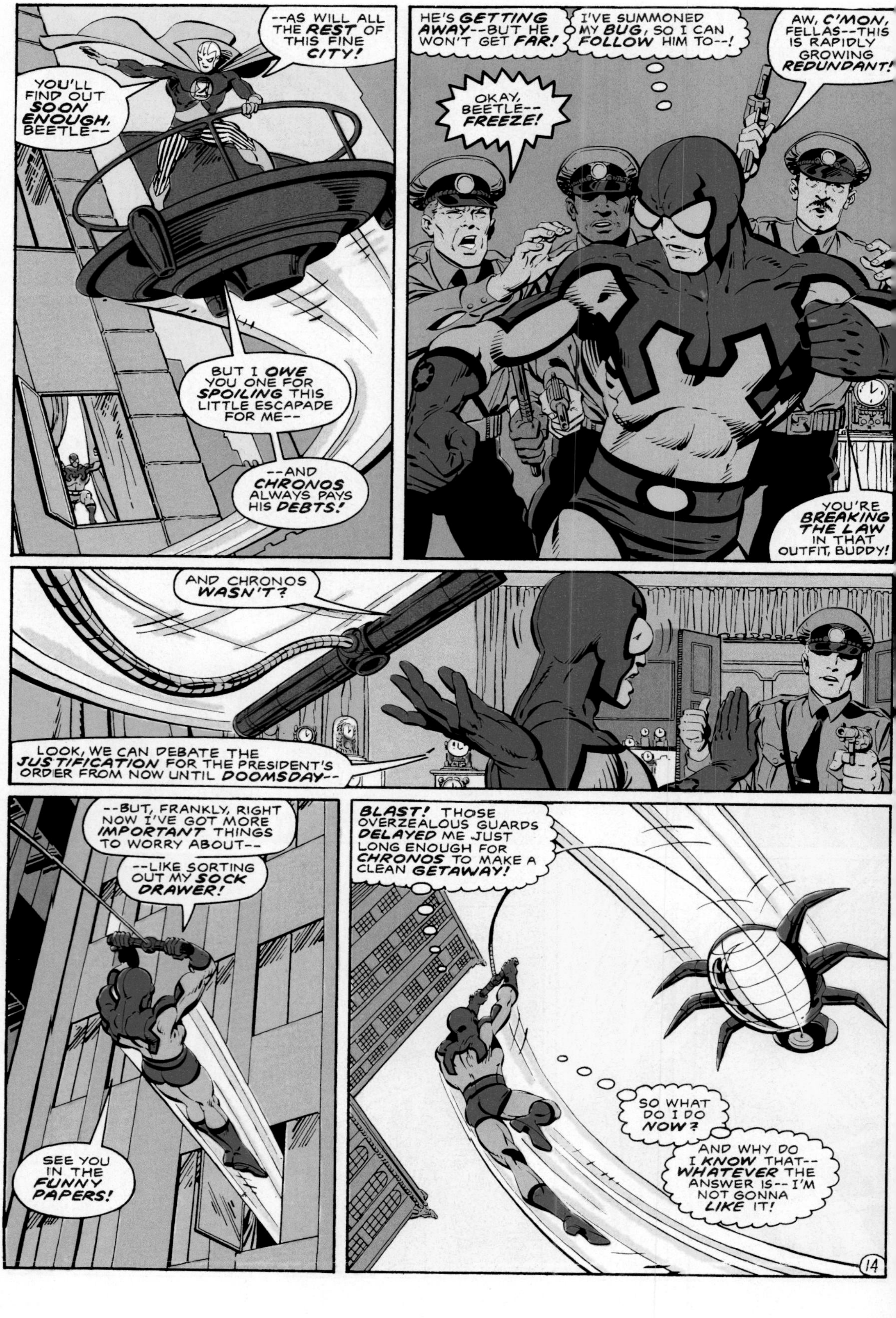
--AS WILL ALL THE REST OF THIS FINE CITY!
YOU'LL FIND OUT SOON ENOUGH, BEETLE--
BUT I OWE YOU ONE FOR SPOILING THIS LITTLE ESCAPADE FOR ME--
--AND CHRONOS ALWAYS PAYS HIS DEBTS!
HE'S GETTING AWAY--BUT HE WON'T GET FAR!
I'VE SUMMONED MY BUG, SO I CAN FOLLOW HIM TO--!
AW, C'MON, FELLAS--THIS IS RAPIDLY GROWING REDUNDANT!
OKAY, BEETLE--FREEZE!
YOU'RE BREAKING THE LAW IN THAT OUTFIT, BUDDY!
AND CHRONOS WASN'T?
LOOK, WE CAN DEBATE THE JUSTIFICATION FOR THE PRESIDENT'S ORDIER FROM NOW UNTIL DOOMSDAY--
--BUT, FRANKLY, RIGHT NOW I'VE GOT MORE IMPORTANT THINGS TO WORRY ABOUT--
--LIKE SORTING OUT MY SOCK DRAWER!
SEE YOU IN THE FUNNY PAPERS!
BLAST! THOSE OVERZEALOUS GUARDS DELAYED ME JUST LONG ENOUGH FOR CHRONOS TO MAKE A CLEAN GETAWAY!
SO WHAT DO I DO NOW?
AND WHY DO I KNOW THAT--WHATEVER THE ANSWER IS--I'M NOT GONNA LIKE IT!

SALEM, MASSACHUSETTS: ON A WINDSWEPT HILL ABOVE THE WITCH-HAUNTED CITY STANDS A COLD AND LONELY *TOWER*--

--A TOWER WITHOUT *DOORS* OR *WINDOWS*--

--WHICH, FOR SEVERAL *DECADES* NOW, HAS SERVED AS HOME AND HEADQUARTERS TO THE MAN CALLED *KENT NELSON*...

I SEE BY THE *CRYSTAL ORB OF NABU* THAT THE SITUATION IS GROWING *WORSE*...

THOSE ONCE WORSHIPPED AS *HEROES* ARE NOW OUTLAWED AND *REVILED*...

DOWN WITH 'HEROES'

A HERO AIN'T NOTHING BUT A SANDWICH

WE DON'T NEED 'HEROES'

DUMP THE DO-GOODERS

DON'T NEED HEROES

...*MOBS* RAMPAGE THROUGH THE STREETS LIKE *ANIMALS*...

I'VE BEEN *OUT* THERE, KENT--I'VE *SEEN* IT!

IT'S *TIME*, ISN'T IT?

TIME FOR-- *HIM!*

I HAVE NO OTHER *CHOICE*, INZA!

THERE IS *MADNESS* IN THE STREETS--AND *HE* ALONE MAY HAVE THE POWER TO SET IT *RIGHT!*

BUT EVERY TIME YOU PUT ON THAT CURSED GOLDEN *HELMET*--EVERY TIME YOU LET *HIM* POSSESS YOU--

--I FEAR *KENT NELSON* WON'T BE COMING *BACK* TO ME!

I'LL *ALWAYS* COME BACK, INZA--SO LONG AS I KNOW YOU'RE *WAITING* FOR ME.

KENT, I-- I *LOVE* YOU!

I *KNOW*, HONEY...

THAT'S WHAT GIVES ME THE STRENGTH TO *DO* THIS!

SEE YOU *SOON*.

15

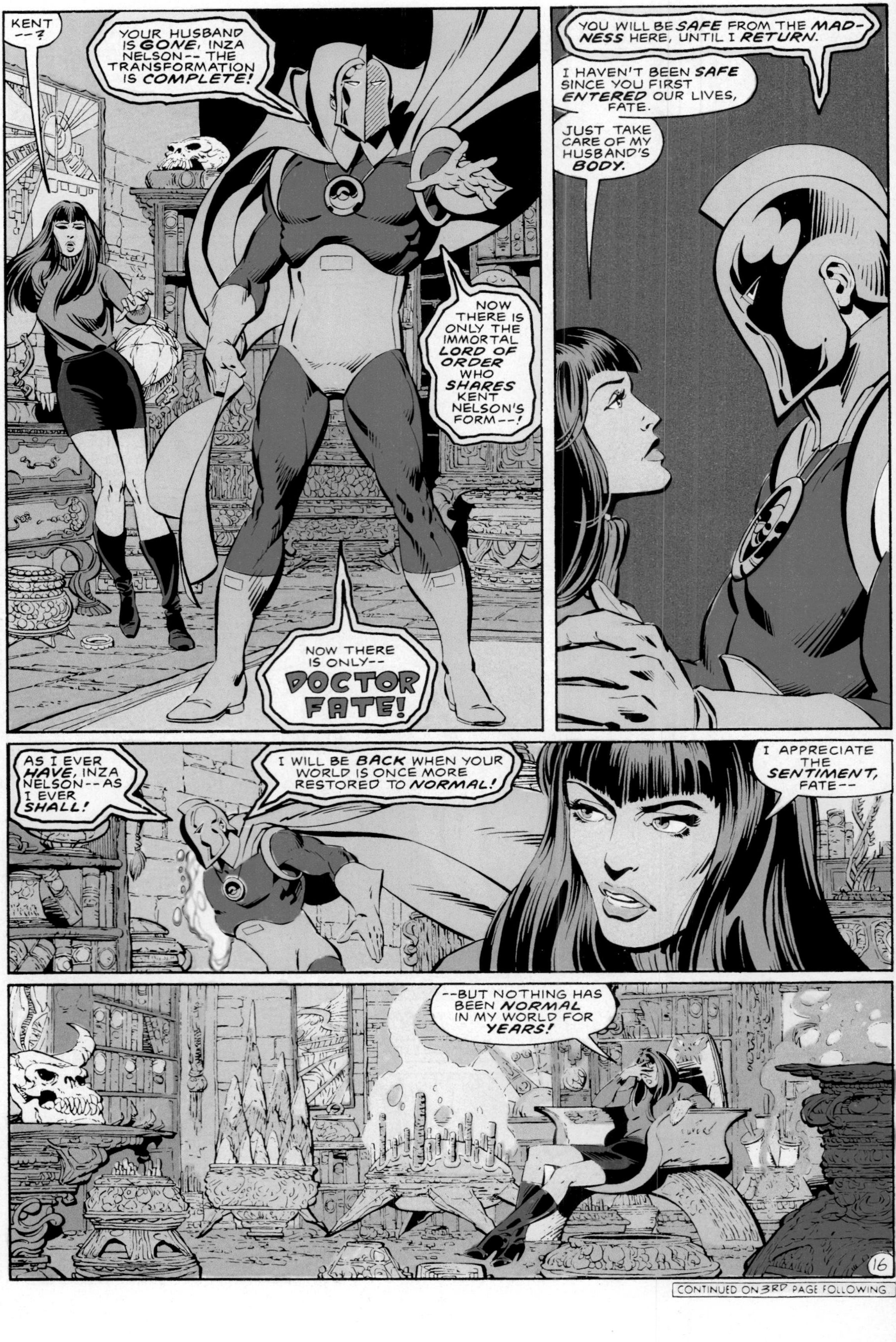
KENT--?
YOUR HUSBAND IS GONE, INZA NELSON-- THE TRANSFORMATION IS COMPLETE!
NOW THERE IS ONLY THE IMMORTAL LORD OF ORDER WHO SHARES KENT NELSON'S FORM--!
NOW THERE IS ONLY--
DOCTOR FATE!
YOU WILL BE SAFE FROM THE MADNESS HERE, UNTIL I RETURN.
I HAVEN'T BEEN SAFE SINCE YOU FIRST ENTERED OUR LIVES, FATE.
JUST TAKE CARE OF MY HUSBAND'S BODY.
AS I EVER HAVE, INZA NELSON--AS I EVER SHALL!
I WILL BE BACK WHEN YOUR WORLD IS ONCE MORE RESTORED TO NORMAL!
I APPRECIATE THE SENTIMENT, FATE--
--BUT NOTHING HAS BEEN NORMAL IN MY WORLD FOR YEARS!
16
CONTINUED ON 3RD PAGE FOLLOWING

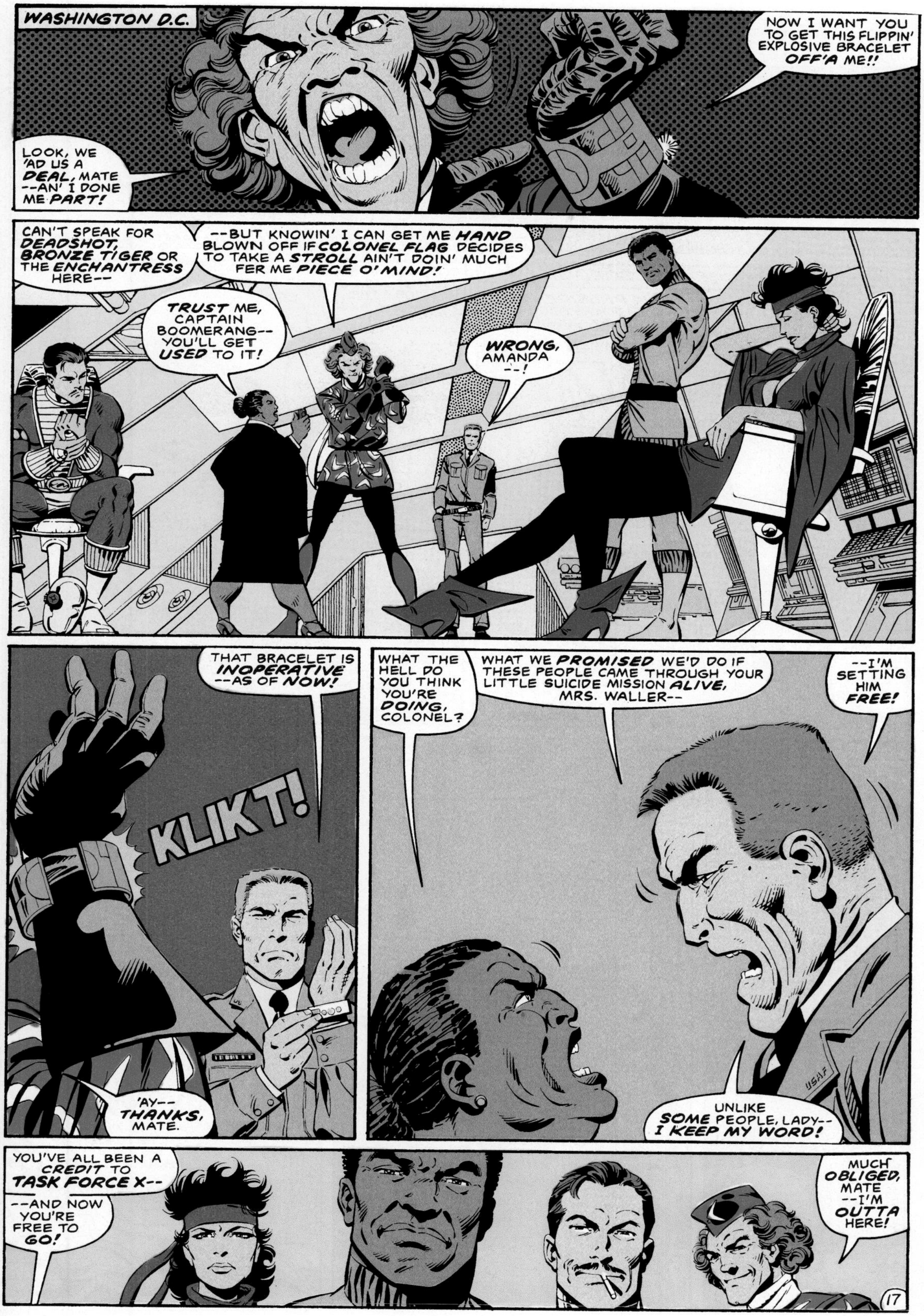
WASHINGTON D.C.
NOW I WANT YOU TO GET THIS FLIPPIN' EXPLOSIVE BRACELET OFF'A ME!!
LOOK, WE 'AD US A DEAL, MATE --AN' I DONE ME PART!
CAN'T SPEAK FOR DEADSHOT, BRONZE TIGER OR THE ENCHANTRESS HERE--
--BUT KNOWIN' I CAN GET ME HAND BLOWN OFF IF COLONEL FLAG DECIDES TO TAKE A STROLL AIN'T DOIN' MUCH FER ME PIECE O' MIND!
TRUST ME, CAPTAIN BOOMERANG-- YOU'LL GET USED TO IT!
WRONG, AMANDA --!
THAT BRACELET IS INOPERATIVE --AS OF NOW!
KLIKT!
'AY-- THANKS, MATE.
WHAT THE HELL DO YOU THINK YOU'RE DOING, COLONEL?
WHAT WE PROMISED WE'D DO IF THESE PEOPLE CAME THROUGH YOUR LITTLE SUICIDE MISSION ALIVE, MRS. WALLER--
--I'M SETTING HIM FREE!
UNLIKE SOME PEOPLE, LADY-- I KEEP MY WORD!
YOU'VE ALL BEEN A CREDIT TO TASK FORCE X--
--AND NOW YOU'RE FREE TO GO!
MUCH OBLIGED, MATE --I'M OUTTA HERE!

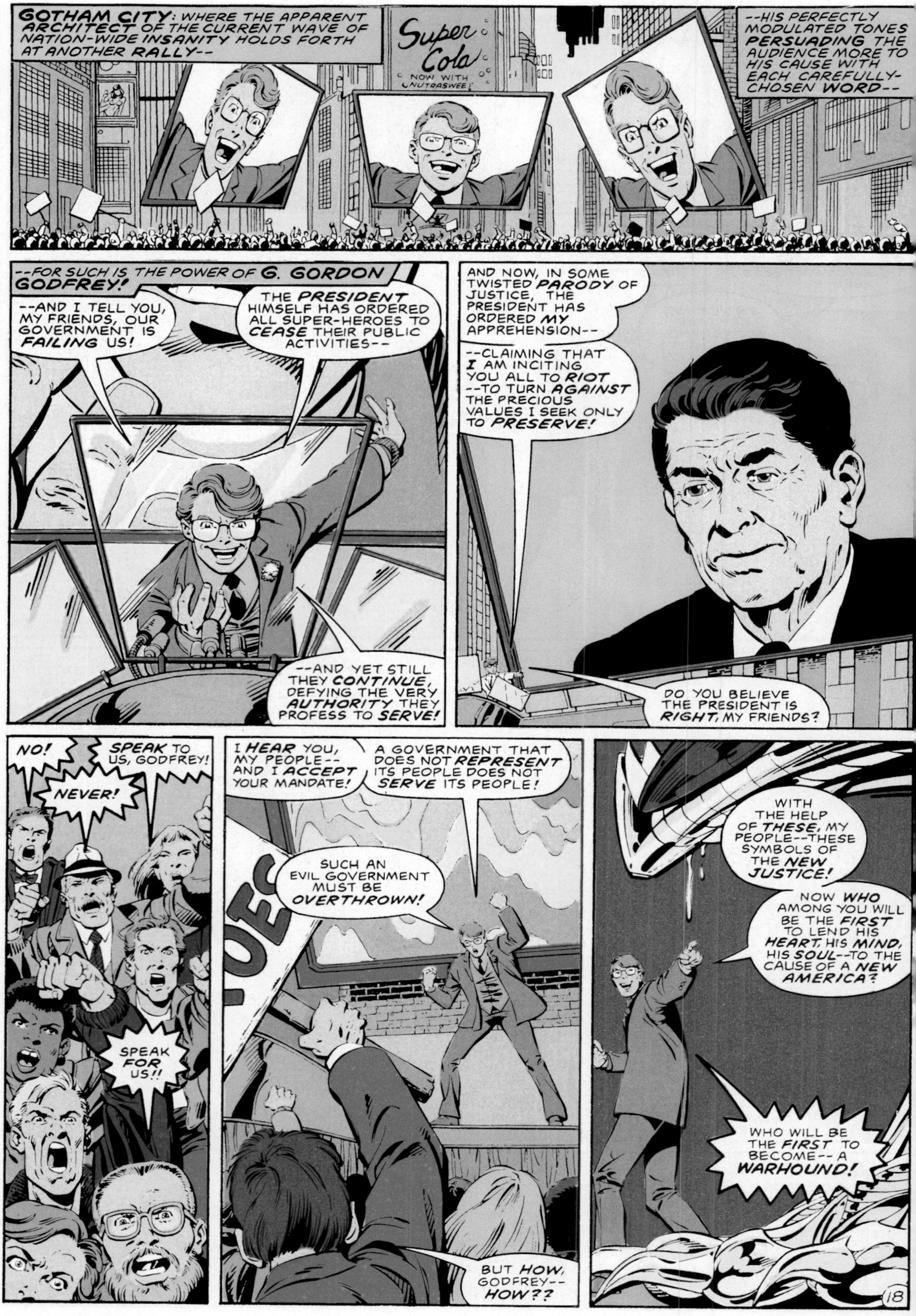
GOTHAM CITY: WHERE THE APPARENT ARCHITECT OF THE CURRENT WAVE OF NATION-WIDE INSANITY HOLDS FORTH AT ANOTHER RALLY--
Super Cola NOW WITH NUTRASWEET
--HIS PERFECTLY MODULATED TONES PERSUADING THE AUDIENCE MORE TO HIS CAUSE WITH EACH CAREFULLY-CHOSEN WORD--
--FOR SUCH IS THE POWER OF G. GORDON GODFREY!
--AND I TELL YOU, MY FRIENDS, OUR GOVERNMENT IS FAILING US!
THE PRESIDENT HIMSELF HAS ORDERED ALL SUPER-HEROES TO CEASE THEIR PUBLIC ACTIVITIES--
--AND YET STILL THEY CONTINUE, DEFYING THE VERY AUTHORITY THEY PROFESS TO SERVE!
AND NOW, IN SOME TWISTED PARODY OF JUSTICE, THE PRESIDENT HAS ORDERED MY APPREHENSION--
--CLAIMING THAT I AM INCITING YOU ALL TO RIOT --TO TURN AGAINST THE PRECIOUS VALUES I SEEK ONLY TO PRESERVE!
DO YOU BELIEVE THE PRESIDENT IS RIGHT, MY FRIENDS?
NO!
SPEAK TO US, GODFREY!
NEVER!
SPEAK FOR US!!
I HEAR YOU, MY PEOPLE-- AND I ACCEPT YOUR MANDATE!
A GOVERNMENT THAT DOES NOT REPRESENT ITS PEOPLE DOES NOT SERVE ITS PEOPLE!
SUCH AN EVIL GOVERNMENT MUST BE OVERTHROWN!
BUT HOW, GODFREY-- HOW??
WITH THE HELP OF THESE, MY PEOPLE--THESE SYMBOLS OF THE NEW JUSTICE!
NOW WHO AMONG YOU WILL BE THE FIRST TO LEND HIS HEART, HIS MIND, HIS SOUL--TO THE CAUSE OF A NEW AMERICA?
WHO WILL BE THE FIRST TO BECOME-- A WARHOUND!
18

NEW YORK CITY: WHERE THE RANDOM RIOTING IN THE CROWDED STREETS HAS SUDDENLY BEGUN TO PALE BEFORE VIOLENCE OF A FAR MORE CALCULATING KIND...

THAT'S *RIGHT*, YOU BLEEDIN' COBBERS-- *RUN!*

RUN LIKE YOUR MISERABLE *LIVES* DEPENDED ON IT--'CAUSE THEY *DO!*

AS OF *NOW*, THIS STREET BELONGS T'-- *CAPTAIN BOOMERANG!*

STILL CAN'T BELIEVE THEM *OTHER* JACKS WOULDN'T COME *WITH* ME WHEN I QUIT FLAG'S *SUICIDE SQUAD--!*

BUT, *HEY* --THAT'S *THEIR* LOSS!

BOOM!

CHOOM!

WHOOM!

"I GOT MORE *IMPORTANT* THINGS TO CONCERN ME RIGHT NOW--

GEMW...

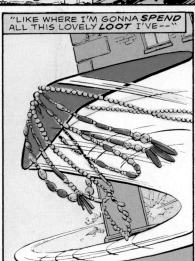

"LIKE WHERE I'M GONNA *SPEND* ALL THIS LOVELY *LOOT* I'VE--"

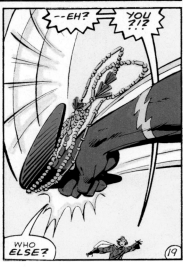

--EH?

YOU ?!?

WHO ELSE?

19

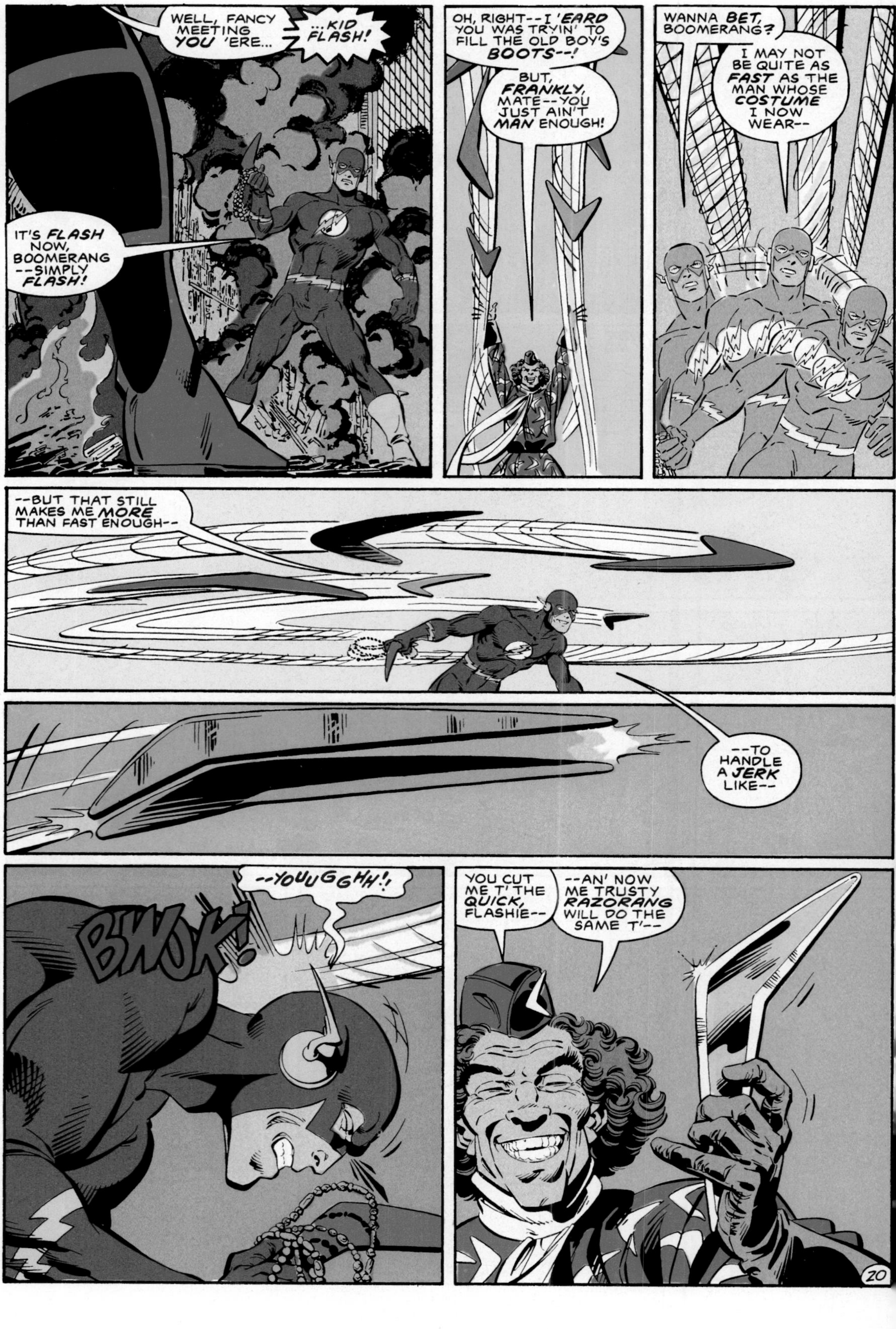

WELL, FANCY MEETING YOU 'ERE...
...KID FLASH!
IT'S FLASH NOW, BOOMERANG --SIMPLY FLASH!
OH, RIGHT--I 'EARD YOU WAS TRYIN' TO FILL THE OLD BOY'S BOOTS--!
BUT, FRANKLY, MATE--YOU JUST AIN'T MAN ENOUGH!
WANNA BET, BOOMERANG?
I MAY NOT BE QUITE AS FAST AS THE MAN WHOSE COSTUME I NOW WEAR--
--BUT THAT STILL MAKES ME MORE THAN FAST ENOUGH--
--TO HANDLE A JERK LIKE--
--YOUUGGHH!!
BWOK!
YOU CUT ME T' THE QUICK, FLASHIE--
--AN' NOW ME TRUSTY RAZORANG WILL DO THE SAME T'--

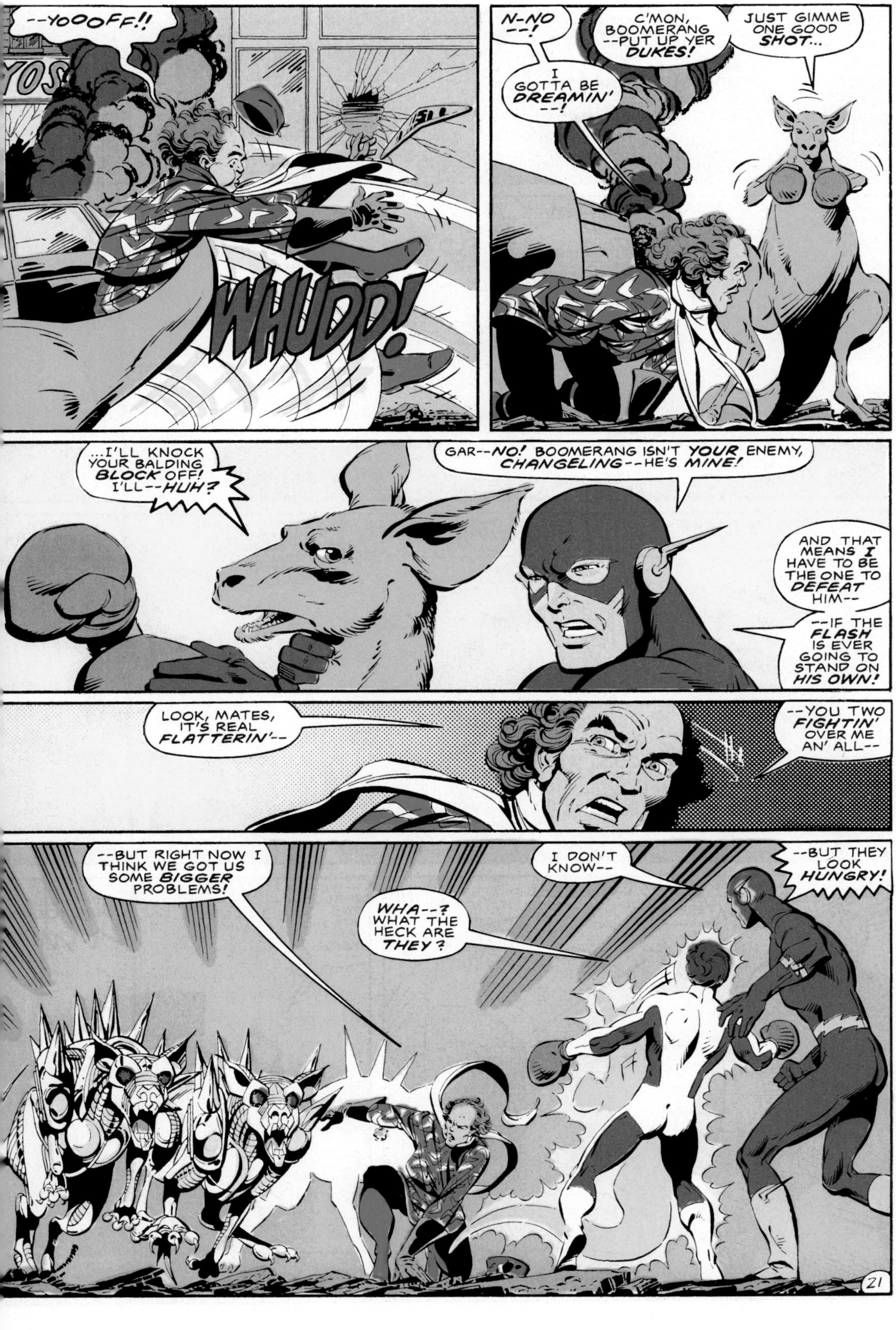
--YOOOFF!!
WHUDD!
N-NO --!
I GOTTA BE DREAMIN' --!
C'MON, BOOMERANG --PUT UP YER DUKES!
JUST GIMME ONE GOOD SHOT...
...I'LL KNOCK YOUR BALDING BLOCK OFF! I'LL--HUH?
GAR--NO! BOOMERANG ISN'T YOUR ENEMY, CHANGELING--HE'S MINE!
AND THAT MEANS I HAVE TO BE THE ONE TO DEFEAT HIM--
--IF THE FLASH IS EVER GOING TO STAND ON HIS OWN!
LOOK, MATES, IT'S REAL FLATTERIN'--
--YOU TWO FIGHTIN' OVER ME AN' ALL--
--BUT RIGHT NOW I THINK WE GOT US SOME BIGGER PROBLEMS!
WHA--? WHAT THE HECK ARE THEY?
I DON'T KNOW--
--BUT THEY LOOK HUNGRY!

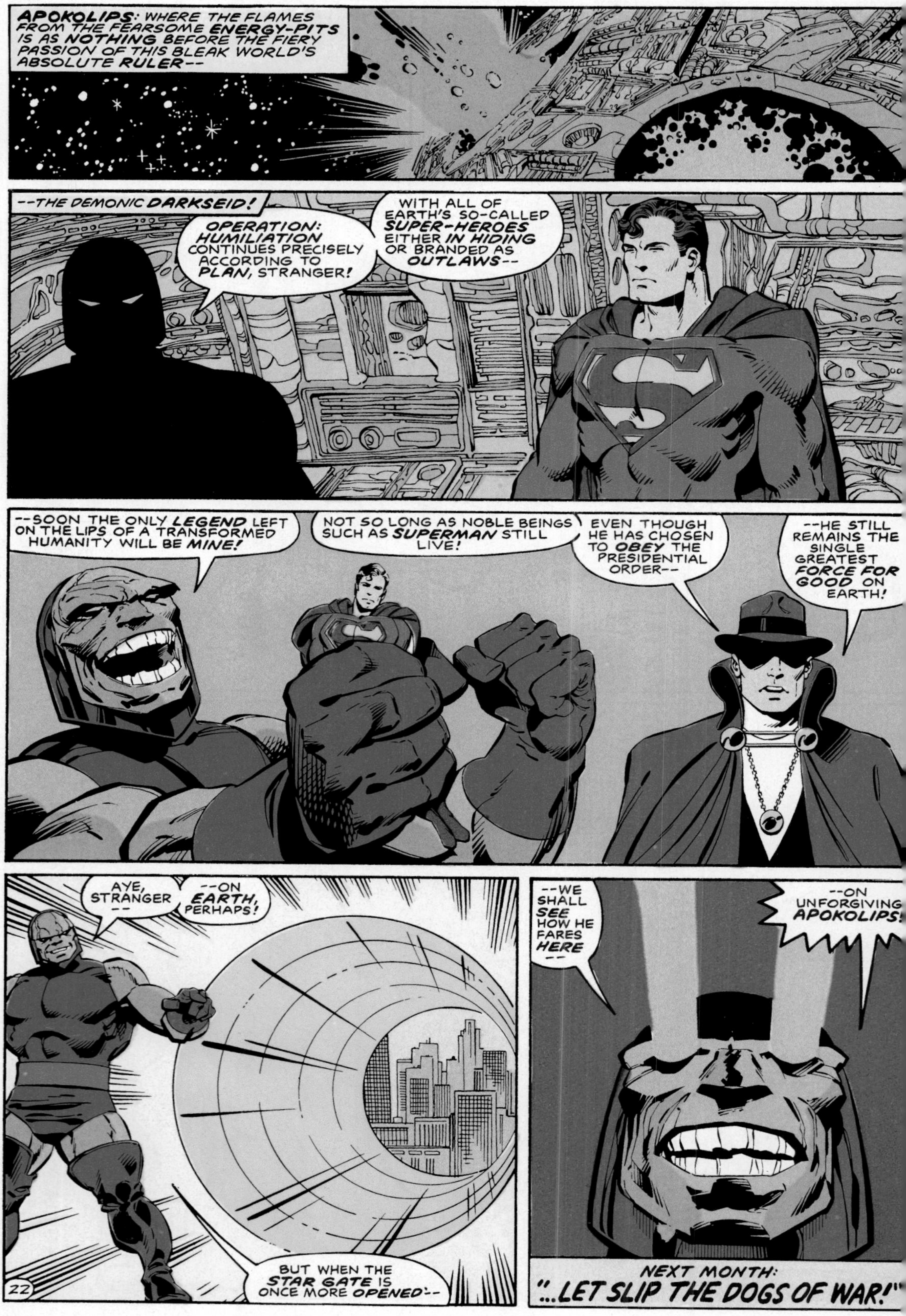
APOKOLIPS: WHERE THE FLAMES FROM THE FEARSOME ENERGY-PITS IS AS NOTHING BEFORE THE FIERY PASSION OF THIS BLEAK WORLD'S ABSOLUTE RULER--
--THE DEMONIC DARKSEID!
OPERATION: HUMILIATION CONTINUES PRECISELY ACCORDING TO PLAN, STRANGER!
WITH ALL OF EARTH'S SO-CALLED SUPER-HEROES EITHER IN HIDING OR BRANDED AS OUTLAWS--
--SOON THE ONLY LEGEND LEFT ON THE LIPS OF A TRANSFORMED HUMANITY WILL BE MINE!
NOT SO LONG AS NOBLE BEINGS SUCH AS SUPERMAN STILL LIVE!
EVEN THOUGH HE HAS CHOSEN TO OBEY THE PRESIDENTIAL ORDER--
--HE STILL REMAINS THE SINGLE GREATEST FORCE FOR GOOD ON EARTH!
AYE, STRANGER --
--ON EARTH, PERHAPS!
BUT WHEN THE STAR GATE IS ONCE MORE OPENED--
--WE SHALL SEE HOW HE FARES HERE --
--ON UNFORGIVING APOKOLIPS!
NEXT MONTH:
"...LET SLIP THE DOGS OF WAR!"

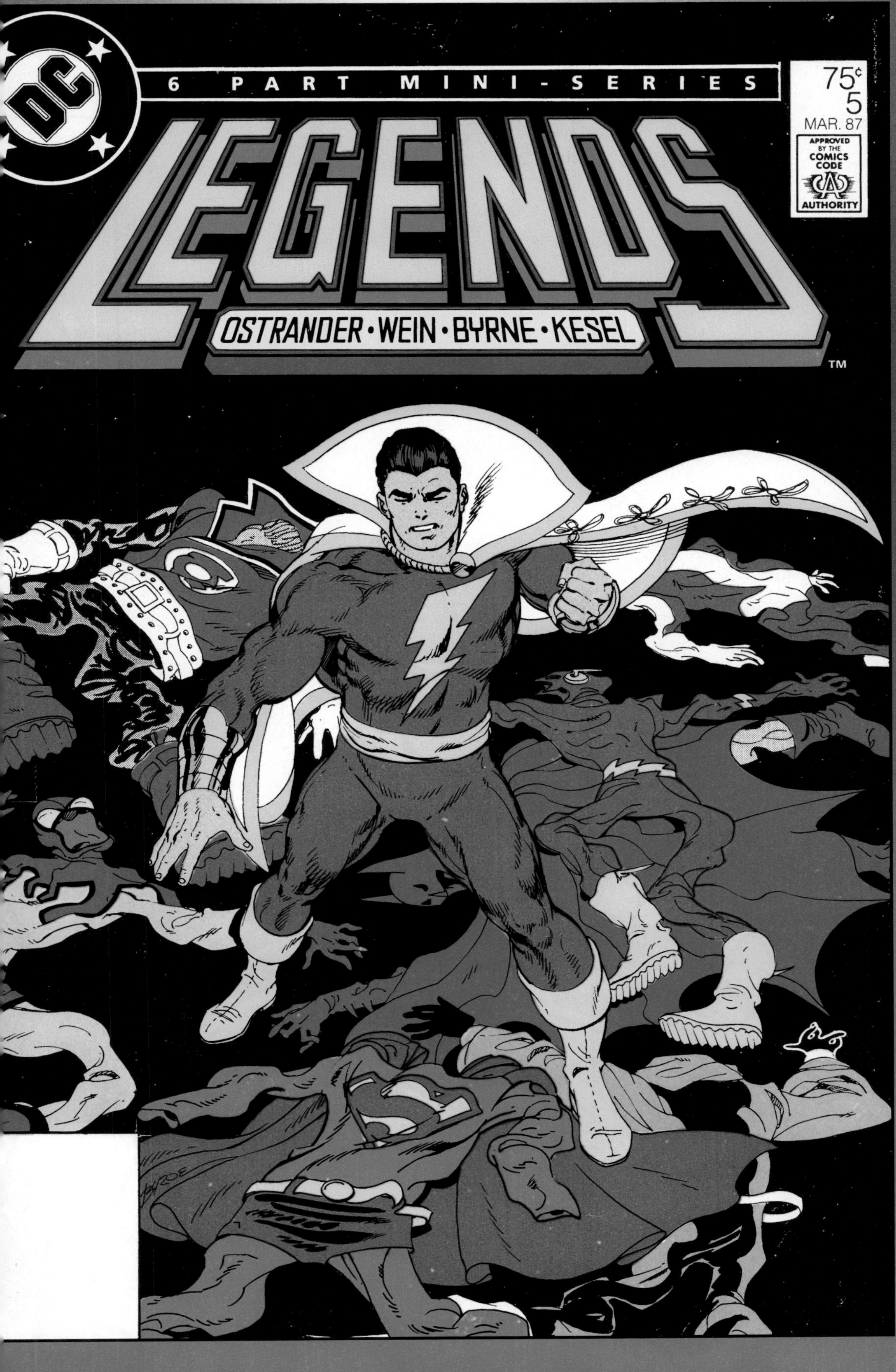
DC
6 PART MINI-SERIES
75¢
5
MAR. 87
APPROVED BY THE COMICS CODE AUTHORITY
LEGENDS
OSTRANDER • WEIN • BYRNE • KESEL
TM

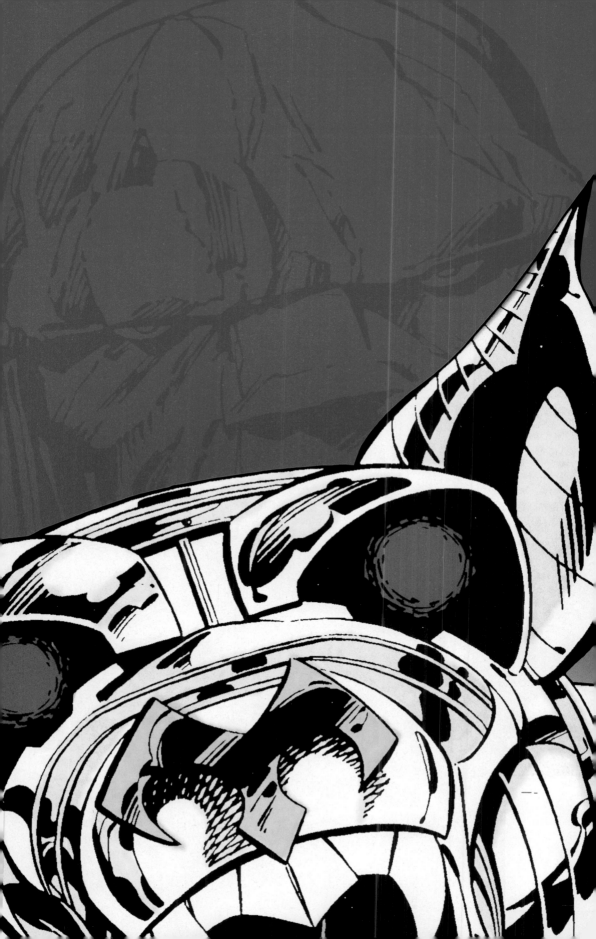

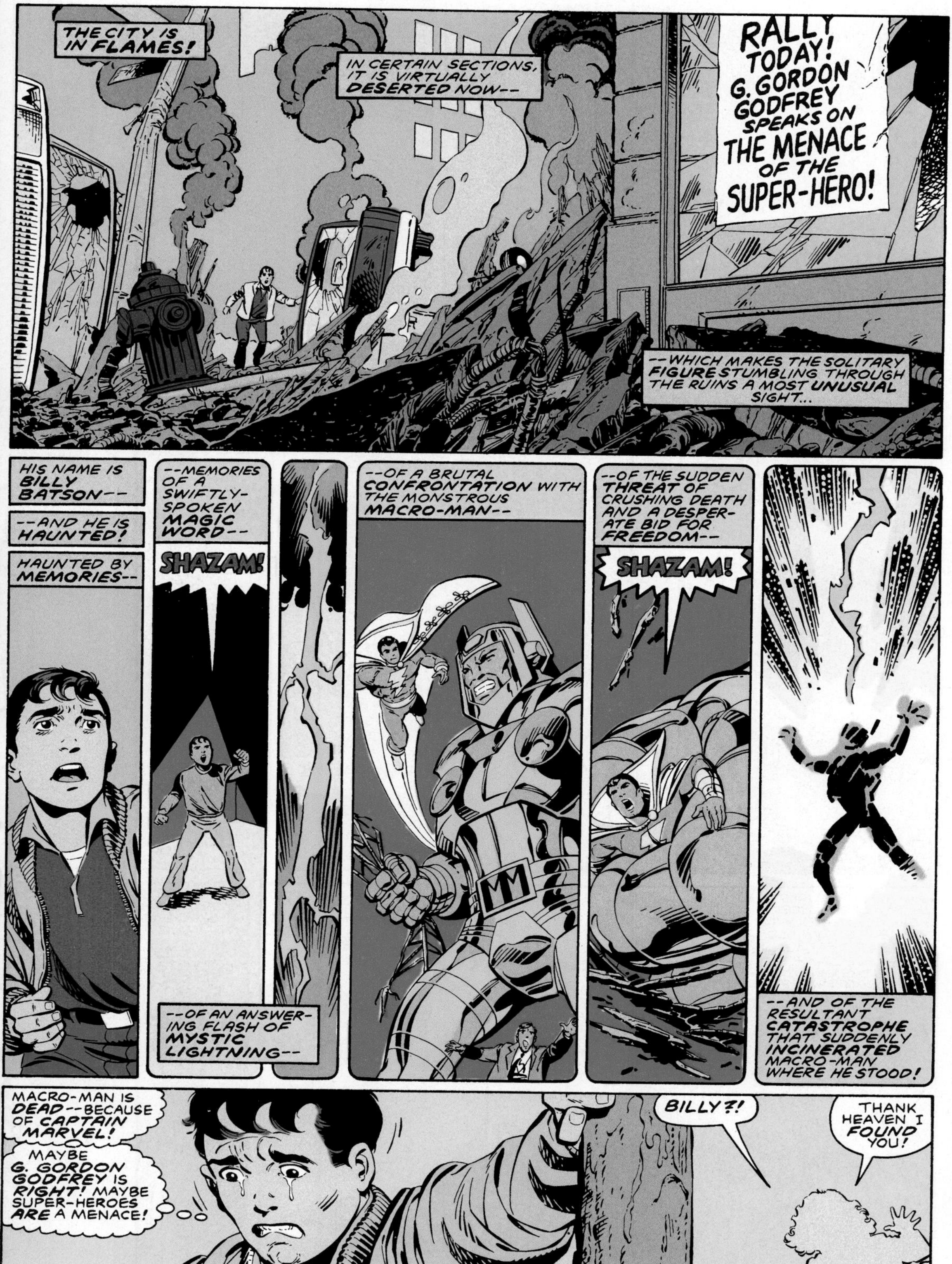
THE CITY IS IN FLAMES!
IN CERTAIN SECTIONS, IT IS VIRTUALLY DESERTED NOW--
RALLY TODAY! G. GORDON GODFREY SPEAKS ON THE MENACE OF THE SUPER-HERO!
--WHICH MAKES THE SOLITARY FIGURE STUMBLING THROUGH THE RUINS A MOST UNUSUAL SIGHT...
HIS NAME IS BILLY BATSON--
--AND HE IS HAUNTED!
HAUNTED BY MEMORIES--
--MEMORIES OF A SWIFTLY-SPOKEN MAGIC WORD--
SHAZAM!
--OF AN ANSWERING FLASH OF MYSTIC LIGHTNING--
--OF A BRUTAL CONFRONTATION WITH THE MONSTROUS MACRO-MAN--
--OF THE SUDDEN THREAT OF CRUSHING DEATH AND A DESPERATE BID FOR FREEDOM--
SHAZAM!
--AND OF THE RESULTANT CATASTROPHE THAT SUDDENLY INCINERATED MACRO-MAN WHERE HE STOOD!
MACRO-MAN IS DEAD--BECAUSE OF CAPTAIN MARVEL!
MAYBE G. GORDON GODFREY IS RIGHT! MAYBE SUPER-HEROES ARE A MENACE!
BILLY?!
THANK HEAVEN I FOUND YOU!
1

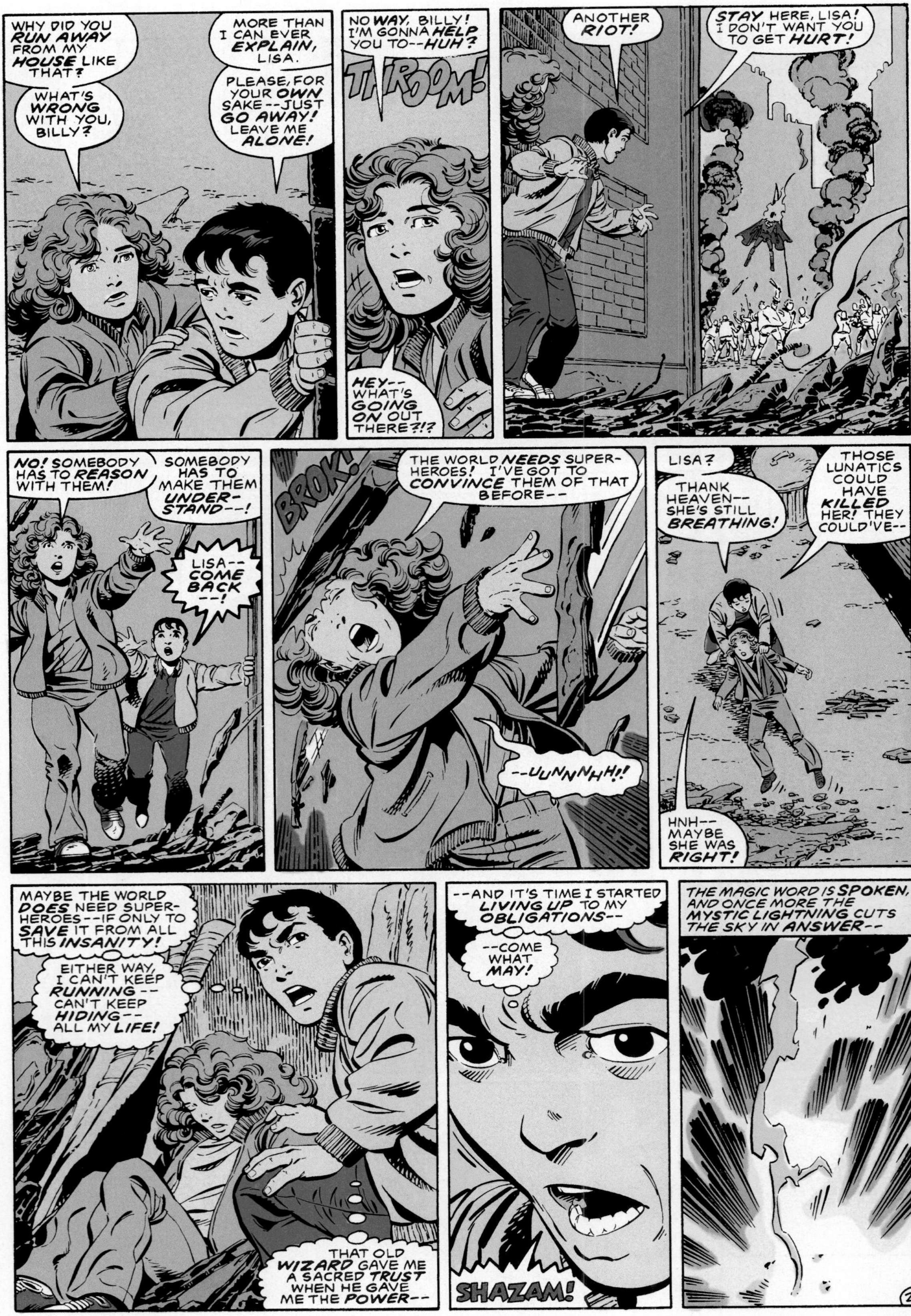
WHY DID YOU RUN AWAY FROM MY HOUSE LIKE THAT?
WHAT'S WRONG WITH YOU, BILLY?
MORE THAN I CAN EVER EXPLAIN, LISA.
PLEASE, FOR YOUR OWN SAKE--JUST GO AWAY! LEAVE ME ALONE!
NO WAY, BILLY! I'M GONNA HELP YOU TO--HUH?
THROOOM!
HEY--WHAT'S GOING ON OUT THERE?!?
ANOTHER RIOT!
STAY HERE, LISA! I DON'T WANT YOU TO GET HURT!
NO! SOMEBODY HAS TO REASON WITH THEM!
SOMEBODY HAS TO MAKE THEM UNDER-STAND--!
LISA--COME BACK--!
BROK!
THE WORLD NEEDS SUPER-HEROES! I'VE GOT TO CONVINCE THEM OF THAT BEFORE--
--UUNNNHH!!
LISA?
THANK HEAVEN--SHE'S STILL BREATHING!
THOSE LUNATICS COULD HAVE KILLED HER! THEY COULD'VE--
HNH--MAYBE SHE WAS RIGHT!
MAYBE THE WORLD DOES NEED SUPER-HEROES--IF ONLY TO SAVE IT FROM ALL THIS INSANITY!
EITHER WAY, I CAN'T KEEP RUNNING--CAN'T KEEP HIDING--ALL MY LIFE!
THAT OLD WIZARD GAVE ME A SACRED TRUST WHEN HE GAVE ME THE POWER--
--AND IT'S TIME I STARTED LIVING UP TO MY OBLIGATIONS--
--COME WHAT MAY!
SHAZAM!
THE MAGIC WORD IS SPOKEN, AND ONCE MORE THE MYSTIC LIGHTNING CUTS THE SKY IN ANSWER--

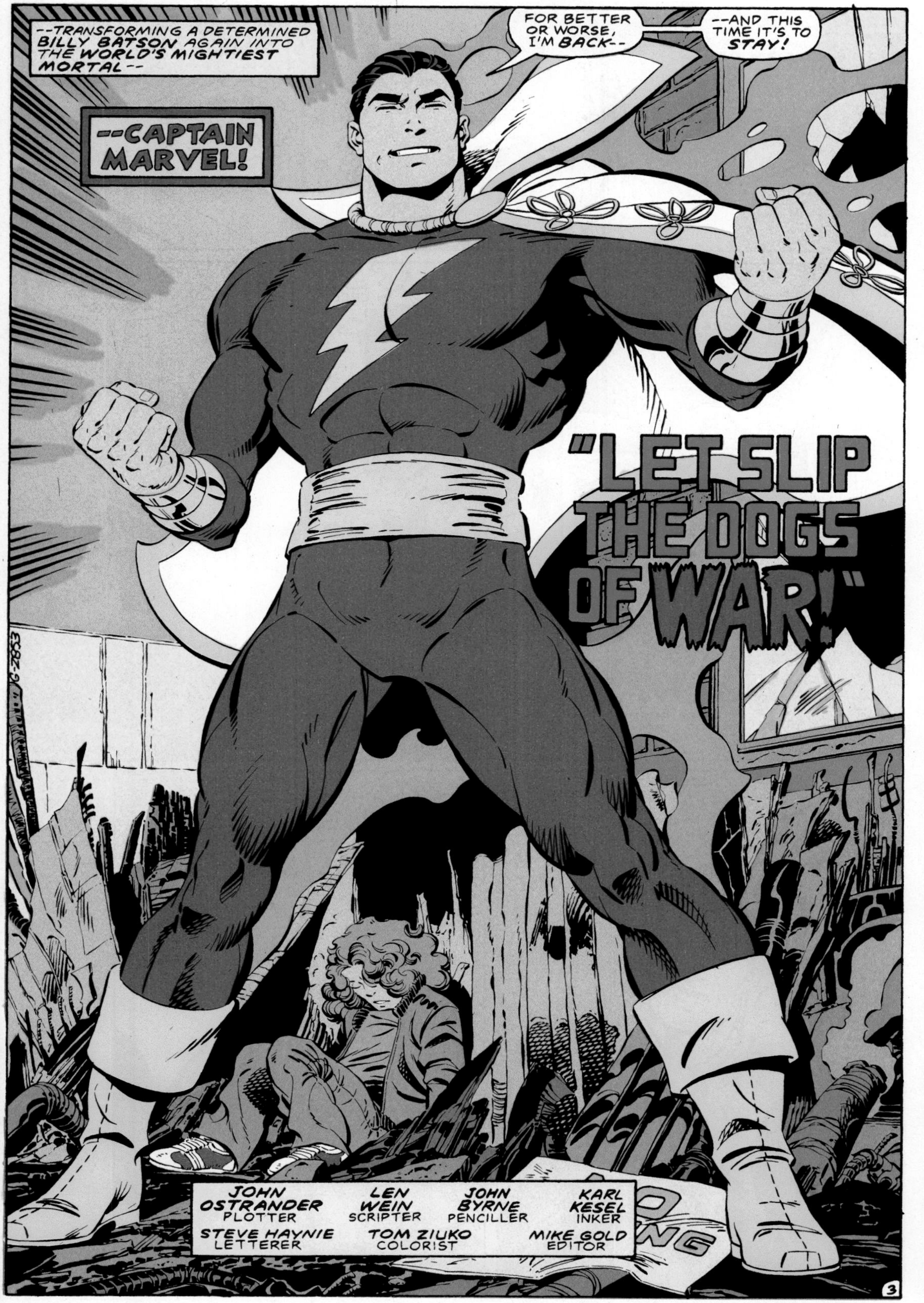
--TRANSFORMING A DETERMINED BILLY BATSON AGAIN INTO THE WORLD'S MIGHTIEST MORTAL--
FOR BETTER OR WORSE, I'M BACK--
--AND THIS TIME IT'S TO STAY!
--CAPTAIN MARVEL!
"LET SLIP THE DOGS OF WAR!"
JOHN OSTRANDER PLOTTER
LEN WEIN SCRIPTER
JOHN BYRNE PENCILLER
KARL KESEL INKER
STEVE HAYNIE LETTERER
TOM ZIUKO COLORIST
MIKE GOLD EDITOR
3

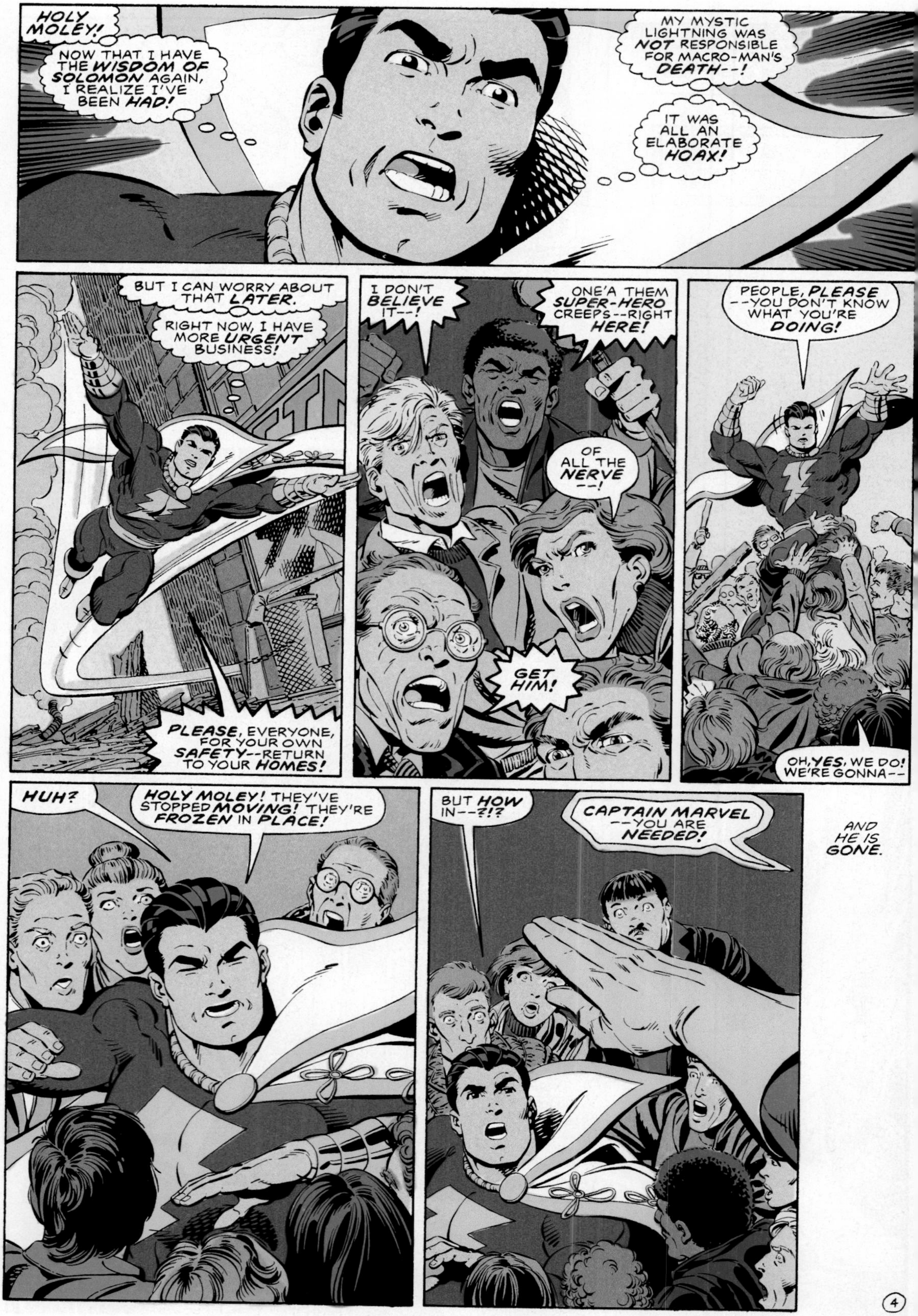
HOLY MOLEY!
NOW THAT I HAVE THE WISDOM OF SOLOMON AGAIN, I REALIZE I'VE BEEN HAD!
MY MYSTIC LIGHTNING WAS NOT RESPONSIBLE FOR MACRO-MAN'S DEATH--!
IT WAS ALL AN ELABORATE HOAX!
BUT I CAN WORRY ABOUT THAT LATER.
RIGHT NOW, I HAVE MORE URGENT BUSINESS!
PLEASE, EVERYONE, FOR YOUR OWN SAFETY--RETURN TO YOUR HOMES!
I DON'T BELIEVE IT--!
ONE'A THEM SUPER-HERO CREEPS--RIGHT HERE!
OF ALL THE NERVE--!
GET HIM!
PEOPLE, PLEASE--YOU DON'T KNOW WHAT YOU'RE DOING!
OH, YES, WE DO! WE'RE GONNA--
HUH?
HOLY MOLEY! THEY'VE STOPPED MOVING! THEY'RE FROZEN IN PLACE!
BUT HOW IN--?!?
CAPTAIN MARVEL--YOU ARE NEEDED!
AND HE IS GONE.

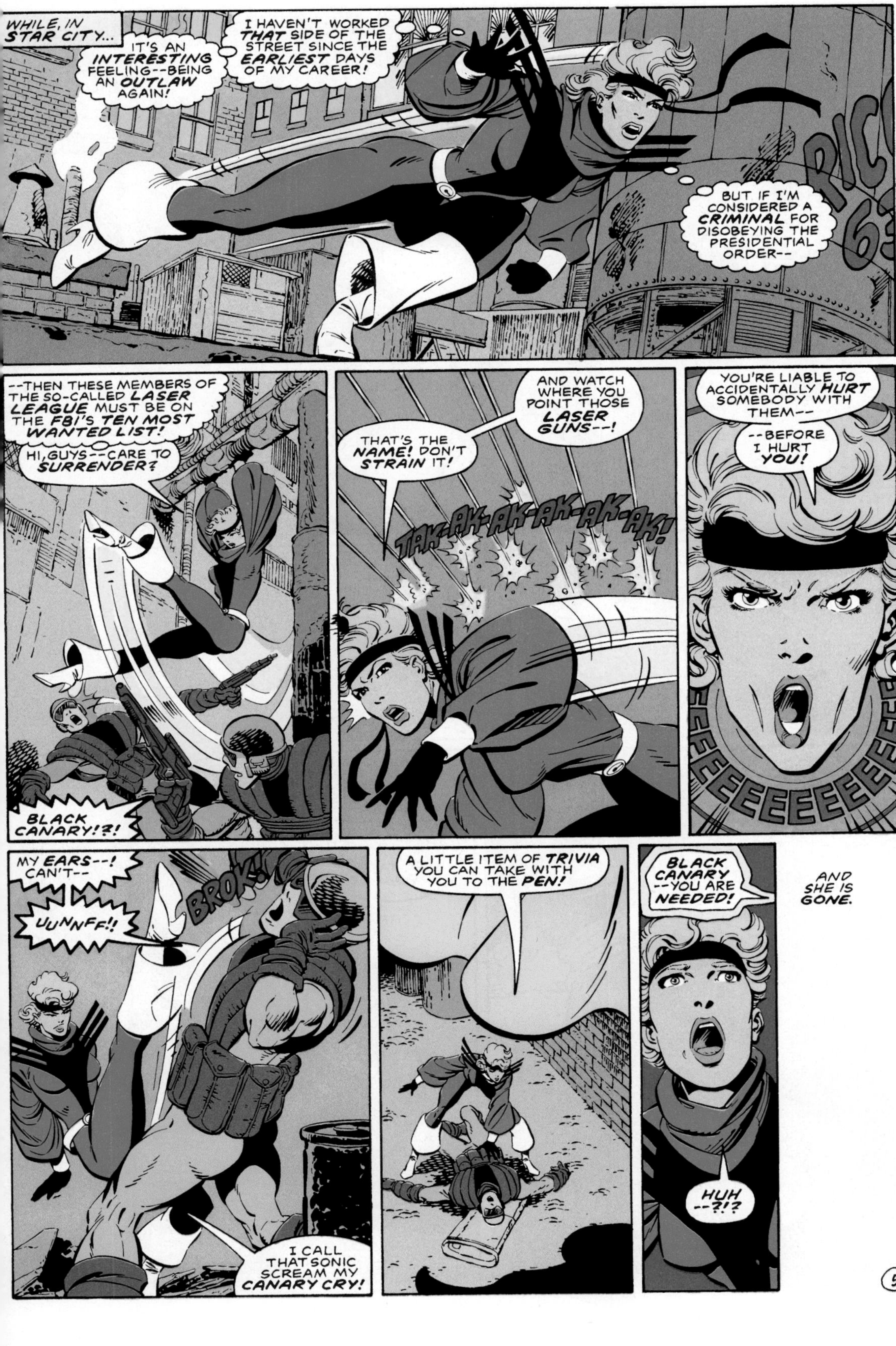
WHILE, IN STAR CITY...
IT'S AN INTERESTING FEELING--BEING AN OUTLAW AGAIN!
I HAVEN'T WORKED THAT SIDE OF THE STREET SINCE THE EARLIEST DAYS OF MY CAREER!
BUT IF I'M CONSIDERED A CRIMINAL FOR DISOBEYING THE PRESIDENTIAL ORDER--
--THEN THESE MEMBERS OF THE SO-CALLED LASER LEAGUE MUST BE ON THE FBI'S TEN MOST WANTED LIST!
HI, GUYS--CARE TO SURRENDER?
BLACK CANARY!?!
THAT'S THE NAME! DON'T STRAIN IT!
AND WATCH WHERE YOU POINT THOSE LASER GUNS--!
TAK-AK-AK-AK-AK-AK!
YOU'RE LIABLE TO ACCIDENTALLY HURT SOMEBODY WITH THEM--
--BEFORE I HURT YOU!
EEEEEEEEEEEEEEEEE
MY EARS--! CAN'T--
BROK!
UUNNFF!!
I CALL THAT SONIC SCREAM MY CANARY CRY!
A LITTLE ITEM OF TRIVIA YOU CAN TAKE WITH YOU TO THE PEN!
BLACK CANARY--YOU ARE NEEDED!
HUH--?!?
AND SHE IS GONE.

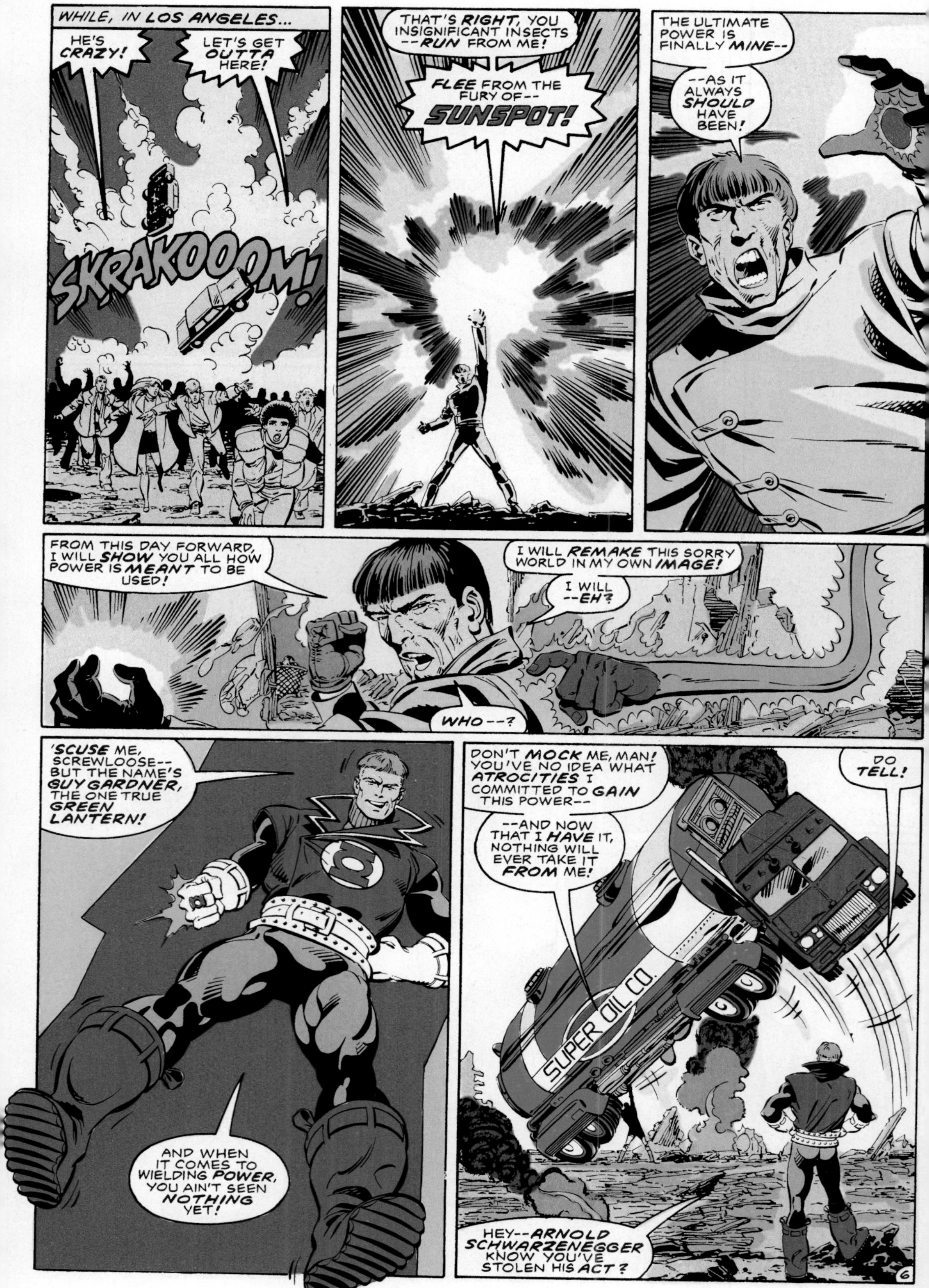
WHILE, IN LOS ANGELES...
HE'S CRAZY!
LET'S GET OUTTA HERE!
SKRAKOOOM!
THAT'S RIGHT, YOU INSIGNIFICANT INSECTS --RUN FROM ME!
FLEE FROM THE FURY OF-- SUNSPOT!
THE ULTIMATE POWER IS FINALLY MINE--
--AS IT ALWAYS SHOULD HAVE BEEN!
FROM THIS DAY FORWARD, I WILL SHOW YOU ALL HOW POWER IS MEANT TO BE USED!
I WILL REMAKE THIS SORRY WORLD IN MY OWN IMAGE!
I WILL --EH?
WHO--?
'SCUSE ME, SCREWLOOSE-- BUT THE NAME'S GUY GARDNER, THE ONE TRUE GREEN LANTERN!
AND WHEN IT COMES TO WIELDING POWER, YOU AIN'T SEEN NOTHING YET!
DON'T MOCK ME, MAN! YOU'VE NO IDEA WHAT ATROCITIES I COMMITTED TO GAIN THIS POWER--
--AND NOW THAT I HAVE IT, NOTHING WILL EVER TAKE IT FROM ME!
DO TELL!
SUPER OIL CO.
HEY--ARNOLD SCHWARZENEGGER KNOW YOU'VE STOLEN HIS ACT?
6

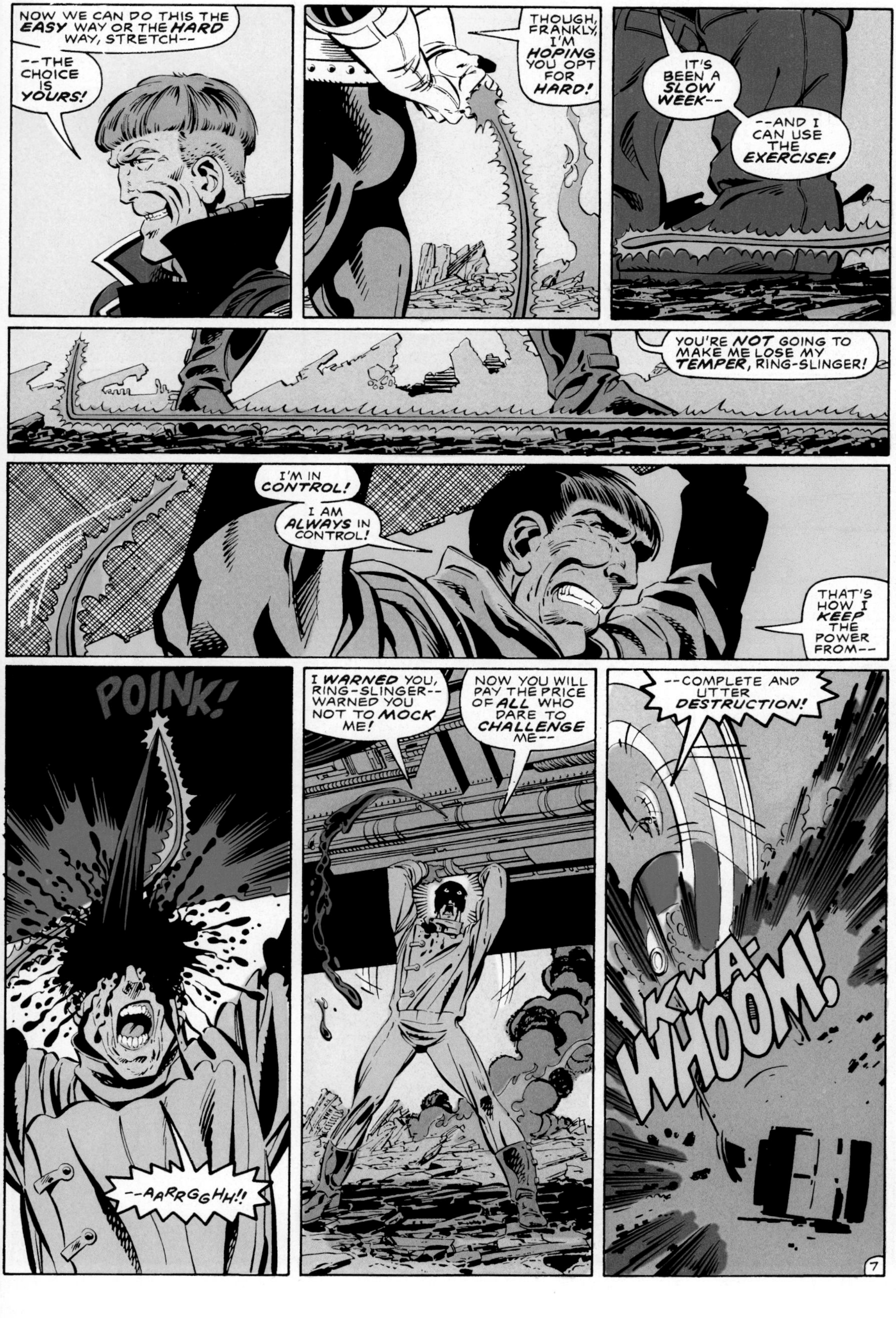
NOW WE CAN DO THIS THE EASY WAY OR THE HARD WAY, STRETCH--
--THE CHOICE IS YOURS!
THOUGH, FRANKLY, I'M HOPING YOU OPT FOR HARD!
IT'S BEEN A SLOW WEEK--
--AND I CAN USE THE EXERCISE!
YOU'RE NOT GOING TO MAKE ME LOSE MY TEMPER, RING-SLINGER!
I'M IN CONTROL!
I AM ALWAYS IN CONTROL!
THAT'S HOW I KEEP THE POWER FROM--
POINK!
--AARRGGHH!!
I WARNED YOU, RING-SLINGER-- WARNED YOU NOT TO MOCK ME!
NOW YOU WILL PAY THE PRICE OF ALL WHO DARE TO CHALLENGE ME--
--COMPLETE AND UTTER DESTRUCTION!
KWA-WHOOM!

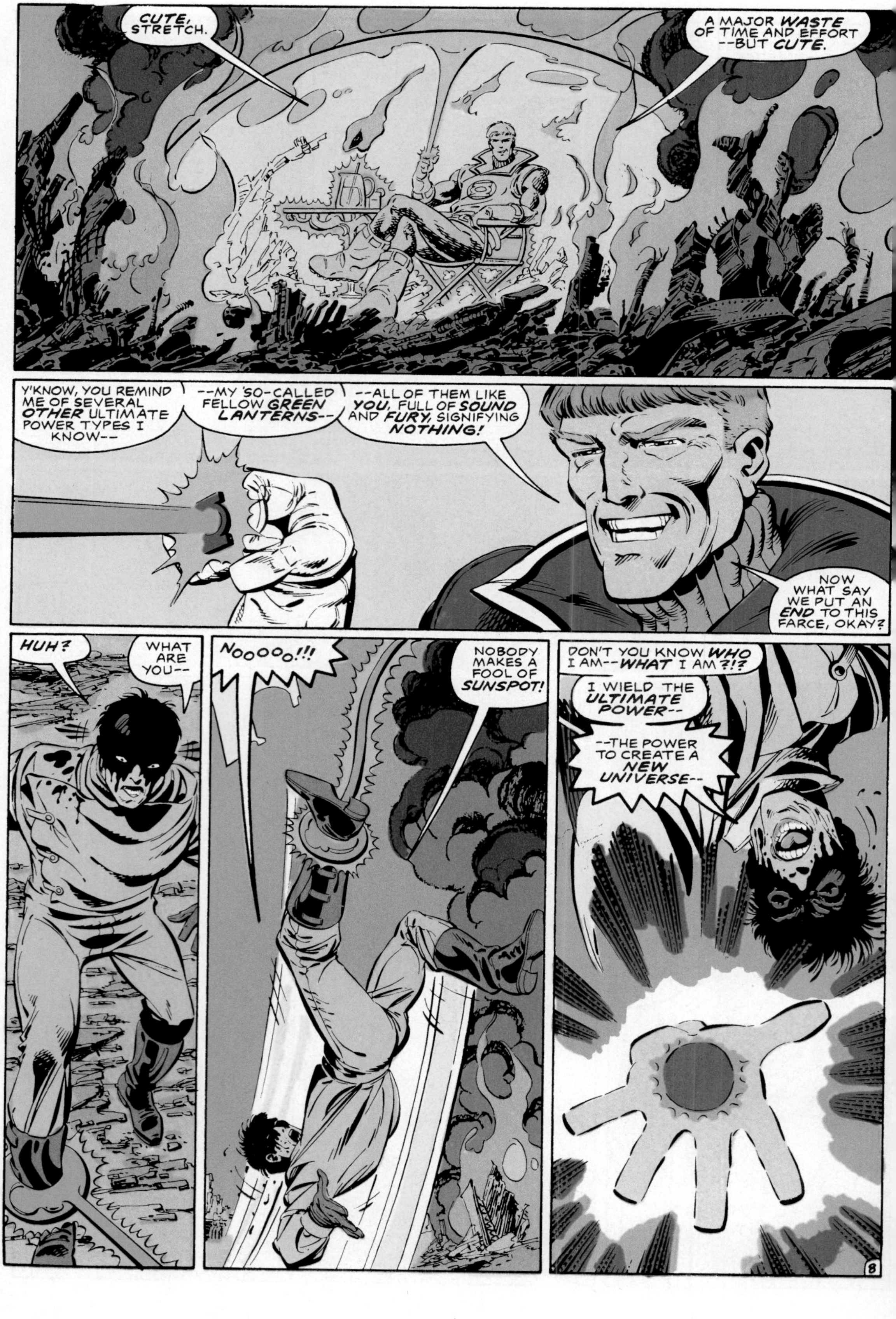

CUTE, STRETCH.
A MAJOR WASTE OF TIME AND EFFORT --BUT CUTE.
Y'KNOW, YOU REMIND ME OF SEVERAL OTHER ULTIMATE POWER TYPES I KNOW--
--MY 'SO-CALLED FELLOW GREEN LANTERNS--
--ALL OF THEM LIKE YOU, FULL OF SOUND AND FURY, SIGNIFYING NOTHING!
NOW WHAT SAY WE PUT AN END TO THIS FARCE, OKAY?
HUH?
WHAT ARE YOU--
NOOOOO!!!
NOBODY MAKES A FOOL OF SUNSPOT!
DON'T YOU KNOW WHO I AM--WHAT I AM?!?
I WIELD THE ULTIMATE POWER--
--THE POWER TO CREATE A NEW UNIVERSE--
8

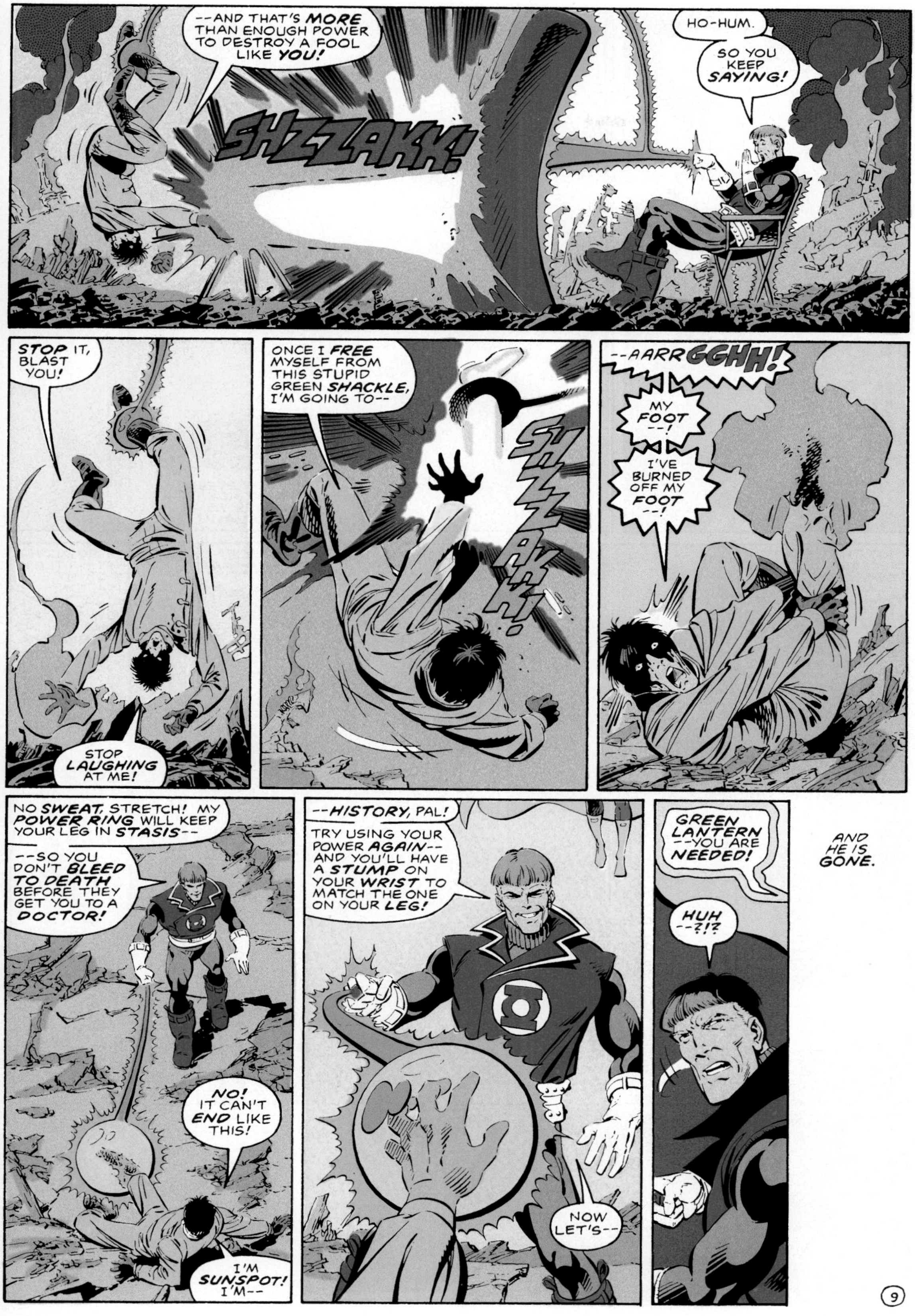

--AND THAT'S MORE THAN ENOUGH POWER TO DESTROY A FOOL LIKE YOU!
SHZZAKK!
HO-HUM.
SO YOU KEEP SAYING!
STOP IT, BLAST YOU!
STOP LAUGHING AT ME!
ONCE I FREE MYSELF FROM THIS STUPID GREEN SHACKLE, I'M GOING TO--
SHZZAKK!
--AARRGGHH!
MY FOOT--!
I'VE BURNED OFF MY FOOT--!
NO SWEAT, STRETCH! MY POWER RING WILL KEEP YOUR LEG IN STASIS--
--SO YOU DON'T BLEED TO DEATH BEFORE THEY GET YOU TO A DOCTOR!
NO! IT CAN'T END LIKE THIS!
I'M SUNSPOT! I'M--
--HISTORY, PAL!
TRY USING YOUR POWER AGAIN--AND YOU'LL HAVE A STUMP ON YOUR WRIST TO MATCH THE ONE ON YOUR LEG!
NOW LET'S--
GREEN LANTERN--YOU ARE NEEDED!
HUH--?!?
AND HE IS GONE.

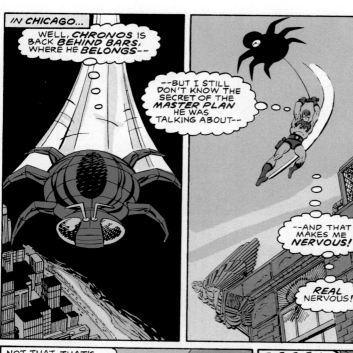

IN CHICAGO...

WELL, *CHRONOS* IS BACK *BEHIND BARS*, WHERE HE *BELONGS*--

--BUT I STILL DON'T KNOW THE SECRET OF THE *MASTER PLAN* HE WAS TALKING ABOUT--

--AND THAT MAKES ME *NERVOUS!*

REAL NERVOUS!

I DEFIED THE *EXECUTIVE ORDER* SO I COULD TRACK DOWN THAT TREACHEROUS *TIME-THIEF*--

--SO I GUESS THAT NOW MAKES ME AN *OUTLAW!*

NOT THAT THAT'S NECESSARILY SUCH A *TERRIBLE* THING, MIND YOU!

I MEAN, IT PUTS ME IN PRETTY CHOICE *COMPANY*...

...ROBIN HOOD... WILLIAM TELL... ZORRO...THE SCARLET PIMPERNEL...

I COULD THINK OF *WORSE* FOLKS TO BE COMPARED TO!

EEEEEEEK!

IT'S A *PEEPING TOM!*

POLICE! POLICE!!!

OOPS.

UHHH-- *SORRY* ABOUT THAT, LADY.

'BYE NOW.

GREAT! SO MUCH FOR WHAT LITTLE IS *LEFT* OF MY REPUTATION!

NOW THEY'RE GONNA CALL ME A *PERVERT!*

CUTE *TUSH,* THOUGH.

AND HE IS GONE.

BLUE BEETLE --YOU ARE *NEEDED!*

HUH --?!?

GOTHAM CITY...

IT IS *QUIET*--

--FOR THE *MOMENT*.

BUT IT'S NOT GOING TO *LAST*--

--NOT SO LONG AS *G. GORDON GODFREY* KEEPS STIRRING THE PEOPLE UP *AGAINST* US!

IN *MY* CASE, ACCOMPLISHING THAT WAS *EASY*-- --I'VE ALWAYS *WANTED* THE PEOPLE TO *FEAR* ME--

--BUT TO TURN THEM AGAINST *SUPERMAN*, AND SOME OF THE REST--?

THERE'S A LOT *MORE* TO THIS THAN THE *OBVIOUS*--

--SOMETHING *UNREAL*, SOMETHING *UNNATURAL*--

--AND IT'S TIME I FOUND OUT EXACTLY *WHAT* THAT SOMETHING *IS!*

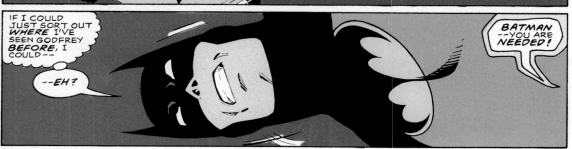

IF I COULD JUST SORT OUT *WHERE* I'VE SEEN GODFREY *BEFORE*, I COULD--

--EH?

BATMAN --YOU ARE *NEEDED!*

AND HE IS *GONE*.

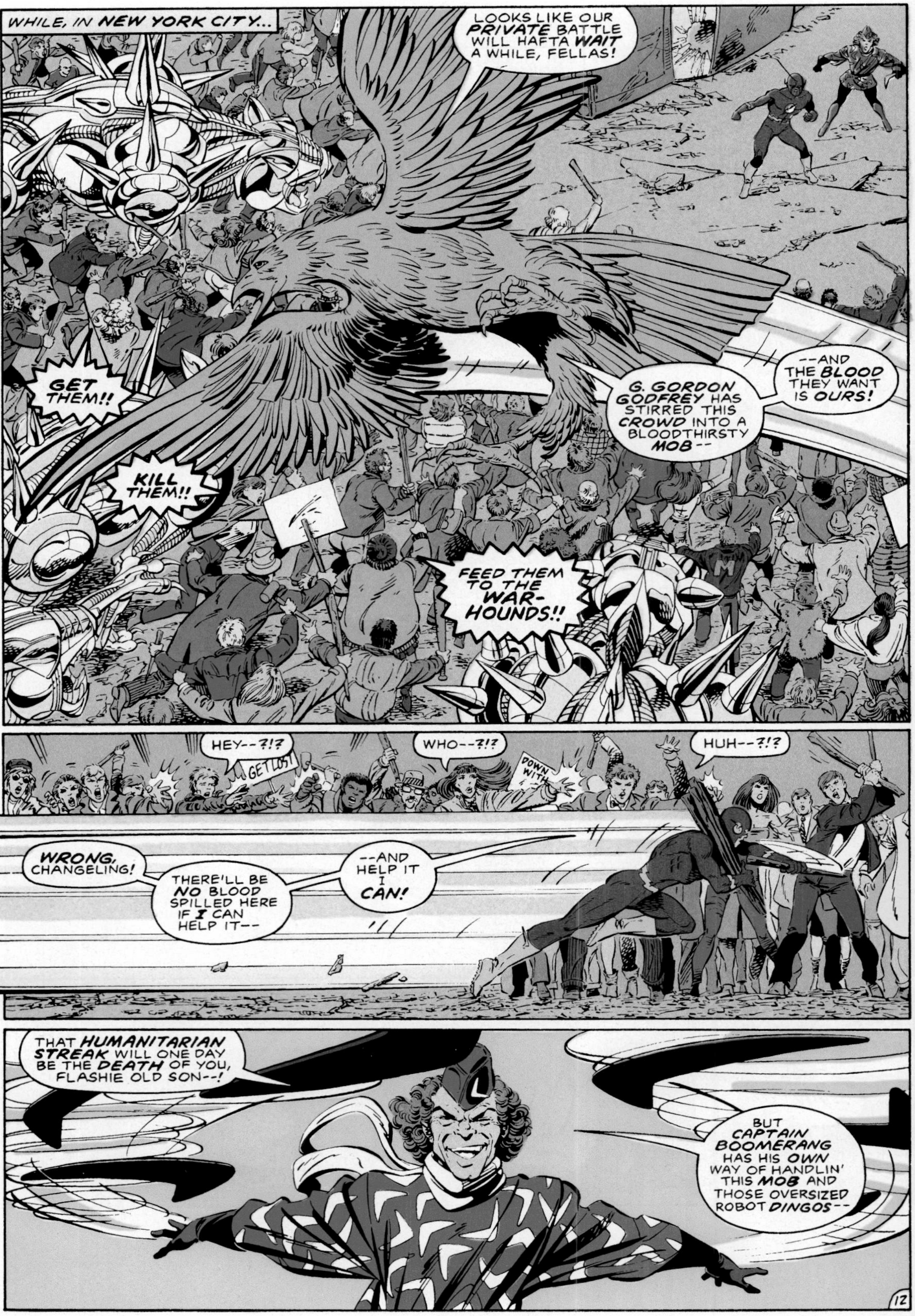
WHILE, IN NEW YORK CITY...
LOOKS LIKE OUR PRIVATE BATTLE WILL HAFTA WAIT A WHILE, FELLAS!
GET THEM!!
KILL THEM!!
G. GORDON GODFREY HAS STIRRED THIS CROWD INTO A BLOODTHIRSTY MOB--
--AND THE BLOOD THEY WANT IS OURS!
FEED THEM TO THE WAR-HOUNDS!!
HEY--?!?
GET LOST
WHO--?!?
DOWN WITH
HUH--?!?
WRONG, CHANGELING!
THERE'LL BE NO BLOOD SPILLED HERE IF I CAN HELP IT--
--AND HELP IT I CAN!
THAT HUMANITARIAN STREAK WILL ONE DAY BE THE DEATH OF YOU, FLASHIE OLD SON--!
BUT CAPTAIN BOOMERANG HAS HIS OWN WAY OF HANDLIN' THIS MOB AND THOSE OVERSIZED ROBOT DINGOS--
12

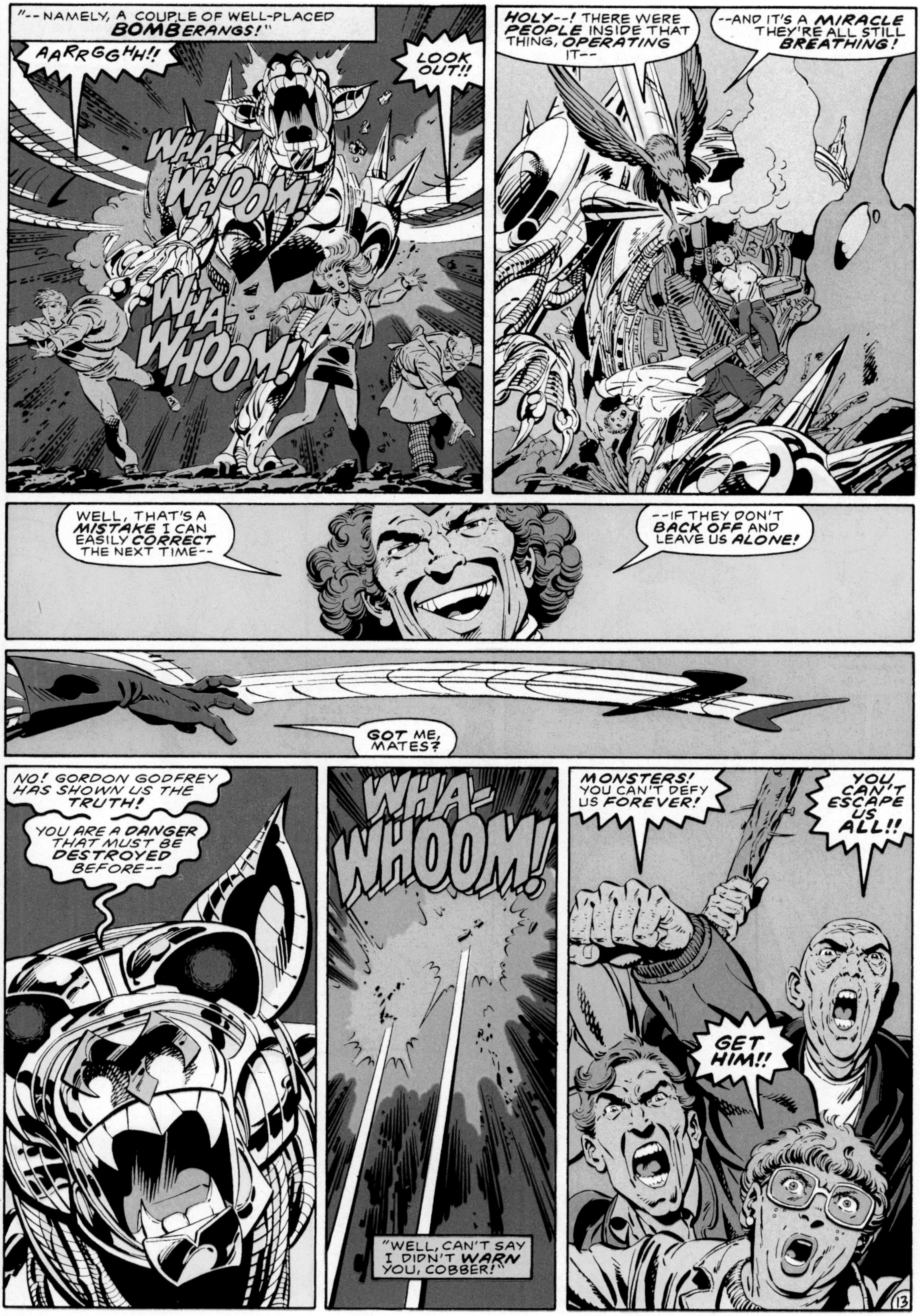
"--NAMELY, A COUPLE OF WELL-PLACED BOMBERANGS!"
AARRGGHH!!
LOOK OUT!!
WHA-WHOOM!
WHA-WHOOM!
HOLY--! THERE WERE PEOPLE INSIDE THAT THING, OPERATING IT--
--AND IT'S A MIRACLE THEY'RE ALL STILL BREATHING!
WELL, THAT'S A MISTAKE I CAN EASILY CORRECT THE NEXT TIME--
--IF THEY DON'T BACK OFF AND LEAVE US ALONE!
GOT ME, MATES?
NO! GORDON GODFREY HAS SHOWN US THE TRUTH!
YOU ARE A DANGER THAT MUST BE DESTROYED BEFORE--
WHA-WHOOM!
"WELL, CAN'T SAY I DIDN'T WARN YOU, COBBER!"
MONSTERS! YOU CAN'T DEFY US FOREVER!
YOU CAN'T ESCAPE US ALL!!
GET HIM!!
13

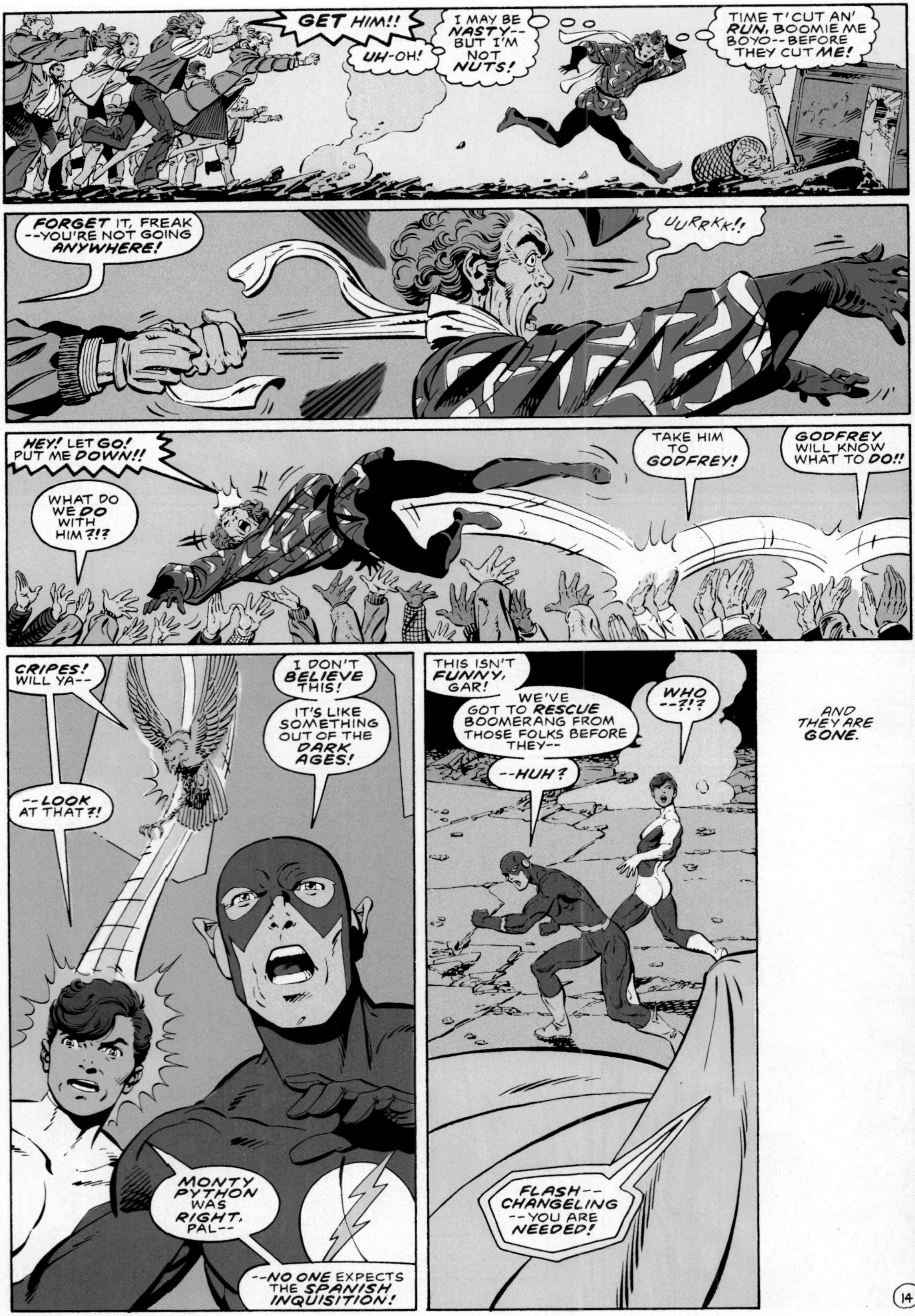

GET HIM!!
UH-OH!
I MAY BE NASTY-- BUT I'M NOT NUTS!
TIME T' CUT AN' RUN, BOOMIE ME BOYO--BEFORE THEY CUT ME!
FORGET IT, FREAK --YOU'RE NOT GOING ANYWHERE!
UURRKK!!
HEY! LET GO! PUT ME DOWN!!
WHAT DO WE DO WITH HIM?!?
TAKE HIM TO GODFREY!
GODFREY WILL KNOW WHAT TO DO!!
CRIPES! WILL YA--
--LOOK AT THAT?!
I DON'T BELIEVE THIS!
IT'S LIKE SOMETHING OUT OF THE DARK AGES!
MONTY PYTHON WAS RIGHT, PAL--
--NO ONE EXPECTS THE SPANISH INQUISITION!
THIS ISN'T FUNNY, GAR!
WE'VE GOT TO RESCUE BOOMERANG FROM THOSE FOLKS BEFORE THEY--
--HUH?
WHO--?!?
FLASH--CHANGELING--YOU ARE NEEDED!
AND THEY ARE GONE.

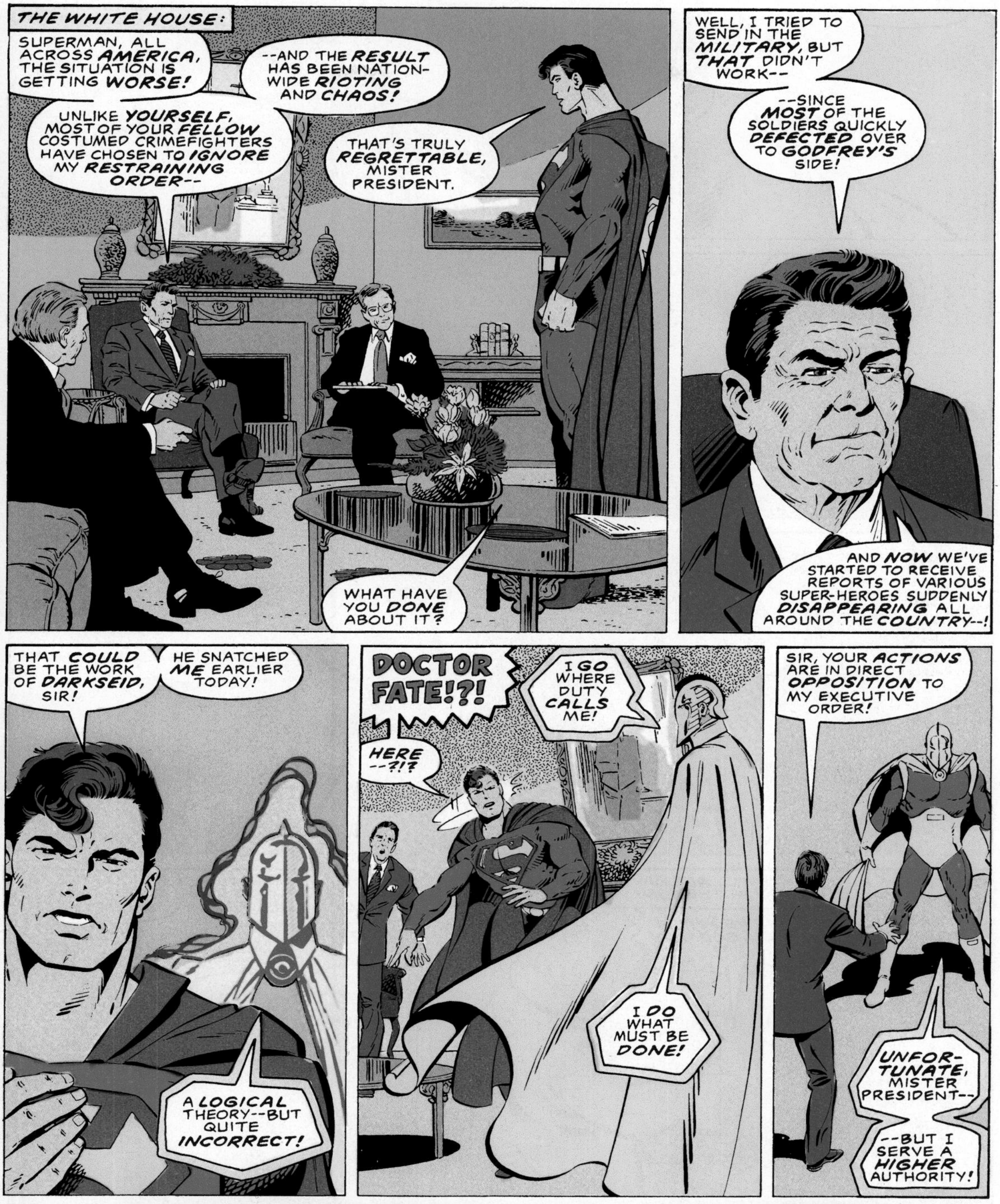
THE WHITE HOUSE:
SUPERMAN, ALL ACROSS AMERICA, THE SITUATION IS GETTING WORSE!
--AND THE RESULT HAS BEEN NATION-WIDE RIOTING AND CHAOS!
UNLIKE YOURSELF, MOST OF YOUR FELLOW COSTUMED CRIMEFIGHTERS HAVE CHOSEN TO IGNORE MY RESTRAINING ORDER--
THAT'S TRULY REGRETTABLE, MISTER PRESIDENT.
WHAT HAVE YOU DONE ABOUT IT?
WELL, I TRIED TO SEND IN THE MILITARY, BUT THAT DIDN'T WORK--
--SINCE MOST OF THE SOLDIERS QUICKLY DEFECTED OVER TO GODFREY'S SIDE!
AND NOW WE'VE STARTED TO RECEIVE REPORTS OF VARIOUS SUPER-HEROES SUDDENLY DISAPPEARING ALL AROUND THE COUNTRY--!
THAT COULD BE THE WORK OF DARKSEID, SIR!
HE SNATCHED ME EARLIER TODAY!
A LOGICAL THEORY--BUT QUITE INCORRECT!
DOCTOR FATE!?!
HERE --?!?
I GO WHERE DUTY CALLS ME!
I DO WHAT MUST BE DONE!
SIR, YOUR ACTIONS ARE IN DIRECT OPPOSITION TO MY EXECUTIVE ORDER!
UNFOR-TUNATE, MISTER PRESIDENT--
--BUT I SERVE A HIGHER AUTHORITY!
THE FATE OF YOUR ENTIRE WORLD IS AT STAKE HERE--
--AND FATE IS MY PROVINCE!
SUPER-MAN --YOU ARE NEEDED!

AND THEY ARE GONE.

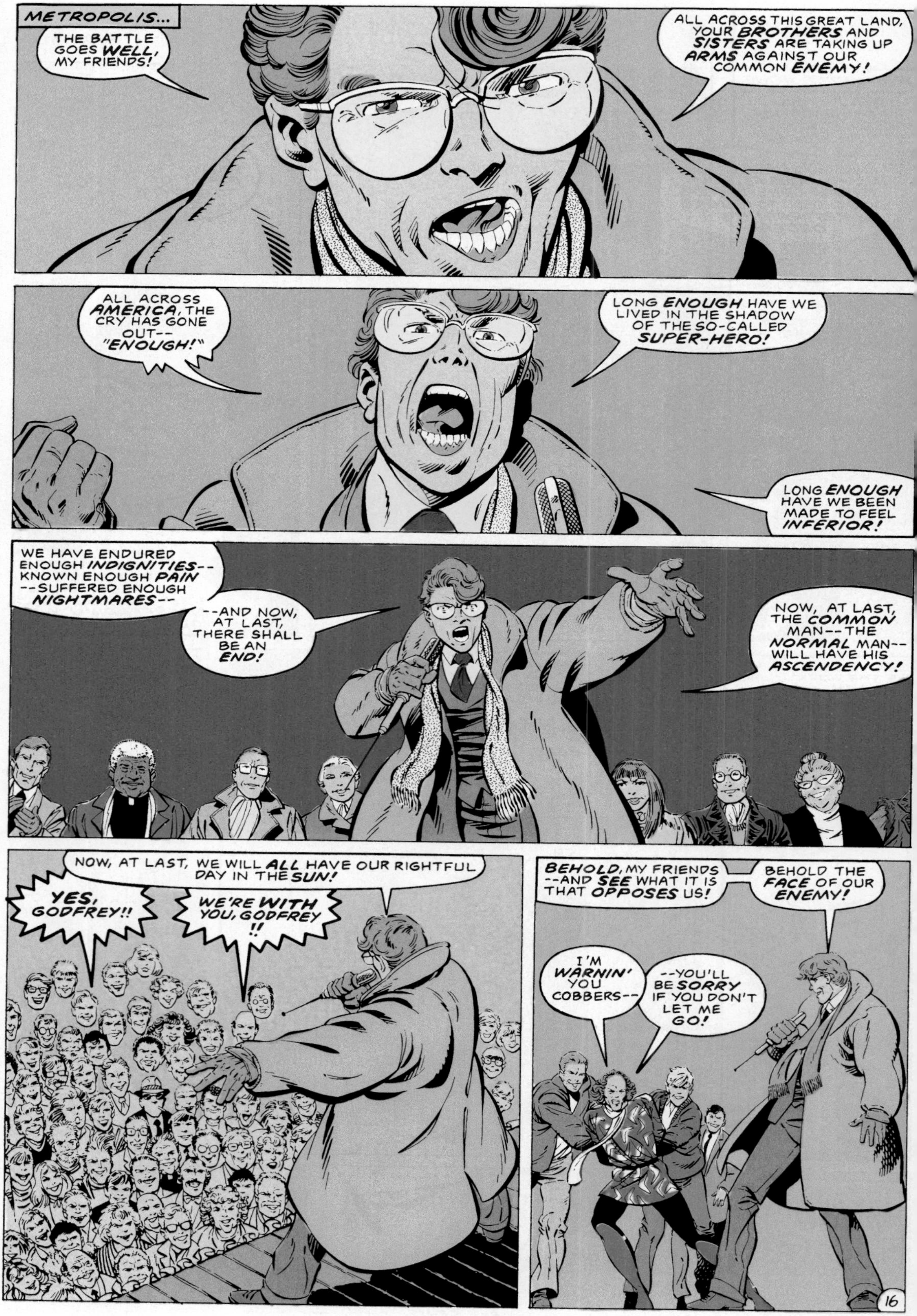
METROPOLIS...
THE BATTLE GOES WELL, MY FRIENDS!
ALL ACROSS THIS GREAT LAND, YOUR BROTHERS AND SISTERS ARE TAKING UP ARMS AGAINST OUR COMMON ENEMY!
ALL ACROSS AMERICA, THE CRY HAS GONE OUT-- "ENOUGH!"
LONG ENOUGH HAVE WE LIVED IN THE SHADOW OF THE SO-CALLED SUPER-HERO!
LONG ENOUGH HAVE WE BEEN MADE TO FEEL INFERIOR!
WE HAVE ENDURED ENOUGH INDIGNITIES-- KNOWN ENOUGH PAIN --SUFFERED ENOUGH NIGHTMARES--
--AND NOW, AT LAST, THERE SHALL BE AN END!
NOW, AT LAST, THE COMMON MAN--THE NORMAL MAN-- WILL HAVE HIS ASCENDENCY!
NOW, AT LAST, WE WILL ALL HAVE OUR RIGHTFUL DAY IN THE SUN!
YES, GODFREY!!
WE'RE WITH YOU, GODFREY!!
BEHOLD, MY FRIENDS --AND SEE WHAT IT IS THAT OPPOSES US!
BEHOLD THE FACE OF OUR ENEMY!
I'M WARNIN' YOU COBBERS--
--YOU'LL BE SORRY IF YOU DON'T LET ME GO!

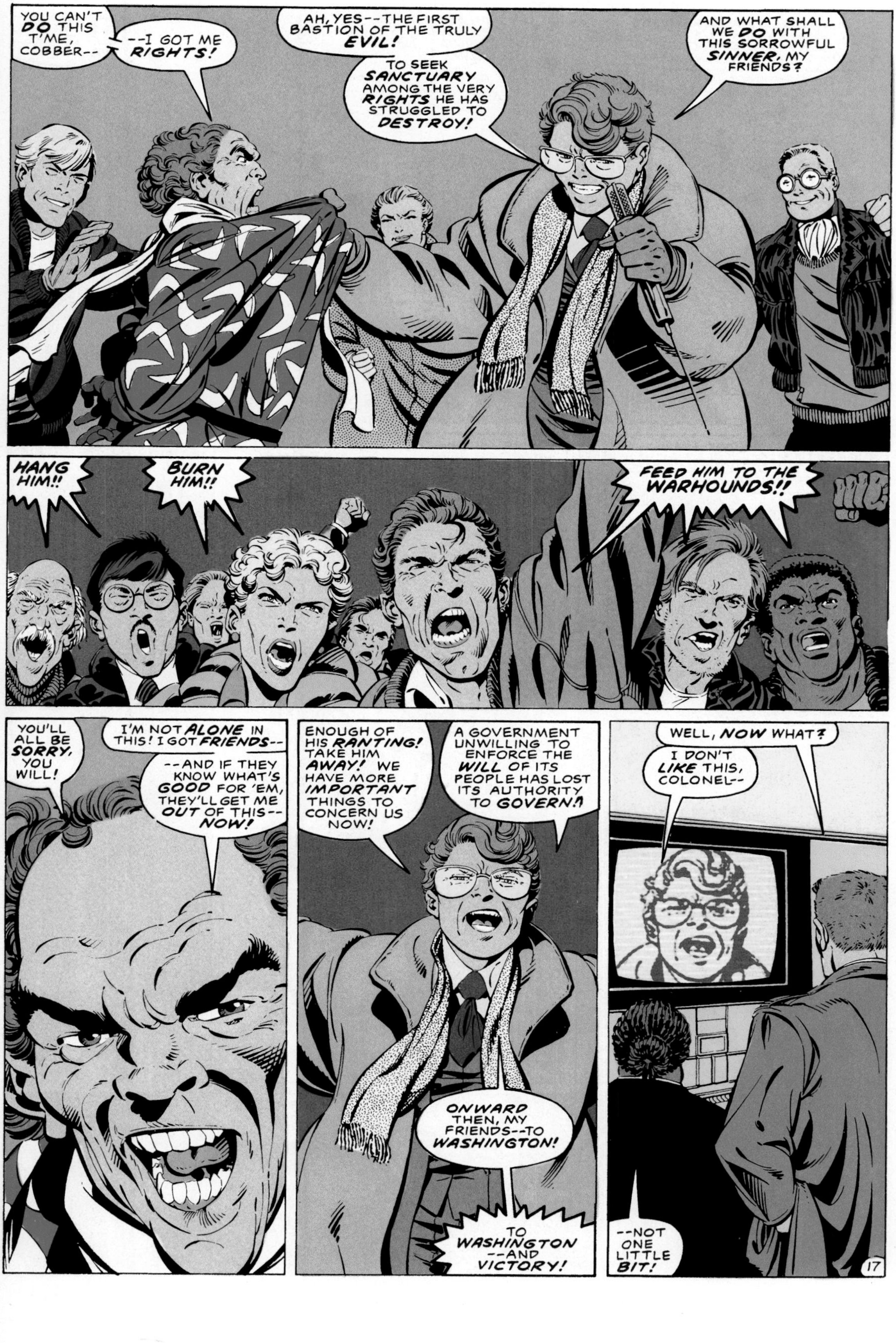

YOU CAN'T DO THIS T'ME, COBBER--
--I GOT ME RIGHTS!
AH, YES--THE FIRST BASTION OF THE TRULY EVIL!
TO SEEK SANCTUARY AMONG THE VERY RIGHTS HE HAS STRUGGLED TO DESTROY!
AND WHAT SHALL WE DO WITH THIS SORROWFUL SINNER, MY FRIENDS?
HANG HIM!!
BURN HIM!!
FEED HIM TO THE WARHOUNDS!!
YOU'LL ALL BE SORRY, YOU WILL!
I'M NOT ALONE IN THIS! I GOT FRIENDS--
--AND IF THEY KNOW WHAT'S GOOD FOR 'EM, THEY'LL GET ME OUT OF THIS--NOW!
ENOUGH OF HIS RANTING! TAKE HIM AWAY! WE HAVE MORE IMPORTANT THINGS TO CONCERN US NOW!
A GOVERNMENT UNWILLING TO ENFORCE THE WILL OF ITS PEOPLE HAS LOST ITS AUTHORITY TO GOVERN!
ONWARD THEN, MY FRIENDS--TO WASHINGTON!
TO WASHINGTON--AND VICTORY!
WELL, NOW WHAT?
I DON'T LIKE THIS, COLONEL--
--NOT ONE LITTLE BIT!

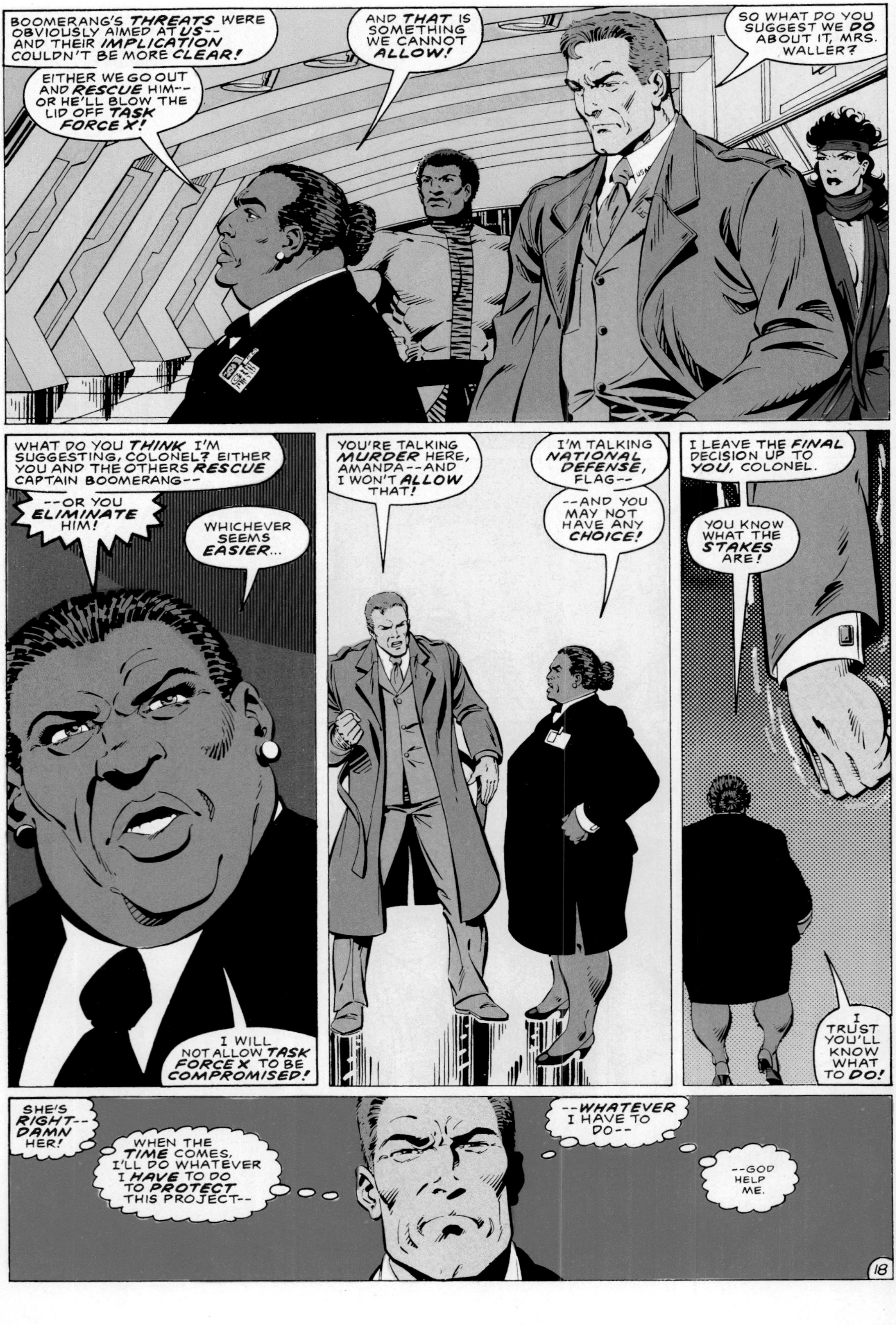
BOOMERANG'S THREATS WERE OBVIOUSLY AIMED AT US-- AND THEIR IMPLICATION COULDN'T BE MORE CLEAR!
EITHER WE GO OUT AND RESCUE HIM-- OR HE'LL BLOW THE LID OFF TASK FORCE X!
AND THAT IS SOMETHING WE CANNOT ALLOW!
SO WHAT DO YOU SUGGEST WE DO ABOUT IT, MRS. WALLER?
WHAT DO YOU THINK I'M SUGGESTING, COLONEL? EITHER YOU AND THE OTHERS RESCUE CAPTAIN BOOMERANG--
--OR YOU ELIMINATE HIM!
WHICHEVER SEEMS EASIER...
I WILL NOT ALLOW TASK FORCE X TO BE COMPROMISED!
YOU'RE TALKING MURDER HERE, AMANDA--AND I WON'T ALLOW THAT!
I'M TALKING NATIONAL DEFENSE, FLAG--
--AND YOU MAY NOT HAVE ANY CHOICE!
I LEAVE THE FINAL DECISION UP TO YOU, COLONEL.
YOU KNOW WHAT THE STAKES ARE!
I TRUST YOU'LL KNOW WHAT TO DO!
SHE'S RIGHT-- DAMN HER!
WHEN THE TIME COMES, I'LL DO WHATEVER I HAVE TO DO TO PROTECT THIS PROJECT--
--WHATEVER I HAVE TO DO--
--GOD HELP ME.

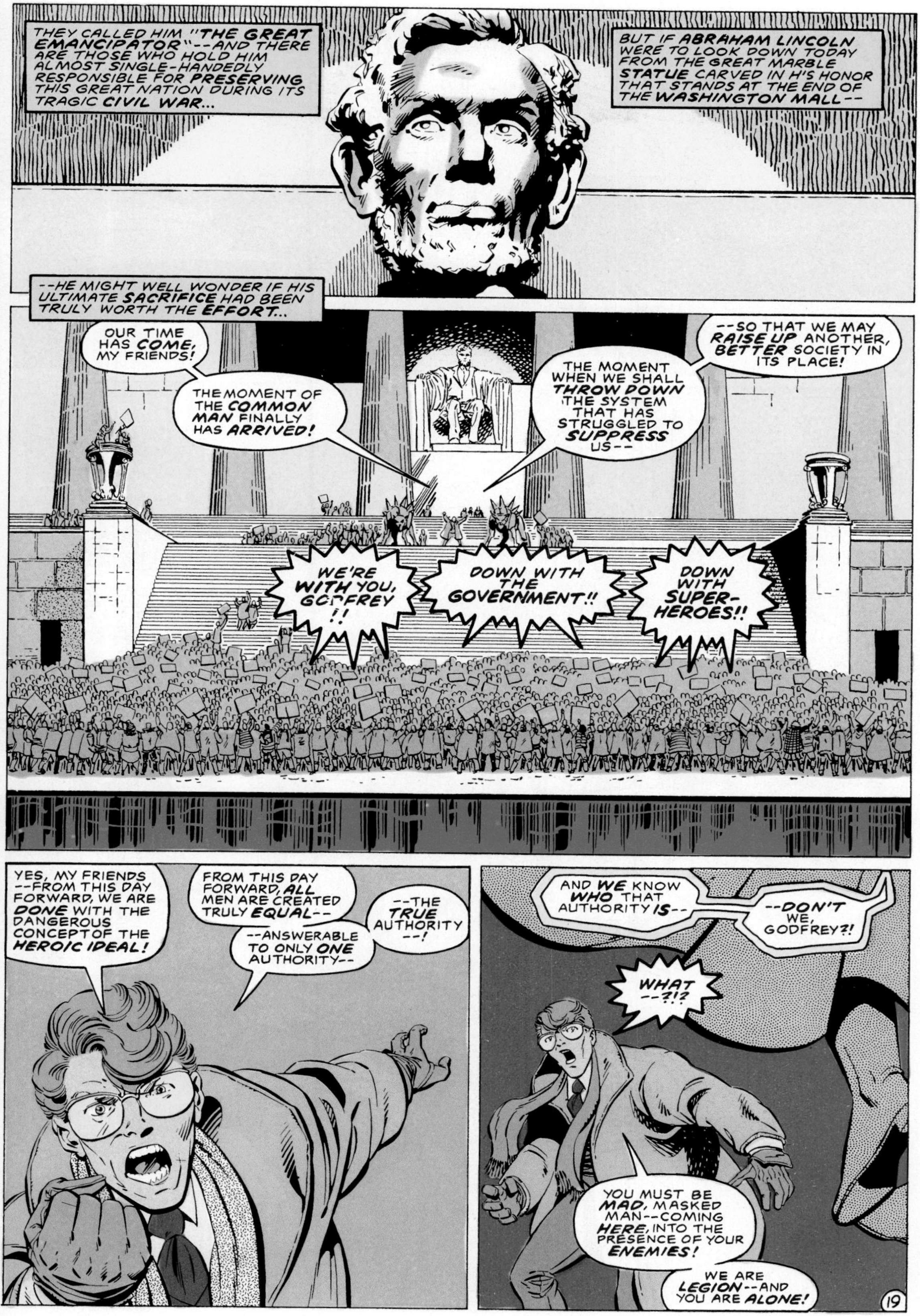

THEY CALLED HIM "THE GREAT EMANCIPATOR"--AND THERE ARE THOSE WHO HOLD HIM ALMOST SINGLE-HANDEDLY RESPONSIBLE FOR PRESERVING THIS GREAT NATION DURING ITS TRAGIC CIVIL WAR...
BUT IF ABRAHAM LINCOLN WERE TO LOOK DOWN TODAY FROM THE GREAT MARBLE STATUE CARVED IN H'S HONOR THAT STANDS AT THE END OF THE WASHINGTON MALL--
--HE MIGHT WELL WONDER IF HIS ULTIMATE SACRIFICE HAD BEEN TRULY WORTH THE EFFORT...
OUR TIME HAS COME, MY FRIENDS!
THE MOMENT OF THE COMMON MAN FINALLY HAS ARRIVED!
THE MOMENT WHEN WE SHALL THROW DOWN THE SYSTEM THAT HAS STRUGGLED TO SUPPRESS US--
--SO THAT WE MAY RAISE UP ANOTHER, BETTER SOCIETY IN ITS PLACE!
WE'RE WITH YOU, GODFREY !!
DOWN WITH THE GOVERNMENT!!
DOWN WITH SUPER-HEROES!!
YES, MY FRIENDS --FROM THIS DAY FORWARD, WE ARE DONE WITH THE DANGEROUS CONCEPT OF THE HEROIC IDEAL!
FROM THIS DAY FORWARD, ALL MEN ARE CREATED TRULY EQUAL--
--ANSWERABLE TO ONLY ONE AUTHORITY--
--THE TRUE AUTHORITY --!
AND WE KNOW WHO THAT AUTHORITY IS--
--DON'T WE, GODFREY?!
WHAT--?!?
YOU MUST BE MAD, MASKED MAN--COMING HERE, INTO THE PRESENCE OF YOUR ENEMIES!
WE ARE LEGION--AND YOU ARE ALONE!
19

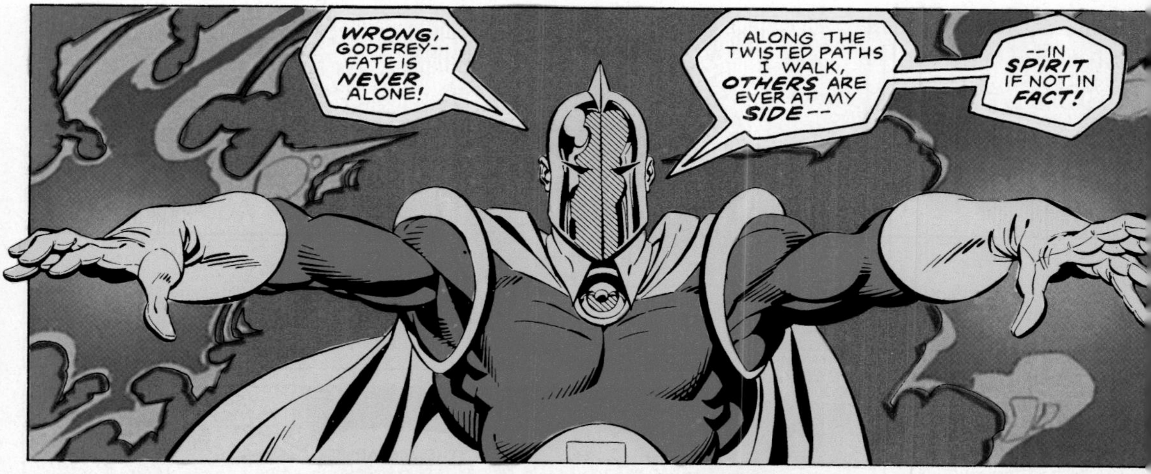
WRONG, GODFREY-- FATE IS NEVER ALONE!
ALONG THE TWISTED PATHS I WALK, OTHERS ARE EVER AT MY SIDE--
--IN SPIRIT IF NOT IN FACT!

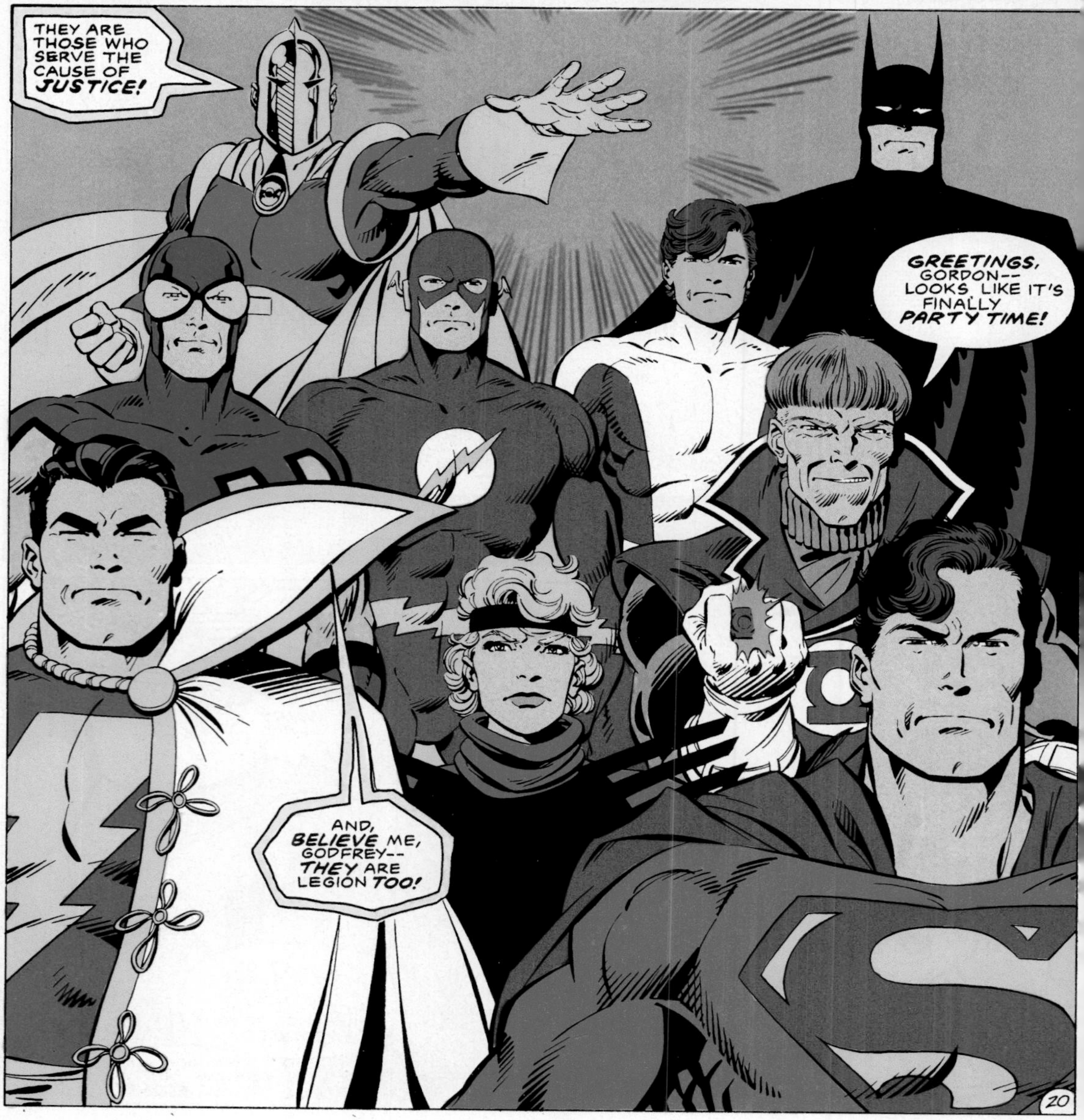
THEY ARE THOSE WHO SERVE THE CAUSE OF JUSTICE!
GREETINGS, GORDON-- LOOKS LIKE IT'S FINALLY PARTY TIME!
AND, BELIEVE ME, GODFREY-- THEY ARE LEGION TOO!

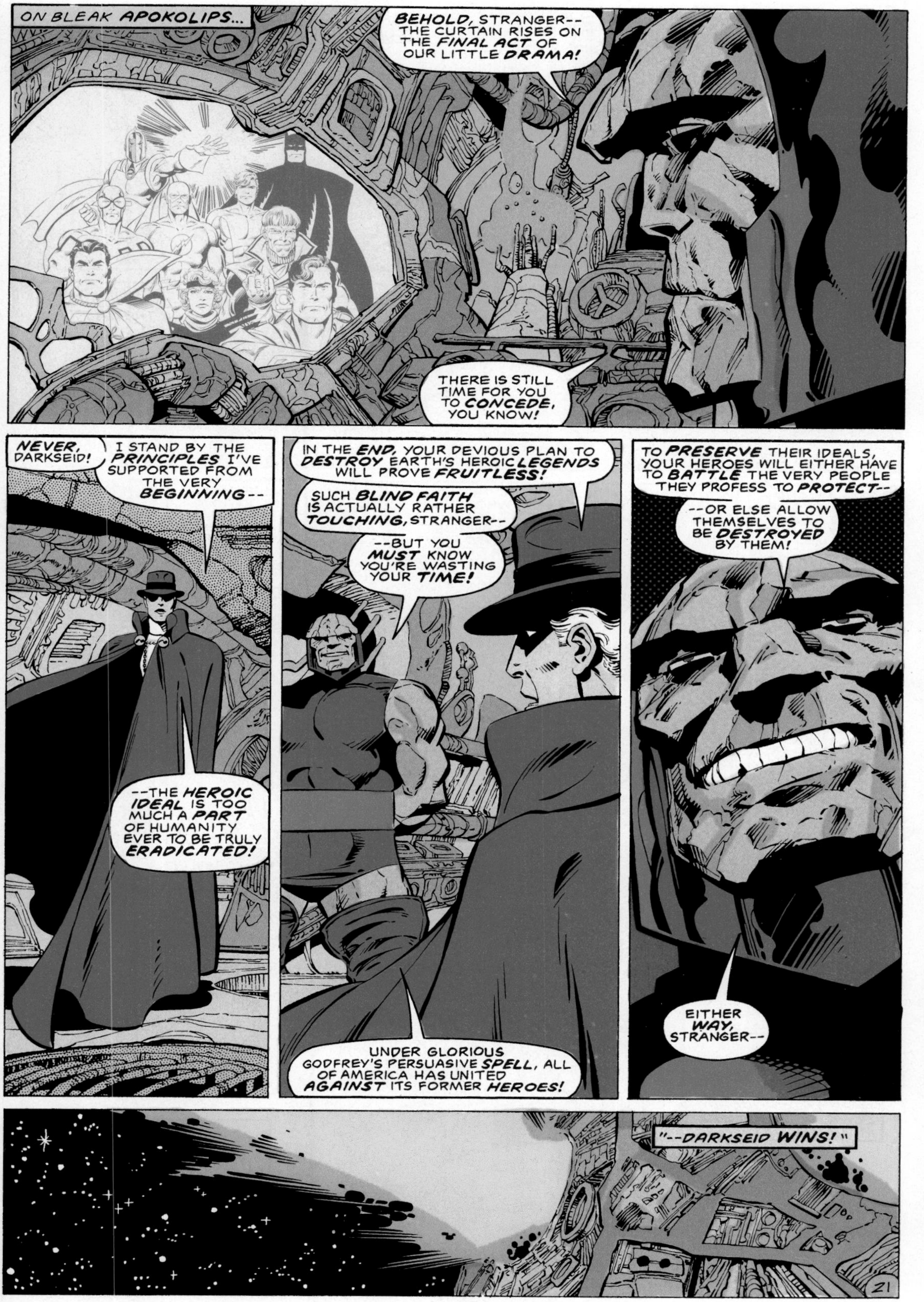
ON BLEAK APOKOLIPS...
BEHOLD, STRANGER-- THE CURTAIN RISES ON THE FINAL ACT OF OUR LITTLE DRAMA!
THERE IS STILL TIME FOR YOU TO CONCEDE, YOU KNOW!
NEVER, DARKSEID!
I STAND BY THE PRINCIPLES I'VE SUPPORTED FROM THE VERY BEGINNING--
--THE HEROIC IDEAL IS TOO MUCH A PART OF HUMANITY EVER TO BE TRULY ERADICATED!
IN THE END, YOUR DEVIOUS PLAN TO DESTROY EARTH'S HEROIC LEGENDS WILL PROVE FRUITLESS!
SUCH BLIND FAITH IS ACTUALLY RATHER TOUCHING, STRANGER--
--BUT YOU MUST KNOW YOU'RE WASTING YOUR TIME!
UNDER GLORIOUS GODFREY'S PERSUASIVE SPELL, ALL OF AMERICA HAS UNITED AGAINST ITS FORMER HEROES!
TO PRESERVE THEIR IDEALS, YOUR HEROES WILL EITHER HAVE TO BATTLE THE VERY PEOPLE THEY PROFESS TO PROTECT--
--OR ELSE ALLOW THEMSELVES TO BE DESTROYED BY THEM!
EITHER WAY, STRANGER--
"--DARKSEID WINS!"
21

AND, IN *GOTHAM CITY...*

IT JUST KEEPS GETTING *WORSE!*

I WAS ONE OF THE *FIRST* TO FALL BEFORE GODFREY'S MINDLESS *MOBS*--

--BUT IT LOOKS LIKE I WON'T BE THE *LAST!*

BATMAN AND THE OTHERS ARE MAKING A *LAST STAND* AGAINST THEM--

--WHILE I JUST LIE HERE IN COMPARATIVE *SAFETY!*

WELL-- *NO MORE!*

G. GORDON GODFREY'S *INSANITY* THREATENS *ALL* OF US--

--ADULTS AND KIDS *ALIKE*--

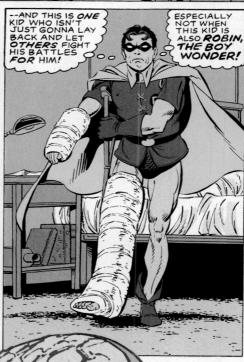

--AND THIS IS *ONE KID* WHO ISN'T JUST GONNA LAY BACK AND LET *OTHERS* FIGHT HIS BATTLES FOR HIM!

ESPECIALLY NOT WHEN THIS KID IS ALSO *ROBIN, THE BOY WONDER!*

I'VE GOTTA DO WHAT I CAN TO *HELP*--

--EVEN IF IT *KILLS* ME!

AND, BACK ON DESOLATE *APOKOLIPS,* DARKSEID'S HUMBLE *HUNGER DOGS* HEAR THE SHUDDERING *ECHO* OF THEIR MASTER'S MOCKING *LAUGHTER*--

--AND PULL THEIR SHUTTERS *TIGHT* AGAINST THE COMING *STORM!*

NEXT MONTH: "FINALE!" BE HERE!

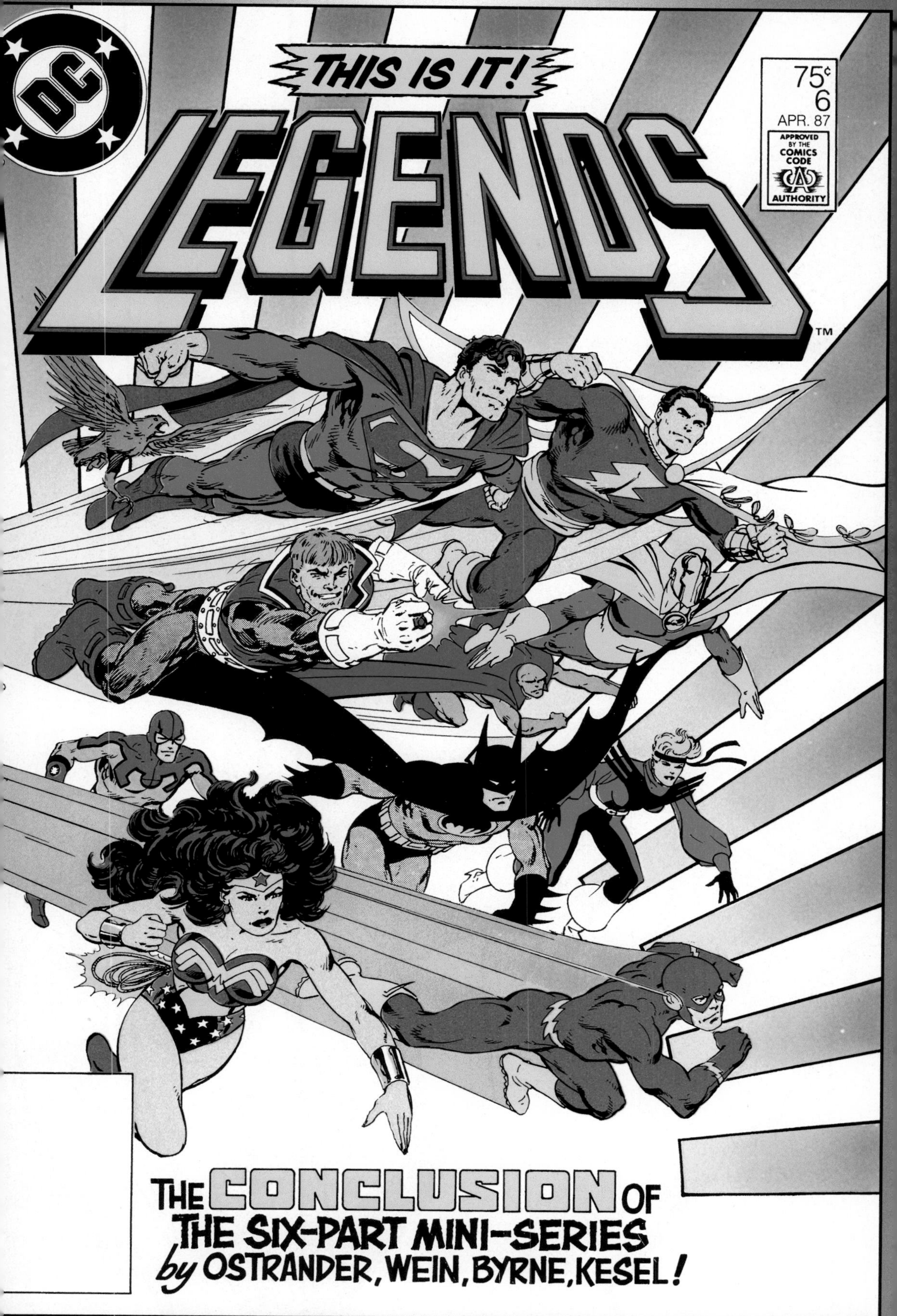
DC
THIS IS IT!
75¢
6
APR. 87
APPROVED BY THE COMICS CODE AUTHORITY
LEGENDS
TM
THE CONCLUSION OF
THE SIX-PART MINI-SERIES
by OSTRANDER, WEIN, BYRNE, KESEL!

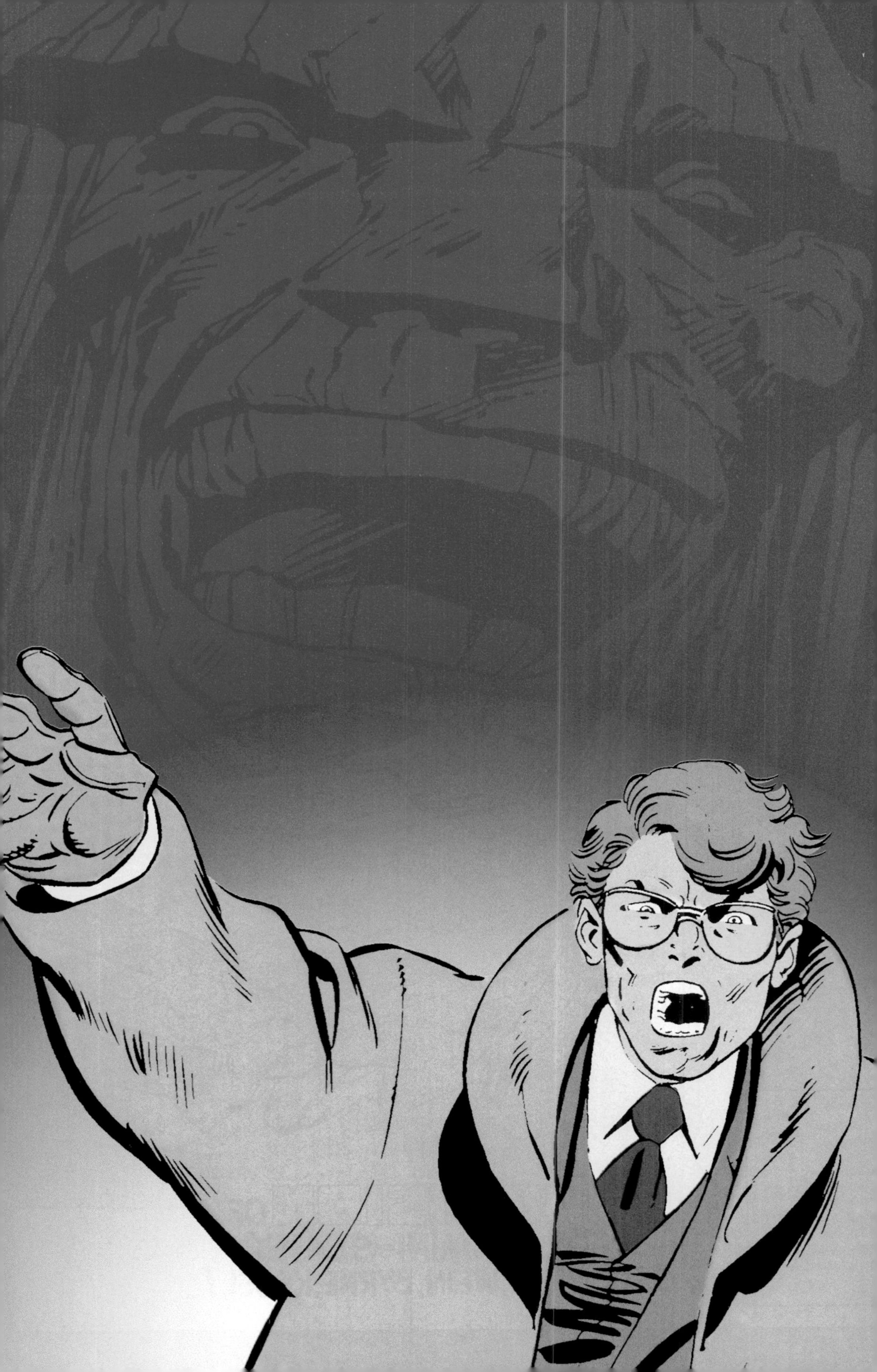

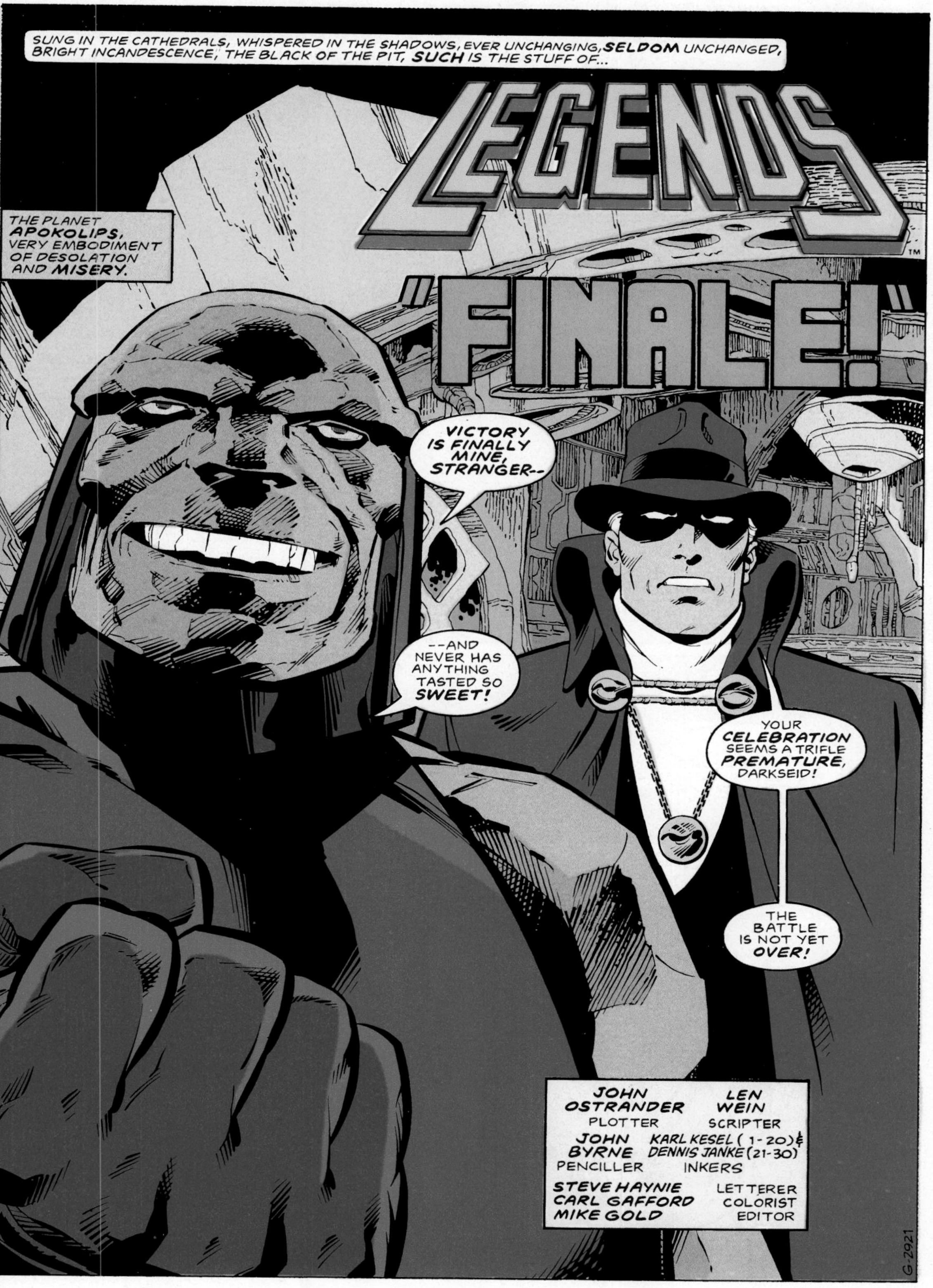
SUNG IN THE CATHEDRALS, WHISPERED IN THE SHADOWS, EVER UNCHANGING, SELDOM UNCHANGED, BRIGHT INCANDESCENCE, THE BLACK OF THE PIT, SUCH IS THE STUFF OF...
LEGENDS™
THE PLANET APOKOLIPS, VERY EMBODIMENT OF DESOLATION AND MISERY.
"FINALE!"
VICTORY IS FINALLY MINE, STRANGER--
--AND NEVER HAS ANYTHING TASTED SO SWEET!
YOUR CELEBRATION SEEMS A TRIFLE PREMATURE, DARKSEID!
THE BATTLE IS NOT YET OVER!
JOHN OSTRANDER PLOTTER
LEN WEIN SCRIPTER
JOHN BYRNE PENCILLER
KARL KESEL (1-20) & DENNIS JANKE (21-30) INKERS
STEVE HAYNIE LETTERER
CARL GAFFORD COLORIST
MIKE GOLD EDITOR
G-2921

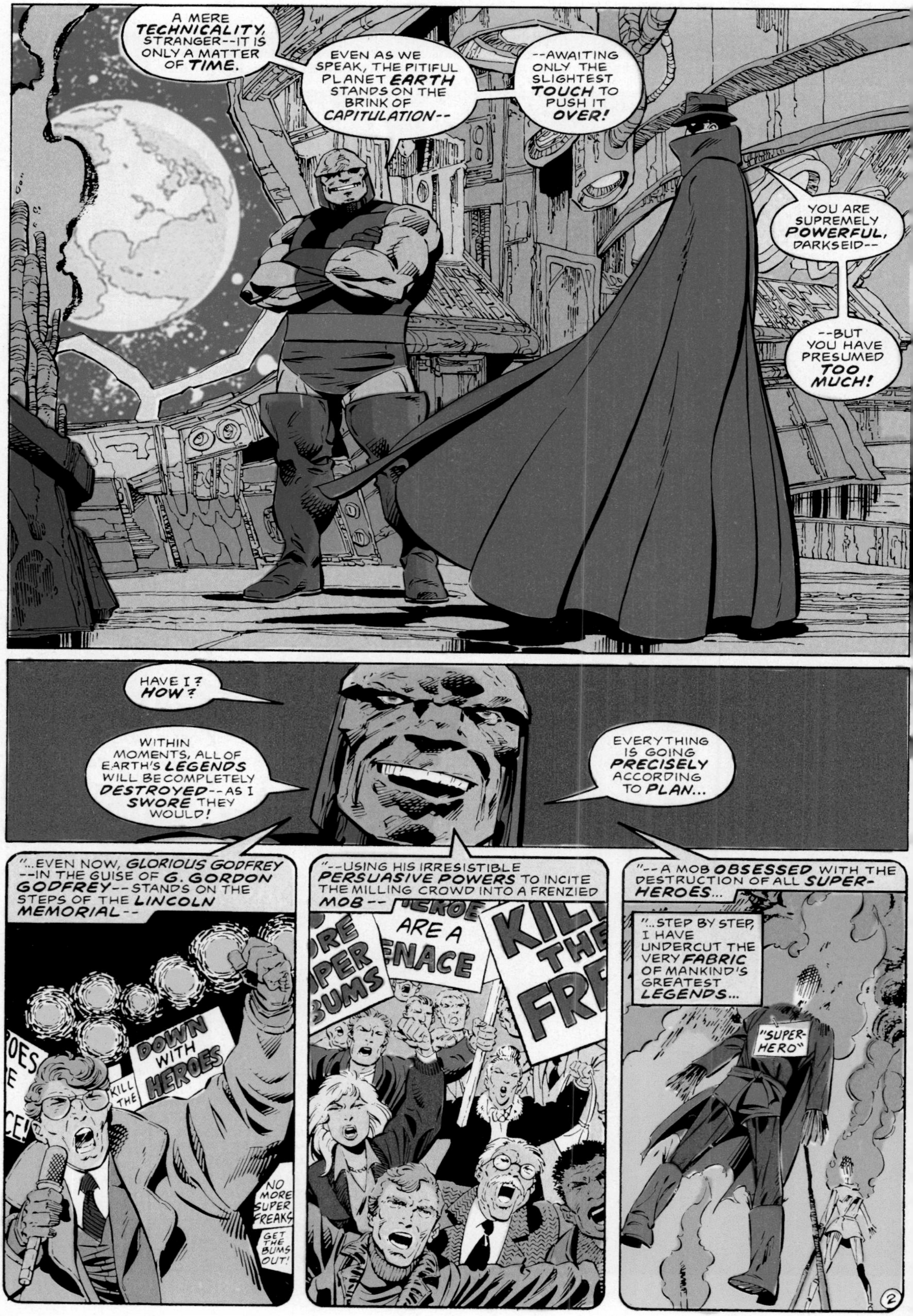

A MERE TECHNICALITY, STRANGER--IT IS ONLY A MATTER OF TIME.
EVEN AS WE SPEAK, THE PITIFUL PLANET EARTH STANDS ON THE BRINK OF CAPITULATION--
--AWAITING ONLY THE SLIGHTEST TOUCH TO PUSH IT OVER!
YOU ARE SUPREMELY POWERFUL, DARKSEID--
--BUT YOU HAVE PRESUMED TOO MUCH!
HAVE I? HOW?
WITHIN MOMENTS, ALL OF EARTH'S LEGENDS WILL BE COMPLETELY DESTROYED--AS I SWORE THEY WOULD!
EVERYTHING IS GOING PRECISELY ACCORDING TO PLAN...
"...EVEN NOW, GLORIOUS GODFREY --IN THE GUISE OF G. GORDON GODFREY--STANDS ON THE STEPS OF THE LINCOLN MEMORIAL--
DOWN WITH HEROES
KILL THE
NO MORE SUPER FREAKS
GET THE BUMS OUT!
"--USING HIS IRRESISTIBLE PERSUASIVE POWERS TO INCITE THE MILLING CROWD INTO A FRENZIED MOB--
ARE A
"--A MOB OBSESSED WITH THE DESTRUCTION OF ALL SUPER-HEROES...
"...STEP BY STEP, I HAVE UNDERCUT THE VERY FABRIC OF MANKIND'S GREATEST LEGENDS...
"SUPER-HERO"

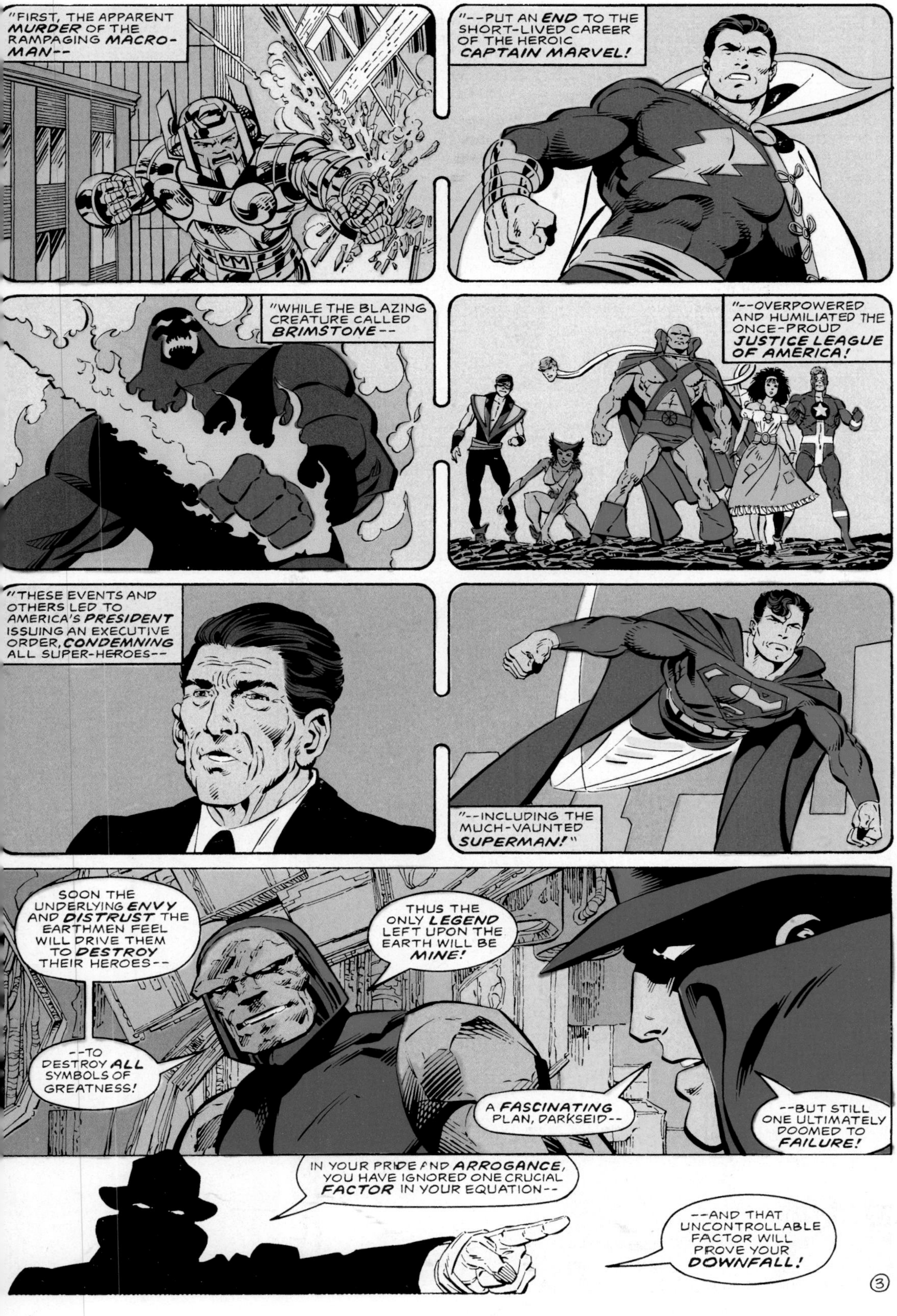
"FIRST, THE APPARENT MURDER OF THE RAMPAGING MACRO-MAN--
"--PUT AN END TO THE SHORT-LIVED CAREER OF THE HEROIC CAPTAIN MARVEL!
"WHILE THE BLAZING CREATURE CALLED BRIMSTONE--
"--OVERPOWERED AND HUMILIATED THE ONCE-PROUD JUSTICE LEAGUE OF AMERICA!
"THESE EVENTS AND OTHERS LED TO AMERICA'S PRESIDENT ISSUING AN EXECUTIVE ORDER, CONDEMNING ALL SUPER-HEROES--
"--INCLUDING THE MUCH-VAUNTED SUPERMAN!"
SOON THE UNDERLYING ENVY AND DISTRUST THE EARTHMEN FEEL WILL DRIVE THEM TO DESTROY THEIR HEROES--
--TO DESTROY ALL SYMBOLS OF GREATNESS!
THUS THE ONLY LEGEND LEFT UPON THE EARTH WILL BE MINE!
A FASCINATING PLAN, DARKSEID--
--BUT STILL ONE ULTIMATELY DOOMED TO FAILURE!
IN YOUR PRIDE AND ARROGANCE, YOU HAVE IGNORED ONE CRUCIAL FACTOR IN YOUR EQUATION--
--AND THAT UNCONTROLLABLE FACTOR WILL PROVE YOUR DOWNFALL!

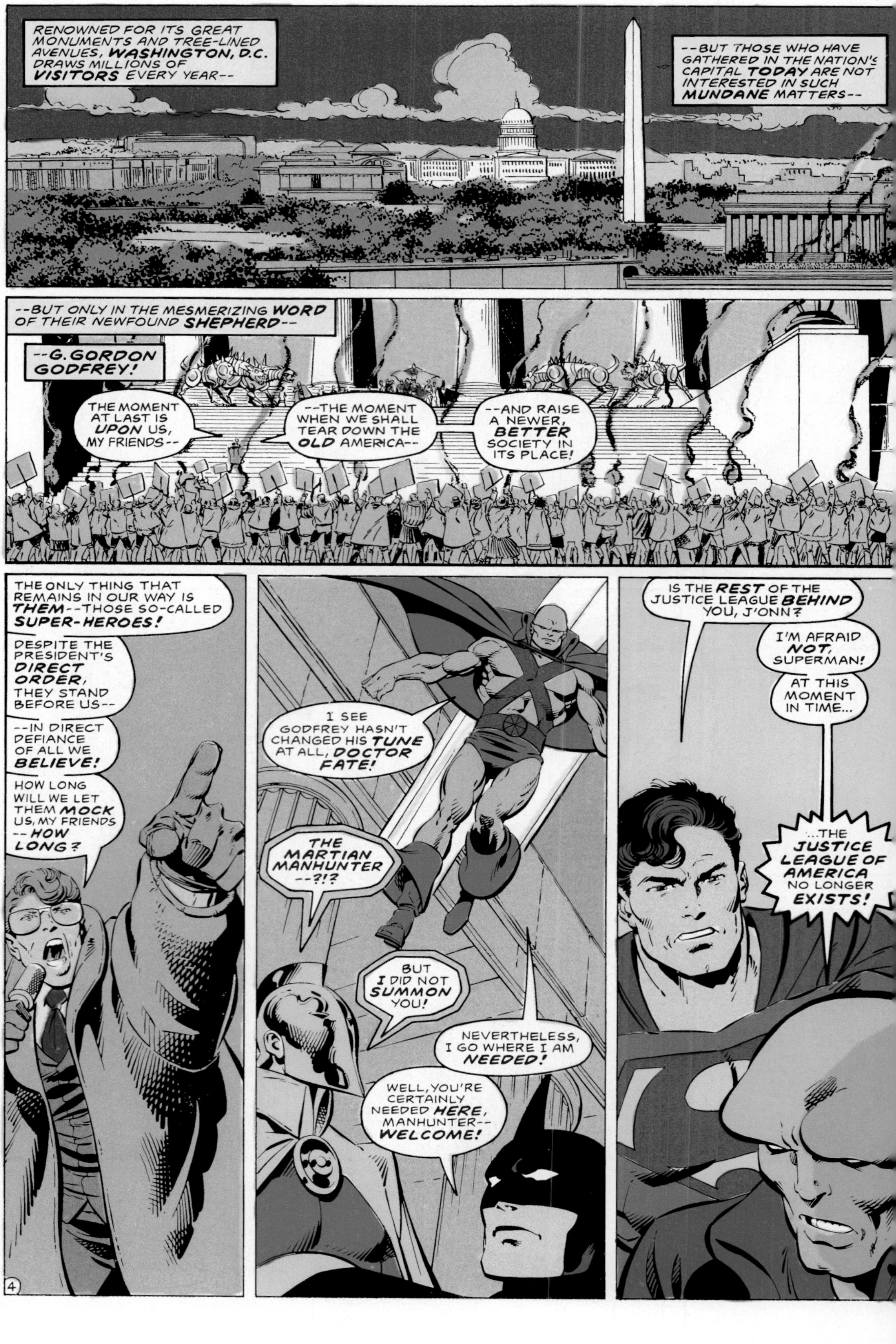
RENOWNED FOR ITS GREAT MONUMENTS AND TREE-LINED AVENUES, WASHINGTON, D.C. DRAWS MILLIONS OF VISITORS EVERY YEAR--
--BUT THOSE WHO HAVE GATHERED IN THE NATION'S CAPITAL TODAY ARE NOT INTERESTED IN SUCH MUNDANE MATTERS--
--BUT ONLY IN THE MESMERIZING WORD OF THEIR NEWFOUND SHEPHERD--
--G. GORDON GODFREY!
THE MOMENT AT LAST IS UPON US, MY FRIENDS--
--THE MOMENT WHEN WE SHALL TEAR DOWN THE OLD AMERICA--
--AND RAISE A NEWER, BETTER SOCIETY IN ITS PLACE!
THE ONLY THING THAT REMAINS IN OUR WAY IS THEM--THOSE SO-CALLED SUPER-HEROES!
DESPITE THE PRESIDENT'S DIRECT ORDER, THEY STAND BEFORE US--
--IN DIRECT DEFIANCE OF ALL WE BELIEVE!
HOW LONG WILL WE LET THEM MOCK US, MY FRIENDS --HOW LONG?
I SEE GODFREY HASN'T CHANGED HIS TUNE AT ALL, DOCTOR FATE!
THE MARTIAN MANHUNTER --?!?
BUT I DID NOT SUMMON YOU!
NEVERTHELESS, I GO WHERE I AM NEEDED!
WELL, YOU'RE CERTAINLY NEEDED HERE, MANHUNTER-- WELCOME!
IS THE REST OF THE JUSTICE LEAGUE BEHIND YOU, J'ONN?
I'M AFRAID NOT, SUPERMAN!
AT THIS MOMENT IN TIME...
...THE JUSTICE LEAGUE OF AMERICA NO LONGER EXISTS!
4

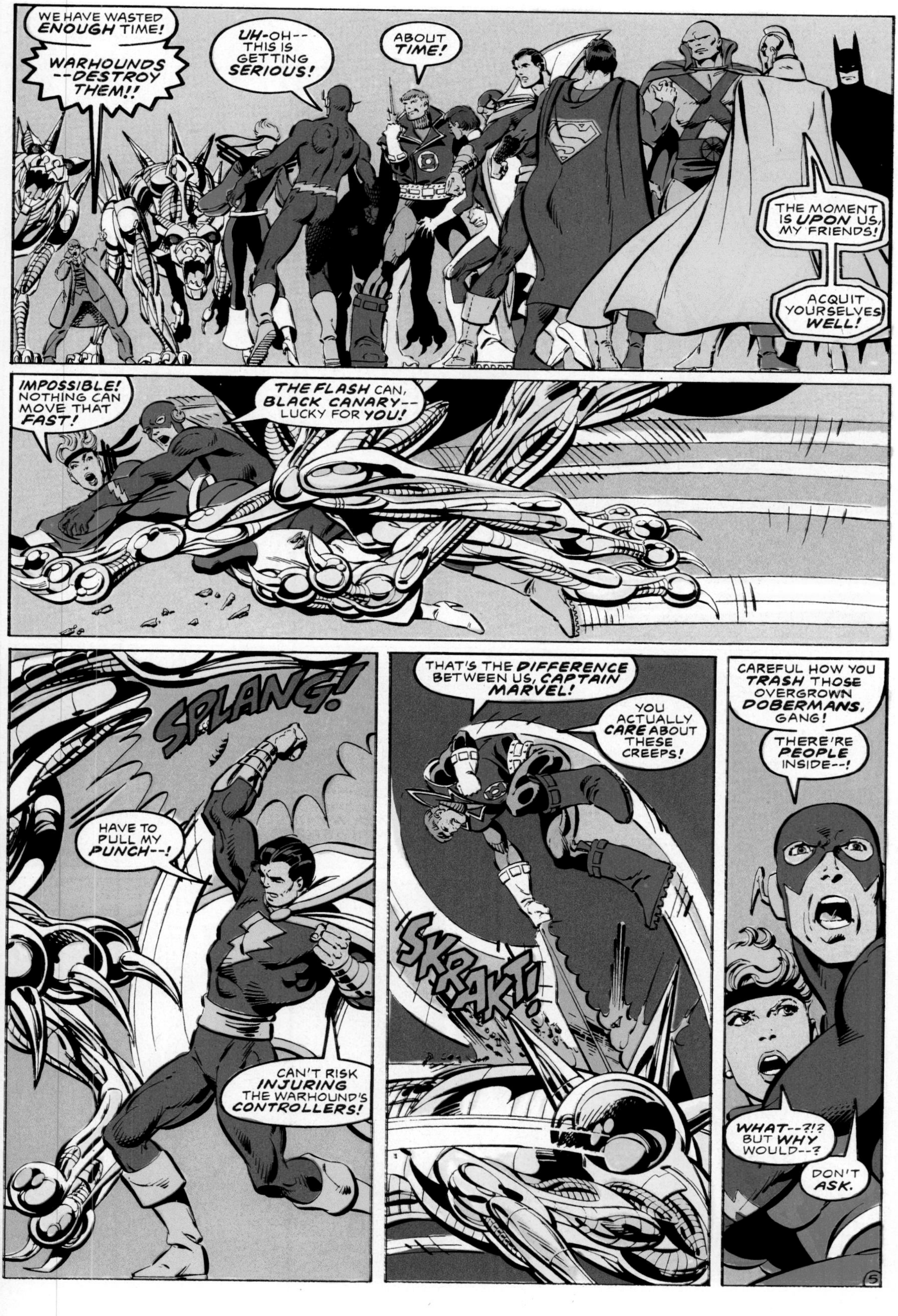

WE HAVE WASTED ENOUGH TIME!
WARHOUNDS --DESTROY THEM!!
UH-OH-- THIS IS GETTING SERIOUS!
ABOUT TIME!
THE MOMENT IS UPON US, MY FRIENDS!
ACQUIT YOURSELVES WELL!
IMPOSSIBLE! NOTHING CAN MOVE THAT FAST!
THE FLASH CAN, BLACK CANARY-- LUCKY FOR YOU!
SPLANG!
HAVE TO PULL MY PUNCH--!
CAN'T RISK INJURING THE WARHOUND'S CONTROLLERS!
THAT'S THE DIFFERENCE BETWEEN US, CAPTAIN MARVEL!
YOU ACTUALLY CARE ABOUT THESE CREEPS!
SKRAKT!
CAREFUL HOW YOU TRASH THOSE OVERGROWN DOBERMANS, GANG!
THERE'RE PEOPLE INSIDE--!
WHAT--?!? BUT WHY WOULD--?
DON'T ASK.

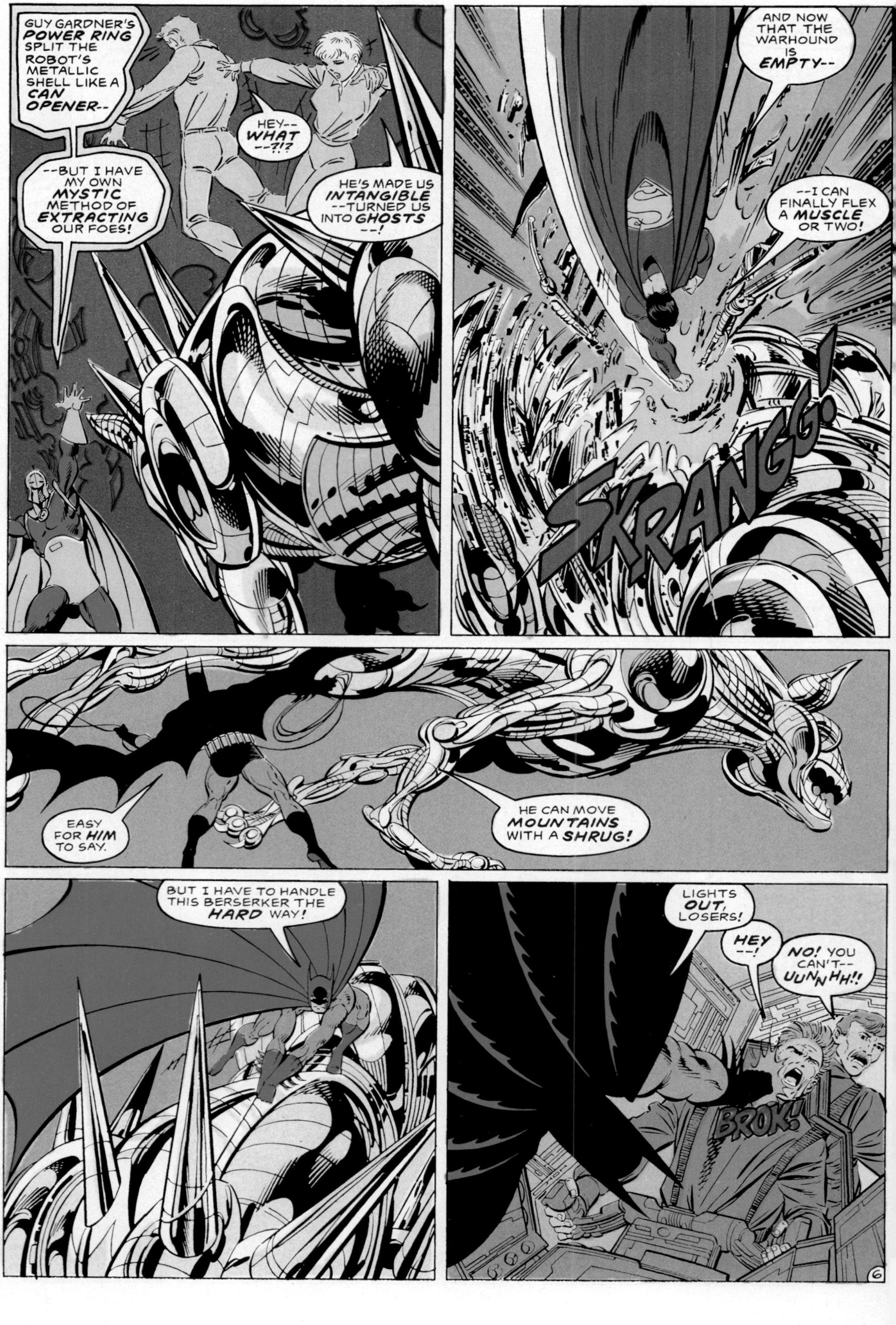
GUY GARDNER'S POWER RING SPLIT THE ROBOT'S METALLIC SHELL LIKE A CAN OPENER--
--BUT I HAVE MY OWN MYSTIC METHOD OF EXTRACTING OUR FOES!
HEY-- WHAT --?!?
HE'S MADE US INTANGIBLE --TURNED US INTO GHOSTS --!
AND NOW THAT THE WARHOUND IS EMPTY--
--I CAN FINALLY FLEX A MUSCLE OR TWO!
SKRANGG!
EASY FOR HIM TO SAY.
HE CAN MOVE MOUNTAINS WITH A SHRUG!
BUT I HAVE TO HANDLE THIS BERSERKER THE HARD WAY!
LIGHTS OUT, LOSERS!
HEY --!
NO! YOU CAN'T-- UUNNHH!!
BROK!

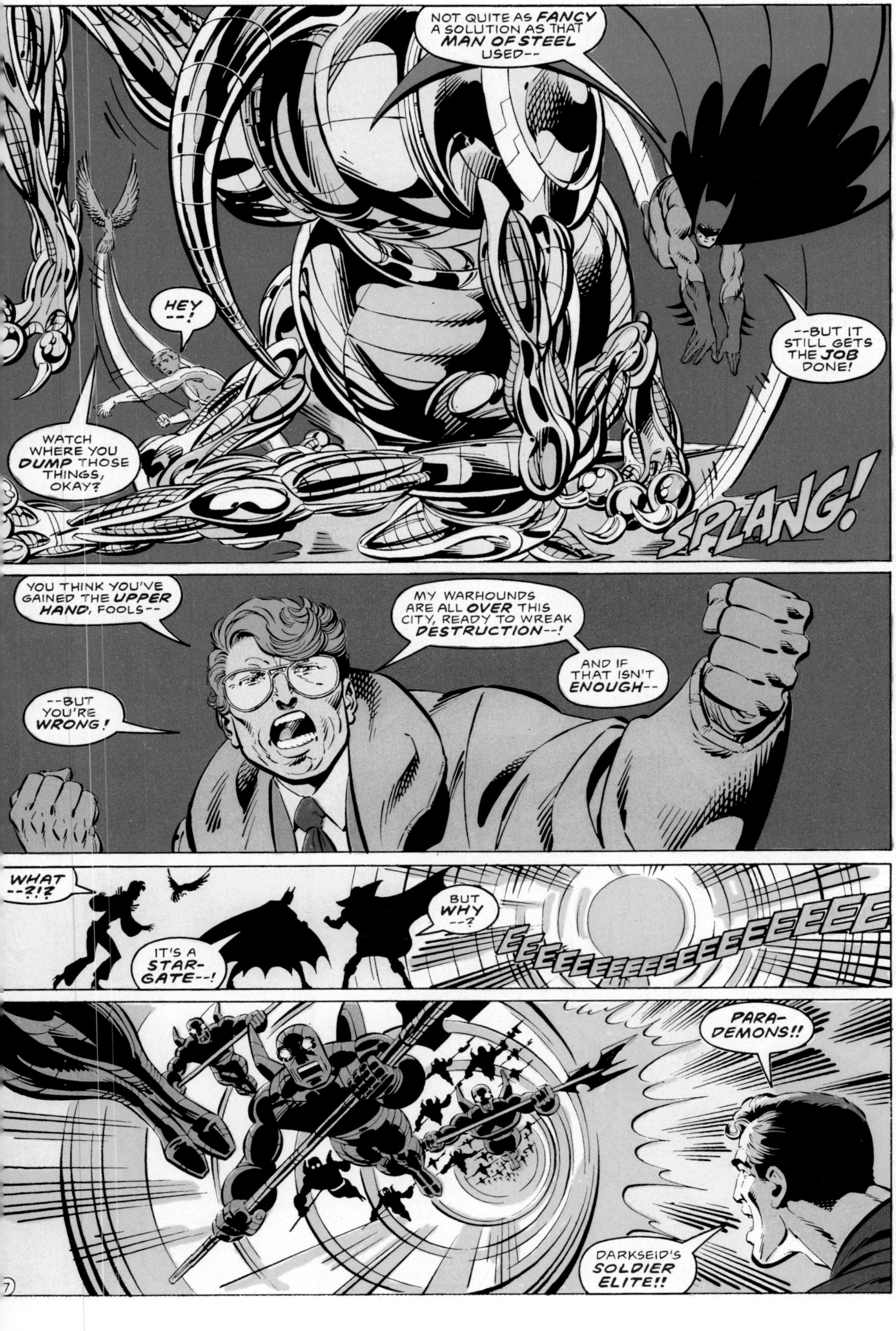
NOT QUITE AS FANCY A SOLUTION AS THAT MAN OF STEEL USED--
--BUT IT STILL GETS THE JOB DONE!
HEY --!
WATCH WHERE YOU DUMP THOSE THINGS, OKAY?
SPLANG!
YOU THINK YOU'VE GAINED THE UPPER HAND, FOOLS--
--BUT YOU'RE WRONG!
MY WARHOUNDS ARE ALL OVER THIS CITY, READY TO WREAK DESTRUCTION--!
AND IF THAT ISN'T ENOUGH--
WHAT --?!?
IT'S A STAR-GATE--!
BUT WHY --?
EEEEEEEEEEEEEEEEEEE
PARA-DEMONS!!
DARKSEID'S SOLDIER ELITE!!

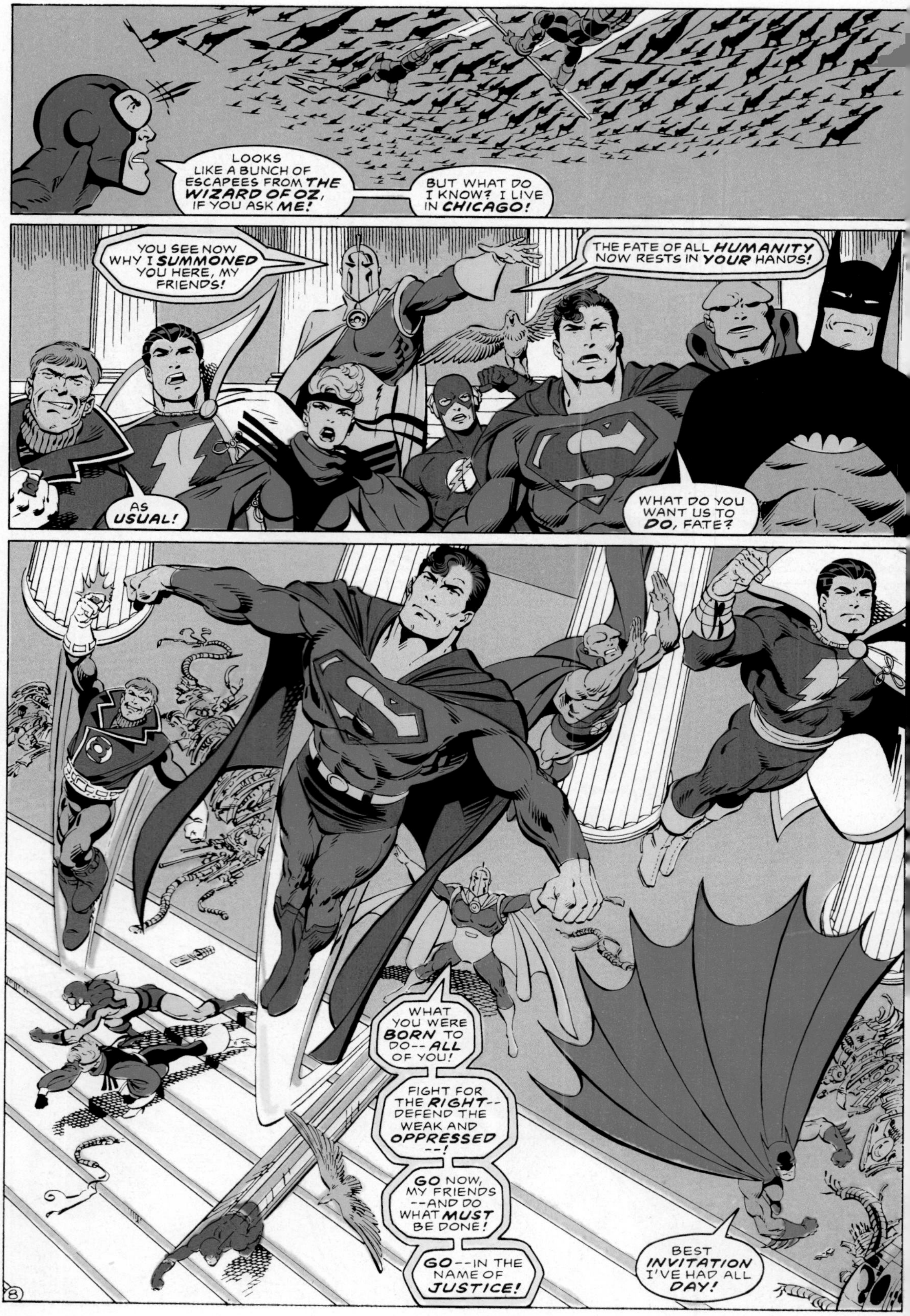

LOOKS LIKE A BUNCH OF ESCAPEES FROM THE WIZARD OF OZ, IF YOU ASK ME!
BUT WHAT DO I KNOW? I LIVE IN CHICAGO!
YOU SEE NOW WHY I SUMMONED YOU HERE, MY FRIENDS!
THE FATE OF ALL HUMANITY NOW RESTS IN YOUR HANDS!
AS USUAL!
WHAT DO YOU WANT US TO DO, FATE?
WHAT YOU WERE BORN TO DO--ALL OF YOU!
FIGHT FOR THE RIGHT-- DEFEND THE WEAK AND OPPRESSED--!
GO NOW, MY FRIENDS --AND DO WHAT MUST BE DONE!
GO--IN THE NAME OF JUSTICE!
BEST INVITATION I'VE HAD ALL DAY!

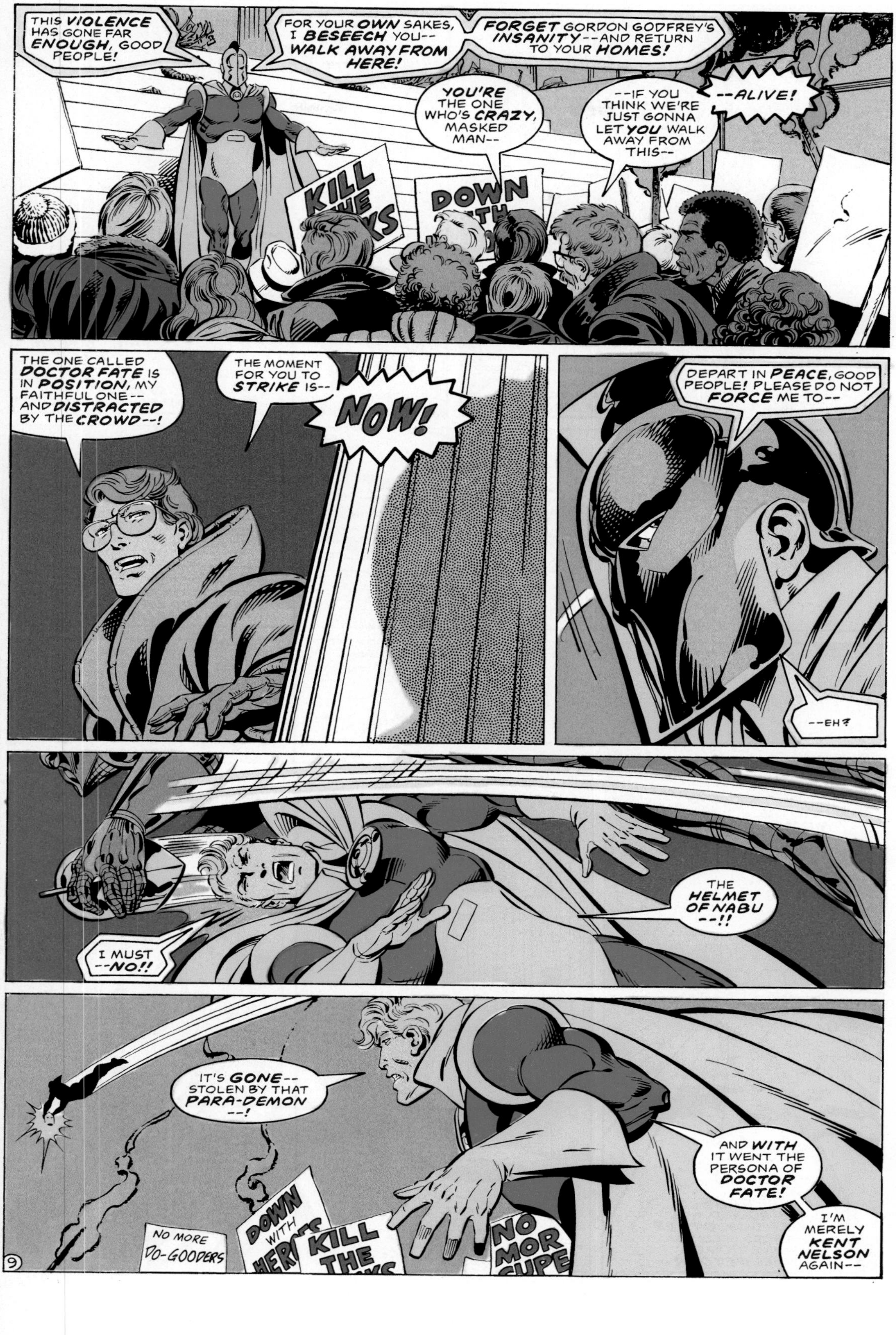
THIS VIOLENCE HAS GONE FAR ENOUGH, GOOD PEOPLE!
FOR YOUR OWN SAKES, I BESEECH YOU-- WALK AWAY FROM HERE!
FORGET GORDON GODFREY'S INSANITY--AND RETURN TO YOUR HOMES!
YOU'RE THE ONE WHO'S CRAZY, MASKED MAN--
--IF YOU THINK WE'RE JUST GONNA LET YOU WALK AWAY FROM THIS--
--ALIVE!
KILL THE
DOWN
THE ONE CALLED DOCTOR FATE IS IN POSITION, MY FAITHFUL ONE-- AND DISTRACTED BY THE CROWD--!
THE MOMENT FOR YOU TO STRIKE IS--
NOW!
DEPART IN PEACE, GOOD PEOPLE! PLEASE DO NOT FORCE ME TO--
--EH?
THE HELMET OF NABU --!!
I MUST --NO!!
IT'S GONE-- STOLEN BY THAT PARA-DEMON --!
AND WITH IT WENT THE PERSONA OF DOCTOR FATE!
I'M MERELY KENT NELSON AGAIN--
NO MORE DO-GOODERS
DOWN WITH
KILL THE
NO MOR

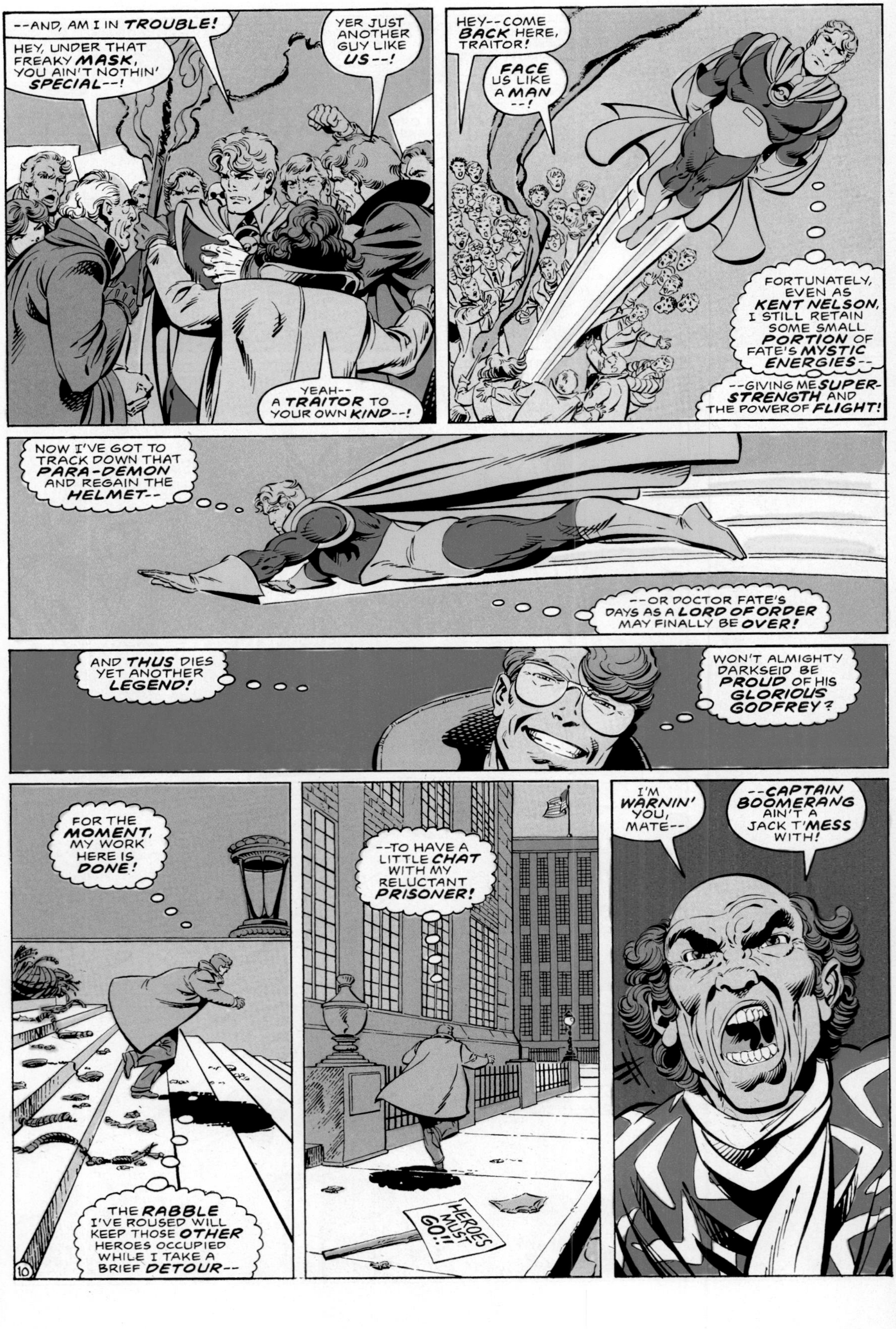

--AND, AM I IN TROUBLE!
HEY, UNDER THAT FREAKY MASK, YOU AIN'T NOTHIN' SPECIAL--!
YER JUST ANOTHER GUY LIKE US--!
YEAH-- A TRAITOR TO YOUR OWN KIND--!
HEY--COME BACK HERE, TRAITOR!
FACE US LIKE A MAN--!
FORTUNATELY, EVEN AS KENT NELSON, I STILL RETAIN SOME SMALL PORTION OF FATE'S MYSTIC ENERGIES--
--GIVING ME SUPER-STRENGTH AND THE POWER OF FLIGHT!
NOW I'VE GOT TO TRACK DOWN THAT PARA-DEMON AND REGAIN THE HELMET--
--OR DOCTOR FATE'S DAYS AS A LORD OF ORDER MAY FINALLY BE OVER!
AND THUS DIES YET ANOTHER LEGEND!
WON'T ALMIGHTY DARKSEID BE PROUD OF HIS GLORIOUS GODFREY?
FOR THE MOMENT, MY WORK HERE IS DONE!
THE RABBLE I'VE ROUSED WILL KEEP THOSE OTHER HEROES OCCUPIED WHILE I TAKE A BRIEF DETOUR--
--TO HAVE A LITTLE CHAT WITH MY RELUCTANT PRISONER!
HEROES MUST GO!!
I'M WARNIN' YOU, MATE--
--CAPTAIN BOOMERANG AIN'T A JACK T'MESS WITH!

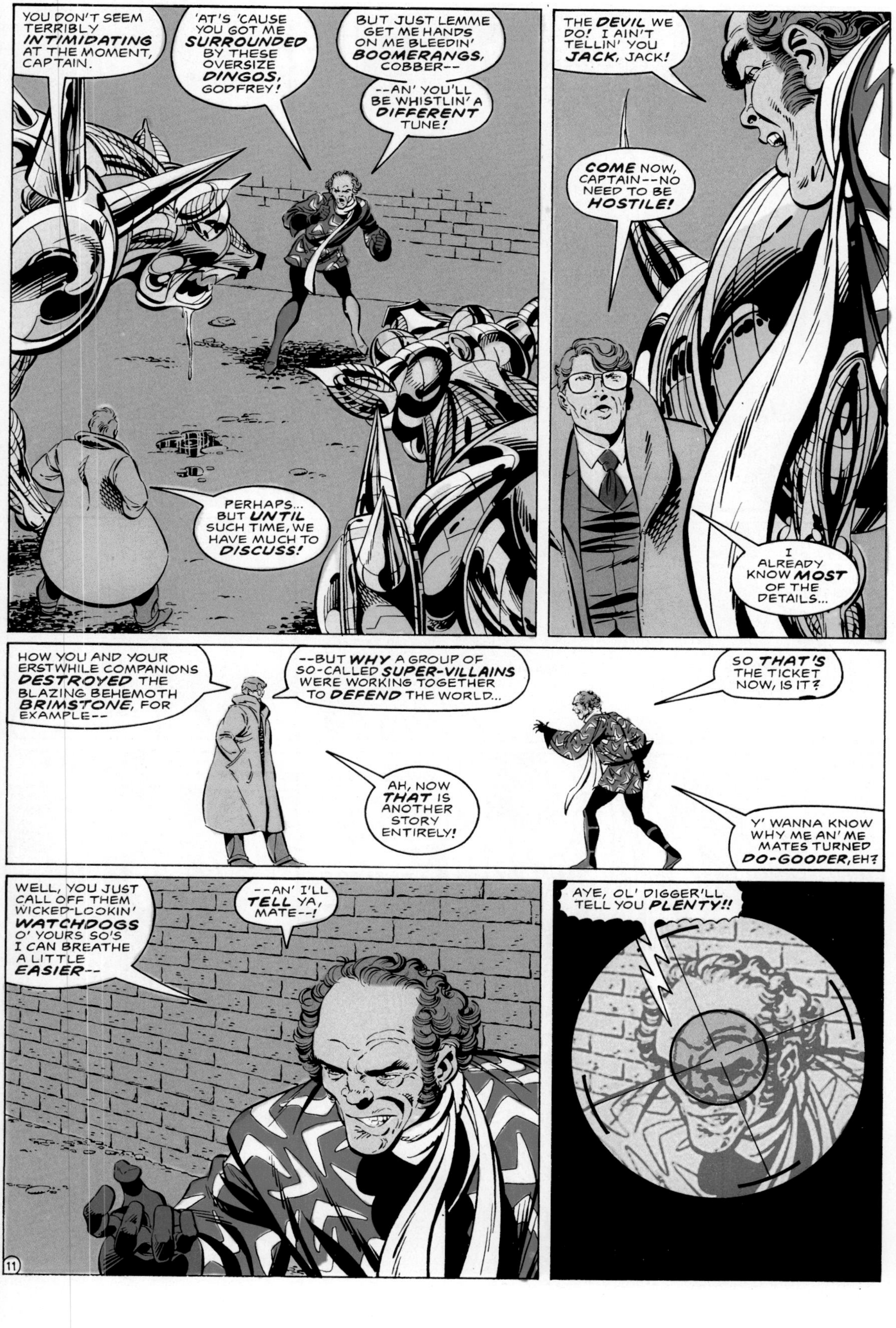

YOU DON'T SEEM TERRIBLY INTIMIDATING AT THE MOMENT, CAPTAIN.
'AT'S 'CAUSE YOU GOT ME SURROUNDED BY THESE OVERSIZE DINGOS, GODFREY!
BUT JUST LEMME GET ME HANDS ON ME BLEEDIN' BOOMERANGS, COBBER--
--AN' YOU'LL BE WHISTLIN' A DIFFERENT TUNE!
PERHAPS... BUT UNTIL SUCH TIME, WE HAVE MUCH TO DISCUSS!
THE DEVIL WE DO! I AIN'T TELLIN' YOU JACK, JACK!
COME NOW, CAPTAIN--NO NEED TO BE HOSTILE!
I ALREADY KNOW MOST OF THE DETAILS...
HOW YOU AND YOUR ERSTWHILE COMPANIONS DESTROYED THE BLAZING BEHEMOTH BRIMSTONE, FOR EXAMPLE--
--BUT WHY A GROUP OF SO-CALLED SUPER-VILLAINS WERE WORKING TOGETHER TO DEFEND THE WORLD...
AH, NOW THAT IS ANOTHER STORY ENTIRELY!
SO THAT'S THE TICKET NOW, IS IT?
Y' WANNA KNOW WHY ME AN' ME MATES TURNED DO-GOODER, EH?
WELL, YOU JUST CALL OFF THEM WICKED-LOOKIN' WATCHDOGS O' YOURS SO'S I CAN BREATHE A LITTLE EASIER--
--AN' I'LL TELL YA, MATE--!
AYE, OL' DIGGER'LL TELL YOU PLENTY!!
11

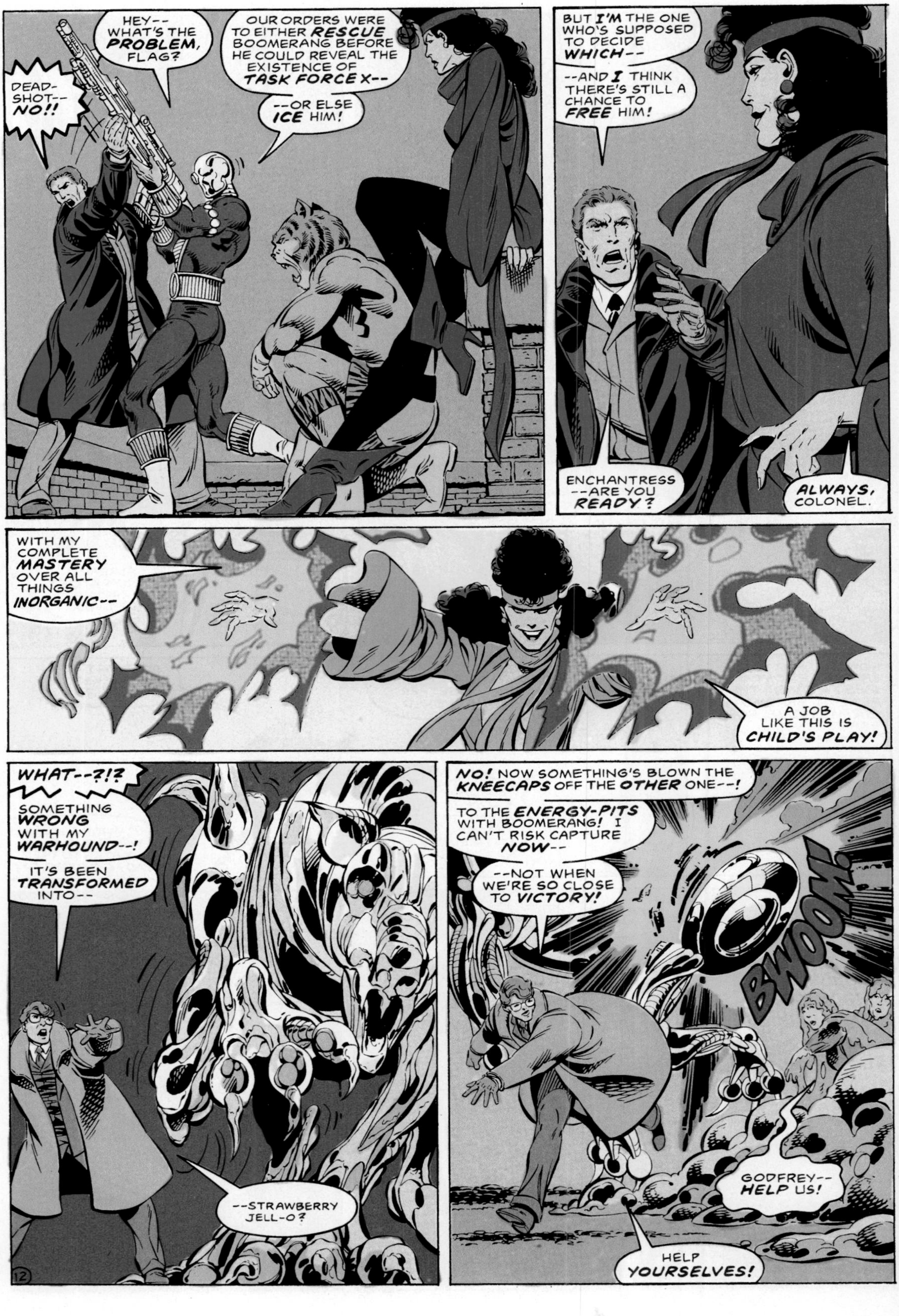
DEAD-SHOT--NO!!
HEY--WHAT'S THE PROBLEM, FLAG?
OUR ORDERS WERE TO EITHER RESCUE BOOMERANG BEFORE HE COULD REVEAL THE EXISTENCE OF TASK FORCE X--
--OR ELSE ICE HIM!
BUT I'M THE ONE WHO'S SUPPOSED TO DECIDE WHICH--
--AND I THINK THERE'S STILL A CHANCE TO FREE HIM!
ENCHANTRESS--ARE YOU READY?
ALWAYS, COLONEL.
WITH MY COMPLETE MASTERY OVER ALL THINGS INORGANIC--
A JOB LIKE THIS IS CHILD'S PLAY!
WHAT--?!?
SOMETHING WRONG WITH MY WARHOUND--!
IT'S BEEN TRANSFORMED INTO--
--STRAWBERRY JELL-O?
NO! NOW SOMETHING'S BLOWN THE KNEECAPS OFF THE OTHER ONE--!
TO THE ENERGY-PITS WITH BOOMERANG! I CAN'T RISK CAPTURE NOW--
--NOT WHEN WE'RE SO CLOSE TO VICTORY!
BWOOM!
GODFREY--HELP US!
HELP YOURSELVES!
12

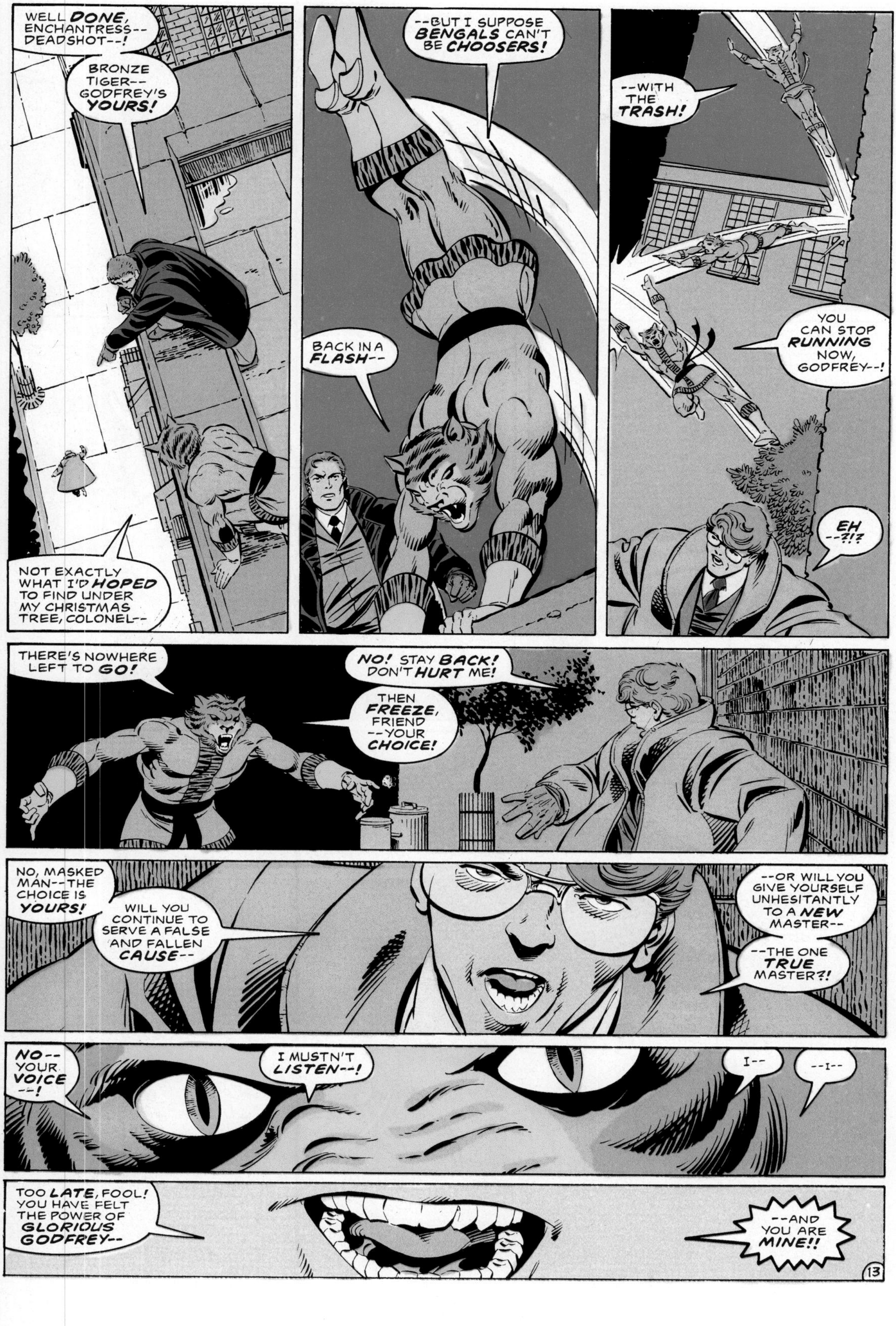

WELL DONE, ENCHANTRESS-- DEADSHOT--!
BRONZE TIGER-- GODFREY'S YOURS!
NOT EXACTLY WHAT I'D HOPED TO FIND UNDER MY CHRISTMAS TREE, COLONEL--
--BUT I SUPPOSE BENGALS CAN'T BE CHOOSERS!
BACK IN A FLASH--
--WITH THE TRASH!
YOU CAN STOP RUNNING NOW, GODFREY--!
EH --?!?
THERE'S NOWHERE LEFT TO GO!
NO! STAY BACK! DON'T HURT ME!
THEN FREEZE, FRIEND --YOUR CHOICE!
NO, MASKED MAN--THE CHOICE IS YOURS!
WILL YOU CONTINUE TO SERVE A FALSE AND FALLEN CAUSE--
--OR WILL YOU GIVE YOURSELF UNHESITANTLY TO A NEW MASTER--
--THE ONE TRUE MASTER?!
NO-- YOUR VOICE --!
I MUSTN'T LISTEN--!
I--
--I--
TOO LATE, FOOL! YOU HAVE FELT THE POWER OF GLORIOUS GODFREY--
--AND YOU ARE MINE!!

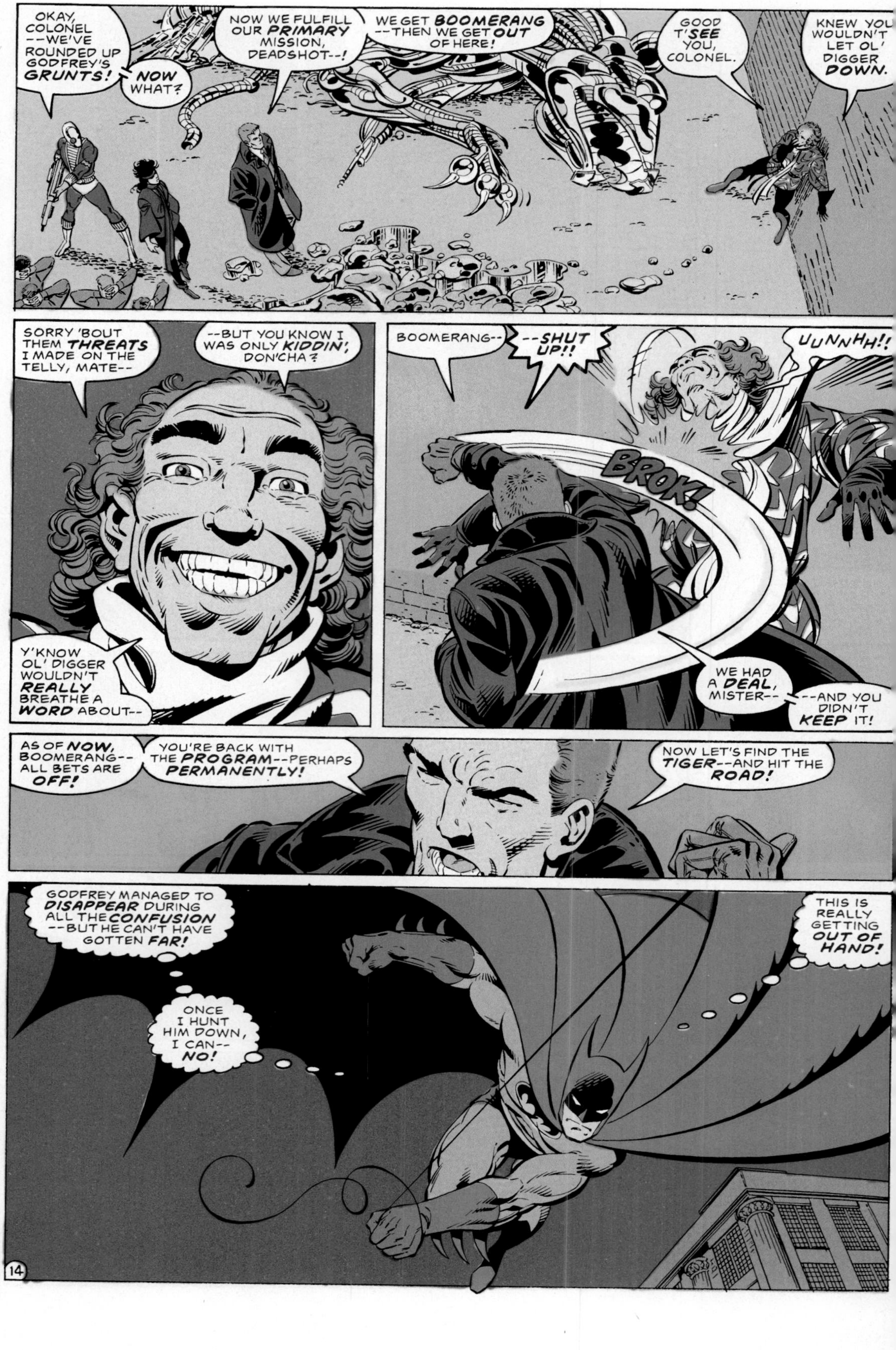
OKAY, COLONEL --WE'VE ROUNDED UP GODFREY'S GRUNTS!
NOW WHAT?
NOW WE FULFILL OUR PRIMARY MISSION, DEADSHOT--!
WE GET BOOMERANG --THEN WE GET OUT OF HERE!
GOOD T'SEE YOU, COLONEL.
KNEW YOU WOULDN'T LET OL' DIGGER DOWN.
SORRY 'BOUT THEM THREATS I MADE ON THE TELLY, MATE--
--BUT YOU KNOW I WAS ONLY KIDDIN', DON'CHA?
Y'KNOW OL' DIGGER WOULDN'T REALLY BREATHE A WORD ABOUT--
BOOMERANG--
--SHUT UP!!
UUNNHH!!
BROK!
WE HAD A DEAL, MISTER--
--AND YOU DIDN'T KEEP IT!
AS OF NOW, BOOMERANG-- ALL BETS ARE OFF!
YOU'RE BACK WITH THE PROGRAM--PERHAPS PERMANENTLY!
NOW LET'S FIND THE TIGER--AND HIT THE ROAD!
GODFREY MANAGED TO DISAPPEAR DURING ALL THE CONFUSION --BUT HE CAN'T HAVE GOTTEN FAR!
THIS IS REALLY GETTING OUT OF HAND!
ONCE I HUNT HIM DOWN, I CAN-- NO!

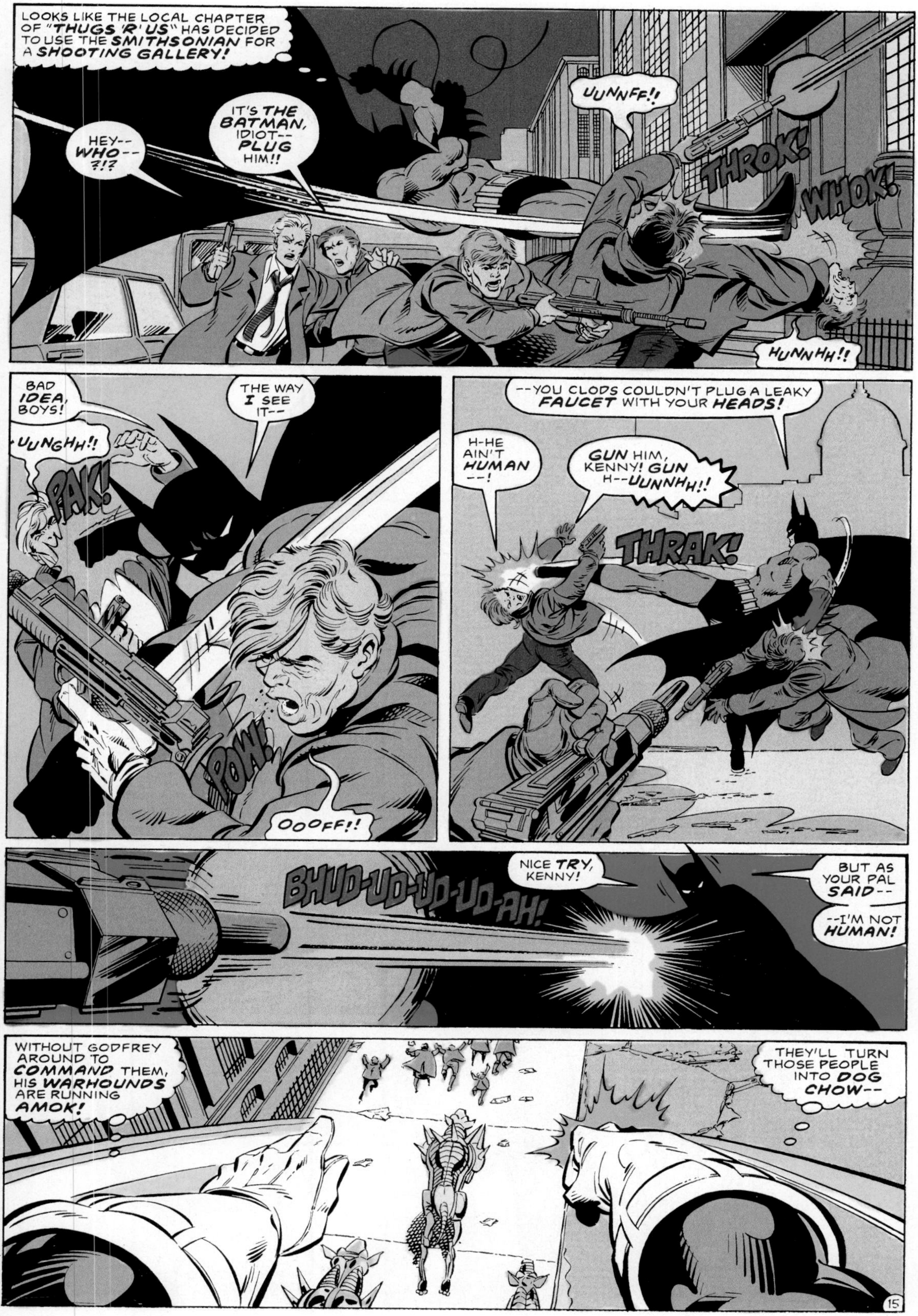

LOOKS LIKE THE LOCAL CHAPTER OF "THUGS 'R' US" HAS DECIDED TO USE THE SMITHSONIAN FOR A SHOOTING GALLERY!
HEY-- WHO-- ?!?
IT'S THE BATMAN, IDIOT-- PLUG HIM!!
UUNNFF!!
THROK!
WHOK!
HUNNHH!!
BAD IDEA, BOYS!
THE WAY I SEE IT--
UUNGHH!!
PAK!
POW!
OOOFF!!
--YOU CLODS COULDN'T PLUG A LEAKY FAUCET WITH YOUR HEADS!
H-HE AIN'T HUMAN --!
GUN HIM, KENNY! GUN H--UUNNHH!!
THRAK!
BHUD-UD-UD-UD-AH!
NICE TRY, KENNY!
BUT AS YOUR PAL SAID--
--I'M NOT HUMAN!
WITHOUT GODFREY AROUND TO COMMAND THEM, HIS WARHOUNDS ARE RUNNING AMOK!
THEY'LL TURN THOSE PEOPLE INTO DOG CHOW--

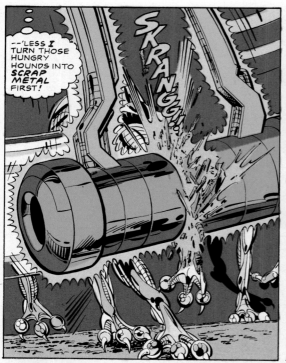

--'LESS *I* TURN THOSE HUNGRY HOUNDS INTO *SCRAP METAL* FIRST!

SKRANGG!

THAT'S ONE HOUND *DOWN*--

--WITHOUT HARMING A SINGLE STUPID *HAIR* ON THE HEADS OF THE MORONS *CONTROLLIN'* IT!

MAYBE *THAT'LL* HELP ME PROVE TO THE *GUARDIANS*--

--THEY GAVE THIS *POWER RING* TO THE *RIGHT*--DARE I SAY IT--*GUY*--

I HAD NOT INTENDED TO REVEAL MY *PRESENCE* IN MAN'S WORLD SO *SOON* AFTER MY ARRIVAL--

--BUT NO AMAZON *WORTHY* OF THE NAME CAN STAND IDLY BY WHILE INNOCENT BLOOD IS AT *RISK!*

COME *AHEAD* THEN, WARHOUND!

THOUGH YOU BE BROTHER TO *CERBERUS* HIMSELF--

16

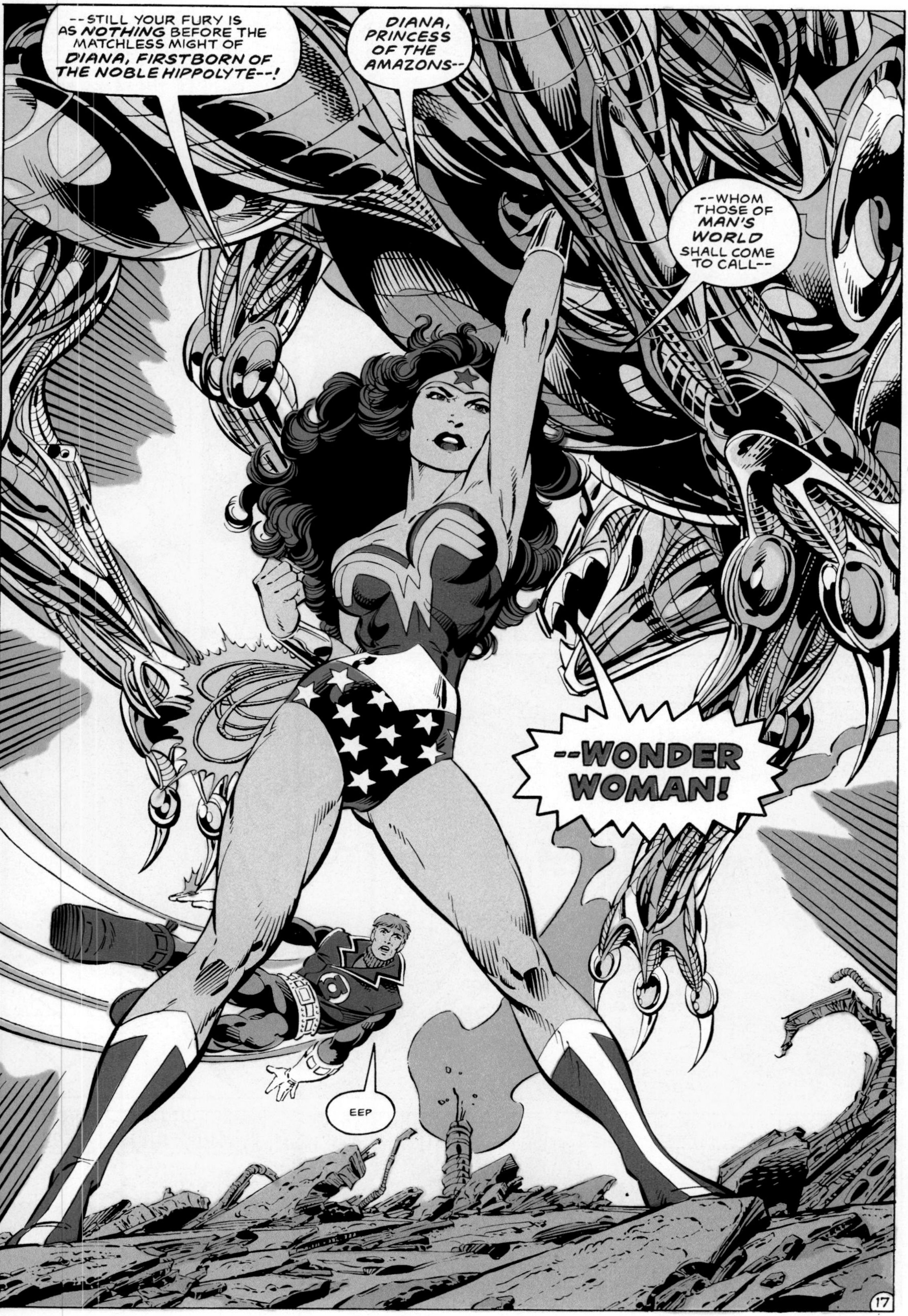
--STILL YOUR FURY IS AS NOTHING BEFORE THE MATCHLESS MIGHT OF DIANA, FIRSTBORN OF THE NOBLE HIPPOLYTE--!
DIANA, PRINCESS OF THE AMAZONS--
--WHOM THOSE OF MAN'S WORLD SHALL COME TO CALL--
--WONDER WOMAN!
EEP

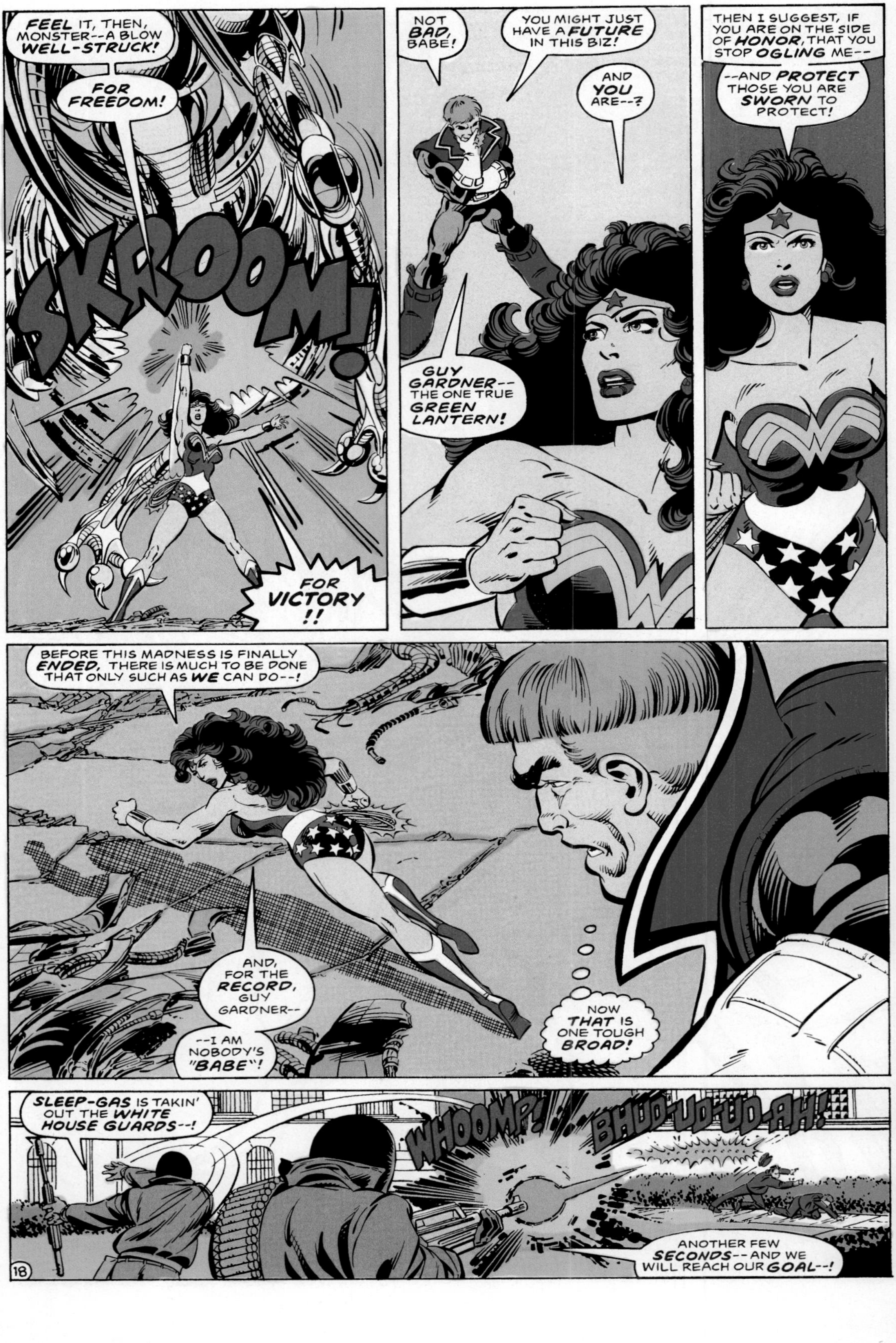

FEEL IT, THEN, MONSTER--A BLOW WELL-STRUCK!
FOR FREEDOM!
SKROOM!
FOR VICTORY !!
NOT BAD, BABE!
YOU MIGHT JUST HAVE A FUTURE IN THIS BIZ!
AND YOU ARE--?
GUY GARDNER-- THE ONE TRUE GREEN LANTERN!
THEN I SUGGEST, IF YOU ARE ON THE SIDE OF HONOR, THAT YOU STOP OGLING ME--
--AND PROTECT THOSE YOU ARE SWORN TO PROTECT!
BEFORE THIS MADNESS IS FINALLY ENDED, THERE IS MUCH TO BE DONE THAT ONLY SUCH AS WE CAN DO--!
AND, FOR THE RECORD, GUY GARDNER--
--I AM NOBODY'S "BABE"!
NOW THAT IS ONE TOUGH BROAD!
SLEEP-GAS IS TAKIN' OUT THE WHITE HOUSE GUARDS--!
WHOOMP!
BHUD-UD-UD-AH!
ANOTHER FEW SECONDS--AND WE WILL REACH OUR GOAL--!

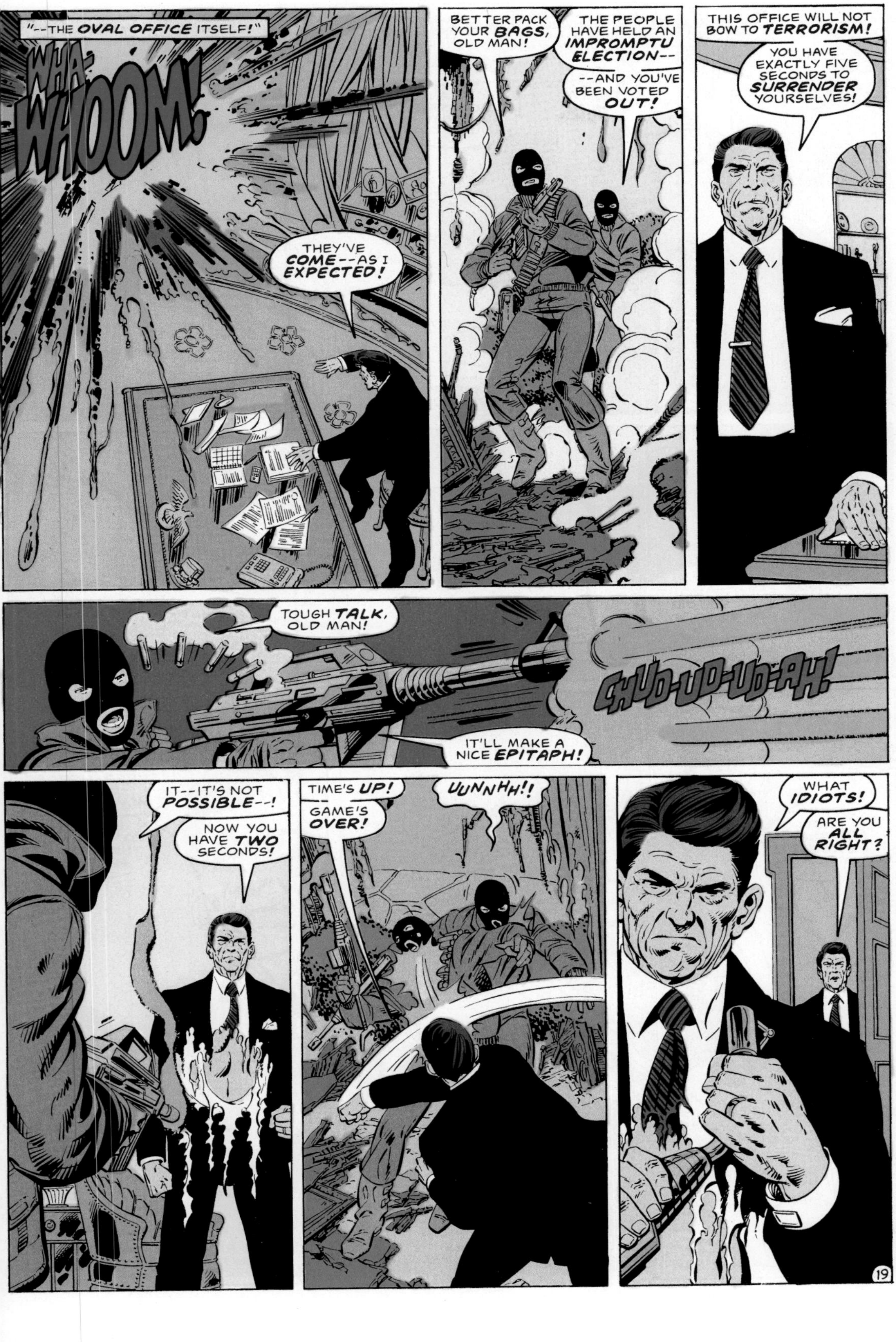
"--THE OVAL OFFICE ITSELF!"
WHA-WHOOM!
THEY'VE COME--AS I EXPECTED!
BETTER PACK YOUR BAGS, OLD MAN!
THE PEOPLE HAVE HELD AN IMPROMPTU ELECTION--
--AND YOU'VE BEEN VOTED OUT!
THIS OFFICE WILL NOT BOW TO TERRORISM!
YOU HAVE EXACTLY FIVE SECONDS TO SURRENDER YOURSELVES!
TOUGH TALK, OLD MAN!
CHUD-UD-UD-AH!
IT'LL MAKE A NICE EPITAPH!
IT--IT'S NOT POSSIBLE--!
NOW YOU HAVE TWO SECONDS!
TIME'S UP!
GAME'S OVER!
UUNNHH!!
WHAT IDIOTS!
ARE YOU ALL RIGHT?

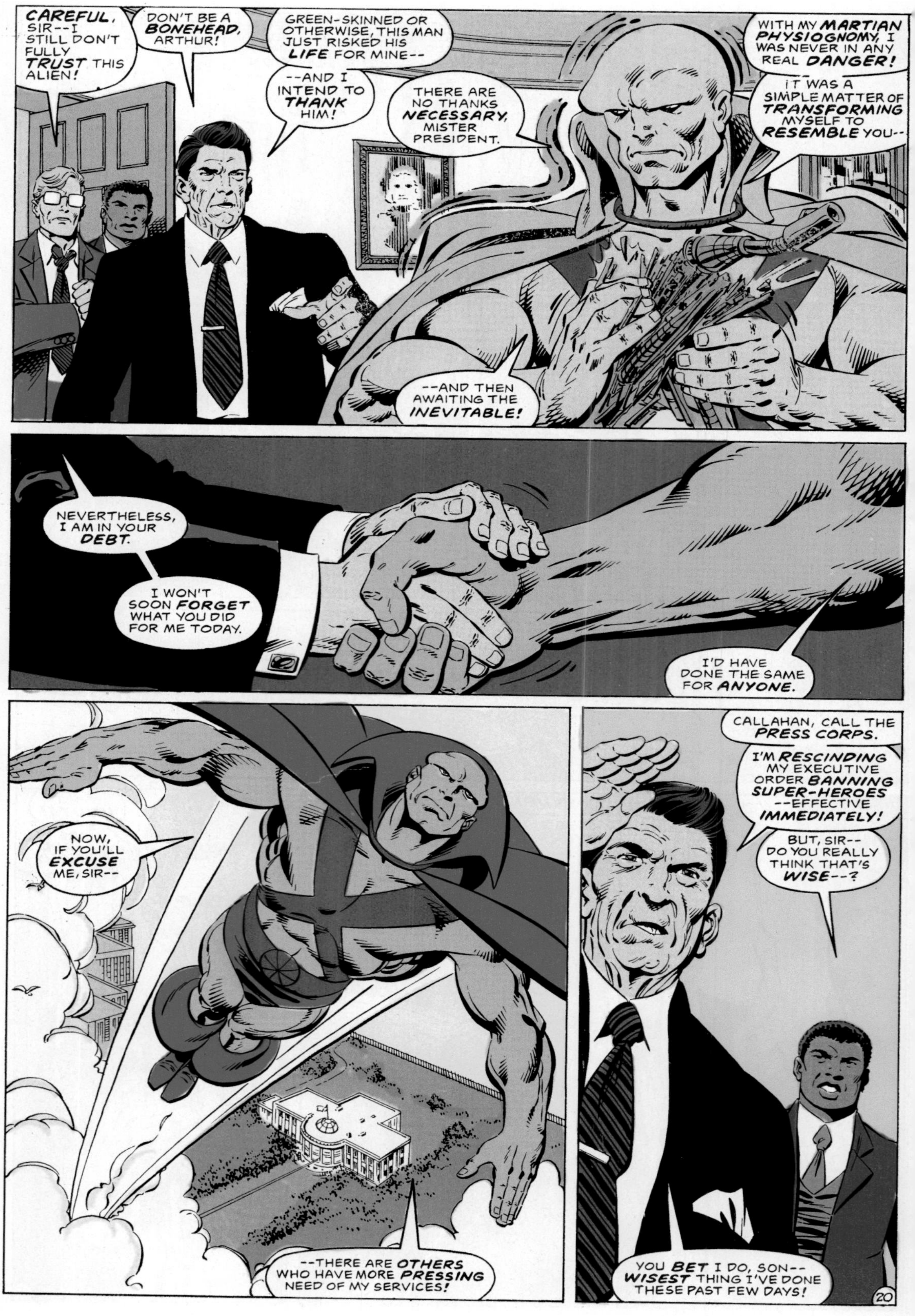

CAREFUL, SIR--I STILL DON'T FULLY TRUST THIS ALIEN!
DON'T BE A BONEHEAD, ARTHUR!
GREEN-SKINNED OR OTHERWISE, THIS MAN JUST RISKED HIS LIFE FOR MINE--
--AND I INTEND TO THANK HIM!
THERE ARE NO THANKS NECESSARY, MISTER PRESIDENT.
WITH MY MARTIAN PHYSIOGNOMY, I WAS NEVER IN ANY REAL DANGER!
IT WAS A SIMPLE MATTER OF TRANSFORMING MYSELF TO RESEMBLE YOU--
--AND THEN AWAITING THE INEVITABLE!
NEVERTHELESS, I AM IN YOUR DEBT.
I WON'T SOON FORGET WHAT YOU DID FOR ME TODAY.
I'D HAVE DONE THE SAME FOR ANYONE.
NOW, IF YOU'LL EXCUSE ME, SIR--
--THERE ARE OTHERS WHO HAVE MORE PRESSING NEED OF MY SERVICES!
CALLAHAN, CALL THE PRESS CORPS.
I'M RESCINDING MY EXECUTIVE ORDER BANNING SUPER-HEROES--EFFECTIVE IMMEDIATELY!
BUT, SIR--DO YOU REALLY THINK THAT'S WISE--?
YOU BET I DO, SON--WISEST THING I'VE DONE THESE PAST FEW DAYS!

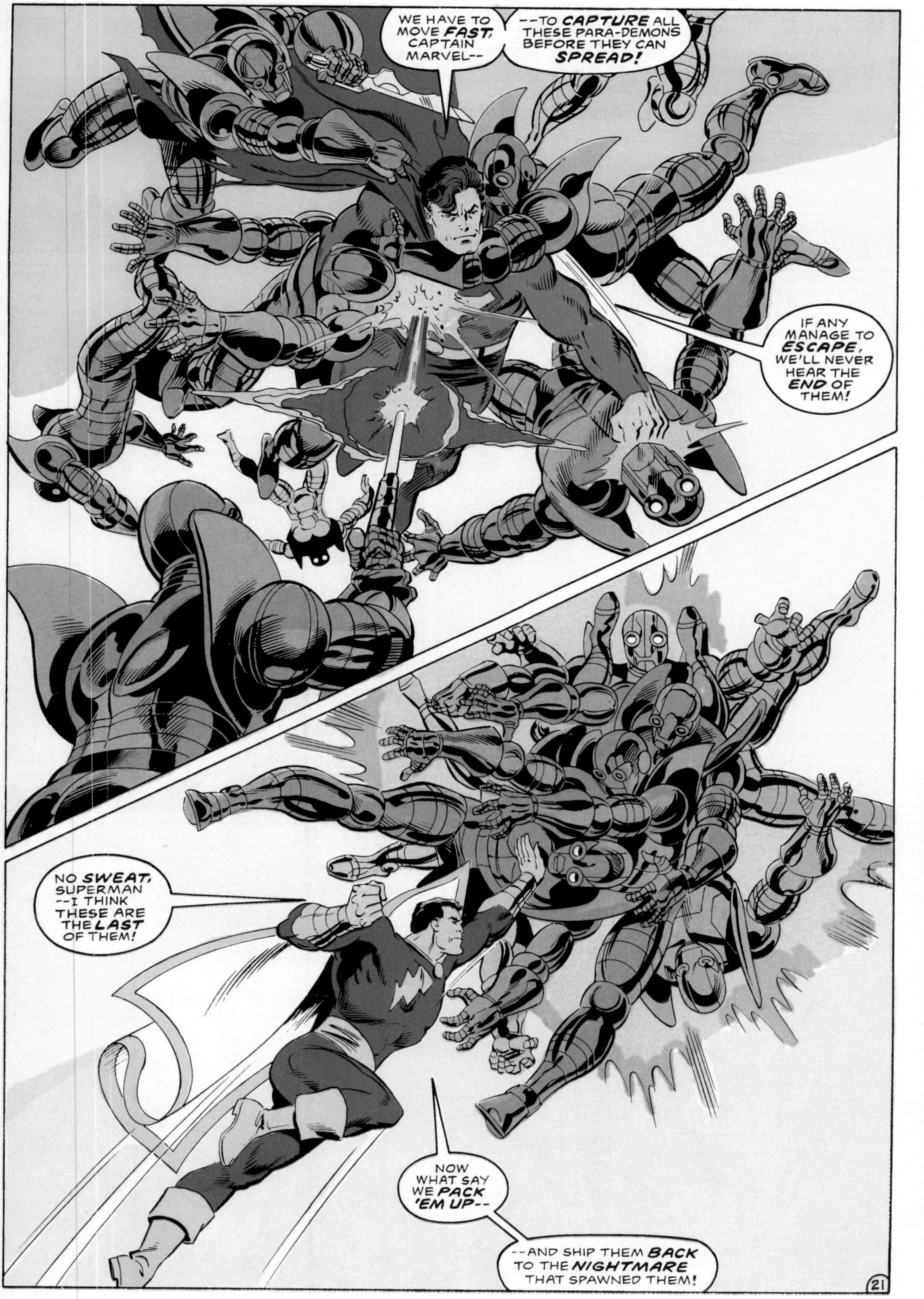
WE HAVE TO MOVE FAST, CAPTAIN MARVEL--
--TO CAPTURE ALL THESE PARA-DEMONS BEFORE THEY CAN SPREAD!
IF ANY MANAGE TO ESCAPE, WE'LL NEVER HEAR THE END OF THEM!
NO SWEAT, SUPERMAN --I THINK THESE ARE THE LAST OF THEM!
NOW WHAT SAY WE PACK 'EM UP--
--AND SHIP THEM BACK TO THE NIGHTMARE THAT SPAWNED THEM!
21

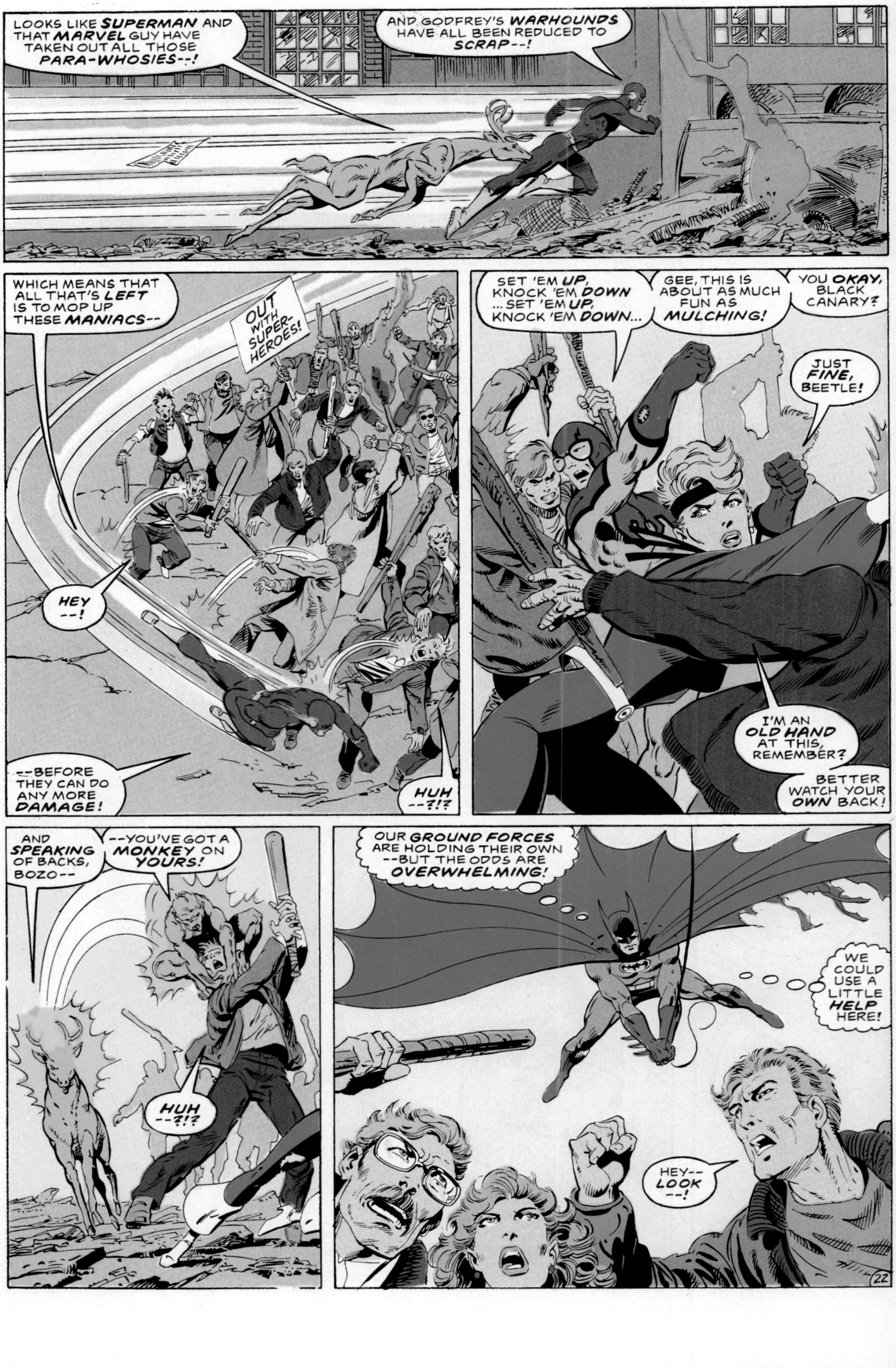
LOOKS LIKE SUPERMAN AND THAT MARVEL GUY HAVE TAKEN OUT ALL THOSE PARA-WHOSIES--!
AND GODFREY'S WARHOUNDS HAVE ALL BEEN REDUCED TO SCRAP--!
WHICH MEANS THAT ALL THAT'S LEFT IS TO MOP UP THESE MANIACS--
OUT WITH SUPER-HEROES!
HEY--!
--BEFORE THEY CAN DO ANY MORE DAMAGE!
HUH--?!?
SET 'EM UP, KNOCK 'EM DOWN ...SET 'EM UP, KNOCK 'EM DOWN...
GEE, THIS IS ABOUT AS MUCH FUN AS MULCHING!
YOU OKAY, BLACK CANARY?
JUST FINE, BEETLE!
I'M AN OLD HAND AT THIS, REMEMBER?
BETTER WATCH YOUR OWN BACK!
AND SPEAKING OF BACKS, BOZO--
--YOU'VE GOT A MONKEY ON YOURS!
HUH--?!?
OUR GROUND FORCES ARE HOLDING THEIR OWN --BUT THE ODDS ARE OVERWHELMING!
WE COULD USE A LITTLE HELP HERE!
HEY-- LOOK--!

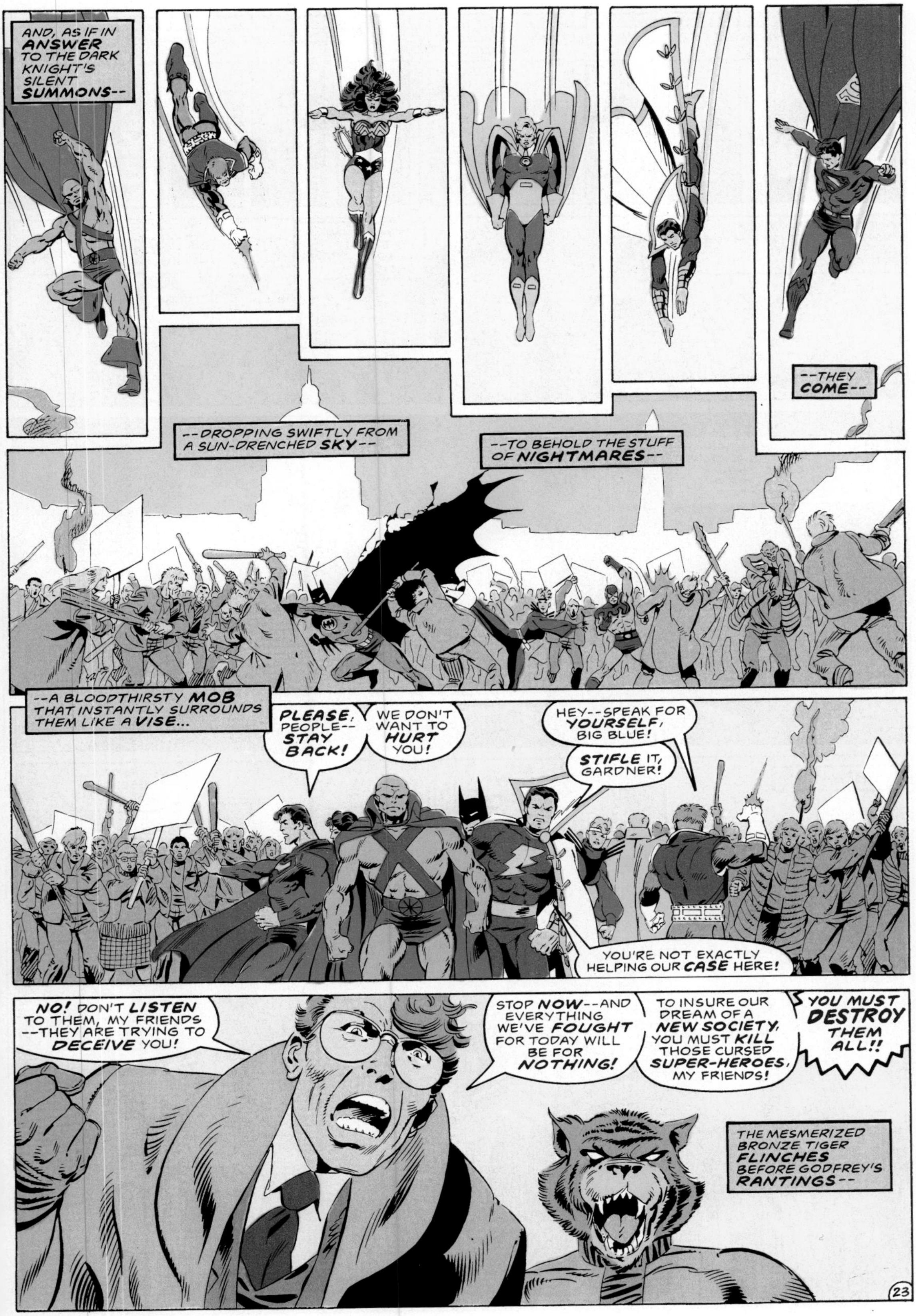

AND, AS IF IN ANSWER TO THE DARK KNIGHT'S SILENT SUMMONS--
--THEY COME--
--DROPPING SWIFTLY FROM A SUN-DRENCHED SKY--
--TO BEHOLD THE STUFF OF NIGHTMARES--
--A BLOODTHIRSTY MOB THAT INSTANTLY SURROUNDS THEM LIKE A VISE...
PLEASE, PEOPLE-- STAY BACK!
WE DON'T WANT TO HURT YOU!
HEY--SPEAK FOR YOURSELF, BIG BLUE!
STIFLE IT, GARDNER!
YOU'RE NOT EXACTLY HELPING OUR CASE HERE!
NO! DON'T LISTEN TO THEM, MY FRIENDS --THEY ARE TRYING TO DECEIVE YOU!
STOP NOW--AND EVERYTHING WE'VE FOUGHT FOR TODAY WILL BE FOR NOTHING!
TO INSURE OUR DREAM OF A NEW SOCIETY, YOU MUST KILL THOSE CURSED SUPER-HEROES, MY FRIENDS!
YOU MUST DESTROY THEM ALL!!
THE MESMERIZED BRONZE TIGER FLINCHES BEFORE GODFREY'S RANTINGS--

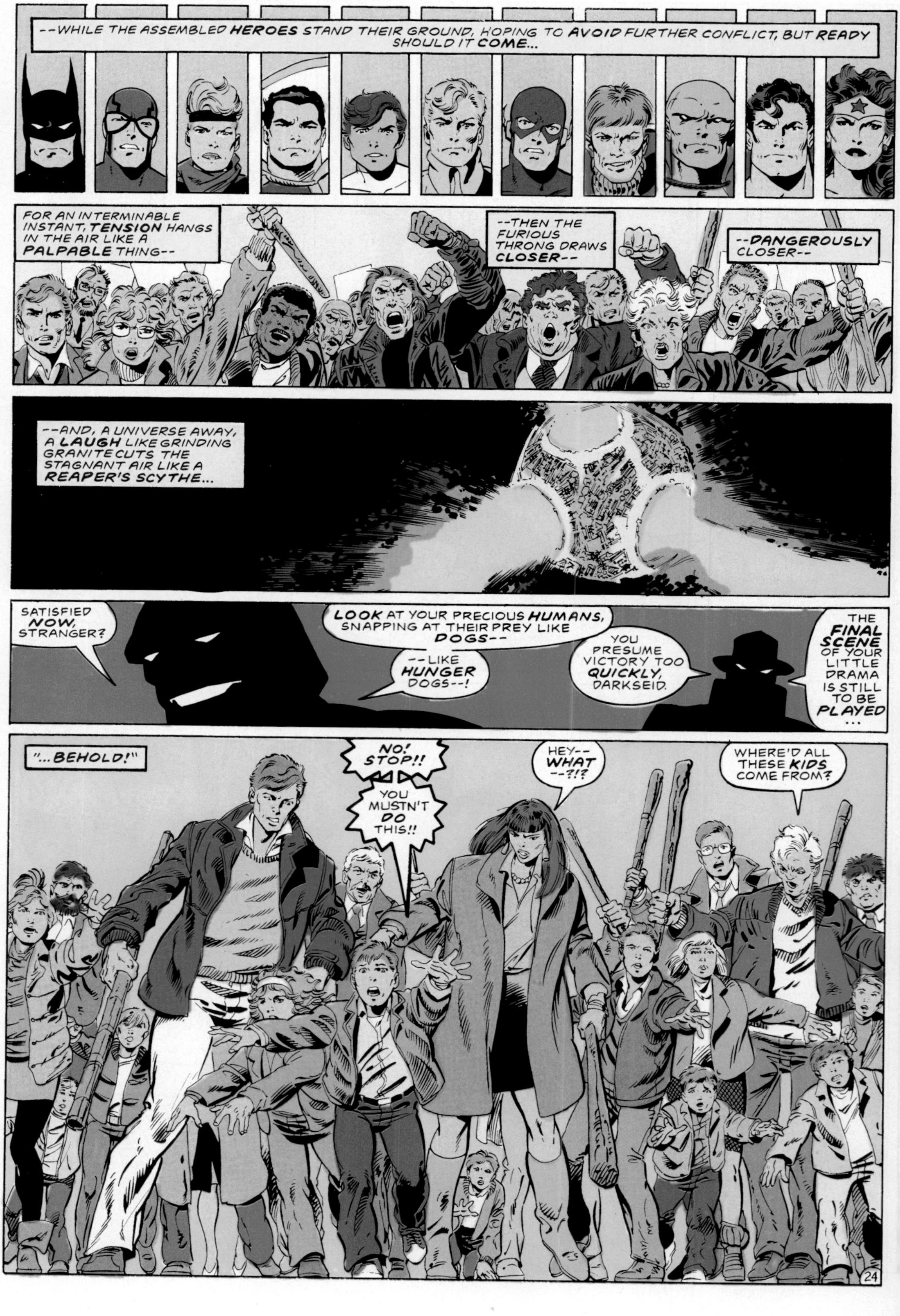

--WHILE THE ASSEMBLED HEROES STAND THEIR GROUND, HOPING TO AVOID FURTHER CONFLICT, BUT READY SHOULD IT COME...
FOR AN INTERMINABLE INSTANT, TENSION HANGS IN THE AIR LIKE A PALPABLE THING--
--THEN THE FURIOUS THRONG DRAWS CLOSER--
--DANGEROUSLY CLOSER--
--AND, A UNIVERSE AWAY, A LAUGH LIKE GRINDING GRANITE CUTS THE STAGNANT AIR LIKE A REAPER'S SCYTHE...
SATISFIED NOW, STRANGER?
LOOK AT YOUR PRECIOUS HUMANS, SNAPPING AT THEIR PREY LIKE DOGS--
--LIKE HUNGER DOGS--!
YOU PRESUME VICTORY TOO QUICKLY, DARKSEID.
THE FINAL SCENE OF YOUR LITTLE DRAMA IS STILL TO BE PLAYED...
"...BEHOLD!"
NO! STOP!!
YOU MUSTN'T DO THIS!!
HEY-- WHAT --?!?
WHERE'D ALL THESE KIDS COME FROM?

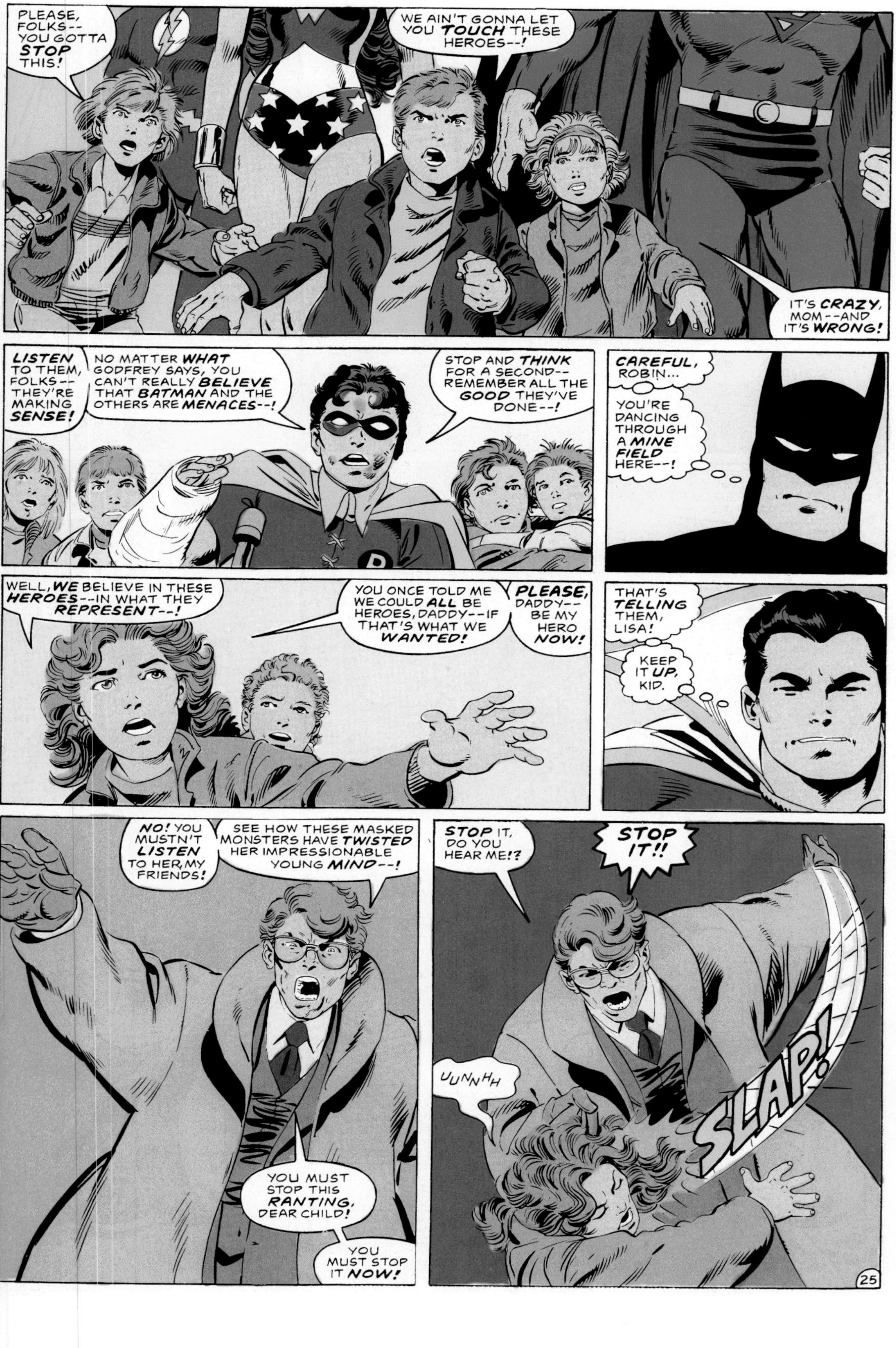

PLEASE, FOLKS-- YOU GOTTA STOP THIS!
WE AIN'T GONNA LET YOU TOUCH THESE HEROES--!
IT'S CRAZY, MOM--AND IT'S WRONG!
LISTEN TO THEM, FOLKS-- THEY'RE MAKING SENSE!
NO MATTER WHAT GODFREY SAYS, YOU CAN'T REALLY BELIEVE THAT BATMAN AND THE OTHERS ARE MENACES--!
STOP AND THINK FOR A SECOND-- REMEMBER ALL THE GOOD THEY'VE DONE--!
CAREFUL, ROBIN...
YOU'RE DANCING THROUGH A MINE FIELD HERE--!
WELL, WE BELIEVE IN THESE HEROES--IN WHAT THEY REPRESENT--!
YOU ONCE TOLD ME WE COULD ALL BE HEROES, DADDY--IF THAT'S WHAT WE WANTED!
PLEASE, DADDY-- BE MY HERO NOW!
THAT'S TELLING THEM, LISA!
KEEP IT UP, KID.
NO! YOU MUSTN'T LISTEN TO HER, MY FRIENDS!
SEE HOW THESE MASKED MONSTERS HAVE TWISTED HER IMPRESSIONABLE YOUNG MIND--!
YOU MUST STOP THIS RANTING, DEAR CHILD!
YOU MUST STOP IT NOW!
STOP IT, DO YOU HEAR ME!?
STOP IT!!
SLAP!
UUNNHH

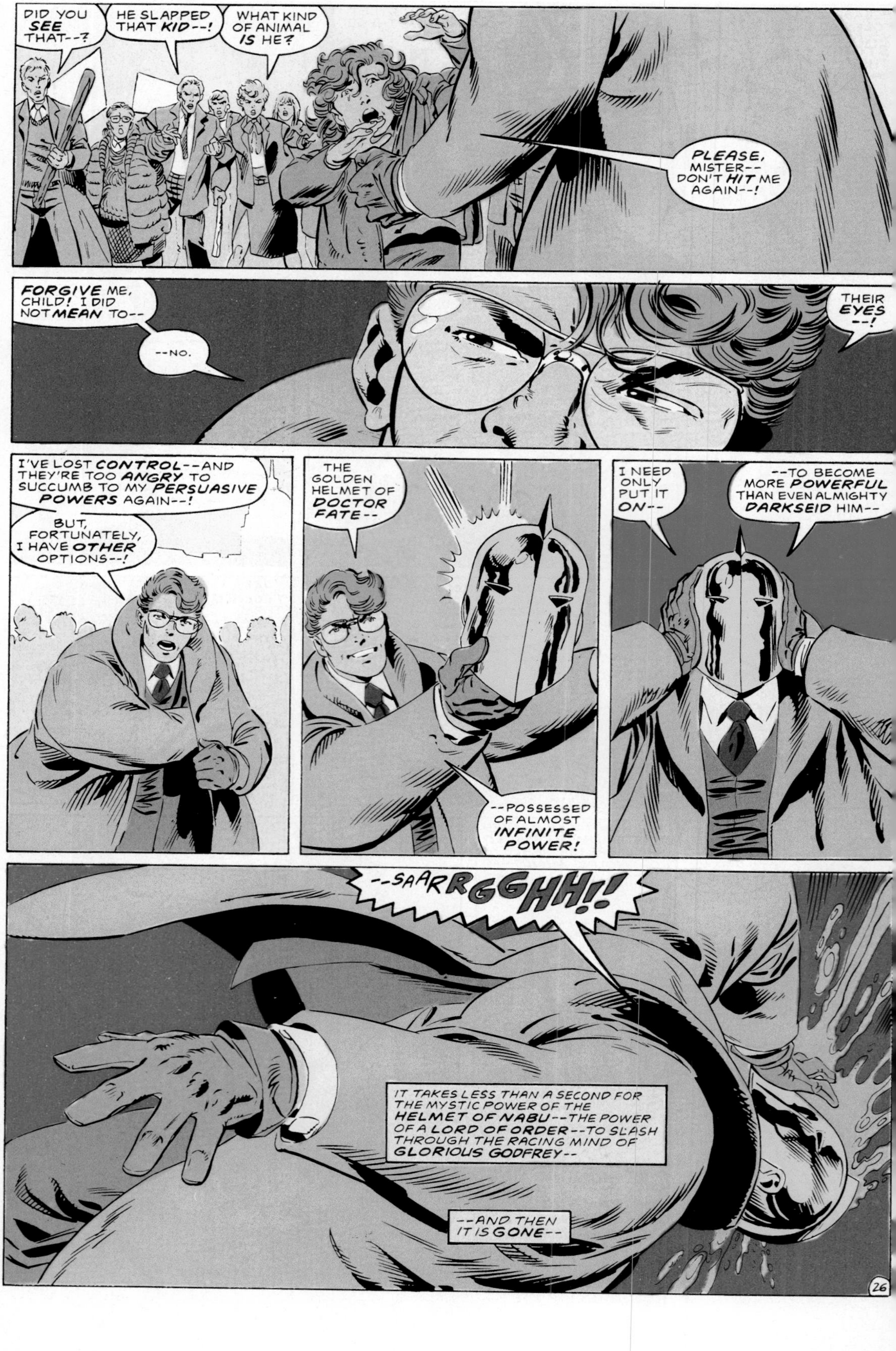
DID YOU SEE THAT--?
HE SLAPPED THAT KID--!
WHAT KIND OF ANIMAL IS HE?
PLEASE, MISTER-- DON'T HIT ME AGAIN--!
FORGIVE ME, CHILD! I DID NOT MEAN TO--
--NO.
THEIR EYES--!
I'VE LOST CONTROL--AND THEY'RE TOO ANGRY TO SUCCUMB TO MY PERSUASIVE POWERS AGAIN--!
BUT, FORTUNATELY, I HAVE OTHER OPTIONS--!
THE GOLDEN HELMET OF DOCTOR FATE--
--POSSESSED OF ALMOST INFINITE POWER!
I NEED ONLY PUT IT ON--
--TO BECOME MORE POWERFUL THAN EVEN ALMIGHTY DARKSEID HIM--
--SAARRGGHH!!
IT TAKES LESS THAN A SECOND FOR THE MYSTIC POWER OF THE HELMET OF NABU--THE POWER OF A LORD OF ORDER--TO SLASH THROUGH THE RACING MIND OF GLORIOUS GODFREY--
--AND THEN IT IS GONE--

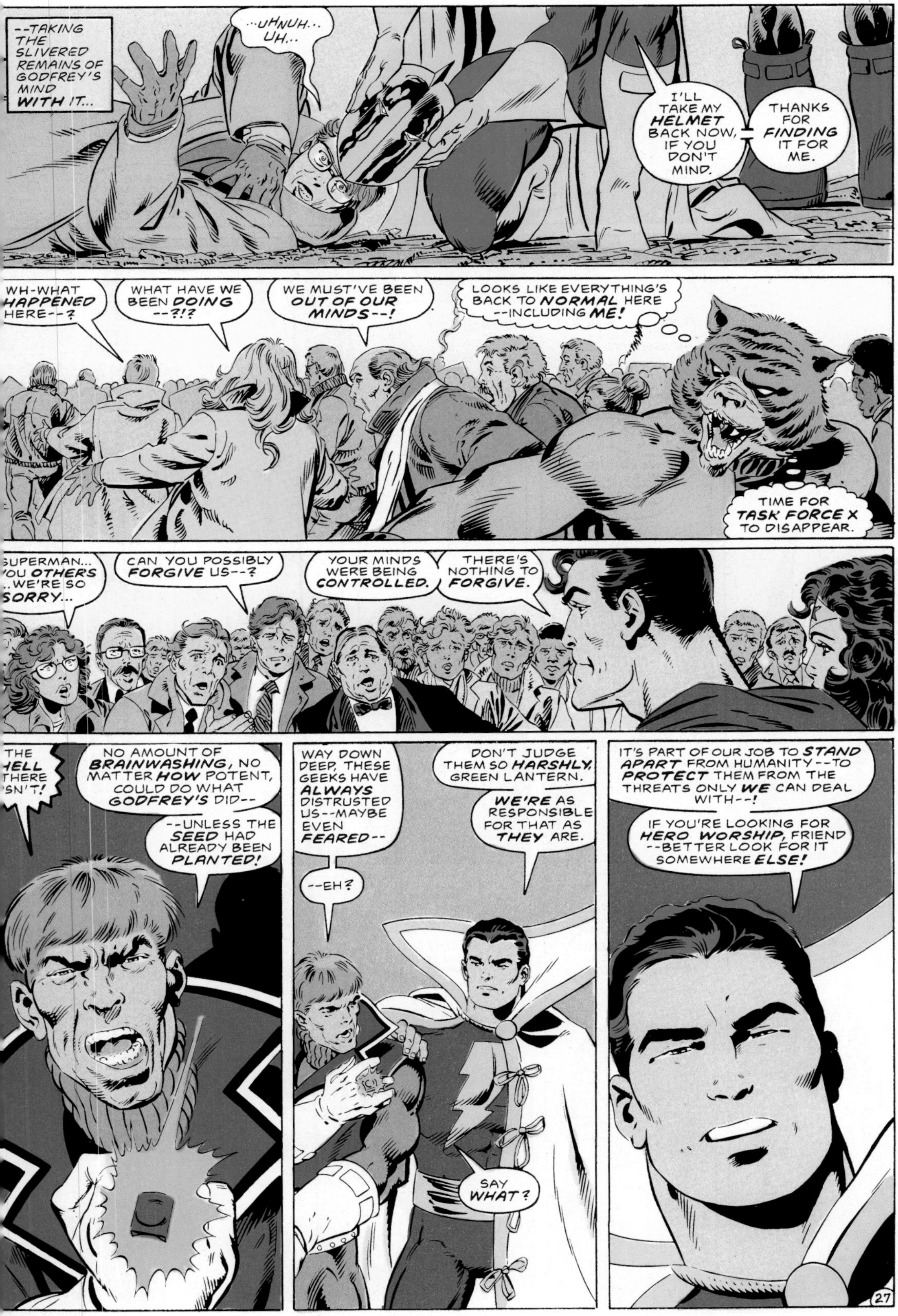
--TAKING THE SLIVERED REMAINS OF GODFREY'S MIND WITH IT...
...UHNUH... UH...
I'LL TAKE MY HELMET BACK NOW, IF YOU DON'T MIND.
THANKS FOR FINDING IT FOR ME.
WH-WHAT HAPPENED HERE--?
WHAT HAVE WE BEEN DOING --?!?
WE MUST'VE BEEN OUT OF OUR MINDS--!
LOOKS LIKE EVERYTHING'S BACK TO NORMAL HERE --INCLUDING ME!
TIME FOR TASK FORCE X TO DISAPPEAR.
SUPERMAN... YOU OTHERS ...WE'RE SO SORRY...
CAN YOU POSSIBLY FORGIVE US--?
YOUR MINDS WERE BEING CONTROLLED.
THERE'S NOTHING TO FORGIVE.
THE HELL THERE ISN'T!
NO AMOUNT OF BRAINWASHING, NO MATTER HOW POTENT, COULD DO WHAT GODFREY'S DID--
--UNLESS THE SEED HAD ALREADY BEEN PLANTED!
WAY DOWN DEEP, THESE GEEKS HAVE ALWAYS DISTRUSTED US--MAYBE EVEN FEARED--
DON'T JUDGE THEM SO HARSHLY, GREEN LANTERN.
WE'RE AS RESPONSIBLE FOR THAT AS THEY ARE.
--EH?
SAY WHAT?
IT'S PART OF OUR JOB TO STAND APART FROM HUMANITY--TO PROTECT THEM FROM THE THREATS ONLY WE CAN DEAL WITH--!
IF YOU'RE LOOKING FOR HERO WORSHIP, FRIEND --BETTER LOOK FOR IT SOMEWHERE ELSE!
27

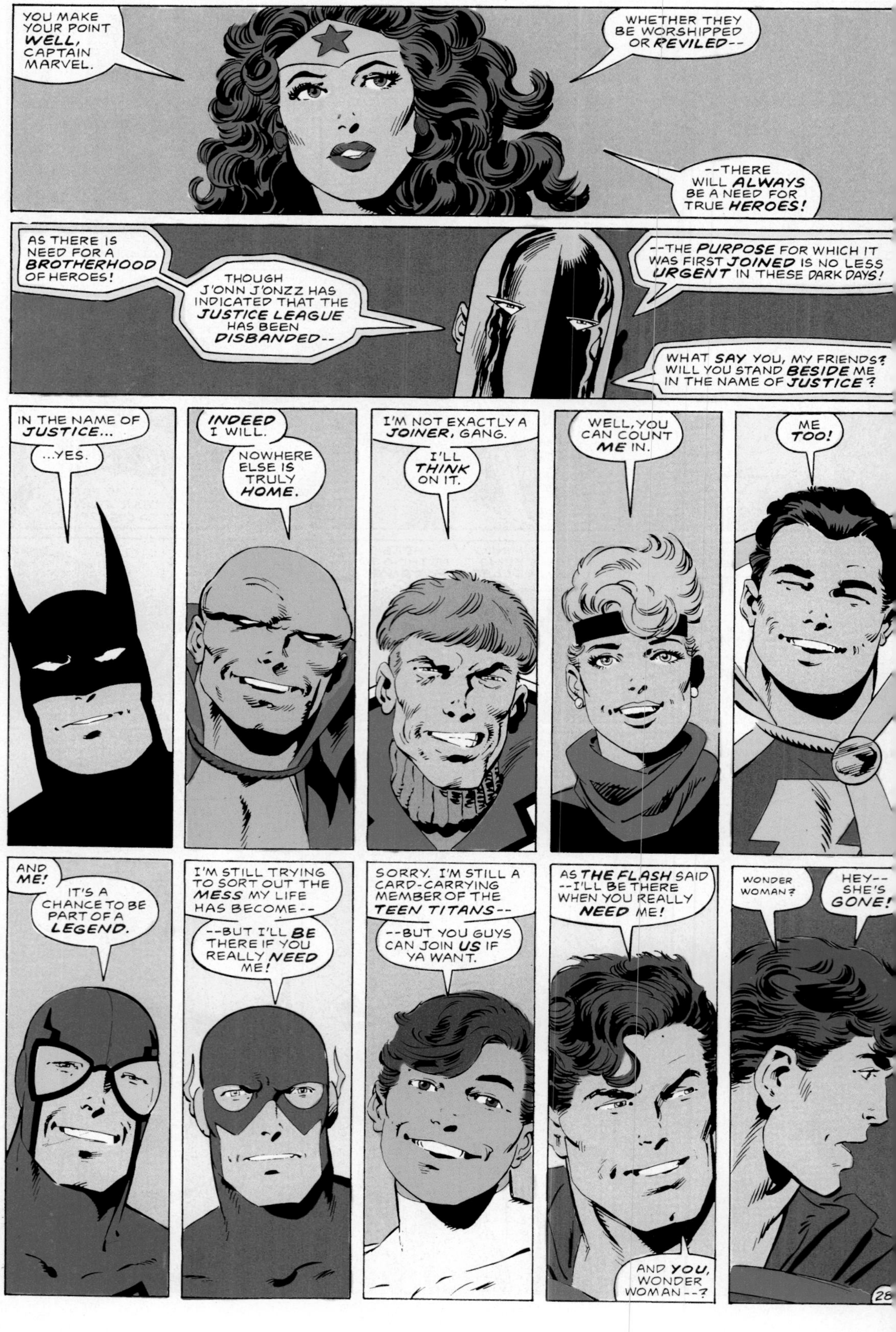

YOU MAKE YOUR POINT WELL, CAPTAIN MARVEL.
WHETHER THEY BE WORSHIPPED OR REVILED--
--THERE WILL ALWAYS BE A NEED FOR TRUE HEROES!
AS THERE IS NEED FOR A BROTHERHOOD OF HEROES!
THOUGH J'ONN J'ONZZ HAS INDICATED THAT THE JUSTICE LEAGUE HAS BEEN DISBANDED--
--THE PURPOSE FOR WHICH IT WAS FIRST JOINED IS NO LESS URGENT IN THESE DARK DAYS!
WHAT SAY YOU, MY FRIENDS? WILL YOU STAND BESIDE ME IN THE NAME OF JUSTICE?
IN THE NAME OF JUSTICE...
...YES.
INDEED I WILL.
NOWHERE ELSE IS TRULY HOME.
I'M NOT EXACTLY A JOINER, GANG.
I'LL THINK ON IT.
WELL, YOU CAN COUNT ME IN.
ME TOO!
AND ME!
IT'S A CHANCE TO BE PART OF A LEGEND.
I'M STILL TRYING TO SORT OUT THE MESS MY LIFE HAS BECOME--
--BUT I'LL BE THERE IF YOU REALLY NEED ME!
SORRY. I'M STILL A CARD-CARRYING MEMBER OF THE TEEN TITANS--
--BUT YOU GUYS CAN JOIN US IF YA WANT.
AS THE FLASH SAID --I'LL BE THERE WHEN YOU REALLY NEED ME!
AND YOU, WONDER WOMAN--?
WONDER WOMAN?
HEY-- SHE'S GONE!

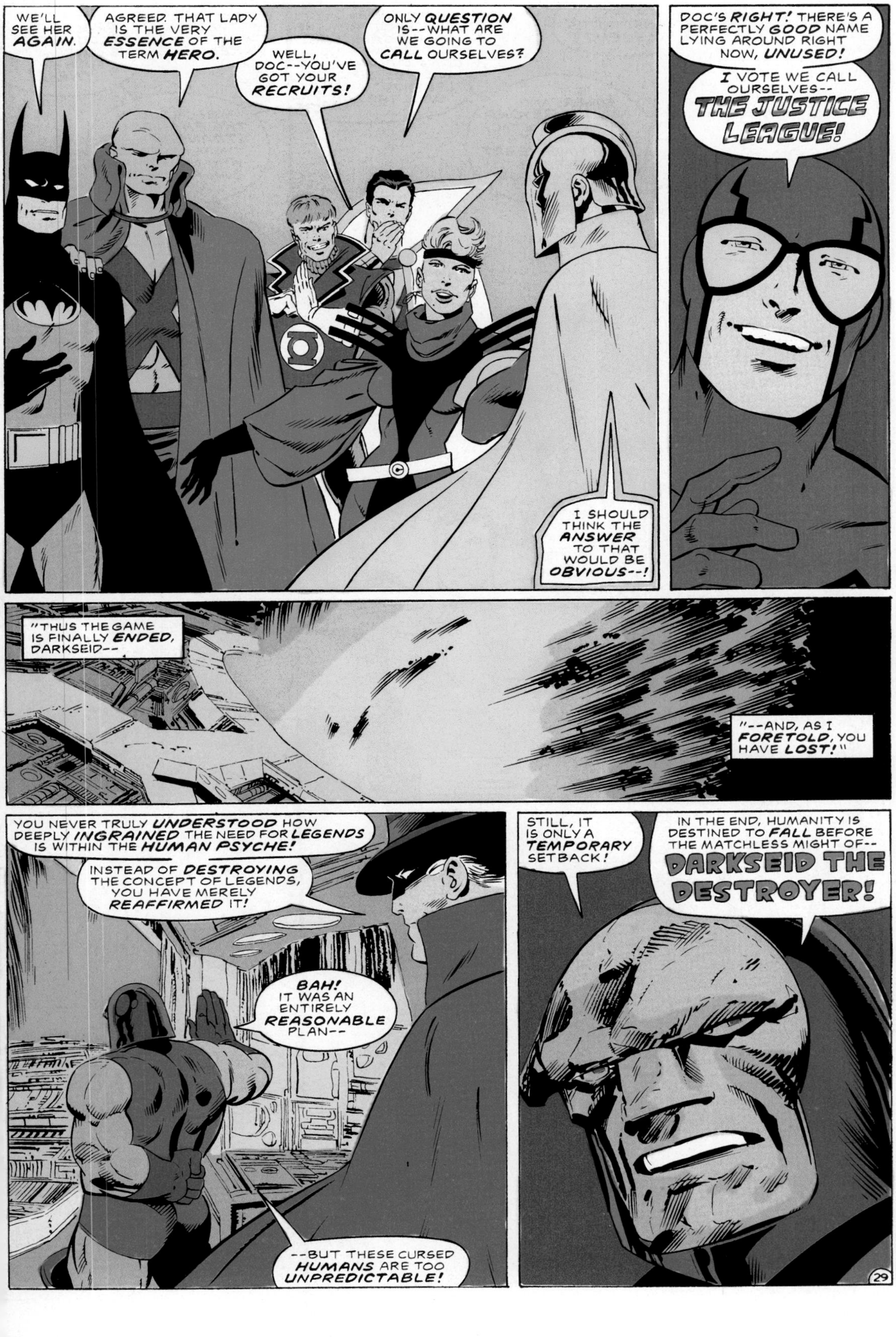
WE'LL SEE HER AGAIN.
AGREED. THAT LADY IS THE VERY ESSENCE OF THE TERM HERO.
WELL, DOC--YOU'VE GOT YOUR RECRUITS!
ONLY QUESTION IS--WHAT ARE WE GOING TO CALL OURSELVES?
I SHOULD THINK THE ANSWER TO THAT WOULD BE OBVIOUS--!
DOC'S RIGHT! THERE'S A PERFECTLY GOOD NAME LYING AROUND RIGHT NOW, UNUSED!
I VOTE WE CALL OURSELVES-- THE JUSTICE LEAGUE!
"THUS THE GAME IS FINALLY ENDED, DARKSEID--
"--AND, AS I FORETOLD, YOU HAVE LOST!"
YOU NEVER TRULY UNDERSTOOD HOW DEEPLY INGRAINED THE NEED FOR LEGENDS IS WITHIN THE HUMAN PSYCHE!
INSTEAD OF DESTROYING THE CONCEPT OF LEGENDS, YOU HAVE MERELY REAFFIRMED IT!
BAH! IT WAS AN ENTIRELY REASONABLE PLAN--
--BUT THESE CURSED HUMANS ARE TOO UNPREDICTABLE!
STILL, IT IS ONLY A TEMPORARY SETBACK!
IN THE END, HUMANITY IS DESTINED TO FALL BEFORE THE MATCHLESS MIGHT OF-- DARKSEID THE DESTROYER!
29

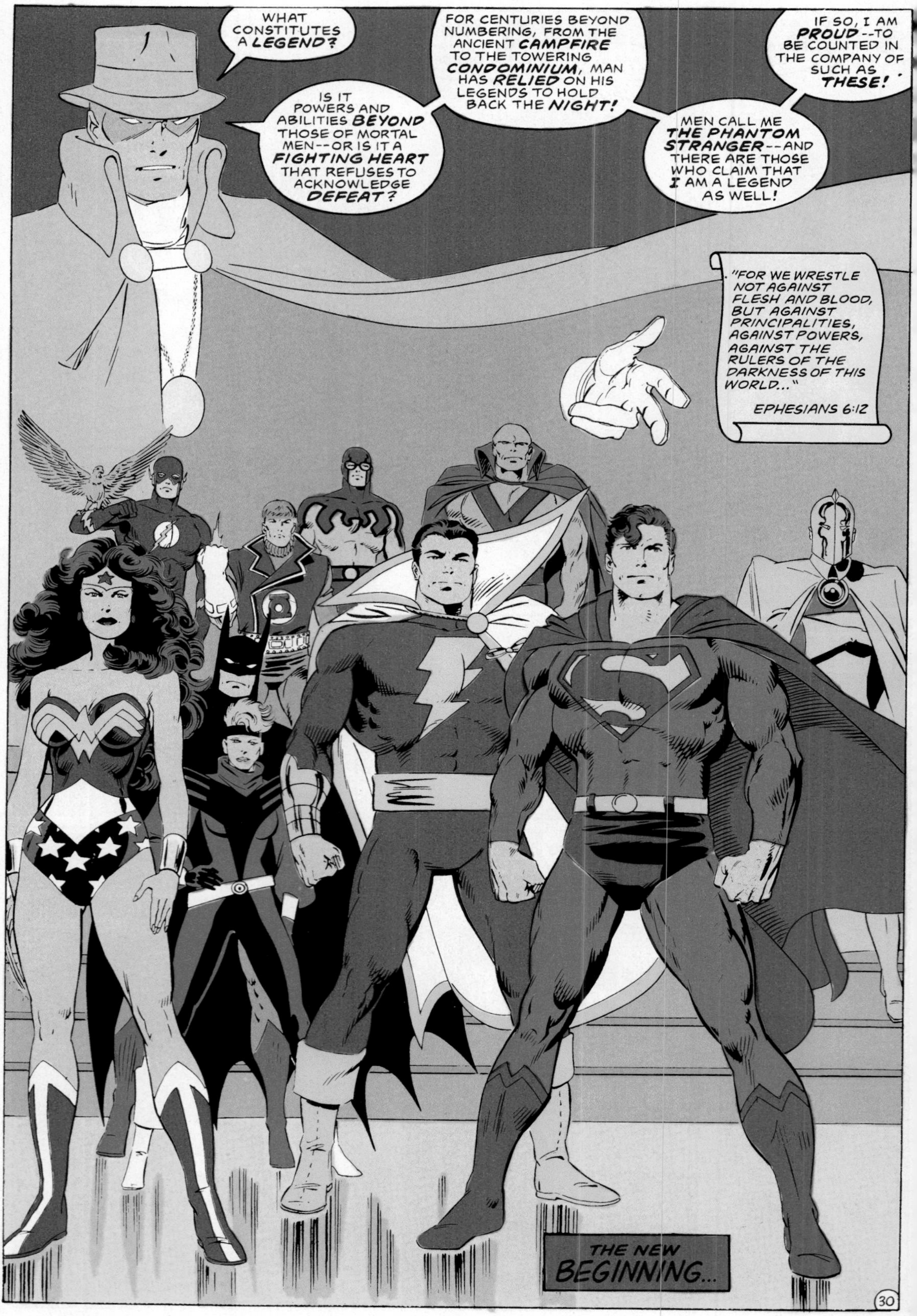

WHAT CONSTITUTES A LEGEND?
IS IT POWERS AND ABILITIES BEYOND THOSE OF MORTAL MEN--OR IS IT A FIGHTING HEART THAT REFUSES TO ACKNOWLEDGE DEFEAT?
FOR CENTURIES BEYOND NUMBERING, FROM THE ANCIENT CAMPFIRE TO THE TOWERING CONDOMINIUM, MAN HAS RELIED ON HIS LEGENDS TO HOLD BACK THE NIGHT!
MEN CALL ME THE PHANTOM STRANGER--AND THERE ARE THOSE WHO CLAIM THAT I AM A LEGEND AS WELL!
IF SO, I AM PROUD--TO BE COUNTED IN THE COMPANY OF SUCH AS THESE!
"FOR WE WRESTLE NOT AGAINST FLESH AND BLOOD, BUT AGAINST PRINCIPALITIES, AGAINST POWERS, AGAINST THE RULERS OF THE DARKNESS OF THIS WORLD..."
EPHESIANS 6:12
THE NEW BEGINNING...

LEGENDS™

THE COLLECTION™

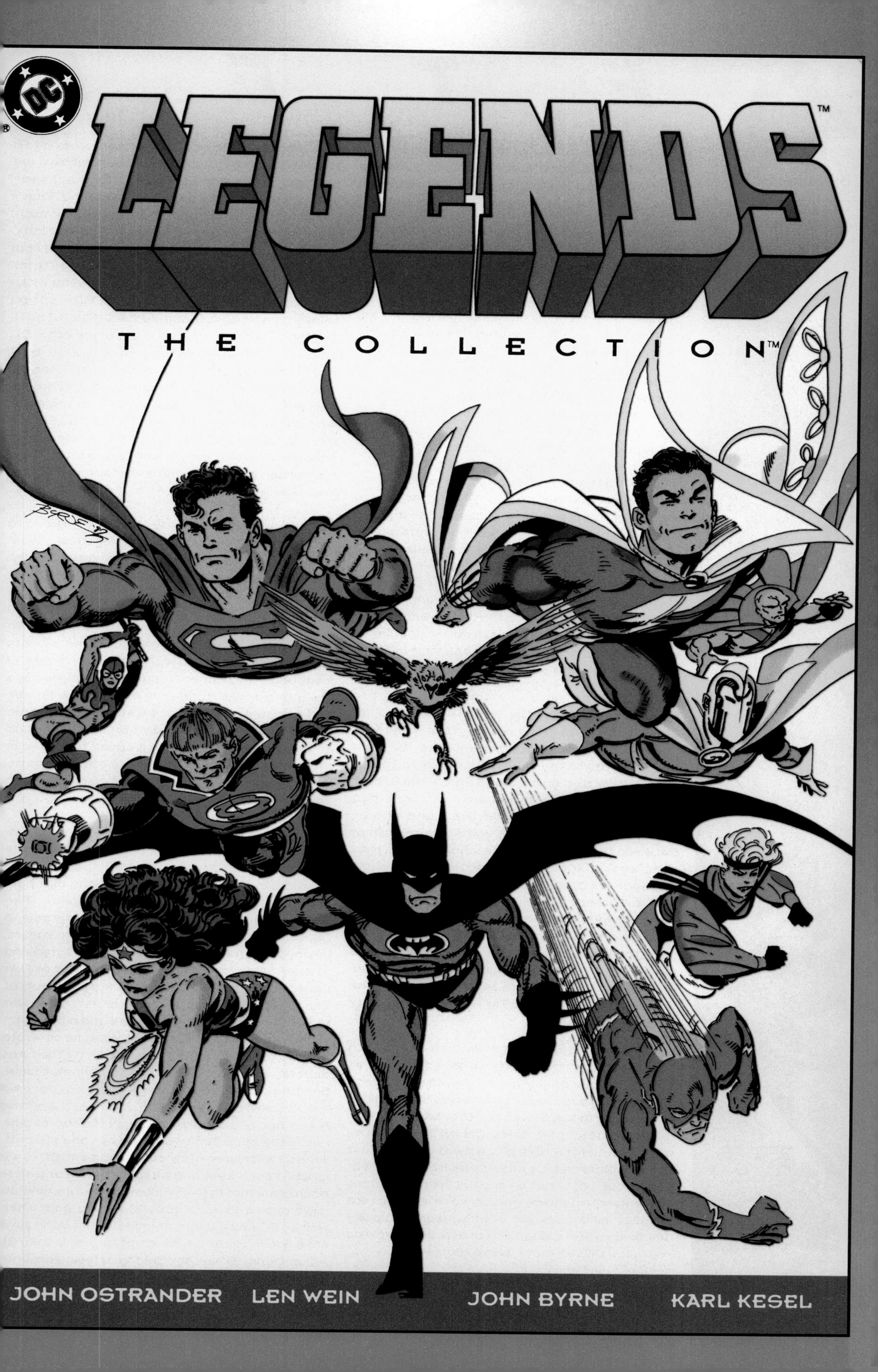

JOHN OSTRANDER LEN WEIN JOHN BYRNE KARL KESEL

AFTER

by Mike Gold

Former
Group Editor/
Director of
Development
for DC Comics.

What do you do after you destroy the universe? Or, to quote Lord Cumulus in the comics-inspired stage play *Warp*, "Destroy the universe? Where are you going to live?"

Well, where would you want to live? Amongst the legends, of course. That was just the situation DC faced back in the fall of 1985, as its Earths-shattering miniseries CRISIS ON INFINITE EARTHS was coming to an end. The purpose of CRISIS was to allow for a major house-cleaning of the confusing and often contradictory parallel universes. The task was one fraught with peril.

I'm not talking about the creative side of the matter, although the accomplishment of writer Marv Wolfman and artists George Pérez, Dick Giordano and Jerry Ordway was no mean feat, to say the least. Their effort speaks for itself, and all but the most anal retentive of mid-1980s comics fans regard the series as one of the greats of the decade. No, the task was dangerous because of a quirk in the makeup of comics fans—a group of which I proudly count myself an enthusiastic member. We have this tendency to organize everything, including those things that were not meant to be organized. Once we have built our own house of cards, we move in and we bring our entire comic book collection along with us. It's no wonder that, once in, we never want to move out. Schlepping all those comics is a royal pain; sandblasting all those memories will knock over the house.

And sandblasting away memories was the by-product of CRISIS ON INFINITE EARTHS. A lot of us who grew up in the 1950s and the 1960s really liked our memories the way they were. We knew our way around the Multiverse. We liked Earth-1 and Earth-2 and Earth-3 and Earth-Prime, that oddly familiar dimension where Julius Schwartz, Cary Bates and Elliot Maggin lived, and where I used to work. We liked the various relationships between the denizens of the infinite Earths. Most of all, we liked Supergirl and The Flash. The people we regarded as the real Supergirl and The Flash. Not Lex Luthor's shape-shifting paramour, not the hormone-laden Kid Flash—and no offense meant to these fine characters, one of whom I used to edit (the hormone-laden one, of course). But to us—gasp—baby boomers, Supergirl was Linda Lee Danvers and the Flash was Barry Allen, and by the end of CRISIS ON INFINITE EARTHS, Linda and Barry were dead.

It is understandable that some fans had a hard time dealing with their losses. We were getting older, having families, paying mortgages, struggling with insurance and retirement plans and tax forms, so it was tough to see that the ol' DC Universe wasn't feeling so hot either. CRISIS ON INFINITE EARTHS was an unquestionable hit and was an important building block in DC's late-80s revitalization, but its purpose was to put an end to certain confusing elements within the mythos. So we're left with Lord Cumulus' immortal question. But we weren't alone—DC Comics was in the same fix as its readers. How do you follow CRISIS? That's where I came in.

In the autumn of 1985, I was deep in employment negotiations with DC's vice-president/executive editor/house legend Dick Giordano. "Deep in nego-tiations" meant I flew to New York, had a wonderful

meal with Giordano and Pat Bastienne, swapped a lot of stupid jokes about some of our mutual close personal friends, and while waiting for the cheese-cake, batted a few salary figures around. That's the meaning of life, folks: cheesecake and cash. A few more formalities, another trip to New York, a pleasant meeting with Jenette Kahn and Paul Levitz, and I accepted the job and returned to my native Chicago to pack. I was barely home when Dick called and politely asked, "Say, Mike, do you think you can do a sequel to CRISIS ON INFINITE EARTHS?" I was aware that a couple of other DC editors had ideas that were kicking around, but I was informed that, for one reason or another, DC was looking for something different. And where better to look than to the outside, to someone who didn't have to live through the daily night-mare of doing a company-wide crossover featuring a million different characters and impacting upon four million different editors, writers, and artists. You know, a virgin.

Always enjoying a foolhardy challenge, I agreed to the assignment. I had a significant logistical advan-tage over my new comrades in New York: I was still in Chicago, so I could do the plotting work without having to constantly run back and forth between those four million people. I could assemble an editorial team, we could plot out our story in peace and quiet, and then we could share it with half the comics industry phone book for refine-ment and coordination. Besides, Dick assigned Bob Greenberger the position of my in-house liaison, and he could run back and forth between those four million people. A gifted writer and editor and an aggressive kibitzer, Bob's greatest talents lie in those coordination efforts. These efforts, in part, led to his eventual promotion to his current position as DC's manager of editorial scheduling.

Bob sent me a set of photocopies of the as-yet-unpublished issues of CRISIS (talk about being the first one on my block). I already had an edito-rial team in mind, but after reading the big finish, I was able to kick back and get a few ideas. Then I called John Ostrander. Whereas he was new to DC, Johnny O. was hardly a newcomer to comics, having written *Starslayer* and having created and written *GrimJack* and *Munden's Bar* over at First Comics, along with numerous other assignments at First and 4Winds/Eclipse. I edited John's work over at First, I was a fan of John's work as a playwright-in particular, a play called *Bloody Bess* he co-wrote over at the Organic Theater Company that was directed by Stuart Gordon, of Re-Animator fame, and had starred Joe Mantegna, who has become a major movie star. Better still, John was a longtime friend, and one of the pleasures of the comics busi-ness is the opportunity to work with one's friends. John already knew of my association with DC as we lunched each week and we spoke before and after each of my trips to New York. He hoped my new job might open a door for him at DC. Indeed, back when I joined DC's staff during my mid-70s stint, John gave me a Green Lantern spec script to give to then GL editor Denny O'Neil. It would be a few years until John would make it in comics—let alone DC—but his enthusiasm and his desire had been there since he had been a zygote. At the time, he lived about two miles south of me.

W O R D

"Hey, John. How would you like to read the final issues of CRISIS ON INFINITE EARTHS?" John said sure, I hung up the telephone, my doorbell rang, and John said, "Well? Where is it?" Enthusiasm. I gave him the photocopies, he looked at them as though they were a chilled case of Coca-Cola and he was in the middle of the Sahara, and I didn't even try to get his attention until he was finished. "So," I said patiently. "How would you like to write the plot for the sequel?" John's response was something to the effect of "Sure. Who would you like me to kill?" This is an offer not to be taken lightly in Chicago, so after reaching our decision, we started to plot. I had a simple starting point: what was DC all about? Superman, Batman, Wonder Woman: legends. The Flash, Green Lantern, Hawkman, Green Arrow, The Legion of Super-Heroes, the Justice League of America. Legends, one and all. We decided that the story should be phrased as a traditional superhero story—not the bleak dystopian stuff that was becoming popular at the time. After all, what could be more dystopian than the destruction of the multiverse and the death of Supergirl and The Flash? We didn't want LEGENDS to be cut from the same cloth as CRISIS. We then took that philosophy one step further: if the purpose of CRISIS was to put an end to sundry elements within the DC mythology, it should be the purpose of LEGENDS to create new elements. Our goal was to establish several series that would spin off from LEGENDS. Dick had already asked me to come up with a new FLASH title, so using LEGENDS as the launchpad provided no difficulty. John already had been discussing pitching a new version of SUICIDE SQUAD—coincidentally, the editor he was working with was Bob Greenberger. Tantalizingly, DC had decided something should be done to energize JUSTICE LEAGUE OF AMERICA, so we decided a new Justice League could be created from LEGENDS. Furthermore, we could give some exposure to a few characters who deserved the light—we decided upon Cosmic Boy of the Legion and Captain Marvel of Shazam! And spin-off miniseries were scheduled for these guys as well.

We worked out our theme, our approach and our goals; we needed some subtext. Stories need to be about something, and the fact that we were doing a traditional superhero story did not mean we had to turn our backs on subtext. The issue of how superheroes would be treated in our society was one that intrigued both of us—Paul Levitz handled it brilliantly in his "Last Days of The Justice Society" story eight years earlier. How had our culture changed from the McCarthyesque setting of Paul's story? In the middle of the Reagan Administration, we felt not, and we wanted to experiment with this issue in LEGENDS. All we needed to come up with were trivial little details like a story and a villain. Simple, right?

While John was doing his creative thing, I moved on to assemble the other members of our team. We needed a dialogist who knew how the various DC characters spoke: asking John to learn the rhythms and patterns of about a million characters would have fried his brain and overtaxed our deadlines. I wanted to work with a guy who had written virtually every major DC character, and Len Wein fit the bill. In fact, Len had also written every major Marvel character, and was to go on to edit every major Disney character. Coincidentally, he was Dick's first choice as well. Better yet, he was available. Whereas Len and I had been friends for a decade, I really hadn't had the privilege of working with him in the comics medium. I'll let you in on a little secret, one that will embarrass Len no end. Len Wein is the most successful new comics creator in the past two dozen years. I'm defining "new comics creator" as somebody who co-created (with an artist) a character that hadn't been around before, that had survived some real test of time, and whose appeal had gone past the cloistered comics medium. Virtually all successful titles launched in the past two dozen years were spin-offs of other peoples' creations: look at all of the new Superman, Batman, X-Men, Green Lantern, Spider-Man, and Justice League titles. What are we left with? The Punisher, Swamp Thing, Ghost Rider, and Wolverine. Ghost Rider doesn't quite make it by the above definition, as his (their?) success has been confined to comics, and that success has suffered lengthy interruptions. That leaves us with Swamp Thing, star of tube, screen, and comics, and Wolverine, star of tube, comics, and comics (and comics, and comics) and The Punisher, star of comics and home video. Two of those three were created by Len Wein (the third was created by Len's roommate, but that doesn't count). Clearly, he was a useful guy to have on a project like LEGENDS. Our work was significantly enhanced by Len's involvement, as his contributions were based on his years of professional involvement with the DC Universe.

Okay, so we had our plotter and were working towards finishing our plot, and we had our dialogist who couldn't dialog until he'd got pencilled pages. So, logically, we needed a penciller. Logically, I called up John Byrne. At that precise moment in time, Mr. Byrne was winding up his sundry assignments over at Marvel Comics. Here was another guy I had known for a considerable length of time, and another former neighbor (Byrne lived about halfway between my apartment and Ostrander's, and had been a member in good standing of the Big Pit Appreciation Society and Marching Band), and another guy I always wanted to work with. J.B. was in an interesting position: he grew up with the DC characters but had not had the opportunity to draw the majority of them professionally thus far. LEGENDS appealed to him for that very reason, but, despite his renowned speed, it would have been tough for him to squeeze it into his schedule along with his waning Marvel commitments and the commencement of his work drawing and writing two monthly Superman titles. There are only so many hours in the day, and John likes to spend at least a few of them watching *Soap* reruns with his wife Andi. "Is there anything you can do to help me with my compensation?" John asked of me. It is part of an editor's job to represent the company in negotiating the talent terms, but I wasn't even on DC's staff yet, so I wasn't familiar with the nuances of their operation methods; however, I was familiar enough with the realities of comicbook publishing to know that John Byrne already received the top page rates in his categories. Royalty deals are standard across the board, so I didn't have a lot of room for negotiation. Then something occurred to me. John told me he had written a gothic novel, but he hadn't shown it to any publishers or agents. I made

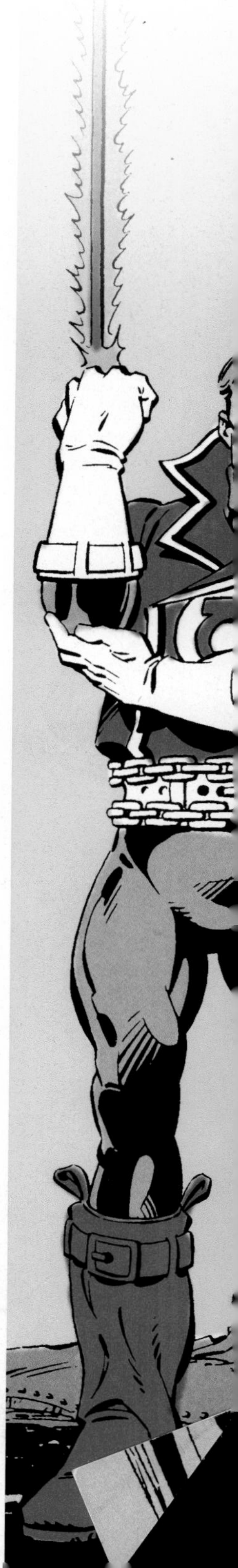

a quick phone call to Dick, who held a quick conference with Paul and Jenette. Dick called me back, I called John back.

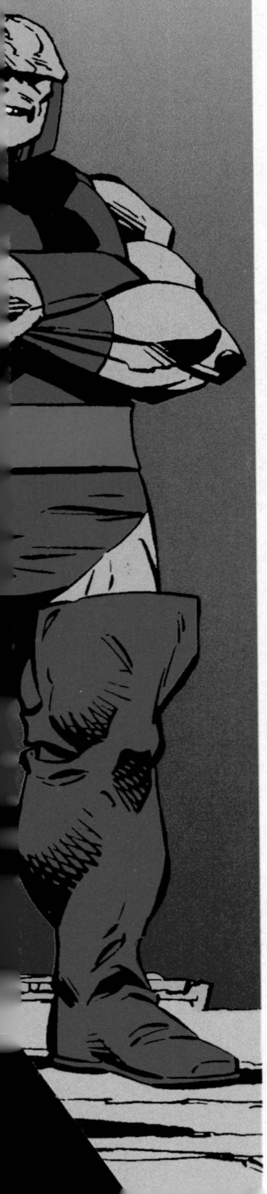

"Okay here's the deal. Let me read your manuscript. If I think it has any potential, DC will open the doors for you with its (then) sister company, Warner Books. If they think the book stinks, it's up to you to work it out." John agreed. Actually, his novel was quite good—particularly as the first draft of a first novel. I wasn't an expert on the genre, but I'd been reading novels for about 30 years and editing stuff for 18, so I held a somewhat informed opinion. Being editor by habit as well as predilection, though, I made a few suggestions, some of which were incorporated into his revised manuscript over the next few months. Warner liked the book, worked with him on making it even better, and it was published as if it were any other novel. John has since written as many short stories and novels as his comics schedule would permit. By this time, the other John had completed the LEGENDS plot and I had become ensconced in DC's New York office. It was time to show the plot to the other DC editors.

Most editors were enthusiastic. Some were relieved that they didn't have the headache of doing the massive crossover in addition to their own already busy schedules. By that time, I had GREEN ARROW in development with Mike Grell, and the beginnings of FLASH mark III in development with Mike Baron, so my workload wasn't as busy as, say, that of Andy Helfer, who was relaunching all three Superman titles, working with us on winding up JUSTICE LEAGUE OF AMERICA and launching the new post-LEGENDS title, and handling other books like GREEN LANTERN CORPS and about a million Keith Giffen projects.

Barbara Randall made serious and significant suggestions that went far beyond that which was requested of her, revealing an editorial expertise that has served her in good stead at both DC and Dark Horse. Andy and I held many long meetings to coordinate the end of the JLA and the launch of the new JL. This was challenging work, as the characters we needed to band together in order to complete the LEGENDS storyline weren't necessarily the best characters to commit to an enduring Justice League. Just as things were beginning to calm down, we hit a problem. Editor Karen Berger was in the midst of revamping Wonder Woman, and she requested we remove the character from LEGENDS. It was impossible to do a DC-wide crossover without Wonder Woman, but we did move her from the very beginning of the first issue to the middle of the last. By that time, Karen and writer/artist George Pérez had a chance to establish their new version of the Amazon in several issues of her own title. We needed to complete our editorial team. Dick suggested asking Karl Kesel to ink the series; I had neither worked with nor met Karl before, but I sure was a fan of his stuff, so I enthusiastically offered him the gig. Continuing our run of luck, Karl agreed.

All I needed was a letterer and a colorist. I had worked with Steve Haynie for several years when we both were at First Comics; the quality of his work speaks for itself.

I knew I'd need a guy who could work fast when necessary, as there's a tendency to run late when you're working on a company-wide crossover involving thousands of approvals each step of the way. Steve fit the bill perfectly. We needed a colorist whose familiarity with all of the characters was absolute: the colorist is at the end of the food chain of comics, and it is often up to him or her to help make up whatever time was lost along the way. We didn't want a person who had to go dig out dozens of different comics for reference each and every time we introduced a character; Tom Ziuko and Carl Gafford knew the denizens of the DC Universe like the backs of their hands. And if you're a colorist, you spend a lot of time looking over the back of your hand.

So we had our team. We had our plot. We had our first issue well under way. And we were working on our marketing plans and the mandatory crossover appearances in other books, some of which came off quite nicely, although a few were admittedly rather minor. We did introduce a few interesting ideas along this front. For one thing, we numbered our crossover appearances—a first for the form. We established three LEGENDS subsets. For one month an important story element involving the Man of Steel flowed from the main series to the sundry Superman titles, and then back to the main series. The COSMIC BOY series started off in LEGENDS and then took the time traveling hero forward to the very end of time. And, finally, we employed the end of the Justice League of America as a subset to LEGENDS: their breakup was a significant part of the main storyline.

We also used the SECRET ORIGINS title as a sidebar to the LEGENDS miniseries, providing important backstory elements for the Phantom Stranger and Suicide Squad that were part of the LEGENDS fabric. If you look carefully at each of the appearances in other titles, you will see that some are labeled "crossover" and others "spin-off." We decided against numbering the first issues of JUSTICE LEAGUE, THE FLASH, and SUICIDE SQUAD as spin-offs from LEGENDS, although, clearly, they were. Since we hoped for long and healthy runs for each of these new ongoing series, we didn't want their images to be obscured by the LEGENDS hype.

So all we had to do was print our comics and sell them—some 31 different issues over about eight months. Talk about hitting the ground running: a company-wide crossover is just about the most difficult thing a superhero comics editor can do. Just ask any of us who have tried it. Actually, you should ask Andy Helfer, who did it twice (MILLENNIUM and INVASION!) and then retired from the DC Universe.

In these reprint book essays, it seems mandatory to say how much fun it was to do whatever it was that is being reprinted. Well, let me tell you, LEGENDS was a hell of a lot of hard work—not just for Len, Karl, Steve, Carl, Tom, Bob, the two Johns and myself, but for the entire DC editorial team and the artists and writers of the spin-offs, crossovers, and the new launch series that were in the wake of LEGENDS. It was also a hell of a lot of work for DC's production and marketing departments.

But, you know something? It was a hell of a lot of fun...one of the most enjoyable projects during my nine years at DC Comics. It was my very first job as an editor at DC Comics—the company that employed such legendary editors as Sheldon Mayer, Julius Schwartz, Mort Weisinger, Robert Kanigher, Joe Orlando and Dick Giordano. My first time at bat, and I had Superman, Batman, Wonder Woman, and the real Captain Marvel on my team. I had the opportunity to work with one of my closest and dearest friends, and to establish working relationships with some of the finest people around.

From a continuity standpoint, it was an important project. From my own personal standpoint, LEGENDS was a once-in-a-lifetime event.